Rainbow
Fly Fishing

A Guide for Still Waters

For Intermediate to Advanced Fly Fishers and Other Anglers

by Ron Newman

An In-Depth Look at Rainbow Trout And Their Environment From an Angler's Perspective

Frank Amato
PORTLAND

All inquiries should be addressed to:
Frank Amato Publications, Inc. • P.O. Box 82112 • Portland, Oregon 97282
503-653-8108 • www.amatobooks.com

Book Design: Ron Newman
Cover Design: Tony Amato

ISBN-13: 978-1-57188-439-8 • UPC: 0-81127-00274-0
Printed in Hong Kong

1 3 5 7 9 10 8 6 4 2

Contents

Contents

Contents

Contents

Contents

Contents

Contents

Preface – Notes to the Reader

Go ahead and flip through this book. You won't find my favorite fly patterns, recipes for cooking fish, knots, the latest fishing gear or my favorite fishing stories. That information can be found in any run-of-the-mill book or magazine on fishing. Instead, this book helps improve your angling success and knowledge about the sport.

As a predator, you need to understand your prey to be consistently successful. You need to know where it hides, where it feeds, when it's active, its physical attributes and so on. An angler who is knowledgeable about the fish will consistently catch more than a novice. Just ask any professional Bass fisherman. This book provides you with a wealth of knowledge about Rainbow Trout and their environment from an angler's perspective.

I fly fish so this book is biased toward the fly fishers' point of view. However, most information is also useful to other anglers including ice fishermen, trollers and spin-casters. I have narrowed the location of these trout to pristine lakes. By "pristine", I'm referring to lakes that tend to be small, free of competing fish species, hold insectivorous trout and are ideally suited for the fly fisher. The fish in these types of waters tend to behave differently than Rainbows in other habitats.

This book has been thoroughly researched over many years. I usually rely on two or more sources to confirm a piece of information or else I use my own computerized records on which to base conclusions. For further information on material contained in this book, try some online searches and readings through scientific journals. The word "ichthyology" or the study of fish is a good place to start. Also, try searches on various terms presented in this book and they will often take you to a variety of unusual sites.

You will find some important points discussed more than once in this book. I won't apologize for this approach. I was taught to tell your audience what you are going to tell them, then tell them and then tell them what you have told them. It helps you to remember a point. If you use this book as a future reference, it also helps to have certain relevant points repeated where applicable.

I don't always agree with the scientific community (e.g.: the lateral line) or always follow general trends (e.g.: use of stomach pumps) so I suspect that most readers will find something in this book on which to disagree. That's probably good. But keep your mind open and consider the possibility of new ideas. I try to provide you with information that is "most likely" to improve your knowledge and fishing success. It's up to you to put this information to good use.

Good Fishing
From Ron Newman

Paul Kollerer

1   9-24-2009

Chasing Rainbows

I've heard it said that 20% of the anglers catch about 80% of the fish. That may sound ridiculous but it's probably an accurate statement. Folks who know what they are doing are the ones who consistently catch fish. Sure, you can catch fish if you just grab your rod and head out a few times a year, but great trips with lots of fish will be few and far between. Consistently successful anglers are those who study and know their prey.

Tournament anglers are a good example. Dumb luck isn't what gets them into competitions. On any given day, they have a good idea of how the fish are likely to behave, what waters they will frequent and what they are likely to be eating. The same can be said for good fishing guides. Knowledge of their prey is essential for consistent success.

> **Did You Know**
> 80% of the fish are caught by about 20% of the anglers.
> Author unknown

Every species of fish has different habits, quirks and peculiarities. These will even change for a single species of fish, such as Rainbow Trout, depending on its environment and circumstances. Rainbows in a stream, for example, will behave differently than those in a lake. And Rainbows in a large deep lake will behave differently than those in a small shallow lake. So let's narrow down which Rainbows we are chasing. We will examine Rainbow Trout that live in the smaller shallower lakes that are free of competing fish species and are insectivorous making the lake ideal for fly fishing imitations of aquatic invertebrates. I call these pristine lakes.

I grew up fishing Rainbows in streams. I learned to read the streams and know where and when to catch trout in that environment. At that time I detested fishing in the lakes because, I thought, there weren't any clues to read. A lake was just a flat body of water without riffles, holds and feeding channels and anyone who caught trout in a lake was just lucky. In the years since my boyhood I've discovered how wrong I was. A lake is a little more subtle and complex to read but the clues that these still waters provide can point you to the fish. But you need to know what to look for and have an understanding of how the trout behave in the environment of a pristine lake.

As this book progresses we will examine Rainbow Trout and pristine lakes in some detail. However, this is presented from the angler's perspective. Extraneous data not of importance to fishing has been filtered out while pertinent information is examined for its importance to angling. It is unlikely that you could discover as much about fishing for Rainbow Trout in any other single document.

Rainbow Origins

The Pacific Salmon species are the closest genetic relatives to the Rainbow Trout. Bows and salmon are native to the cool, snow-melt waters that flow into the Pacific. These fish evolved in Russia, Canada and the western part of the United States long before the first fly rod was invented.

Originally, these trout were only found in the moving waters of streams and rivers or those lakes directly linked to these mainstream waterways. Most Rainbows migrated to the Pacific Ocean to feed and grow. They only returned to their native stream to spawn. However, a few found adequate food and shelter in the fresh water and began to spend their entire life cycle in a lake without a trip to the ocean. In particular, the smaller lakes at the headwaters of a watershed offered good habitat plus a stream in which to lay eggs. The shallow water of these small lakes was rich in nutrients and provided an abundance of aquatic invertebrates on which to feed.

Settlers eventually moved into the Pacific Rim watersheds and discovered the Rainbow Trout. At first they fished the lakes, streams and rivers strictly for food. They found that Rainbows were not only good to eat but had exceptional strength and stamina. They were, in fact, enjoyable to catch. Folks began to angle for these fish as a sport. The land was tamed, lifestyles improved and the settlers soon had more leisure time to pursue this new pastime. They began to transport these strong fish to lakes that were previously barren of fish. These new lakes had a super abundance of aquatic invertebrates and more importantly, lacked other species of fish to compete for the bugs. As expected the fish grew fast, big and strong. Fish of 18 pounds were being caught from lakes after the third year from a stocking of fingerlings. At Jewel Lake in southern British Columbia a Rainbow was caught that reportedly tipped the scales at 53 pounds. And of course there were still those seagoing Rainbow Trout (Steelhead) to be caught in the rivers and it wasn't uncommon to catch those in excess of 30 pounds.

Their large size, combined with their strength and stamina are the things that create angling legends. Then as now, the anglers told stories of the days catch or the one that got away. Word spread and soon the wealthy from around the world were traveling to the waters of the Pacific Rim in quest of Rainbow Trout. A couple of small hatcheries were established and more lakes were stocked. Soon these fish were transported to other countries far from their native waters.

Today, Rainbow Trout are common around the world. They have been introduced to many waters that meet a basic set of conditions for the fish to survive. However, survival conditions are not the same as good habitat. These fish have been stocked into large water bodies, small water bodies, productive waters, barren waters, warm waters, and cold waters. There have been success stories but also failures that resulted in weak or small fish bearing little resemblance to their legendary ancestors.

Notable success stories include the stocking of Rainbows into New Zealand, Chili and numerous small lakes in British Columbia. The later is where I live and fish. Some of these small lakes are not much bigger than a football field and can produce Bows in excess of ten pounds.

Types of Trout

There are many types of trout. Cutthroat Trout, Brook Trout, Rainbow Trout, Brown Trout, and Lake Trout are the most commonly known. However, just because a fish is called a trout doesn't mean those types of fish are closely related. The Brook Trout and Lake Trout for example are a 'char' belonging to the genus *Salvelinus*. The genus for trout is *Salmo* and pacific salmon belong to the genus *Oncorhynchus*.

Until fairly recently Rainbow Trout were called *Salmo gairdneri* and considered a member of the trout genus. However, in its wisdom the scientific community decided Rainbow and Cutthroat Trout were more closely related to the pacific salmon than to fish such as the Brown Trout (*Salmo trutta*). So the scientific name of Rainbow Trout is now *Oncorhynchus mykiss* and the Cutthroat Trout is *Oncorhynchus clarki*. I'm not sure of the details regarding these reclassifications but suspect it has something to do with Rainbows and Cutthroat migrating to the ocean while the other trout species don't. If you want to look up further information about the trout, whitefish and salmon, they all belong to the family *Salmonidae* in the order of *Salmoniformes*.

Fish that hatch in fresh water, migrate to the ocean and then return to fresh water to spawn are said to be anadromous. An anadromous Rainbow Trout is called a Steelhead. Genetically, Rainbow Trout and Steelhead are identical.

Did You Know
Cutthroat and rainbow trout are cross-breeding in many locations. These hybrids are taking on the characteristics of both species until it is sometimes difficult to identify one species from the other.

They are the same fish. However, the offspring of a Steelhead will inevitably migrate to the ocean and the offspring of a Rainbow will stay in fresh water even though it has the opportunity and circumstances to reach the ocean. Why this happens is a bit of a mystery.

Did You Know
Even today, rainbow trout in the Kamloops Region are referenced as Kamloops Trout and are internationally known for their fighting abilities, strength and size. These trout grow bigger, faster and are stronger than rainbow trout from most other locations. However, this is strictly a product of the environment. These astounding qualities cannot be transported to another location.

Rainbow Trout will sometimes show differences in physical characteristics and appearance. A prime example of this is the Kamloops Trout. In 1892 a Dr. Jordan of Stanford University was sent samples of trout found in the vicinity of Kamloops, British Columbia that were said to be larger, stronger and physically different than other Rainbow Trout. He examined the fish and found that they were, in fact, different. The head and maxillary process were longer and wider than on other Rainbows. They averaged more rows of scales but had fewer gill rakers, along with fewer rays in the dorsal and anal fins and the branchiostegal rays (the indented lines under each jaw) were fewer. Dr. Jordan was convinced these fish were different from

Salmo gairdneri and gave them the name *Salmo kamloops*. However, in later years, this new species was transported for stocking in other locations and after a while, these characteristic differences disappeared. As it turned out, there weren't any genetic differences in the Kamloops Trout. The physical differences were entirely a result of the environment in which the Kamloops Trout lived and so their physical attributes could not be exported.

Life Stages of a Rainbow

The life cycle of the Rainbow Trout is very similar to its closest relatives. Like salmon, trout need clean flowing water for spawning. Tributary streams rather than mainstream rivers are usually preferred spawning sites. The larger rivers often have problems with silt covering the eggs and suitable gravel can sometimes be hard to find. Rounded gravel about the size of ping-pong balls is about right for most Rainbows. This size isn't too big to move when building the nest (Redd) in which to lay eggs. But the size is large enough to form cavities between each gravel pebble. The eggs are about the size of peas and settle into these cavities where they are sheltered and receive sufficient moving water and oxygen for the egg to develop.

In lakes having inlet or outlet streams the trout will move into these waters for spawning. If a lake doesn't have an associated stream the Rainbows cannot successfully spawn. The mature trout will take on spawning colors, go through the chemical changes within the body, and develop the eggs and sperm for spawning. But without flowing water, the Rainbows will not actually spawn. Instead, the eggs and sperm are re-absorbed into fish's body. That usually retards any further growth of the trout. Occasionally on windy lakes, there is sufficient water movement along gravelly shores to fool trout into dropping their eggs and sperm but these are not likely to survive long enough to hatch.

From the fisheries management perspective, lakes without natural spawning offer a much better opportunity to produce a quality sport fishery. Uncontrolled natural spawning can produce many more fish than the food web can support. The result is many small fish. In stocked lakes without natural spawning,

> **Did You Know**
> To prevent Rainbows from going into the spawning cycle, some are being sterilized in the hatchery. Named Triploids, these fish can grow to a very large size.

fisheries managers can balance the numbers of fish with the food web to target larger fish for the angler. From the fly fishers perspective it is much better to raise Rainbows in a hatchery and subsequently stock suitable lakes. These fish will be stronger, healthier, and larger than where natural spawning has resulted in too many fish.

When the young hatch from the egg they still have the yolk sacs attached and are called *alevins*. The alevins stay within the gravel cavities until the yolk sac is absorbed and they need to go in search of food. When they emerge from the gravel they are called *fry*. As they get larger they are often referred to as fingerlings, parrs, smolts, adults and finally spawners. Adulthood is when the fish are sexually mature and can produce eggs or sperm. Sexual maturity doesn't usually happen until the fish are 3 to 5 years old. Some males "think" they are sexually mature at two years and actually go through the body and color changes without developing the applicable sexual organs. These are called precocious males.

From alevins to adults, Rainbows will grow about a pound per year under reasonably suitable conditions. The color changes that an adult undergoes to signal that it is ripe for spawning can be drastic to subtle depending on the environment. Usually there is a darkening of the belly, body and gill plate while the lateral line becomes a much brighter red. With the chemical changes in the body, the male can even develop a hooked jaw much like a salmon. If you catch a Rainbow with these advanced signs of spawning, I would suggest you gently release it. They aren't particularly good for the dinner table. The flesh becomes soft and they can be anything from tasteless to foul tasting with an odor.

Spawners will congregate in areas with suitable gravel even in a lake environment. Resist the temptation to cast a fly to these larger trout. Rainbows don't necessarily die after spawning but will if they are sick or in a weakened state. Catching and releasing these fish will increase the likelihood of their demise before they can recover and once again become a fish worth catching and suitable for the dinner table.

Fishing Tip

Most good sportsmen and knowledgeable anglers will not intentionally try to catch or otherwise molest spawners. These fish do not have the same strength and stamina to survive "catch & release" as a maiden fish.

An adult female will lay about 800 eggs per every pound of body weight. The eggs are laid into the Redd or gravel nest. The male positions himself over the Redd and emits sperm at about the same time as the eggs are dropped. The eggs are fertilized in the water as they drop into the cavities between the chunks of gravel. If they are healthy and lucky, an adult Rainbow can go through several spawns. However, about 80% won't survive their first spawn.

Basic Rainbow Requirements

The water conditions needed to support a population of Rainbow Trout are not onerous. Within limits, the Rainbows can adapt to a variety of conditions. Within that range, Rainbows can be successfully stocked for sport fishing. However, the best water conditions are those emulating the ancestral waters of these fish.

Naturally, the first thing a Rainbow needs is water. After we put the fish in water, we need to ensure the water is cool, properly oxygenated and not too acidic or polluted. After that, we must guarantee the trout has a steady supply of food on which to grow. All of these requirements must be acceptable to provide a suitable habitat for the Rainbow. Take any one of these factors outside an acceptable range and the fish will not survive. For our Rainbows to thrive, all these factors must be balanced and within the preferred range of the trout. Trout may survive near the edge of one limiting factor or another but under those conditions they will not grow to their full potential.

Temperature Requirements

From its ancestral habitats, it's obvious that Rainbows require cool water. These fish thrive in water that is around 48°F to 55°F (9°C to 13°C). For spawning, these trout prefer water temperatures slightly colder at around 43°F to 48°F. Bows do quite well in water temperatures from 38°F to 60°F. Water that is cooler or warmer can cause stress.

If water temperature rises to about 70°F (21°C), it can kill the trout. These are not warm water fish. Fortunately, for the Rainbow, warm water floats to the surface and cooler water settles to the lake bottom. If the lake is deep enough, the trout can often find acceptable water temperature near the lake bottom even when the surface temperatures reach the lethal limit.

It should be noted that a Rainbow is not likely to freeze. Fresh water freezes at 32°F but a Rainbow won't freeze until the temperature is 30.5°F. Underneath the winter ice cover on a lake, the water is actually warmer than 32°F. In addition, this lower freezing temperature allows the ocean going Rainbows to survive the winters in the salty northern oceans that freeze at less than 32°F.

> **Did You Know**
> Rainbows will not freeze until temperatures reach 30.5F and this isn't likely to happen since water freezes at 32F and then floats thus keeping the deeper water from becoming colder.

Oxygen Requirements

Rainbows thrive in water that has an oxygen content of 6 Parts per Million (ppm) or more. Too much oxygen isn't usually a problem. However, in turbulent water, such as below a dam spillway, super saturation with oxygen can occur and harm the fish. In pristine lakes, we can essentially ignore this problem.

When oxygen levels drop below 6 ppm, trout are increasingly stressed from oxygen deprivation. Then they become progressively more lethargic. When oxygen content in a lake drops below 4 ppm, the trout can die. Water temperature, decaying plant matter, 'turnover' and other factors can reduce oxygen levels. These will be discussed in more detail as we proceed.

It should be noted that Rainbows require more oxygen in warm water than they do in cold water. If oxygen content drops in warm water, the results can be devastating to the trout. To survive, a Rainbow needs about fifty percent more oxygen in water at 68°F as it does in water that is 43°F. To compound the problem, warm water doesn't hold oxygen as well as cold water.

Acidity

Rainbow waters should be clean and free of pollutants and toxins. Trout prefer water that is somewhat alkaline but will tolerate slightly acidic water. Alkalinity below a pH of 8.2 or acidity above a pH of 6.0 is the usual range. Neutral water is 7.0 on the pH scale. Without a testing kit, you can often tell if water is acidic by the presence of Lily Pads which tend to grow in slightly acidic water. Excessive acidity will not only kill the trout but the entire lake. This is happening in some areas subject to acid rain.

Food Requirements

The last of the basic requirements for a Rainbow is the need to obtain sufficient nourishment. In pristine lakes, trout primarily feed on aquatic invertebrates. If this food source becomes limited, the trout will feed on other fish. It cannot survive on a diet of plant material. The trout may nibble plants to supplement certain vitamin and mineral needs but its digestive system is not designed for a plant diet. Trout need enough 'meat' to maintain bodily functions plus some extra for growth and survival under stressful conditions.

The quantity and types of food in a specific lake will depend on many factors. Two of the main factors are nutrient levels in the lake and the amount of shoals or shallow water areas. We will be discussing this in more detail later.

To summarize our discussion on Rainbow requirements, if the basic needs of food, temperature, pH and oxygen are satisfied then the Rainbows are likely to survive. As all these factors approach optimum levels, the trout become strong, healthy and a fish that is of interest to the sportsman.

The Sport of Chasing Rainbows

Fly fishing has existed for over a 1000 years and angling for sport even longer. And for its strength, agility and other sporting qualities the Rainbow Trout is one of the worlds favorite sport fish. This fish can be caught on most any type of gear, in virtually every season. Through stocking programs, it can be caught in most every cool climate country of the world.

Depending upon local environmental conditions, Rainbow Trout will adapt, thrive and offer exceptional angling opportunities and challenges. Pristine lakes (free of competing fish species) offer one type of challenge to the Rainbow angler; large or multi-specie lakes offer another challenge and the various types of streams or rivers offer yet other challenges. And in each of those environments lie thousands of considerations to arrive at the right choice of time, place, lure and presentation to catch one of these elusive trout.

Over the last 100 years there have been significant advances in the art and science of angling. Today's' fishing gear, from hooks and lines to rods and reels, is much better designed for actually getting a fish into the net. The peripheral equipment we use for angling, from boats and motors to sunglasses and life vests is vastly superior and makes it much easier to pursue our sport. Even our attitudes toward the sport have changed.

Not that long ago, angling, and fly fishing in particular, was a past-time for the rich. Big bucks were spent having horse hair braided into a fly line and then getting to good fishing waters. Back then, it seemed almost mandatory to kill virtually every fish landed with little concern for the environment. In today's world, most folks can afford to angle and attitudes toward our sport have changed.

Before we get into the nitty-gritty of knowing our fish, I would like to devote a couple of pages to examine our sport in today's world. The science and sociology of angling is constantly changing. As intermediate to advanced anglers, we should be aware of how these may affect our future angling experiences.

Fisheries Management

We need a healthy community of Rainbow Trout in an accessible lake or stream before we can pursue our sport. That's where fishery management comes into play. And gone are the days when fisheries management simply meant dumping a barrel of live fingerlings into a body of water and hoping for the best.

Fisheries managers in the modern world need to start by assessing and managing very complex ecosystems and habitat. When conditions are suitable the fisheries managers can introduce (stock) fish or manage an existing fish community to provide the maximum benefits to society. Of course, that means that risk assessments and cost/benefit analysis are needed. After we have an established fishery, the managers must establish and enforce fishing regulations that provide the best angling experience to a variety of anglers (not just you) while protecting the environment and the aquatic habitat.

As you can see, fisheries management in today's world gets very complex and requires a substantial background in science as well as other disciplines. Even so, there is a lot that we don't know about the fish and their habitat. Good management becomes an art as well as a science. I would encourage all anglers to work with their fisheries managers to improve our sport. Help these folks by letting your opinions be known and sharing your information on any aspects of angling. And consider some of the multiple complexities before you start bad-mouthing current decisions about existing fisheries management.

And what is the bottom line for sport fishing? Governments provide us with fisheries management and angling opportunities because it is cost effective to do so. They wouldn't continue to stock lakes, for example, if the monies generated from the sale of fishing licenses, taxes associated with fishing, etc. didn't pay for this program. They have no obligation to provide us with stocked lakes in which to fish. Because of recent trends, this could spell disaster for our sport.

It seems that the number of anglers purchasing fishing licenses is declining and the average age of those who do angle is increasing. In short, young folks aren't taking up the sport. In our modern age, I expect that kids are staying at home playing electronic games rather

> The boy who learns to fish will become a better man for it.

than going fishing with the old man or granddad. These trends are currently of concern to fisheries managers and should be of concern to us anglers. Governments may decide to quit funding fisheries management programs if the dollars are not generated from our sport. As a suggestion, promise yourself to take a kid fishing this summer.

Angler Responsibilities

Being responsible for our sport is not just a job for fisheries managers. Every angler has a role in maintaining our sport and making it an enjoyable experience. Many of our responsibilities are just common sense. For an obvious example, every angler must know and abide by the fishing regulations. It goes without saying. For a more subtle example, everyone who uses a boat motor should keep it well maintained to prevent oil and gas from leaking into the lake. For the most part, we don't even need to think about our responsibilities. It's just a part of being an ethical angler.

In the modern world, our angling attitudes have evolved to fit the times. Today's typical angler is often a conservation minded person, local to the area and reasonably well informed on local issues and his responsibilities toward the sport. But in our modern world, anti-hunting and anti-fishing proponents have also evolved. These folks want to force their emotional opinions on everyone else and they are actively lobbying to put an end to our sport.

I don't intend to go into a long dialogue on the specifics of angler responsibility. But we should discuss a few broad topics because the world is changing and this could put our sport in jeopardy.

> ➢ As intermediate to advanced anglers, we are probably the 20% that catch 80% of the fish. We should be setting examples for other anglers and be the ones actively lobbying to improve our sport.
> ➢ Always follow fishing regulations and disassociate yourself from anyone who knowingly violates those regulations or damages the fishing resource.
> ➢ Show respect for the fish, the resource and other anglers on the lake. Be courteous and assist less knowledgeable anglers.
> ➢ Follow a set of angling ethics that are appropriate to the type of fishing and locality being fished. See Appendix 1 for an example pertinent to fly fishing on pristine lakes.
> ➢ Limit the number of fish killed to those destined for your dinner table. Avoid keeping fish in hopes of giving them to your neighbors.
> ➢ When releasing fish, follow proper "catch and release" techniques. See Appendix 2 for a brief overview of the process. I would also suggest that this includes avoiding the use of a stomach pump. See Appendix 3 for reasons.
> ➢ Avoid any unnecessary disturbance to any wildlife including spawning fish, nesting birds or aquatic insects.

> Never put anything into the lake except your anchor, fly and fly line.

9

> ➤ Avoid polluting the lake in any way. As a rule-or-thumb, don't put anything into the lake except your anchor, fly and fly line.
> ➤ Get involved in projects that conserve or enhance the fishery resources.

I could list a lot of others but I'm sure you get the idea. If you value your sport, then be a responsible angler and get involved.

End Notes

To summarize some of this Chapters points on angling success:
> ➤ It is the knowledgeable angler that consistently catches fish.
> ➤ Rainbows will behave differently under different environmental circumstances such as living in a stream, river, common lake or pristine lake.
> ➤ In pristine lakes, other species of foraging fish are absent so Rainbows forage on insects rather than bait fish.
> ➤ Like streams and rivers, lakes offer good clues as to where to fish for larger Bows.
> ➤ Avoid fishing for Rainbows in the spawning stages.
> ➤ Under the right conditions, even very small lakes can produce large Bows.
> ➤ As necessities for trout survival reach their limits, the trout become stressed and are harder to catch.
> ➤ Fisheries management is not an exact science.
> ➤ Anglers have a responsibility to protect their resource and sport.

2

Rainbow Habitats

Rainbow Trout live in a variety of habitats. They are found in the running water of rivers and streams. They are found in the still waters of fresh water lakes and ponds. As Steelhead, they are even found in the ocean. If their basic requirements are satisfied, Rainbows are likely to survive and grow in many types of water. However, in each of these different types of water, conditions vary. Likewise, trout will change their behavior to suit the conditions of their home water.

For the purposes of this book, we have limited our examination of Rainbow Trout to those in pristine lakes. That eliminates the Steelhead, Rainbows that live in streams and rivers, those Rainbows living in very large lakes and the trout living in lakes that have been invaded by non-trout species. Essentially that limits our examination to smaller lakes, with insectivorous trout, that are ideal for fly fishing.

I have made this limitation for the purposes of accuracy. Yes, many of the specifics in this book are applicable to Rainbows living in each water type. But some of the statements are only applicable to Rainbows in pristine lakes. Behavior, food types, fishing strategies and even some of the Rainbows sensory perceptions can vary with their habitat.

In this chapter, we look at the habitat requirements of a Rainbow Trout. Emphasis will be on pristine lakes and the angling techniques suitable to this environment. To gain a basic understanding of the underwater world of the Rainbow we will also need to look at some of the peculiarities of water.

Lake Habitats

Limnology is the study of freshwater lakes. Why, you ask, do we have a whole branch of science dedicated to the study of a depression that contains water? For starters, that definition could apply to a puddle, a pond or an ocean. Secondly, each lake is unique. And thirdly, we anglers need to understand the lake habitats if we are to improve our angling skills. We need to understand the workings of a lake just as a stream angler knows the traits of a stream.

Let's start by deciding what a lake is. A lake is a body of fresh water that is non-flowing and at some point, deep enough that the penetration of sunlight is insufficient to support photosynthesis by bottom dwelling plants. A pond can support bottom dwelling plants throughout the entire water body but a lake can't.

The determination of pond versus lake isn't by size or surface area as many people might expect. It is by light penetration. In addition, the depth of light penetration to support rooted plants will vary with water clarity. We can have small lakes or large ponds according to the strictest of definitions.

Rainbow Trout can live in a pond and this can be a very productive habitat. However, ponds have a basic problem as a continuous Rainbow home. They are too shallow to support a population of trout over a long period. At some time or another, the waters of a pond will either get too warm or else become so depleted of oxygen under natural conditions that the trout will die.

Fly fishers will gladly share their knowledge, flies and even their gear but never their secret fishing lake.

As a rule-of-thumb, let's consider ponds to be water bodies that don't get any deeper than about 25 feet. That's about the average depth sunlight can penetrate for photosynthesis on a typical pristine lake.

Lake Types

When studying lakes, limnologists classify lakes according to the amount of dissolved nutrients they receive. There is a little more to it but that's the basic idea. The more nutrients a lake receives the more likely it is to be a productive producer of fish. Based on the nutrients received, lakes are classified as Oligotrophic, Mesotrophic, Eutrophic or Dystrophic.

Eutrophic means well nourished. Eutrophication is the process by which a body of fresh water becomes enriched with dissolved nutrients that stimulates the growth of aquatic plant life. With bacterial decomposition of dead plants and algae, these lakes can be oxygen poor.

Oligotrophic means poorly nourished. An oligotrophic lake is deficient in nutrients that support plant life. Without abundant plant life, these lakes are usually oxygen rich. And 'meso' means mid or middle and so a lake that is mesotrophic has moderate nutrients to support plant life and has moderate oxygen contents.

Dystrophy means faulty nutrition. A dystrophic water body is usually acidic with brown water and plant materials that are not decomposed. A eutrophic lake that eventually fills in with plants and sediments becomes a dystrophic pond, swamp or bog.

More important than the names is the concept. Different lakes have different productivity levels. In turn, the productivity level of a lake will affect the behavior of the trout and that will affect the tactics utilized by the angler. For example, in a productive lake with lots of nutrients there will be lots of bugs. The trout can be expected to be

Lakes in similar stages of development tend to have similar aquatic invertebrates and food chains.

large, well fed, contented and probably insectivorous. Thus, they will be choosy about a fly presentation and hard to catch because of food abundance.

Table 1 – General Characteristics of Lake Types

Characteristic	Oligotrophic	Mesotrophic	Eutrophic	Dystrophic
Geologic Age	Young	Middle Aged	Old	Over-the-Hill
General Elevation	Upper Watershed	Mid Watershed	Lower Watershed	Flats of Lower Watershed
Shoreline & Lake Bottom	Boulders and Rocks	Rocks, Gravel and Sand	Sand and Mud	Mud to Fine Silt & Muck
Oxygen	Reasonably High	Moderate	Fairly Low	Very Low
Temperature	Cold	Cool	Mild	Warm
Plant Life	Little	Moderate	Heavy	Over Abundant
Nutrients	Few	Moderate	Abundant	Depleted
Shoals and Drop-offs	Few shoals and rapidly drops to deep water	Modest shoal development with some rapid drop-offs and deep portions.	Many shoals with gradual drop-offs and limited deep water.	Entire area in the littoral zone. Likely a shallow basin.
Water Clarity	Very Clear	Clear to Cloudy	Cloudy to Murky	Frequently brown water
Aquatic Invertebrates	Moderate	Abundant	Very Abundant	Can be limited and specialized.
Fish Productivity	Low	Moderate	High	Limited or None
Spawning Streams	Usually	Sometimes	Seldom	Unlikely

Oligotrophic lakes have poorly developed food chains. These lakes can produce some large trout but how they become large is different from the other types of lakes. In Oligotrophic lakes, the small trout are insectivorous but the larger fish tend to become carnivorous and even cannibalistic in order to find sufficient food. These lakes tend to have species of fish other than trout and the use of a lure or flatfish is usually more productive than fly fishing. Streamer flies will be the best bet in these lakes.

The best waters for the fly fisher are the lakes that are in the range from Mesotrophic to Eutrophic. The Eutrophic lakes have lots of food to grow large trout. However, this abundance of food also means it is less likely that the trout will select an artificial fly. Eutrophic lakes can also have temperature

> Every lake offers a unique habitat and the Rainbows find ways to take full advantage of each habitat.

problems in mid-summer, oxygen problems in turnover and potential problems with winter kill. The Mesotrophic lakes offer the best general conditions for Rainbow fishing but they won't tend to produce trout that are quite as large. My personal favorites are those lakes about half way between Eutrophic and Mesotrophic.

Lake Zonations

Lakes come in many sizes, shapes, shoreline structure, productivity levels and so on. But there are also many similarities in most lakes. They have certain stratification layers, basic features, and zones that are important to the fly fisher. We should examine some of these to see how they might affect our fly fishing strategy.

Light Penetration Zones

The amount of light penetration for plants distinguishes a pond from a lake. These are also important considerations within a lake. Scientists have divided a lake into three basic zones depending on the amount of sunlight received.

Littoral Zone - The littoral zone is the shallow area within a lake where light reaches the lake bottom in sufficient quantities to support rooted plant growth. These areas are similar to a pond but are within a lake and connected to deeper water. This zone stretches from the shore, across any shoals or shallows, over the drop-off and then into depths to the point where sunlight cannot

> **Did You Know**
> Eighty to ninety percent of the biomass within a lake lives in the littoral zone. When the trout are intent on feeding, this is where they go.

support plant growth. The littoral zone contains most of the living organic biomass in a lake. Rooted and floating plants along with many groups of animals typify this zone.

Limnetic Zone – This is typically in the 'middle' of the lake out beyond the littoral zone. More specifically, the limnetic zone is the upper portion of the deep water. It receives sufficient light for photosynthesis but the lake bottom does not reach into this zone. Critters that can suspend within the water column such as fish, zooplankton and algae tend to inhabit this zone when in the deep water portions of the lake.

Note: The limnetic zone and the littoral zone both receive sufficient sunlight for photosynthesis but rooted plants cannot grow in the limnetic zone because the bottom is too deep. This zone of light penetration is known as the "photic zone".

Profundal Zone – The profundal zone lies below the limnetic zone. It too is out beyond the littoral zone. In this deep water, light penetration is not sufficient for photosynthesis. It is a dark and gloomy world with cold water and only a few life forms. Organisms tend to be critters such as bloodworms, anaerobic bacteria and fungi. After trout have fed, they will often drop down into the cold waters of the profundal zone to rest and digest their food.

Water Temperature Zones

We will look at the temperature stratification of water in more detail later. For now, it is sufficient to know that during the summer months, the warm water will float to the surface and cooler water will settle below that. This temperature stratification forms three distinct zones in a summertime lake. These are the epilimnion, the thermocline and the hypolimnion.

Epilimnion – The epilimnion is the layer or zone of warmer water near the surface of the lake. This zone has been warmed by the air and sunlight and churned through wind action. The water temperatures and depth of the epilimnion will vary with the seasonal temperatures.

Hypolimnion – The hypolimnion is the layer of cold water that sits on the lake bottom in deep water. This cold water layer will usually include the entire profundal zone and, depending on relative water temperatures, maybe some of the littoral zone. At the bottom of the hypolimnion, the water temperature is usually around 39°F.

Thermocline – The thermocline is the transition layer between the epilimnion and the hypolimnion. In the thermocline, the temperature rapidly changes from warmer to colder water. The 'hard' definition of thermocline is that the water temperature must change by at least a half degree per foot of depth but that rule isn't especially important to anglers.

These temperature layers won't form until after ice-off and turnover. The depth of these layers is continuously changing as the season's progress. The thickness of the epilimnion will be at its greatest in the hottest part of the summer. At times, the hypolimnion will extend into the littoral zone and over the shoals.

In mid-summer, the upper water layers (epilimnion) can reach stressful or lethal temperatures of 60°F to 70°F. To find their preferred water temperatures of 48°F to 55°F, trout will often drop into or below the thermocline where the water is cooler. And that is where the angler should fish. It isn't necessary to be precise about fishing an exact depth but a lot of anglers will carry an underwater thermometer to locate these temperatures.

Rainbows will sometimes move in and out of their preferred temperature range to take advantage of feeding opportunities. They may rest in a deep thermocline and make forays onto the warmer shoals for feeding. If food (your fly) is presented near the thermocline, these summertime fish will often take advantage of an easy meal.

Lake Bottom Structure

We have one more set of zonations to consider. These zonations are the water depths we have already been mentioning. These proceed from shore, to shoal, to drop-off and then to the deep water.

Shore - The shore is where the water meets the land.

Shoal - The shoal is the shallow waters near the shore. This is somewhat ambiguous since "shallow" is a term relative to the total depth in the lake.

Deep Water - Deep water, as the term implies, are the deeper portions of the lake. Usually we are talking about the limnetic and profundal zones together and suggesting water that is more than 25 or 30 feet in depth.

Drop-Off - The drop-off is a transition between shoal and deep water. This structure is defined by a steeper slope than usually occurs on the shoal or the lake bottom. If there is only a gradual slope transition between shore and deep water then we don't usually call it a drop-off.

Lake Profile

Now that we have the names to all the parts, let's look at a small chunk of lake to see how these all fit together. Figure 1 is a typical profile of a eutrophic lake. Not all sections of the shoreline will have this same cross section.

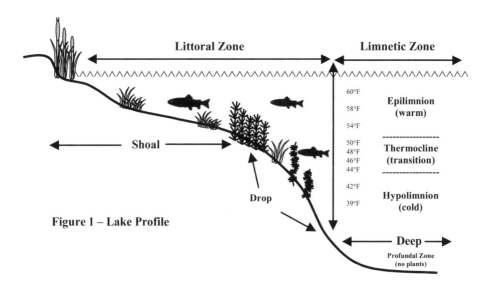

Figure 1 – Lake Profile

The littoral zone, which grows rooted plants, is the most important zone in a lake for the fly fisher. The littoral zone usually includes the shoal and part or all of the drop-off. The shoals and drop-offs are the most productive portions of a lake. Almost all of the aquatic invertebrates live in these areas at least part of the time. Therefore, when its time to feed, guess where the Rainbows are usually found.

The deeper portions of the lake are also important to the trout but not as important to the angler. The hypolimnion, thermocline and profundal zone are areas of cool water and possibly darkness in which the Rainbows will rest and digest their food. These are also havens of cooler water during the hot summer months.

> My fishing records show that over a long period, 50% of Rainbows are caught on the shoal, 30% at the drop-off and only 20% in deep water.

Water Properties Affecting Habitat

The main ingredient in a Rainbows habitat is water. A water environment is totally alien from the world of us air breathers. The properties of water deviate so radically from the properties of air that we terrestrials would find it a crazy place to live. However, as anglers should have some idea of how water properties affect the daily living of aquatic organisms.

Water Density

The density of water combined with the fact that it is a liquid, affects almost everything in the Rainbows environment. Liquid water is about 780 times denser than gaseous air. The "physics" of almost everything in this ecosystem seems different from terrestrial standards. Movement, light, sound, color, temperature and even the effects of gravity appear to take on a new meaning in an underwater environment. The physics don't really change but they do react differently in this "thick" environment.

For example, quick movement can be difficult in water without the proper body engineering for this environment. Try running through water or moving the flat side of your hand through water. The water compresses and makes movement difficult. To compensate, Rainbows have taken on streamline forms that pass easily through water and they can use their fins and tail to push or propel themselves through this dense medium. Scientists say they couldn't design a better shape for moving through water than the form of many fish as engineered by Mother Nature. Even the slime on the Rainbow is designed to reduce water compression, friction and drag.

The density of water also causes anything less dense than water to rise and float. Items lighter than water will not stay on the lake bottom. Trout and some other critters have developed techniques to change their density. Trout use an air bladder to reduce their total density. This density reduction essentially gives the trout the ability to fly or float in their environment. Aquatic invertebrates also take advantage of this property of water. Chironomid, for example, will fill an air sac to reduce its density causing it to float to the water surface where it can hatch.

We should probably mention now that there is a complicating factor to the water density phenomenon. Water reaches its maximum density (is heaviest) at 39.2°F or 4°C. Any water that is colder <u>OR</u> warmer than this temperature will be less dense and thus weigh less. Water that is less dense will float over water than is more dense. This is the primary force in the stratification of water temperatures and the development of an epilimnion, thermocline and hypolimnion.

In a deep enough lake, the water on the lake bottom and in the profundal zone will never rise above a temperature of 39.2°F. We will be discussing this density factor more while discussing water temperatures and the process of turnover.

Water Purity

Pure water is colorless, odorless and tasteless. Seldom do we find pure water in nature. Water is also a good solvent. It dissolves minerals on its way to a lake. As soon as we have minerals in the water, it is no longer pure. As soon as we have water with mineral nutrients, we are likely to have organisms

> **Did You Know**
> In nature, you are unlikely to find pure water. If you do, you are viewing water devoid of nutrients and life.

living in the mixture. Add some light and we are likely to get algae and plants, which further reduce the purity of the water. No matter how clear a water body looks, it is likely to be teaming with life.

Sound in Water

Sound is transmitted better through a dense medium than it is through a permeable medium such as air. The density of water carries sound better and faster than happens in an air environment. Water will carry a sound wave much farther and four times faster than the loosely packed molecules of air (1433

> **Did You Know**
> Sound will travel faster, further and with more clarity in a water environment than in a terrestrial environment.

m/sec versus 335 m/sec). The next time you and your buddy are talking on a lake, just remember that the person in the boat a hundred yards away can probably hear what you are saying. So will the fish and from a much greater distance.

Light in Water

Since water is 780 times denser than air, these molecules are much tighter packed. Water will absorb and disperse light energy much faster than what happens in air. As sunlight enters a lake, the water gradually absorbs the sunlight starting with the shorter (and more energetic) wavelengths first. The first colors to be

> **Did You Know**
> The deep blue to blue-green color reflected from deep water is because those colors have less energy and are not absorbed as rapidly in the water column.

absorbed are the reds, then oranges, then yellows and on into the greens and blues. Since the green and blue wavelengths are longer, they pass through the water molecules with more ease and are the last to be absorbed by the water. They are the wavelengths that will be reflected in deeper water. That's the reason that deep clear waters often appear to be bluish-green or blue in color. Shallow water, on the other hand, will often appear yellowish. This yellowish color, is not necessarily because the reflecting colors are depicting the color of the lake bottom.

Among other things, light absorption in water will also change the color of your fly as it moves down the water column. In less than ten feet of water, a pure red fly (short wave lengths) will appear as dark gray in color and a couple of feet deeper it will appear as black to the trout. There are a number of organisms that live in moderately deep fresh or salt water, that take on a red coloration as a form of camouflage. Lobsters, crabs, starfish and crayfish are a few examples. Unfortunately, the theory that red color on flies and lures makes them more visible to the trout is pretty much a bogus idea. We will examine this aspect of light further when we discuss the vision of trout.

Another aspect of light is when it passes from a medium of one density into a medium of different density the light energy bends in a process called refraction. You've probably seen the straight stick that appears to bend in water. When this process is viewed from underwater and looking toward the surface, something

> **Did You Know**
> Water bends light, reflects light, decreases the intensity of light and changes the color of light with the depth in the water.

strange happens. At 48° from the perpendicular all vision is reflected back down off the bottom of the waters surface. There is only a circular view through the surface to the outside world and that doesn't extend beyond that 48° mark. Again, we will discuss this further when we examine the vision of a trout.

Oxygen In Water

Air contains 35 times more oxygen than water. Therefore, an organism living in water needs to be about 35 times more efficient at retrieving oxygen from its environment. The gills of trout are remarkably efficient at extracting oxygen from water. They are also extremely fragile. If you intend to release a fish, never let anything contact the gills of that fish.

Oxygen gets into lake water through a number of methods. The primary way is via the absorption of oxygen directly from the air at the waters surface. Whitecaps breaking in open water and waves breaking along the shoreline will trap air bubbles. These trapped air bubbles will directly transfer oxygen into the water via osmosis. A running stream gathers oxygen this way. Raindrops falling into a lake surface also provide air bubbles that are plentiful in oxygen. Oxygen is even absorbed from the air just by having direct contact between the two surfaces. In addition, wind and water temperature will actually set up currents in the water that transport the oxygen from the surface to deeper in the lake.

> **Did You Know**
> After a few days of windy weather, oxygen levels in a lake are likely to be higher and the Bows more active. Active fish are more likely to feed than lethargic fish.

Plants and Oxygen

Another source of oxygen in a lake is from plants. Aquatic plants, like terrestrial plants, use the process of photosynthesis to convert sunlight into food and energy. In the photosynthetic process, sugars (carbohydrates) are produced from carbon dioxide and water. The carbon is used to produce the sugar and the oxygen is released back into the water.

Photosynthesis occurs during the daylight hours and during this time, oxygen is released. At night, the plants breathe (respire) and the photosynthetic process is reversed. During respiration, the sugars and oxygen are used and carbon dioxide and water are given off as waste products. As a result, there is slightly more oxygen in the water at sunset than at sunrise. The basic process and daily results are as follows.

Plant Photosynthesis

$$6\ CO_2 + 6\ H_2O = 6O_2 + C_6H_{12}O_6$$

OR >   6 carbon dioxides + 6 waters = 6 oxygen + 1 sugar

Plant Respiration

$$6\ O_2 + C_6H_{12}O_6 = 6CO_2 + 6\ H_2O$$

OR >   6 oxygen + 1 sugar = 6 carbon dioxides + 6 waters

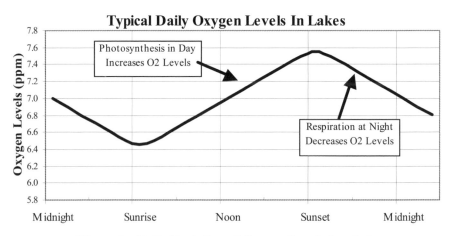

Figure 2 – Daily Variation of Oxygen Levels in a Lake

These daily changes in oxygen levels happen primarily in the shallower water where plants are growing. The formulas and details aren't important to most fly fishers but the concept is. Rainbows are more active and feed better, when the oxygen levels are higher. As Figure 2 shows, this condition happens around sunset. My data shows that the number of Rainbows caught per hour is about 30% higher near sunset than at other times of the day.

Plants are also a primary source of oxygen depletion in a lake. As plants and other organisms die, they settle to the lake bottom where bacteria decompose their bodies. The bacteria use oxygen from the water in this decomposition process.

> **Did You Know**
> Other factors being equal, the trout will become more active and thus feed more as oxygen levels increase in the lake.

The primary period of oxygen depletion is during the winter months when ice covers the lake. The ice prohibits oxygen exchange with the air. In addition, sunlight doesn't penetrate the ice very well and plants need this ingredient in photosynthesis. Without it, they die and the bacteria begin their work. This is a primary factor in fish kills during the spring turnover. The poorly oxygenated water from the lake bottom is brought toward the surface and mixed with water that may already be low in oxygen. If the mix drops to oxygen levels less than 4 ppm, the trout will likely die.

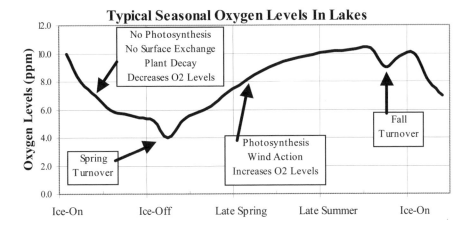

Figure 3 – Seasonal Variation of Oxygen Levels in a Lake

Over the course of a summer, the plants will generate more oxygen through photosynthesis than they consume through respiration. In addition, the wind and wave action is constantly building up oxygen levels over the free water period. So in the fall there is more oxygen than in the spring. Figure 3 gives a picture of what typically happens. However, many factors can affect this profile.

Did You Know
From spring turnover through fall turnover, the level of oxygen in a lake steadily increases. Trout should be more active but warming water temperatures are often an off-setting factor.

Algae blooms and water temperatures (as discussed in the next section) are the two biggest factors affecting summertime oxygen depletion. Algae blooms can cut off the supply of sunlight to rooted plants causing their death. The algae also die and settle to the lake bottom. Again, decomposition begins and oxygen levels subside. The level of oxygen can be significantly affected by algae blooms. Very heavy algae blooms can cause fish kills in the mid-summer or fall.

Water Temperature

Water does not exchange heat nearly as well or rapidly as air. While the air temperature might vary 30°F over the course of a day, the water temperature is only going to be affected by a fraction of a degree, if at all. Even in constantly freezing air, for example, it will take a lake several weeks for an ice layer to form on a lake. Rapidly changing water temperatures is not usually a factor affecting fishing. In addition, water will mix as it changes temperature. Thus, the entire water column must first be cooled and stratified before the surface layer will freeze.

Water temperature does change over time and can have a significant impact on the trout. Rainbows are cold blooded. They take on the temperature of their surroundings. In turn, this affects the metabolism and oxygen intake of the trout. Cold water isn't too much of a problem but warm water is a problem for Bows. As already discussed, water in excess of 70°F can actually kill the trout.

> **Did You Know**
>
> Cold water will hold more oxygen than warm water. However, in warm water trout need more oxygen to function. The trout will seek a location in the water column that balances each of these needs.

A contributing factor in this problem is that warm water holds less oxygen to support metabolism and breathing than cool water. Table 4 provides a sample of how oxygen content changes with water temperature.

The numbers in Table 2 will change with depth, season, and most other lake conditions. However, the table shows graphic reasons why Bows will seek water temperatures that are in the preferred range of 48°F to 55°F. During warm summer conditions, the trout are likely to be found in the deeper and cooler portions of the lake.

Temperature Relationships to Oxygen Content & Consumption

Temp Degrees C	Temp Degrees F	Oxygen Saturation (O2 ppm)	Typical Water O2 Content* (O2 ppm)	Typical Trout O2 Consumption (O2 ppm)
0	32.0	14.6	9.8	4.5
2	35.6	13.8	9.2	4.7
4	39.2	13.1	8.8	5.0
6	42.8	12.4	8.3	5.2
8	46.4	11.8	7.9	5.5
10	50.0	11.3	7.6	5.7
12	53.6	10.8	7.2	6.0
14	57.2	10.3	6.9	6.3
16	60.8	9.8	6.6	6.6
18	64.4	9.4	6.3	7.0
20	68.0	9.0	6.0	7.3
22	71.6	8.7	5.8	7.7
24	75.2	8.4	5.6	8.1
26	78.8	8.1	5.4	8.5
28	82.4	7.8	5.2	8.9
30	86.0	7.5	5.0	9.4

* Prior to oxygen depletion due to decomposition, respiration, etc.

Table 2 – Generalized Temperature to Oxygen Relationship

Water temperature will also affect the activity of other organisms in the lake. Many insects, for example, will await a certain water temperature before commencing to hatch. Algae blooms are often triggered by water temperature and their presence will increase water temperature by intercepting sunlight. Zooplankton will often hold at different levels in a lake based on water temperature.

Water temperature combined with the fact that water reaches its maximum density at 39°F creates a special habitat condition that we should now discuss. This special condition is called "turnover" and is our next topic.

> **Did You Know**
> Many insects will not hatch until the water temperature reaches a certain minimum threshold. Once that lower limit has been achieved, the insects will then use other keys, such as moon position or sun angle, to time their hatch.

Turnover

Many anglers have heard and used the term "turnover" but few actually understand the process. Turnover is when the water near the surface drops to the lake bottom and the lake bottom water rises to the surface. The process happens because water density reaches its maximum density at 39.2°F but "overturn", as some folks call it, will only occur in climates cold enough to form ice on the lake.

In <u>winter</u>, water at 39°F is densest and will be on the bottom of the lake. Water at 38°F is less dense and will be above that. The water temperatures are progressively colder as we go up the water column. At the lake surface, the water will be frozen at 32°F.

> **Did You Know**
> Ice weighs less than the water below it. That is why it floats. Floating ice also acts as an insulator to prevent deeper lake water from freezing.

In <u>summer</u>, this temperature regime is reversed. Water at 39°F will still be on the lake bottom. However, as we move up the water column the temperature get progressively warmer with the warmest water being on the surface. Turnover occurs when these summer and winter conditions are changing places. This happens in both the spring and fall.

Let's look at the springtime turnover first. As the days get warmer, the lake surface ice melts. As it melts, it warms to 33°F. Daily the upper water warms and merges with the cooler water below. In shallow water, penetrating sunlight warms the lake bottom and thus that water. It rises and merges with water of its own temperature. Eventually we have two strata of water temperatures. The upper strata will be at 38°F and the lower strata at 39°F. The lake is now ready to turnover.

The next bit of warmth will warm the surface layer from 38°F to 39°F. Being denser, that water will then drop through the water column. In shallow water, sunlight penetration will also warm the lake bottom causing that water at 39°F to warm to 40°F. Being lighter, that water begins to rise. The upper and lower layers of water are replacing each other and

> **Did You Know**
> For "turnover", the temperature throughout the water column must be at or about 39°F.

23

turnover is in progress. The basics of this process in the springtime are shown in Figure 4. Figure 5 shows the reverse process in the fall.

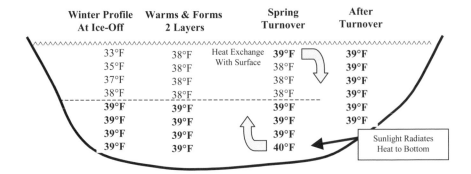

Figure 4 – Water Temperatures During the Spring Turnover Process

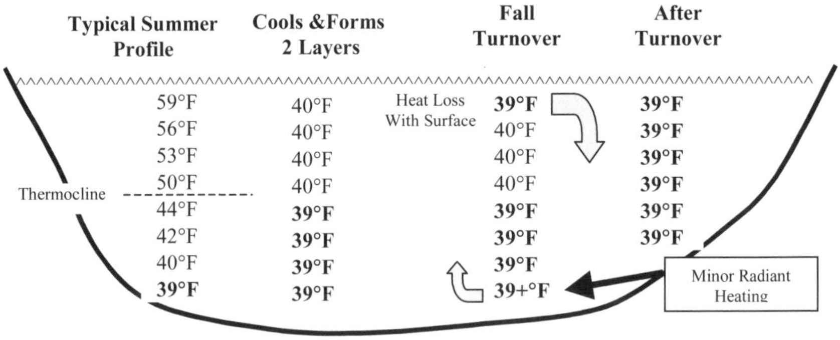

Figure 5 – Water Temperatures During the Fall Turnover Process

In the fall, essentially the same process happens in reverse. At this time of year the upper layer of water is at 40°F, cools to 39°F to become denser. It then sinks through the surrounding water. It should be noted that the radiant energy warming the lake bottom in the fall is less intense due to sun angle. Turnover at this time of year is a slower process. If the weather is cloudy, the fall turnover may be very insignificant. The surface water simply settles to the bottom, gradually displacing the warmer water and there is little circular motion.

Turnover affects the fishing because of oxygen loss throughout the water column. Over winter, oxygen levels have dropped. During winter, ice and snow will cut off about 90% of the light reaching the lake bottom. Rooted plants and algae die and settle to the bottom where they rot and consume oxygen. In addition, the upper layers of water are not in contact with the air

> As you might guess,
> a trout under stress
> isn't going to bite,
> when things aren't right.

and thus oxygen is not being replaced. By the time winter is over, there is a layer of oxygen depleted water around the decomposing plants and the upper water layers lack abundant oxygen.

During spring turnover, the oxygen depleted water is merged with the rest of the lake water. In the mixing process, what little oxygen remains is evenly distributed throughout the water column. The net result is a reduction in adequately oxygenated water throughout the water column. Occasionally the critical oxygen level of 4 ppm is surpassed and the fish die.

Fall turnover is not nearly as drastic or hard on the trout. Wind and wave action over the summer has mixed the water and so the initial oxygen content is high. Most plants are still alive and there isn't a layer of oxygen depleted water near the bottom. The surface water sinking toward the bottom is well oxygenated and the process usually occurs much slower in the fall. Fishing is likely to remain good during a fall turnover.

> **Fishing Tip**
> Bows will often hug the shoreline at sometime during both the spring and fall turnovers. The wise angler will watch for signs of fish in these areas. At both times of year, freshwater shrimp are a favorite on the Rainbows menu.

The quicker a turnover occurs, the more likely it is to result in oxygen depletion and poor fishing. The affects of turnover will generally last two to three weeks depending on the amount of sunlight, air temperature, wind action, and so on. Particularly in the spring but also in the fall, the fishing will improve after turnover.

Under average conditions, it will take a lake five to ten days after ice-off before a lake begins to turnover. Fishing should be good before turnover begins. Bottom materials floating to the surface is a good indicator that turnover is underway. Turnover will occur over the shoals and in the shallow portions of a lake before it does in the middle or deeper portions of the lake.

As turnover begins, the fish are likely to move to the deeper water where oxygen depletion hasn't yet started. And that's where you should fish. But you will probably want to keep your fly in the upper ten feet of water. As the turnover process moves into deeper water, it is probably finishing in the shallow water. At that

> As water turns over
> the oxygen is lower,
> and fish are found
> where waves meet ground.

time, it is wise to try fishing over the shoals. During a rapid spring turnover, the entire lake may have oxygen problems. In these circumstances, the trout will seek any water they can find with sufficient oxygen. This is most likely to be found right along the shoreline.

On windy days, the waves build up and break against the shore on the down wind side of the lake. Each breaking wave is adding oxygen to the water. Rainbows will sometimes congregate in these small areas where underwater currents are providing a continuous flow of oxygenated water from the wave action. These areas are generally small and seldom extend more than 15 feet from shore. If you can find one of these areas of 'oxygen flow', they can provide some excellent fishing in conditions that are otherwise poor. You can also find fish that hug the shoreline in the fall but at this time of year, it seems to be more a matter of comfort and feed availability than dire necessity.

Aquatic Plants

Aquatic plants are the life giving force in a lake. As we have seen, these plants provide oxygen to the lake system. Through photosynthesis, they also provide the food energy for the grazers at the bottom of the food chain. Without this energy from the plants, the higher life forms in a lake, such as Rainbow Trout, could not exist.

Some of these plants will only grow along the shoreline of the lake. Plants such as bulrushes, cattails, sedges and a variety of reeds will have their roots anchored in the water and their upper parts above the water. Numerous invertebrates will live in and around the submerged portions of these plants. I say "in" because some bugs like the bloodworm will bore into the stems of these plants. The out-of-water portions of these plants are also important to bugs such as the damselfly and dragonfly which crawl up theses plant stems to emerge into adults. Many insects will rest on these shoreline plants after feeding or during mating.

Other aquatic plants only grow under the water without any portions intentionally extending above the water. These plants include the Chara weed, coontail, pondweed, milfoil, lily pads and others. As a rule-of-thumb, the population of aquatic invertebrates increases proportionally with the amount of aquatic plants in a lake. And that means the lake can support larger populations of bigger fish.

Essentially rooted aquatic plants need sunlight, nutrients in the water, a specific pH range, and some muck on the lake bottom in which to sink their roots. Different species have different requirements for each of these factors. Lily pads, for instance, prefer slightly acidic water while Chara weeds prefer alkaline water. It's possible but not likely that you will find each of these plants growing in the same lake.

Because a specific species of plant has the same requirements, the individual plants tend to grow in similar places within a lake. These patches or weed beds only extend to certain water depths because of sunlight requirements for photosynthesis. The patches also tend to occur over similar nutrient regimes and soil types on the lake bottom. In different lakes with different conditions, such as water clarity, the same species of plant may grow at different depths or in different locations.

> **Fishing Tip**
>
> From mid July through late August, the sunlight is very bright, aquatic plants have grown tall and aquatic invertebrates are somewhat scarce. Through this period, the Rainbows are especially fond of staying in or near weed beds.

Learning the names and identification of these plants probably isn't important to most anglers. Knowing that these weed patches are some of the primary feeding grounds in the lake is important. An angler who learns a specific lake will know where these aquatic plants are found. When the fishing gets tough it's time to visit some of the more productive of these weed beds.

There is one last aquatic plant to mention before we leave this section. An alga is a plant even though it isn't rooted. Blue-green algae are one of the more common and important algae in our lakes. Algae float near the lake surface. In the warmer water of summer, these plants can flourish to the point that they form thick layers. These thick layers can cut off sunlight to any plants deeper in the water column. They can get so thick that algae near the surface can even cut off sunlight to other algae further down in the layer. Without the sunlight, all these plants will die and begin to decay and consume oxygen. The layer of algae will also restrict oxygen uptake at the lake surface. These combining factors can cause summer-kills of trout.

The Aquatic Food Chain

An important part of the Rainbows habitat is the food chain. When we look at a food chain, we are just looking at what an organism feeds on and then who eats that organism. We will be discussing the foods of Rainbow Trout in more detail in later chapters but we should present the food chain basics here.

As already mentioned, the foundation of a food chain starts with plants that only need sunlight, water and nutrients to survive. Plants are considered the primary producers in the food chain. If a lake doesn't have plants, it can't support any of the higher life forms. Up to a critical point, the more plants we have the more animal life that can be supported.

Did You Know
Photic zone refers to the area of a lake with sunlight penetration through the water column. Essentially, it is a combination of the littoral zone and the limnetic zone.

Aquatic plants can range from microscopic in size, to free floating plants such as algae, to plants rooted on the lake bottom, to plants that inhabit the transition from water to land. But virtually all the plants will live in the photic zone of the lake. Other organisms will live below the photic zone but not usually plants.

When a lake has sufficient quantities of plants, it can support organisms from the animal kingdom that feed on the plants. Animals that feed on plants are generally referred to as grazers. As the grazer population increases, they provide a large enough source of food to sustain other members of the animal kingdom. Scavengers will inhabit the lake and feed on the dead plants and grazers. Scavengers can live below the photic zone and feed on organic materials that settle to the lake bottom. Soon, invertebrate predators that hunt and feed on the grazers and scavengers would be found in the food chain. When there are enough invertebrates, a lake would support a population of vertebrates (fish) that would feed on many of the invertebrates.

That is the quick version of the food chain. In real life, the process isn't quite that simple. There are all kinds of interactions in this process. Some fungi can live without sunlight. Some critters occupy more than one niche. A freshwater shrimp, for example, is a grazer; a scavenger and an invertebrate predator all rolled into one. And then there are the exceptions such as fish that are grazers. These days science tends to call it a food "web" rather than a food chain because of the complexity of these interactions. But the important point to remember is that the entire chain of feeding events starts from plants that are found in the photic zone.

About 50% of Rainbows are caught on the shoal and another 30% at the drop off. By far the best fishing in a lake is in the littoral zone where rooted plants can survive. Because of the propensity of plant life, that is where the vast majority of grazers are found. Naturally, the scavengers and invertebrate predators will be near the grazers, which are their primary

> A hungry trout
> Won't laze about.
> In the shallows it feeds,
> Right next to the weeds.

food source. And thus, the Rainbows frequent the littoral zone when feeding. That's where the Rainbows food is most abundant.

An angler should assess the depth of light penetration and where littoral zones are likely to be found. Angling effort should then be concentrated in or near these areas where rooted plants can survive. Rainbows that aren't feeding will frequent the middle of the lake and deep waters. Non-feeding trout can sometimes be enticed to a fly but the majority of feeding trout will be on or near the shoal where the food chain offers the best opportunity for success. Note that this statement isn't necessarily true for Rainbows that are feeding on baitfish. When present, these minnows become a part of the food chain. They will frequent the middle of the lake and are a food source for the Rainbow. The trout will actively feed on baitfish far from the littoral zone.

Within a lake, large fish are at the top of the food chain. The basic premise of a food chain is that anything smaller than you can be eaten. In reality, the trout is limited to foods that are smaller than about six percent of the Rainbows own body mass. The trout must be able to pass the food through its esophagus and hold that food within the stomach and six percent is about the maximum. To illustrate, an eight-pound Rainbow of 27 inches could eat (with difficulty) a ten-inch Rainbow of 7.5 ounces. As the size of a Rainbow decreases, so does the maximum and average size of its food items. Within the food chain, usually the small Rainbows feed on the very small food items such as Copepods, Daphnia, and water mites. The larger Rainbows in a pristine lake tend to feed on the moderate to larger sized invertebrates. The larger Rainbows are 'able' to feed on the very small invertebrates but prefer to feed when there is an abundance of food items in the larger size classes. Sometimes all it takes to keep those pesky little trout from taking your fly is to put on a larger fly.

Reading a Lake

After you have fished a lake a few times, you generally know what type of lake it is, where the shoals and other structures are, the water clarity and other information to help in deciding where to fish within the lake. Ultimately, you need to get out on a lake to determine this information. However, to some degree, you can determine what to expect and where to fish even if you have never fished a lake.

The surrounding topography will give you the first clue as to what to expect from a lake. A lake generally takes on the form of the surrounding landscape. A lake that sits in the bottom of a steep "V" shaped valley will most likely have the same shape. It will probably be deep, oligotrophic with clear water and few shoals. You can expect a lake that sits on flat to rolling terrain to be geologically older and it will probably be fairly shallow, eutrophic and have large shoals and shallow areas with cloudy to murky water. By looking at the angle at which the land enters the water, you have a good idea as to what the lake bottom is doing. Mesotrophic lakes often have variety in how steep the land enters the lake.

By using adjacent terrain, the angler can also determine the most likely location of shoals and shallows that are the primary trout feeding areas. Where the land enters the lake at a steep angle, the location probably doesn't have a large shoal. It is probably a deep portion of the lake. Conversely, where the land enters the lake at a shallow angle there are probably shoals and it should be a good feeding area. Where the land enters the water as a 'point' there is a good probability that it has a similar topography underwater. An angler can anchor directly off the point and expect deeper water on both sides. Where creeks or drainage patterns enter the lake there is a strong possibility of a shoal even if the land enters the water at a steep angle. When it rains, the water flowing through these drainage patterns will pick up sand and silt which will settle to the bottom on entering the still lake waters. Over years, these build up into shoals.

> **Fishing Tip**
>
> A shoal or drop-off that is near deep water is usually a good place to fish. The shoal provides abundant food while the deep water provides a place for the trout to rest and digest its food.

The shoreline of the lake will also give you good clues as to what the lake bottom will be like in a given location. A rocky shoreline where the land enters the lake at a steep angle will probably have a rocky lake bottom. On a gentle slope into the lake, you can usually expect gravel and small stones as the wave action washes the surrounding dirt into the lake but not the gravel. This washout from the shore will often provide enough soil on the lake bottom for plants to root in the littoral zone. A muddy shoreline will probably have a muddy lake bottom. Muddy or silty bottoms provide a rooting medium for plants and are the most likely locations to have underwater weed patches. They are also more likely to be the areas that are highly productive in aquatic invertebrates.

Deciduous trees and bushes along a shoreline often indicate that the location is rich in organic matter to support underwater plant growth. As the deciduous vegetation sheds its leaves in the fall, these will drop into the lake, settle to the bottom and the bacteria will decompose these materials for the aquatic plants to use. Coniferous trees along the shoreline will shed needles. The bacteria cannot process needles as easily as leaves and coniferous needles are more acidic. The result is that shorelines with conifer trees near the water edge are not usually as productive as shorelines with deciduous vegetation.

A last indicator that I use in reading a lake is the presence of emergent or floating plants along the shoreline. Emergent and floating plants are those that have their roots in water but parts of the plant emerge from or float on the water. These can be seen above the water from a distance and include plants such as cattails, bulrushes, horsetails, lily pads, reeds and so forth. When you see these growing along a portion of the shoreline, it is a good indication that there is an associated feeding shoal. When I am unfamiliar with a lake, I will usually head straight for locations with emergent plants to begin my fishing and exploration of the lake.

When you get to a lake for the first time, look over the lake and read the signs. Select an area that has a substantial feeding shoal with nearby deep water for the Rainbows to shelter. This variety of shallows with deep water will generally provide the conditions most suitable for the trout.

End Notes

From our perspective, the Rainbow Trout's habitat is a strange and unusual place. Each lake is different and the trout need to adapt to the specifics of the lake in which it lives. And yet, some things in these varying environments remain the same. The angler needs to assess the variables and the constants of a lake. Variables such as water clarity will affect the depth of light penetration and thus weed bed depth. Constants such as the trout feeding in or near weed beds will remain the same from lake to lake. With all the unusual properties of water, we shouldn't be surprised that Rainbows have developed some unique ways in which to take advantage of their environment. In the next couple of chapters, we will look at some of the Bows physical and sensory abilities in adapting to their underwater habitat. Some of these are quite astounding.

Figure 6 – A 7 pound 10 ounce Bow from a Pristine Lake

3

The Physical Attributes of Rainbows

When you look at a Rainbow Trout, there really isn't much to it. A head, a body, a tail, some fins and some pretty colors. Yet that is all that is necessary. With these basics, the trout can swiftly and effectively move about its environment to catch prey.

Living in water presents a totally different set of requirements than what is needed for living in a terrestrial environment. By our standards, the underwater world in a lake is an alien ecosystem. It is a sluggish medium to move through without the proper body

> **Did You Know**
> Water is 780 times denser than air and the torpedo shape of fish is the most efficient shape for moving through this dense medium.

shape. Arms and legs work fine in air but only hamper movement in water. In fact, anything that protrudes from the body creates "drag" in water and is a hindrance to movement.

Rainbow Trout and other organisms that live in water have evolved some unique physical adaptations to do more than survive in their underwater world. The Rainbow excels in many physical feats by comparison to land animals. Water being 780 times denser than air plays an important role in these abilities.

I would like to devote this chapter to ensuring that you, as an angler, are familiar with the basic physiology of the Rainbow. More importantly, we should examine the physical strengths and weaknesses of this fish. Understanding how the fish physically functions in its environment is a part of the knowledge needed to consistently hook and land these fish.

The Rainbow Body Structure

The body shape of terrestrial animals generally has a bulbous head with neck, legs and sometimes arms. These don't really function well in water. So Mother Nature decided to streamline the trout's body into something that did function well in this dense environment. The result is a torpedo shaped body.

The head and torso are melded together with a tail and some attached fins. The whole structure is built for speed and the ability to catch prey. For a comparison, in its underwater environment the Rainbow Trout would be considered akin to a bird of prey. It is a hunter and needs speed and maneuverability. And it has tremendous speed and excellent agility. But let's begin with the basics. Figure 7 provides the names of the basic parts of a Rainbow and Figure 8 provides a closer look around the head of this trout.

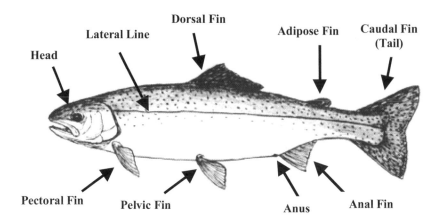

Figure 7 - The Basic Body Parts of a Rainbow Trout.

Basic Body Shape

The Rainbow's body is thickest about one third of the way from the head toward the tail. This fusiform and somewhat torpedo shaped body is about the best design possible for movement through water. Except for the fins, the body lacks extrusions that would create drag or turbulence in the water and even the fins can be closed to fit tight against the body when drag needs to be reduced. The body is laterally compressed from side to side. This sideways flattening of the body assists the fish with movements such as rapid stops or turning and even helps the fish propel itself.

Tail and Muscles

The tail or caudal fin of the trout is the primary means of rapid locomotion. By sweeping the tail back and forth, the fish is propelled through the water. Most of the body undulates as the Rainbow sweeps its tail from side to side. This sidewise motion along with the lateral compression of the body also helps create propulsion through water. Most of the muscle tissue in the trout's body is designed just for this movement.

From behind the head to where the tail starts, the trout's muscles are segmented into overlapping layers. You've seen these layers as you cook a trout. You can flake off individual layers of muscle. Each segmented layer is attached to an individual vertebra in the spinal column and therefore can be controlled separately during movement. The fish can contract these muscles in one direction part way down the body and in the opposite direction further down the body to give the undulations necessary for sweeping the tail and obtaining forward thrust.

Fins

All the fins of the trout are used for stabilization and specialized maneuverability. They act as rudders, keels, sails, brakes, planers and propellers. The single fins (dorsal, adipose and anal) are primarily used for stability and determining direction. The paired

> **Did You Know**
> The boney structures in the fins of a trout are called rays. These are attached to muscles which allow the rays to be extended or flattened next to the body. The webbing between the rays is like the webbing in a ducks foot and can be used to press against the water.

fins (pectoral and pelvic) are matching sets of fins on both sides of the body that are more versatile. The Rainbow can use the pectoral fins, for example, to move slowly and gingerly forwards, sideways or even backwards while approaching or searching for prey. They can be extended at various angles to be used as planers that cause the fish to dive or rise in the water column. If one pectoral fin is flared while the other is held tight to the body, it will assist in turning the trout. If both are extended and flared, they act as brakes to help the fish stop. When the trout is rapidly swimming, most fins are retracted or only slightly extended to provide the necessary direction and stability. For rapid stops, the trout can turn its compressed body sideways to the direction of travel and flare all the fins. In the thick water environment, this maneuver will cause it to come to a rapid stop.

Skin, Scales and Slime

The entire body of the trout is covered with skin, scales and slime. The scales are quite small compared to many other species of fish. Covering the scales is a thin layer of slime. The skin, slime and scales of the trout protect the internal organs and muscles from infections and mechanical damage. Most anglers seem to understand the functions of the skin and scales and seldom complain about these, but the slime is another matter.

As unpleasant as the slime is to touch, it has a number of valuable functions. The slime on the trout sloughs-off as the trout swims. Slime being slippery, plus sloughing-off, reduces friction by about 60% and thus helps the trout move through water with ease. The soughing of the slime has another purpose. Some bodily wastes are deposited in the slime. As it slowly peels away these wastes are removed from the fish along with the slime. These waste products are what sometimes give the Rainbow an iridescent color in sunlight.

The salt content needed in the trout's body is generally higher than the surrounding freshwater. In the salt-water environment of a sea going steelhead the water has a higher salt content than the fish can tolerate. The trout's kidney is the primary organ to control the salt balance, but the slime helps maintain that balance. The next time you are handling a fish destined for release, please remember how important the slime is to the fish. Handle the fish in a manner that removes as little slime as possible.

Lateral Line

The lateral line is sometimes difficult to see on the Rainbow. This structure is a thin line that runs the length of the fish from the mid-point of the tail to the upper portion of the head. The lateral line contains a series of sensory organs that pick up low frequency vibrations in water. There is a lateral line on both sides of the trout's body. These sensory organs also exist in the head of the Rainbow. However, in the trout's head these organs are not in a continuous series and thus are not easily visible to the angler. We will be discussing this sensory organ in much more detail in Chapter 4.

Head

While the body of the Rainbow is primarily designed to move the fish and house the internal organs, the head does most everything else. The head is a bony structure that holds and protects the trout's brain which processes the sensory input received by the fish. As shown in Figure 8, a pair of eyes for vision and a pair of nostrils to assist with smell are located in the head. The trout has an internal ear in the head located just behind the brain but there are no external ears or ear holes.

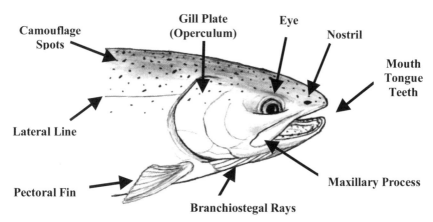

Figure 8 - Head of the Rainbow Trout

The mouth of the trout is the most forward part of the fish and the opening through which angler's flies and the trout's food is ingested. Without hands or other appendages to direct food into this opening, the trout must move forward to engulf the food and then close the mouth to surround the food. The trout's eyes are located slightly behind the mouth to assist in the food gathering process but sufficiently near the mouth to judge the distance to the food item.

The trout has small but sharp teeth on the jaws, tongue and vomer bone on the roof of the mouth. These teeth are not used for chewing the food but rather for grasping and holding the prey so it doesn't escape. In fact, all the teeth point toward the tail of the fish and this helps guide the food into the trout's throat. The trout swallows its food whole.

Those lines under the 'chin' of the trout are called branchiostegal rays and they function with the mouth to help in the feeding process. These muscles help to rapidly open the trout's mouth and gill plate. When rapidly opened, water is sucked into the mouth of the trout and expelled through the gills. This helps to

Fishing Tip

You have probably noticed very soft strikes when fishing flies that resemble an aquatic invertebrate. When the trout is fooled into thinking the fly is a bug, it will often just suck the fly into its mouth rather than strike it hard. Watch for your line or leader to dip or move slightly and then softly set the hook.

guide any small food such as Chironomids, into the trout's mouth. This is the normal ingestion process used by the trout when feeding on small invertebrates in a lake.

Gills

The mouth serves another function. It is the main method of bringing water to the gills for oxygen extraction. The gills are located under the Operculum or the plates that cover the gills. The gills only extract oxygen from the water as the water is moving toward the tail of the fish. When resting, the branchiostegal rays are used to open and close the gill plates. With the mouth slightly open, water is sucked into the mouth when the gill plates are opened. The mouth is then closed and the water is forced over the gills as the gill plates are closing. It almost looks like the fish is gasping when breathing in this manner. When the trout is swimming, both the mouth and gill plates are slightly opened and the movement of the fish forces water over the gills.

Bones

The skeleton of the Rainbow is simple and I'm sure everyone is familiar with the basic design. The spine or backbone runs from the tail to the head of the trout. It runs approximately through the center of the trout and pretty well parallels the lateral line. The spine consists of a series of connected vertebra. The manner in which these vertebras are connected allows the muscles to pull the spine in many directions. The spine of a trout is far more flexible than the spine of a human.

Upright bones originate from each vertebra to help support the tissue above the spine. To help with this tissue support, fine bones also originate from each side of the vertebra. These extend towards the sides and slightly upward. Below the spine from head to anus is the body cavity and that is enclosed by a set of ribs on each side of the fish. From the anus to the tail are firm bones that extend straight down that are similar to those above the spine. Again, each of the ribs and downward spikes are connected to individual vertebra.

The skull in the head of the trout is a complex series of interlocking bony plates plus cavities for the eyes and other organs in the head. The primary design of the bones in the head is to allow for the opening and closing of the mouth and gill plates.

Internal Organs

The body cavity and head of the fish contain the internal organs of the trout. The Rainbow and other fish have the usual assortment of internal organs plus an air bladder. The brain is located just behind and above the eye. The ear in a fish is an internal organ and located just behind the brain. The gills take the place of lungs, found in terrestrial animals, and are located just under the gill plates. The heart pumps oxygenated blood through the fish and for efficiency is located near the gills, where the oxygen is obtained. The liver is fairly large and located behind the heart. That "blood vein" that lies along the spine of the trout and always contains coagulated blood no matter how soon you clean the trout isn't actually a blood vein. That long, narrow, dark colored and hard to remove thing is actually the kidney. The digestive system is much like terrestrials but somewhat shortened. Food comes in the mouth, through an esophagus, into the stomach, then through short intestines and out the anus.

And now let's talk about that air bladder. This organ is next to the spine and is located above most everything else but the kidney. This organ is just an air bag and its function is to provide the trout with buoyancy in the water. It occupies about 8% of the body cavity. By inflating or deflating the air bladder, the trout can obtain just the right amount of air to make it neutrally buoyant. It can then remain suspended at any depth in the water without much fin action.

Did You Know
The density and thus the buoyancy of water act to support the internal organs of a trout. If lifted out of water the full effects of gravity take over and that can damage the trout's internal organs. Try not to remove the fish from water but if you must then always support its tummy.

You would also think that the air bladder would act to keep the trout in an upright position but that isn't the case. If you've seen a dead trout floating in the water it will usually be belly up or floating with its side to the surface rather than floating in the upright position. The reason is that the air bladder is very slightly below the trout's center of gravity. Without frequent and proper fin control (usually just the pectoral fins), the trout will tend to turn upside down. However, the advantage of this arrangement is that it gives the trout greater flexibility for rapid turns, grabbing surface insects and rapidly returning to the depths. This placement gives the trout greater underwater maneuverability. And that's one of the reasons for the great fighting abilities of the Rainbow Trout.

Another point of interest about the air bladder is how the trout can inflate or deflate this organ. Salmonids including Rainbow Trout have a duct between the air bladder and the stomach. Air can be pumped between these two organs. Yep, to a large degree, the trout inflates its air bladder through the stomach and air gets into the stomach by the trout gulping surface air. If you have been observant on the lakes, you may have noticed trout swimming along and gulping air. Most likely, you thought the trout were feeding on some small organisms on the surface. Rainbows are also infamous for making great leaps out of a lake and, much to the chagrin of anglers, this usually happens when they aren't feeding. These episodes often happen when conditions in the lake are rapidly changing (such as turnover). Many anglers have explained this leaping phenomenon by saying that the trout are shaking lice. Far more likely is that the changing water conditions are also changing the buoyancy of the fish. This creates stress in the trout and so they won't feed. The jumping part is so they can rapidly gulp or expel air to match the changing water conditions. To me, this air bladder theory seems to be the most logical explanation for these jumping episodes.

The Colors of a Rainbow

Folks often comment on the beautiful coloration of a Rainbow Trout. And it's true. But those colors may well be different in different lakes as the water changes clarity. The coloration of these trout will also change throughout its different life stages.

Young, the trout have vertical parr marks. As they mature into maiden trout, they become white on the sides, dark green on the back and silvery on the belly. The Bows we most frequently catch have these colors. Then as the trout readies for spawning, the sides of the fish along the lateral line take on the reddish rainbow stripe. The gill plates also become red and the belly darkens. When fully into its spawning colors, the Rainbow can be very dark in color. Anglers will sometimes refer to the trout with these spawning colors as "gum boots" because they can become almost black like an old rubber boot. The spawning colors are visual signals to other mature trout that the fish is ripe and ready for spawning.

We mainly fish for maiden trout that have matured beyond their adolescent coloration but not gone into their adult spawning colors. Even at this same stage of development, the Rainbows will often display different coloration depending upon the type of water in which they live. A maiden Rainbow living in crystal clear water, for example, is usually quite light in color. The same fish raised in murky or dark colored water will usually be much darker in color. It may even become so dark that it begins to look like the dark coloration of a spawner. This lighter or darker coloration is a gradual adjustment that Mother Nature makes to match the trout to its environmental conditions. A dark fish is more obvious in clear water and a silvery fish more obvious in darker water.

> **Did You Know**
> The dark coloration on the back of a Rainbow extends further down the sides of a fish living in shallow water than on a fish living in a deep water lake.

Regardless of the water type or life stage, the coloration of all Rainbows is designed around a single theme. That theme is to provide the trout with camouflage when it is viewed from within the water or from above the water. Camouflage was one of the main considerations of Mother Nature in determining the color scheme of these trout. If you have ever tried to spot a Rainbow in water you can appreciate how well its color scheme hides the fish.

When looking down on the Rainbow you see its dorsal or upper side. The top of the trout's head, its back, dorsal fin and tail are a darkish green to a dark bluish green.

This color usually matches the color deep water appears when looking down. The tail probably takes on this color because it is usually in motion and lighter colors would likely flash in the sunlight. In shallower water, this dark color will usually blend in well with the lake-bottom weeds and algae. White marl shoals are about the only type of bottom against which the trout becomes somewhat visible. Even then, it's still hard to see the fish. Because the trout is laterally compressed and the dark upper surface is quite narrow, there is only a small strip of darker color to contrast with the light bottom of a marl shoal.

Camouflage spots cover the upper half (plus or minus) of the Rainbow. These spots are densest on the back of the fish and gradually lessen as the lateral line is approached. These spots are larger or smaller and extend further down the sides of the fish depending on the environment. The purpose of these spots is to break up the outline of the trout and help to provide transition in the change from a dark upper surface to a silvery belly.

The color of the trout gradually lightens in color towards the underside of the fish. Below the lateral line, the trout is generally white and the underside of the belly is silvery. These lighter colors provide camouflage when the trout is viewed from below. When

Did You Know

In shallow water, sunlight reflects from the lake bottom and strikes the silvery belly of the Rainbow. In turn, the light is then reflected from the fish's belly back toward the lake bottom. This unusual camouflage technique is designed to reduce sharp shadows on sunny days.

looking toward the surface with the sky as the backdrop, everything appears whitish in color from underwater. Thus, the belly of the trout will blend in well with that view. The silver on the belly of the trout serves another function. It reflects light back toward the lake bottom. This helps to reduce any shadows that the trout may cast in shallow water.

Fishing Tip

From underwater, the trout cannot see anything above water at an angle of more than 48 degrees from the perpendicular. You can use this information to determine if the fish can see you. Naturally, this depends on the distance and depth of the fish. Trout near the surface cannot even see close objects unless they are almost overhead. Also, standing up in your boat increases the odds you will be seen.

The transitioning of colors from dark at the top to light on the belly also provides good camouflage when viewing the trout from the side. If you are underwater and look up you can see through the surface. This is where you would see the white belly of the fish. Moving your line of vision down you will find that at 48 degrees you can no longer see through the water's surface. At that point, light is reflected back down like a mirror. The visual effect is that these distant but upper reaches of water appear dark. The middle depths appear lighter and the lake bottom is illuminated with reflecting light often giving it a brighter appearance. Those colors match the coloration of the Rainbow and it becomes hard to spot at a distance. The camouflage spots also break up the outline of the trout in this view from the side.

Color changes in the trout don't happen in a few hours. The changing of color is accomplished via pigment cells in the skin. These cells will lighten or darken over time to match the surroundings of the fish or the stage in its life cycle. In some circles, it is thought that the type of food that the trout eat triggers color change. However, I have seen trout of different coloration in lakes with essentially the same food chain but with different colored water. These color changes may simply be a chemical response to the surroundings of the fish caused by their visual senses rather than what they eat.

The Physical Abilities of a Rainbow

Seldom do folks think about the speed, strength, agility and other physical abilities of a Rainbow Trout. These fish are actually quite amazing in comparison to most other critters. Whenever I'm giving a course that includes a discussion on the abilities of these fish I like to start by saying that they are "faster than a speeding bullet", "stronger than a charging locomotive" and "able to leap tall buildings in a single bound". The abilities of Rainbow Trout are worth comparing to Superman and we anglers normally just take most of these abilities for granted.

You would think that it would be easy to open a book or search the internet to look up the speed and other abilities of a trout. However, Researchers have difficulty measuring these abilities and no two seem to agree on a particular set of numbers. The best we can do is to take some reliable reference points. I have done that and then used these to do my own calculations for speed and other physical abilities. I know that speed increases with trout length and tail width. I have reliable information that a Rainbow fingerling can attain a burst speed of 10 mph, which is faster than some of the literature gives credit. I have reliable information that steelhead can jump to 3.4 meters in height and can calculate the necessary speed to achieve that height. I had to bring out my old Physics books but I've managed to calculate speeds, jumping heights, gravitational pull, energy expenditure, and other physical attributes that are consistent with these reliable reference points. In turn, this will give you some idea of just what you are up against when you have one of these marvelous fish on your rod.

Another consideration in presenting the physical abilities of trout is that the abilities aren't consistent. For example, an increase in water temperature of 10°C will decrease the water viscosity or density about 22%. That presumably allows the trout to move faster through the water and affects other abilities. Another factor affecting ability is the physical condition of a specific fish. For example, a trout that is fat or unhealthy won't have the same abilities as a fish in prime condition. The maximum abilities are most interesting and what I intend to provide. But keep in mind that these are not necessarily precise numbers but are probably the best you are going to find. So let's look at some of the high-end abilities of these amazing creatures.

Speed

In different literature sources, I have seen the top speed of Rainbow Trout listed at 10 miles per hour (mph), 12 mph, 23 mph and so forth. With these different numbers being bantered about, someone has to be wrong. So I started gathering more information on the subject and found out that I was the one who was wrong. In fact, "all" those speeds were correct. What the literature neglected to mention or didn't understand was that the top speed of a Rainbow increases with size. There are also three types of speed to consider. 'Cruising speed' is the maximum speed that the trout can sustain over long periods such as an hour. Then there is 'sustained speed' which is a speed that can be maintained for moderate intervals of time such as ten to twenty minutes. And then there is 'burst speed' which is the speed of most interest to fly fishers.

Burst speed is the maximum speed that the trout can attain over a short distance and only maintain for a few seconds. You experience that speed when the fly is set, the trout begins its initial run and your reel begins to scream as fly line is rapidly removed. I find it sort of interesting that no one has bothered to set standards for measuring these factors. For example, if all researchers used 5 seconds to measure burst speed then there would probably be some consistency in the numbers. In addition, Researchers always insist on using small trout (less than 12 inches) as the subjects of their studies. If larger trout were used, we would have some reliable information for trout of a size of interest to us fly fishers. Anyway, following is the best information I've been able to calculate and assemble on the speed of Rainbow Trout.

Table 3 – Estimated Speeds of Rainbows by Length

Rainbow Length	10 inches	12 inches	14 inches	16 inches	18 inches	20 inches	22 inches	24 inches	26 inches	28 inches
Cruising Speed	2.4 mph	2.6 mph	2.8 mph	3.0 mph	3.2 mph	3.4 mph	3.5 mph	3.7 mph	3.9 mph	4.0 mph
Sustained Speed	5.9 mph	6.5 mph	7.0 mph	7.5 mph	8.0 mph	8.5 mph	8.9 mph	9.3 mph	9.7 mph	10.0 mph
Burst Speed	**17.3 mph**	**18.9 mph**	**20.4 mph**	**21.8 mph**	**23.2 mph**	**24.4 mph**	**25.6 mph**	**26.7 mph**	**26.0 mph**	**28.0 mph**
Distance Traveled in Burst	25.3 ft/sec	27.7 ft/sec	30.0 ft/sec	32.0 ft/sec	34.0 ft/sec	35.8 ft/sec	37.6 ft/sec	39.2 ft/sec	40.8 ft/sec	42.4 ft/sec

For the sake of comparison, an Olympic sprinter who runs the 100-yard dash in 9.7 seconds will average 21 mph and the athlete who runs a four-minute mile will average 15 mph. If our Rainbow Trout were the size of an athlete, say six feet, it would theoretically attain a burst speed of around 46 mph. So Rainbow Trout aren't actually faster than a speeding bullet but do achieve more than respectable speeds.

Even more impressive than the speed of a Rainbow is the acceleration or time it takes the trout to achieve its top burst speed. The trout can go from a stand still to

> **Did You Know**
> Rainbows can accelerate form a stand still to top speed in about one second.

top burst speed in approximately one second. That means that a 16-inch trout, for example, will pull about one "G" (gravitational force) in the first second of acceleration. In the first two seconds of being hooked, it can travel about 48 feet if we ignore the drag created by your fly line. After a few seconds, the trout will begin to slow down although it may make subsequent bursts at slightly slower accelerations. Again, for comparison, a dragster that achieves 130 mph in 6.5 seconds has an average acceleration rate of 20 mph/sec compared to 21.8 mph/sec in the first second for our 16-inch trout. Of course, our trout only accelerates for the first second. It then reaches peak speed, only maintains that for a few seconds and then begins to slow down.

There is a practical application of this information for the fly fisher. Most "nice" trout that break your leader do so in the first one or two seconds after the fly is set. The force of an accelerating two-pound trout can easily break a six-pound leader. Whenever you set the fly, be prepared to give the fish all the line it needs. The rod tip must be kept high after the fly is set. Keeping the tip

> **Did You Know**
> Of the Rainbows anglers accidentally lose, about 80% are lost within two minutes of being hooked.

high allows the spring action of the rod to absorb the initial acceleration shock and subsequent energy release. Hopefully you have nicely coiled the fly line in the bottom of boat so that it doesn't tangle while being rapidly stripped through the guides of the rod. And your reel should have bearings capable of these kinds of forces. If you managed to hang onto a nice Rainbow for the first few seconds, you can brace yourself for some of the other physical attributes of these amazing fish.

Note: I mention the bearings in your reel because the first Steelhead I caught on the fly actually destroyed the bearings in my fly reel and popped three guides off my fly rod.

Agility

When we were talking about the internal organs of a trout, I mentioned that the air bladder of the trout is slightly below the center of gravity and that this arrangement helped the trout make rapid turns and dives. That may have been a little bit of an understatement. The Rainbow can make 90-degree turns in the middle of a steep dive or vertical rise. It can stop on a dime and with its acceleration capability be traveling at 20 mph in the opposite direction almost instantaneously. Zigs and zags, circles and loops and walking on water are all within the fighting capability of this fish. A Chinese acrobat doesn't have quite the agility that most Rainbow Trout possess.

> When on the ground
> The cows lay down
> The fish are deep
> And fast asleep.

For landing these trout, the first three or four minutes are the most critical. During that time, let a nice trout run where it wants, keep your fly line tight line and just hang on. After the fish starts to tire a little, you can begin to bring the trout toward the boat. It will often take a little rest during this period. When you have the fish within about ten to twenty feet from the boat, be prepared for another series of runs and dives.

Jumping

A Rainbow Trout can put on quite a display of aerial acrobatics when hooked. It's one of the qualities that make Bows such a popular sport fish. The broader tails of larger trout help them to jump higher than smaller fish but the addition of weight soon limits these heights due to the pull of gravity. As a rule-of-thumb, expect Rainbows to jump to heights of about three times their body length. I have seen Rainbows exceed this general rule. Conversely, don't expect fat or unhealthy fish to reach those heights. Jumps of 3.4 meters or 11.1 feet have been reliably recorded for Steelhead.

The height that a Rainbow jumps is determined by the speed of the fish when it breaks free of the water and the angle at which the fish exits the water. Maximum heights are obtained when the fish leaves the water at a vertical angle. Jumping heights are reduced at lower angles even though the same exit speed is maintained. Down to an angle of 45 degrees, the horizontal distance traveled across the water surface will increase. At less than 45 degrees, the horizontal distance decreases. To obtain a vertical jump the trout must be about three or more body lengths under the surface.

> Trout have shown me that you can get into trouble by opening your mouth.

When the trout moves upward in the water to jump, it must fight the pull of gravity. That means that it no longer reaches its top burst speed. The maximum burst speeds are achieved when the fish is swimming horizontally or diving. The air bladder makes the trout neutrally buoyant in the water but that doesn't help when rapidly moving in an upward direction. When the trout moves upward, the force it exerts is the same as horizontal burst speeds but speed is reduced proportional to the pull of gravity. When the trout breaks free of the water, the only factors determining the height of the jump are exit speed and gravity.

Table 6 provides estimates of the maximum jumping height you might expect from one of these fish under ideal conditions. However, don't expect a fish you have on the line to necessarily achieve these heights. The

> Don't judge an angler by the size of his rod.

following are maximums expected and even the drag of your fly line through the water can significantly reduce jumping height.

Some critters in the animal kingdom such as grasshoppers, frogs and cats, are designed for jumping. Most, including humans, are not and are only capable of leaps that are about equivalent to one body length. At three body lengths, the Rainbow isn't the worlds best jumper and not actually able to leap tall buildings, but it ranks high in its ability to thwart the affects of gravity.

The most prolific jumpers seem to be those Rainbows in the range from 16 to 22 inches. Larger and smaller fish jump but not as frequently and with such abandon as these mid size fish. An average "jumper" will probably take three to five leaps.

However, I've had Rainbows make a series of 10 to 12 leaps with every one nearing the maximum jumping height.

Table 4 – Maximum Jumping Heights of Rainbows by Length

Rainbow Length	10 inches	12 inches	14 inches	16 inches	18 inches	20 inches	22 inches	24 inches	26 inches	28 inches
Vertical Jump Height	2.6 Feet	3.2 Feet	3.7 Feet	4.3 Feet	4.9 Feet	5.4 Feet	6.0 Feet	6.5 Feet	7.1 Feet	7.6 Feet
45 Degree Jump Height	1.9 Feet	2.3 Feet	2.6 Feet	3.0 Feet	3.4 Feet	3.8 Feet	4.2 Feet	4.6 Feet	5.0 Feet	5.4 Feet
Exit Speed from Water	8.9 mph	9.7 mph	10.6 mph	11.3 mph	12.0 mph	12.7 mph	13.3 mph	13.9 mph	14.5 mph	15.1 mph
Exit Speed from Water	13.0 Ft/Sec	14.3 Ft/Sec	15.5 Ft/Sec	16.6 Ft/Sec	17.6 Ft/Sec	18.6 Ft/Sec	19.5 Ft/Sec	20.4 Ft/Sec	21.3 Ft/Sec	22.1 Ft/Sec

When you hook into a jumper, there are no hard and fast rules for handling the fish. They shake their head and may be jumping toward you one second and away from you the next second. The line should be kept taut enough to maintain pressure on a barbless hook but not so taut that a shake of the head can dislodge the fly or break a leader. If given the chance, I try to get the rod tip high, the fly line on or above the water surface and then apply just enough pressure to keep the line taut until the fish decides to try another tactic.

Strength

For the burst speeds we have determined, I've done the force and energy calculations for Rainbow Trout. While horsepower may have some meaning, I doubt that joules, ergs, Newton's and foot pounds would mean much to most of us. For those interested, the force in Newton's and the horsepower of work exerted by our Rainbows is provided in the following table.

Table 5 – Estimated Rainbow Strength at Burst Speed by Length

Rainbow Length	10 inches	12 inches	14 inches	16 inches	18 inches	20 inches	22 inches	24 inches	26 inches	28 inches
Force in Newton's	1.69 nt	3.06 nt	5.08 nt	7.91 nt	11.7 nt	16.7 nt	23.0 nt	30.8 nt	40.4 nt	51.9 nt
Work (Energy) in Horsepower	0.009 H.P.	0.017 H.P.	0.031 H.P.	0.052 H.P.	0.081 H.P.	0.122 H.P.	0.176 H.P.	0.247 H.P.	0.337 H.P.	0.450 H.P.

43

Translated into angler language, if you point your rod directly at a hooked trout, you can expect to break off even moderate sized fish. A Rainbow of 15 inches or about 1.5 pounds can break six-pound test leader if we don't use the spring action of the rod tip to reduce the shock of impact. Always retrieve your fly with the rod tip pointed 30 or more degrees away from the location of your fly. That will allow the rod to absorb some of the initial shock even if you're asleep at the helm. When you set the fly, move the rod tip directly above your head. This will provide the maximum spring action from your rod. When my wife hits a nice fish, I always remind her to "keep the rod tip high". When she doesn't she often loses the fish.

So how does this strength relate to something we know? Again, if we grow our trout to a six-foot length and attached legs, it would weigh about 14% as much as a horse but have the strength of 18 horses. One horsepower is equal to 550 foot pounds of work per second. That isn't stronger than a charging locomotive but pound for pound is stronger than a horse.

> The heavy handed angler and his fish are soon parted.

The Size of Rainbows

One of the physical attributes of a Rainbow that we anglers appreciate most is the size potential of these fish. Sure, most of the Rainbows we catch are about 12 inches or weigh in at about three quarters of a pound. But in a pristine lake with a reasonable food supply, these fish can grow to ten or fifteen pounds and more. With their strength and agility, even a two pound Rainbow (17 inch) is a lot of fish to bring in on light tackle.

> **Did You Know**
> The length of a Rainbow is measured from the tip of the nose to the "fork" in the tail. The girth around the fish is taken just in front of the dorsal fin.

We Canadians tend to express the size of our fish in terms of pounds and ounces. We can always tell when an American angler is on the lake. He will relate the size of his fish to his buddies in "inches". The weight estimate is actually a much better indicator of fish size. For example, a 20 inch trout will average 3lbs 5oz but the expected range from a slim to a fat trout is from 2 pounds 13 ounces up to 4 pounds 2 ounces. That is quite a weight variation for a single trout length.

To weigh your fish there are a number of good scales on the market. Often these come in both imperial (pounds and ounces) and metric (kilograms). A good tubular scale that weighs fish to the nearest ounce is not cheap. However, a cheap scale is not accurate and a waste of money. About twelve to fifteen pounds is the maximum weight capacity for these good scales.

However, a word of caution if you buy a good scale and have previously been *estimating* the weight of your fish. Expect the average weight of your "nice" fish to be cut almost in half. Invariably we anglers tend to overestimate the weight of a large fish by a factor of almost two. When I first purchased my scale, I had to weigh a five-pound bag of sugar just to confirm that my scale was providing the correct weight. That "five pound trout" of many anglers who *estimate* weight is about the same as my fish that weigh in at two and a half to three pounds. If another angler brags a little too much, I will sometimes offer to weigh the fish on my good scales. If you want to keep the average size of your catch large, then you may NOT want to buy a set of scales.

If you don't want to invest in a good set of scales to weigh your fish, there are a number of good formulas for determining the weight of your trout. Sturdy's Formula is quite accurate. Essentially you take four-thirds the length of your trout in inches times the girth in inches squared and divide that quantity by 1,000 or $(4/3*L*G^2)/1000$. It gives you the weight in tenths of pounds. However, to get all these measurements requires a dead fish or a lot of extra fish handling.

I use a formula that doesn't require the girth measurement and that means less handling of the fish. The formula takes the length in inches, add one and cube that quantity. Then divide by 2750 which is a "form constant" for a typically shaped Rainbow. The formula becomes $(L+1)^3/2750$ and the result is the weight of the fish in tenths of pounds for a typical trout. By typically shaped I mean that it has the normal torpedo shape you expect from a Rainbow. If the trout is slim, the "form constant" is 3250. If the fish is fat, the "form constant" is 2215. About 90% of the fish I've checked will fall within the slim to fat range. Fish that are shaped like snakes or footballs will fall outside the typical range. To get a good estimate of weight, all you need is length and an estimate of how typically the fish is shaped.

> Never criticize a meal prepared by the camp cook unless you are prepared to take over his job.

Typical Shaped Rainbow >

The following table provides good estimates of trout weights by length.

Table 6 – Typical Rainbow Weights by Length and Body Shape

Rainbow Length	10 inches	12 inches	14 inches	16 inches	18 inches	20 inches	22 inches	24 inches	26 inches	28 inches
Slim Body Build	0 lbs 6 oz	0 lbs 10 oz	1 lbs 0 oz	1 lbs 8 oz	2 lbs 1 oz	2 lbs 13 oz	3 lbs 11 oz	4 lbs 12 oz	6 lbs 0 oz	7 lbs 8 oz
Typical Body Shape	0 lbs 7 oz	0 lbs 12 oz	1 lbs 3 oz	1 lbs 12 oz	2 lbs 7 oz	3 lbs 5 oz	4 lbs 6 oz	5 lbs 10 oz	7 lbs 1 oz	8 lbs 13 oz
Fat Body Build	0 lbs 9 oz	0 lbs 15 oz	1 lbs 8 oz	2 lbs 3 oz	3 lbs 1 oz	4 lbs 2 oz	5 lbs 7 oz	7 lbs 0 oz	8 lbs 14 oz	11 lbs 0 oz

So as a rule-of-thumb, your fish will need to be about 13 inches to reach a pound, 17 inches to make two pounds and 23 inches to hit the five pound category.

Size Distributions

Pristine lakes that are ideal for fly fishing are normally stocked by the Fisheries Management folks. In lakes where the numbers of fish are in balance with the food chain, we can anticipate encountering Rainbows in excess of five pounds. Since most of us like to catch big Bows I would like to take a few minutes to discuss the size distributions of fish in these lakes and what sizes you might expect to catch.

Normally a stocked lake will have one or two stockings of fry or fingerlings during a year. Stocking these fish typically occurs during the spring or fall. The fish stocked during a particular year comprise an "age class" and these fish will be somewhat the same size. I say "somewhat" because trout are individuals and each will be more or less aggressive and grow faster or slower than their stocking mates.

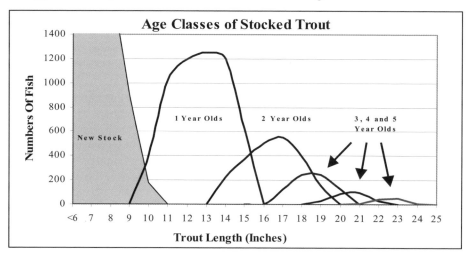

Figure 9 – Typical Age Class Distribution of Rainbows

Because of their differing aggressiveness, and thus growth rates, the size and length of individual fish within an age class will start to vary significantly among an age class. It doesn't take long before the size of fish in one age class is overlapping with the size of fish in the next age class as show in Figure 9. The result is fish of most every size showing up in the anglers catch.

> Expect about 60% mortality in each age class for each year they are in a lake.

Often a particular age class of Rainbows will hang out together, group for protection and feed together. This is especially true of the younger age classes. One day you may catch several two year olds and the following day catch a batch of one year olds.

Each year you can expect the numbers of fish in a given age class to drop significantly through mortality. The rate of decrease is about 60% per year in each age class. Younger and smaller fish are highly susceptible to disease, trauma and predation. Older and larger fish face a high mortality rate from angler success.

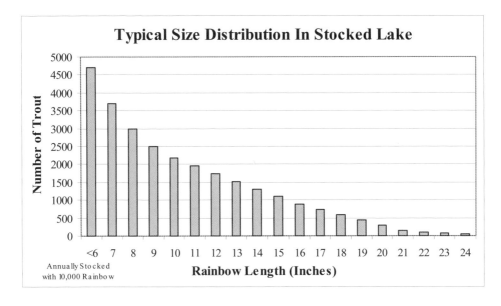

Figure 10 – Typical Size Distribution of Rainbows

This high mortality rate and the fact that the same aged trout will grow at different rates produces a steadily declining size distribution in a lake. A typical size distribution in pristine lakes will be something like what is shown in Figure 10.

> **Fishing Tip**
> Small Rainbows are opportunistic, easy to catch and can waste the time of a serious angler. If you see a lot of little fish rising and feeding in one location then try fishing in another location with less activity but providing the chance for some larger fish.

OK, so what does that mean to you as an angler? Well, in a typical lake such as shown in Figure 10, what are your chances of catching one of those 24 inch Rainbows? Not counting the newly stocked fish there would be over 27,000 fish of various sizes and only about 45 would be 24 inches or larger. And those bigger fish are the ones who are very lucky or very cunning. Those larger fish will probably be taken by the angler who knows his prey.

The size of fish you catch will generally be proportional to the numbers of fish of those sizes in the lake. The numbers of trout you catch that are smaller than one-pound will depend on your personal fishing style. I try to avoid the smaller fish. Even so, my catch of trout less than a pound is still about 30% of the

> **Did You Know**
> Two strikes per hour can be expected while fly fishing pristine lakes. Expect the landing of one fish per hour averaging about one pound. Expect to be skunked (no fish) about 30% of your hours fished. You can use these averages to rate your fishing success.

total. Small trout are opportunistic feeders and feed more frequently than large trout so it is sometimes hard to keep them off the line. If your fishing style is something like mine, then Figure 11 represents the typical catch you can expect over a long period.

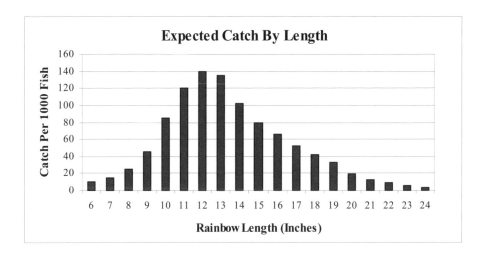

Figure 11 – Average Size Distribution of Catch

In looking at the previous graphs, a consistent theme emerges. The larger the fish, the fewer there are and the less likely we are to catch one. In a lake that is initially stocked with 20,000 fingerlings, we can only expect about 1.2% (250 fish) to survive to the fourth year and only about 0.05% (100 fish) to survive until the fifth year.

> Even with a lot of skill, sometimes it takes a little luck to get what you want.

The Growth of Rainbows

How fast a fish grows is a topic that should be discussed along with fish size. An average rate of growth would be about one pound per year in a typical pristine lake. However, other factors come into play that should be of interest to the fly fisher and even help to improve your fishing success.

In lakes that are eutrophic to mesotrophic (see Chapter 2) with a reasonable abundance of food and moderate levels of competition the one pound per year rule is common. Thus, a five-year-old fish can be expected to weigh around five pounds. However, nutrient poor lakes will not normally produce five-pound fish and conversely a super productive lake may produce five-year-old fish that

> Expect Rainbows to put on one pound of growth per year. But that can be doubled in productive waters.

are 15 pounds. Steelhead that feed and grow in the ocean can be expected to weigh in at 15 to 30 pounds after 4 to 5 years. But remember that Steelhead typically have lots of available food items under ideal conditions.

Food to Weight Gain Ratios

Scientists often use a ratio when examining the expected growth rates of animals. This ratio expresses of the amount of food it takes to put on one pound of weight. For warm-blooded animals, a 10:1 ratio is usually cited. Meaning that, ten pounds of food are required for an animal to put on one pound of weight. To put that into other words, if a 100-pound person eats 2.75 pounds of food each day they will consume 1000 pounds of food in a year and can be expected to gain ten pounds in weight. For each 10 pounds of food eaten, 1 pound of weight has been gained and that is the 10:1 ratio. However, qualifiers need to be put on these kinds of statements. That ratio is just an average and primarily aimed at animals in their immature growing years.

> **Did You Know**
> Small, young trout require proportionally more food to survive and grow than do the large, old trout.

Rainbow Trout are not warm-blooded and the 10:1 ratio does not apply. Trout are cold-blooded and a ratio of about 3:1 applies to small trout whereas a ratio of about 5:1 applies to larger trout. A small trout must eat about three ounces of food to gain one ounce in weight (ratio of 3:1). A large trout must eat about 5 ounces of food, to put on that same ounce in weight (ratio of 5:1). This is because the larger body mass of big Rainbows requires more energy for maintenance. For both, food consumption must be over a reasonably short period of time that allows the trout to maintain bodily functions plus have extra energy to apply toward weight gain. If the period between feeds is too long, all the energy goes into maintaining the trout and nothing is left over for growth.

As a part of the growth rate equation, the stomach of a trout will hold about 6% of the trout's body weight. That means a small trout must feed frequently to put on weight. That's because a small amount of food will fill its stomach and the energy from that is quickly used. Six percent of a large trout's volume is a lot more food and thus a lot more energy for maintenance and growth. After a good meal, a large trout can wait significant periods without feeding and still gain weight. Near the end of this book, I will present some information on how long it takes trout of

> **Did You Know**
> A Rainbows stomach will hold about 6% of the total volume of the fish. Also, smaller fish need more food to grow than larger fish.

different sizes to go into feeding frenzies. This section should also shed some light on why you tend to catch smaller fish.

Because it is cold-blooded, a trout does not need to maintain a minimum core body temperature like warm-blooded animals. Maintaining a core body temperature is one of the reasons that warm-blooded animals require so much more food. Allowing the body temperature to fluctuate with the surrounding environment allows more food energy to be directed toward growth in the trout. This also allows the trout to go for extended periods without eating. If you want an example of this, then consider the spawning Steelhead that enters a river and won't eat for months until the spawn is completed.

Metabolism and Growth

Metabolism is the processes of converting food to energy for body maintenance and growth. Higher metabolic rates mean that more food is required to maintain the body and thus less food goes toward growth. As you might expect, water temperature is a big factor affecting trout growth. In cold-blooded creatures, colder water means that metabolism slows and in warmer water metabolism increases. The water temperature that seems to optimize the metabolism and grow rate of trout is in the range of 48°F to 55°F (9°C to 13°C). This is the preferred water temperature for Rainbows.

> **Did You Know**
> In water that is too warm, the trout can die due to increased metabolic rates.

The time it take for a trout to digest food is a good indicator of a trout's metabolism rate. In water near freezing, it will take a small trout about nine days to digest its food. At optimum temperature levels, digestion takes one or two days. Digestion proportionally speeds up with increasing water temperature. In warmer water near lethal temperatures, the digestion rate is down to four or five hours. The trout can actively feed in high water temperatures and still not get enough food to maintain bodily functions. It won't be able to ingest food fast enough to keep up with the metabolic demands of its body. What's worse, the trout isn't likely to be actively feeding during warm water conditions.

> Our trout have marvelous growth rates. They double in size each time the story of their catch is retold.

Oxygen use is another good indicator of metabolism. In warmer water, the trout's metabolism increases and more oxygen is consumed. A big problem with this scenario is that warm water holds less oxygen than cold water. The following table shows these trends of oxygen consumption and digestion rates at different water temperatures.

Table 7 – Metabolism Indicators at Different Water Temperatures

Water Temperature	33 °F	37 °F	41 °F	45 °F	49 °F	53 °F	57 °F	61 °F	65 °F	69 °F
Avg. # Days to Digest Food	9.0	6.2	4.3	2.9	2.0	1.4	1.0	0.7	0.5	0.3
Trout Oxygen Consumption	4.5 ppm	4.8 ppm	5.0 ppm	5.3 ppm	5.6 ppm	5.9 ppm	6.2 ppm	6.6 ppm	6.9 ppm	7.3 ppm

Let's summarize this section on trout growth rates. Numerous factors such as water temperature, digestion rates, food conversion rates, and oxygen consumption rates affect the growth of trout. And we haven't even mentioned factors such as food availability, energy requirements to catch their food, the presence of trace elements needed by the trout, and so on. You can see some of the problems the fisheries managers face in producing a quality fishery. Let's just stick to the average that a Bow puts on about a pound of weight per year in a pristine Rainbow lake.

And there are several points to remember from the angler's perspective. In very cold water the trout will not need to feed as frequently as when the water warms. Conversely, during the warm water conditions of a hot summer the trout become lethargic to conserve oxygen and will not feed as frequently. Angling is best when water temperatures range from 48°F to 55°F (9°C to 13°C).

Aggression and Growth

Previously, we said that some siblings in an age class grow fast while some of their stocking mates don't. I like to categorize those fish that grow faster than average into two types.

A wind knot is a casting knot made when there were no witnesses.

The first type is the "aggressive" feeder. These are characterized as fish that will be the first to dart out of a school of its siblings to grab a morsel of food. Aggressive feeders will indeed grow faster but their aggressive behavior also means they will be among the first trout caught by an angler. By the time we are into the fourth or fifth year after stocking, there will be few of these trout remaining in the lake. Their aggression will most likely have placed them on someone's or something's dinner table.

The second type of faster growing trout is the "efficient" feeder. These fish are cautious. They are also more effective at finding a meal than their siblings. While other trout are waiting for a tidbit of food to become available, these fish will be busy scrounging through the weeds to find something to eat. Efficient feeders will often be the fish that cautiously eats when the others have decided that it isn't a feeding time. By their fourth or fifth year, these will be the larger fish in the lake. They are the least likely to have been previously hooked by an angler and most likely to make up the bulk of the fish remaining in an older age class.

The size of a fish is directly proportional to its intelligence and inversely proportional to its killer instincts.

If you like to target larger fish then it pays to consider the factors that allowed them to become large. A standard fly presentation may not entice these fish into a take and these fish may be feeding when the other fish in the lake are inactive. To get these efficient feeders it sometimes takes an unusual fly pattern. Odds are that these larger fish have become apprehensive of the standard fly patterns in use. It is also likely that these efficient feeders will be rummaging in or near the weeds rather than cruising in the open waters. More than once my daily take has consisted of one or two large fish with little activity among any of the smaller fish.

End Notes

Physical attributes of the Rainbow such as speed, strength, agility and stamina become important once the trout is on the line. These trout are not fish that you can just haul into the boat. They have a strong instinct for predator avoidance and you are a predator. They are capable of breaking a leader even after you think the fight is over.

Physical attributes such as size and growth usually depend on factors like habitat, food availability and so forth. Assessing when and where to fish is something else that we want to discuss in later chapters. The knowledgeable angler needs the skill to select a time and place that will most likely produce results.

> Life is more than a can of worms
> but less than a Royal Coachman.

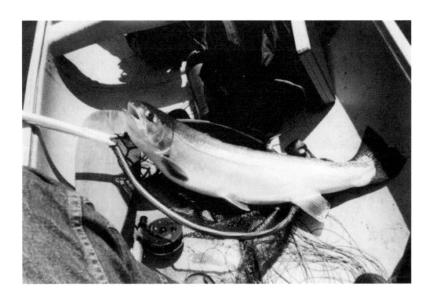

Figure 12 – A Ten Pound Rainbow From a Small Pristine Lake
It took about 45 minutes to land this fish on a 7 lb tippet.

4

Sensory Perceptions of Rainbows

In the previous chapters, we have looked at the physical attributes and abilities of Rainbow Trout. We have examined their habitat and some of the peculiarities of water. And intentionally in these chapters, I didn't go into too many aspects regarding the sensory perceptions of Rainbows. Many aspects of their sensory abilities are astounding and I wanted to present these all at once.

It is through their sensory abilities that Rainbows locate prey and your fly. As anglers, we need to know how trout accomplish this task and how they perceive the world in which they live. Can a Rainbow distinguish color, how far can it see and under what light conditions? How well does a trout hear, smell, taste and how do these affect the way you stalk the fish? The list goes on, but by knowing the limits of their sensory perceptions, you are more likely to understand how trout approach your fly.

Normally we think of "the" five senses as vision, hearing, taste, smell and touch. Anything beyond that is normally considered as Extra-Sensory Perception (ESP). The Rainbows have at least one more perception called distant touch. And the average range for several Rainbow senses are well beyond what is considered normal for a human. From this basic definition, we can say that Rainbows have ESP. So, let's start with vision and work our way through how the trout perceive their world.

Rainbow Vision

Many of the Rainbow Trout's sensory perceptions are well above average. However, seeing at a distance isn't in that category. These fish are nearsighted. They can see well up to fifteen or twenty feet but their vision isn't very good beyond that.

Despite this handicap, Rainbows are primarily "sight" feeders. The trout will use other sensory abilities to help detect and locate food from a distance. But when they are within their good vision range, they primarily rely on eyesight to make their final approach to a morsel of food.

Naturally, vision is not always possible for the final approach. In the darkness of the profundal zone, or on a pitch black night or even in some very murky waters the trout must rely on other sensory perceptions to make that final strike on their prey. But given the chance, the trout like to look over what they are eating before putting it in their mouth. I know some people who like to do the same thing.

Besides being nearsighted, the vision of a Rainbow differs from our own in other ways. Eye shape and placement on the head are a couple reasons. Another reason is because of the properties of water including water density. Some strange things happen to light in water which affects how the trout view their world. Let's begin by examining the eyes of the Rainbow.

> **Did You Know**
> While a Rainbow Trout is primarily a sight feeder, it is also somewhat nearsighted. It can only see well up to about 15 or 20 feet.

The Eyes of a Rainbow

The eyes are located behind and above the mouth as shown in Figure 8 in Chapter 3. The eyes are on opposite sides of the head and slightly bulge out from the head. This positioning of the eyes allows the Rainbow to watch its food right up to the point it enters the mouth. When prey is going through erratic escape movements, this positioning allows the best chance of actually catching the prey.

The eye of the trout is the organ that receives light and thus produces vision. Light comes through the cornea or outer covering of the eye, passes through the lens which focuses the light and the visual image is received at the retina or inside surface of the back of the eye.

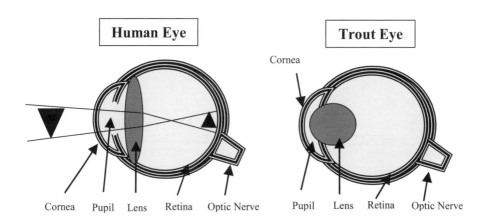

Figure 13 – Basic Design of the Human and Trout Eye

The retina has millions of light receptor cells known as cones and rods. There are three different types of cone cells. Each type receives different wavelengths of light. Each color of light comes in a different wavelength. And so the cone cells are responsible for color vision. The rod cells are about 1000 times more sensitive to light than cone cells. With their extra sensitivity to light, the rod cells allow the trout to see well at night and under other low light conditions. The information from both cones and rods is transferred to the brain through nerves and the brain interprets this information as vision.

The construction of the Rainbow's eye differs from a human eye as well. As shown in Figure 13, the lens in the human eye is oblong (lens shaped) in cross section and flush with the pupil opening. In the trout, the lens is spherical and slightly protrudes through the pupil opening. This difference in shape has both good and bad points. On the plus side, the spherical and protruding lens allows light to enter the eye from a sharp angle and greatly increases the trout's range of peripheral vision. On the negative side, this lens shape is what causes the trout to be nearsighted.

Each of the Rainbows eyes can move forward, backward, up or down within the eye socket. Each eye can make those movements independent of movement in the other eye. One eye can be looking up and forward while the other eye is looking down and backward. There is a need for this range of eye motion. Light that enters straight through the lens gives the clearest picture on the retina. Like our own vision, an object is more in focus when a Rainbow looks directly at it. An object gets out of focus the further it gets from the direct line of sight. At the extremes, peripheral vision can detect movement and little else. With this movement in the eye socket, a Rainbow can focus on objects it only detected with its peripheral vision. It can focus on two objects in opposite directions at the same time. We humans cannot comprehend this ability with our own limited visual senses.

The Direction of Sight

With the protruding lens adding extra peripheral vision and the bulging eyes on opposite sides of the head, the trout has an extraordinary range of vision. Each eye can see directly forward, to the side, and almost directly behind the fish. The fish has a blind spot directly towards the tail because the body behind the head is slightly wider than the protruding eye. Each eye can also see very well in the upward direction and almost directly below the fish, but there is a blind spot directly below the fish as well. See figures 14 and 15. Except for these blind spots, the trout can see in a complete sphere around itself.

The blind spots of the trout only range from underneath the head, toward the tail, and then slightly above the tail. The trout can see about 320 out of a possible 360 degrees. The undulating motion of a swimming trout reduces the size of this blind spot even further. So, except for underneath and behind itself, the Rainbow can see virtually everything going on around it. That is how a trout views the world.

When it attacks its prey, a Rainbow will usually approach from underneath and behind (behind would be opposite the direction of prey progress). From the trout's perspective, this is a bug's blind spot. From behind and below is the direction the trout believes is easiest to catch its prey.

Depth Perception

Depth perception is the ability to judge distance with the eyes. This ability requires that both eyes view the object. The brain interprets the angles of the eyes when focused at a certain distance. Sharper angles mean an object is closer and decreased angles mean the object is further away. A single eye cannot accurately judge distances.

When an eye on one side of the trout is viewing something that isn't also seen by the other eye it is said to be using monocular vision with "mono" meaning one. Monocular vision has no depth perception. When both eyes can see the same thing it is referred to as binocular vision with "bi" meaning two. Binocular vision allows depth perception. The Rainbows have monocular vision, binocular vision and a blind spot in that visual sphere around their body.

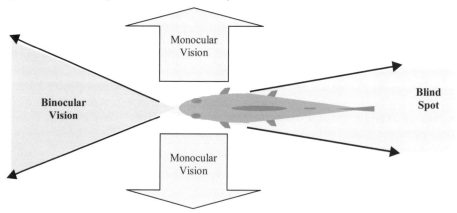

Figure 14 – Binocular Vision, Monocular Vision and the Blind Spot

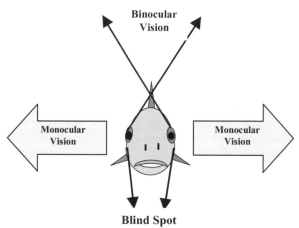

Figure 15 – Binocular Vision, Monocular Vision and the Blind Spot

Depth perception is an essential component of trout feeding. Can you imagine the scene as a mighty Rainbow cautiously stalks its prey without binocular vision? It gets closer and closer, then lunges and closes those powerful jaws around – empty water. The prey was a little further away than expected. So it tries another approach. It gets closer and closer – and bumps into the prey before that gaping mouth has even opened. This time the prey was closer than expected. At that rate, it may take six or seven tries before the Rainbow could successfully grab your fly.

Each eye of the trout is constantly moving forward, backward, up and down in search of predators and prey. Thus, it is looking at the world with monocular vision most of the time. When movement is detected, the Rainbow will instantly try to determine if it is predator or prey. If a predator is even suspected, the trout will immediately flee.

If detected motion appears to be a possible food item, a hungry trout will try to get the prey into its zone of binocular vision. This allows an estimate of distance and how best to approach its next meal. It will then slowly approach the prey and stalk it from behind and below if possible. From experience, the trout will usually know if the final approach can be slow and lazy such as when it catches a Chironomid or if the final thrust must be rapid to grasp a fast moving prey.

> **Fishing Tip**
>
> To detect soft strikes by Rainbows, the fly fisher needs to ensure that coils are not present in the leader. Coils form when the leader is wrapped around the reel. During a strike these act like a spring and need to be straightened before angling starts.

For most of the Rainbows that forage on aquatic invertebrates, the final approach is generally slow as the trout gently sucks a food item into its mouth. A fly fisher not paying attention to the line will often miss these soft strikes or may not even be aware they had a strike. The upside of these soft strikes is that the fly fisher can be certain that the trout are indeed being fooled into thinking the chosen fly is a morsel of food.

The Visual Trigger

Over eons of evolutionary development, any slight movement or contrast detected by the eyes of the Rainbow causes the fish to become excited. This is not just a "wow and whoopee" but more like an adrenaline rush in humans. The movement may be a swimming Otter or the shadow of a diving Osprey. The contrast may be the black and white colors of a Loon or a large predatory fish hiding in the weeds.

Contrast or movement detection by the eyes will cause chemical reactions in the fish that readies it for instant body action. This physical excitation has probably developed because of the need to "feed or flee" at the slightest indication of movement or unusual contrast. I call this phenomenon the "visual trigger".

This behaviour pattern is genetic programming in the trout. It is instinct if you like. It is not something the trout can control. The trout see something suspicious such as movement or unusual contrast and their body is immediately on high alert.

Besides the "feed or flee" reactions to visual stimulus, the trout sometimes have a third reaction. If the trout aren't hungry, and have decided that your fly isn't going to eat them, they may become curious. Sometimes even your best-tied flies will invoke nothing but curious looks by the trout.

Fishing Tip
If a variety of flies haven't worked, try varying your retrieve of the fly. This may activate the trout's visual trigger and cause an interest in your fly.

You have probably seen one or more Rainbows following a trout you are landing. Part of the reason is the sound vibrations emitted by the hooked trout. But the main reason is the "visual trigger". As the hooked trout rapidly dashes about with flanks reflecting sunlight, other trout in the vicinity will become excited and come to investigate. Sometimes they will even nip at the hooked trout.

This is the principle that trolling hardware employs through the use of flashers, willow-leafs and the like. The visual trigger also works when trout see other fish feeding or giving chase. They become excited and may also give chase. A number of very successful flies use the same concept. They have sharply contrasting colors such as black and white. This contrast will serve to attract the trout. A wise fly fisher will have a few such flies in the fly box.

We fly fishers can use our knowledge of the visual trigger to improve our fishing. Without changing your fly you can try changing your retrieve. Try your usual slow retrieve but then rapidly retrieve the fly about ten feet or if you are Chironomid fishing with a dry line then just raise the rod tip from the horizontal to the vertical position in one sweeping motion. The suddenly faster movement of your fly will sometimes entice the trout into taking a nip.

Even if the trout aren't taking your fly, you can be certain that it has been observed. If the trout aren't taking your fly then change it. I usually plan on ten minutes per fly or until I have satisfactorily worked a fly through my area of fishing. If that still isn't working, then try changing your fly to one

Fishing Tip
Contrast in its environment will get a trout's attention. Always have a few flies in your box that have lots of contrast such as white on black.

with sharply contrasting color (such as black and white). Sometimes the sharp contrast will stimulate the visual trigger and be effective. And if nothing else is working, you can always try a contrasting fly with a variable retrieve at different depths.

Night and Low Light Vision

Do Rainbows feed at night? You bet. My records show that evening fishing (6 pm to 11 pm) is about 30% better than daytime fishing. I have even caught Rainbows on pitch-black nights with no moon.

When discussing the eye structure of the Rainbow we saw that rod cells are primarily designed for non-color or night vision. There are about 20 times as many rod cells as cone cells and they are about 1,000 times more sensitive to light than the cone cells. Humans have an Iris in the eye that opens and closes to let in more or less light and helps to protect the sensitive rod cells. Rainbows do not have an Iris. For the Rainbow to protect these sensitive cells, the rods are withdrawn into the retina during daylight and extended for use only at night for night vision. In a protruded position, these cells are more effective at gathering the scarce light under conditions of darkness.

Thus, Rainbows can see much better at night than humans and many other critters with an Iris. It is estimated that these fish can see sufficiently well to feed on a small, slow moving insect at 0.0001 lux when the rod cells are fully extended. That is the amount of light present on a clear starlit night. That amount of light isn't sufficient for Rainbows to efficiently chase down and capture fast moving prey such as minnows, but it is adequate to forage on the slow moving insects and crustaceans in the lake.

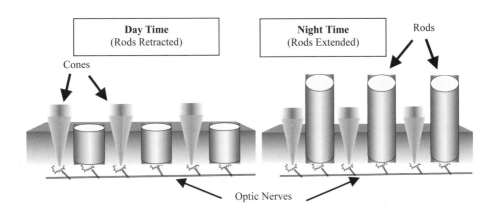

Figure 16 – Rod Cells Extending in a Rainbows Cornea

Another factor influencing night feeding and vision is the position of a Rainbow in relation to available light. At night when you are sitting in your boat and looking down into the water, it is as black as the Ace of Spades. Even if you hold your hand above the water surface, it can be hard to see with any clarity. How can a small bug be detected in that murky blackness?

If you hold your hand up to the night sky, you can see a silhouette fairly clearly. When feeding after dark, this is the view the trout will usually try to get of their prey. Most often, the trout will cruise in the shallow water of a shoal but near the bottom and search out prey

Fishing Tip
Rainbows actively feed on bugs at night. When fishing at these times, use a dark fly with a sharp silhouette and slowly retrieve it on a dry line fairly high in the water column.

swimming above them. They are able to pick out the silhouette of prey or a fly above them much easier than if the prey is below.

Day and Bright Light Vision

If the sun becomes too bright, we humans may squint or even close our eyes to protect them from the sun. Have you ever seen a Rainbow close its eyes, squint or even blink? I doubt it because Rainbows don't have eyelids. When the light gets too bright, the trout don't have any immediate method of protecting their eyes. The best they can do is move into a shaded weed patch or into deeper water where the amount of sunlight is filtered to a reasonable level of tolerance. Bright sunshine may be an enjoyable time for us to angle but it isn't the best time for the trout to feed. Most of their feed is in or near the shallow water but the level of sunlight is also highest in those areas.

Sunlight is brightest when the skies are clear and the sun is directly overhead. As cloud cover increases, light levels decrease. As the angle of the sun decreases and the sun moves lower in the sky, the intensity of sunlight will also decrease. More and more sunlight is reflected off the water surface the closer the sun is to the horizon. The following table will give some idea of the amount of sunlight entering the water under differing conditions. Note that "lux" is a measure of light illumination similar to a foot-candle. One lux converts to 0.0929 foot-candles. It is the amount of light received per square meter from a candle at a distance of one meter.

Table 8 – Approximate Light Levels (Lux) Under Different Conditions

Cloud Cover (noon)	0%	30%	60%	90%	Overcast	Heavy Overcast
Lux	127,000	90,000	30,000	10,000	1,500	500
Sun Angle (No Clouds)	90° Noon	60° Early After-noon	30° Late After-noon	10° Near Sunset	0° Sunset	-5° (twilight)
Lux	127,000	110,000	57,500	12,500	750	10
Moon Conditions	Full Moon At 60°	Full Moon At 30°	Full Moon At 15°	Quarter Moon At 60°	Quarter Moon At 30°	Quarter Moon At 15°
Lux	0.30	0.133	0.053	0.075	0.033	0.013
General	Air Glow at Sunset	Civil Twilight	Nautical Twilight	Starlight + Air Glow	Total Starlight	Overcast Night
Lux	750	10	0.04	0.002	0.0002	0.0001

Table 8 shows the tremendous range in brightness under differing conditions. I haven't seen any researched numbers but I suspect the most suitable light levels for Rainbow feeding are between 1,000 lux and 0.001 lux. And because of the lack of eyelids, I suspect that Rainbows will actively avoid light when light levels in the water exceed about 5,000 to 10,000 lux. Those numbers seem to agree reasonably well with information I have regarding water clarity.

In practical terms for the fly fisher, on bright sunny days it is best to angle in deeper water or near weed patches and other areas offering shelter from the bright sunlight. Rainbows don't necessarily stop feeding during bright light conditions but they will seek an area to feed that minimizes their exposure to excessively bright

> If the sun is bright,
> The fish won't bite.
> They're reluctant to rise
> When sun hurts their eyes.

light. As cloud cover increases, the trout will forage further from their shelter and into shallower water. On numerous occasions, I have watched Rainbows feed while a cloud is passing over the sun and stop feeding as soon as direct sunlight returns. And as we saw in the last section, after sunset is one of the better times to fish the shallows.

Water Clarity and Vision

As water clarity decreases, so does the distance the trout can see. Water clarity is also an important factor in the reduction of excessively bright sunlight. As the turbidity (cloudiness) of the water increases, the particles of suspended matter in the water intercept more and more of the sunlight. These suspended particles include things such as algae, plankton and suspended silt or mud. Even in water that appears clear there are millions of tiny particles. Through shear numbers, they block the sunlight.

The water itself also slows and absorbs sunlight. By the time a beam of sunlight has traveled 30 feet down into a lake with very clear water, the light intensity is less than 1% of what it was entering the lake. In lakes with very murky water, there is insufficient light to feed by at a depth of 15 feet.

Table 9 provides approximate light levels in different water clarity situations on bright sunny days with the sun directly overhead. This table offers valuable insight regarding water depths to fish. Since fishing is probably best where light levels are between 1,000 and 0.001 (one one-thousandths) lux and Rainbows tend to avoid light over 5,000 to 10,000 lux, you

Fishing Tip
In murky water the amount of sunlight rapidly decreases with water depth. Under these conditions, keep your fly fairly high in the water column where enough sunlight is present for the fly to be viewed.

can determine appropriate depths to place your fly.

The last row of Table 9 provides the approximate depth you can see into the water to help give you some idea of the relative water clarity. For example, if you can see the lake bottom or your anchor down to a depth of about 16 feet then the water would be considered "cloudy". Using Table 8, we can estimate the amount of light entering the lake, and Table 9 would tell us what happens to the light after it enters different water clarity situations.

On a lake with clear to very clear water, Table 9 tells us we should be fishing in deep water when it is bright and sunny. As water gets cloudier, the range of underwater brightness decreases and we can effectively fish in shallower water during bright conditions.

> **Fishing Tip**
> In turbid water with restricted vision, slow down the speed of your retrieve. The trout will need the time to locate and inspect your fly. A fast retrieve doesn't provide that opportunity.

When we get into murky to very murky water, the trout are not likely to be feeding in deep water because the nighttime rod cells are not extended and there is insufficient light in deeper water to see the food. In murky water the fish are likely to frequent the shallows even in bright sunlight but will only be able to see your fly from a very short distance. In this type of water, it is probably best to angle on bright sunny days rather than when light levels are too low.

Table 9 – Approximate Light Levels (Lux) By Depth and Water Clarity

Water Depth	Relative Water Clarity					
	Very Clear	Clear	Cloudy	Very Cloudy	Murky	Very Murky
(feet)	(lux)	(lux)	(lux)	(lux)	(lux)	(lux)
At Surface	127,000	127,000	127,000	127,000	127,000	127,000
1	107,950	92,250	82,550	69,850	50,800	25,400
3	77,990	53,580	34,880	21,130	8,130	1,020
6	47,900	22,600	9,580	3,520	520	8
9	29,420	9,540	2,630	590	35	0.07
12	18,070	4,030	720	100	2	0.0005
15	11,090	1,700	200	16	0.15	
18	6,810	720	55	3	0.009	
21	4,180	300	15	0.5	0.0005	
24	2,570	130	4	0.07		
27	1,580	55	1	0.01		
30	970	25	0.3	0.002		
Depth of Vision	42 Feet	24 Feet	16 Feet	11 Feet	7 Feet	4 Feet

Note: these light levels would be at noon on a bright sunny day.

The Visual Window

When trout look up at a starlit sky or the clouds on a sunny afternoon, they view the incoming light through a "visual window". From within a lake, light and vision are reflected off the bottom of the water surface when the viewing angle is greater than 48° from the perpendicular (see Figure 17). This happens because light bends as it enters mediums of different densities through a process called "refraction".

In water, this critical refraction angle for light going into air is 48°. From the perpendicular to 47°, the trout can see objects above the waters surface but at 49°, there is a mirror effect off the underside of the water. Objects above but away from the window can still be seen because of this bending of light. Even objects just slightly above the water surface can be seen outside the window. This gives the trout a somewhat distorted view of the world above the water.

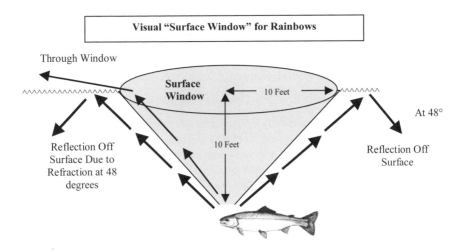

Figure 17 – The Trout's Visual Window

The visual window is approximate twice as wide as the swimming depth of the fish. A trout swimming at 10 feet down will have a visual window with a diameter of about 20 feet. Normally vision above the water isn't very meaningful for the trout except for detecting predators. However, viewing things such as food items that are 'on' the water surface is an important consideration. A food item outside the 48° window will be hard for the trout to detect visually. An item within the window will form a nice silhouette against the sky. Fly fishers intending to angle with a dry fly need to be aware of this visual window.

When searching for surface bugs, the Rainbow will usually cruise at a depth appropriate for the lake and the amount of surface food. In clear water with little surface food, the trout may cruise down around the 15-foot mark to expand their view of the surface. And because they are nearsighted, they won't go much deeper than this when searching the surface. If surface food is plentiful in clear water, they will just stay near the surface. An angler can see a series of surface rings as the trout swim along rising to grab bugs. Cruising depth will be close to the surface in water that is cloudy or murky because the distance of vision is restricted. But once again, if the food is plentiful the angler can see a series of surface rings as the trout feeds.

A trout swimming close to the surface, is more likely to be spooked by a fly landing directly within its visual window than a fish down deeper. The fly fisher should avoid dropping a fly directly over a rising Rainbow. It is better to watch the direction of travel via the series of surface rings and estimate where the fish is going to rise in a few seconds. Cast your fly some distance in front of fish and allow the

> **Fishing Tip**
>
> If you know where a trout is surface feeding, avoid dropping a fly directly into its surface window. A splash-down directly in the window may spook the fish via the visual trigger.

fish to swim to the fly rather than taking the chance that you will startle it with an offering placed directly on its head.

Color Vision

Yes, Rainbows can see in color. As already mentioned, the cone cells in the eye of the trout are for daylight and color vision while the rod cells are for night vision and primarily detect black and white.

Color vision in water, however, is a bright light phenomenon. Under conditions of darkness, it is difficult to see in color. Also, as the intensity of light is reduced, colors take on more of a gray hue and the colors are not as bright. As the intensity of sunlight disappears, the colors of things underwater turn darker gray or even black. Several factors affect the intensity of sunlight and thus the perception of color. Let's look at these.

The first factor is, naturally, a lack of sunlight. After sunset and before sunrise the trout will view most everything underwater in the black and gray tones. When the sun is near the horizon, more light is reflected off the water surface and less light (and thus less color) is apparent in the lake. And as we saw from table 9, light intensity is reduced by cloud cover. Under these reduced light levels, the colors perceived in the lake become progressively less distinctive. But under the surface of the water, additional filtering of light and color is also occurring even in bright sunlight.

Suspended sediments in a lake and even the water itself will absorb sunlight. Table 10 gave us a good idea of how light intensity changes with water clarity and depth. As the lux level decreases in a lake, you can expect the perception of color to decrease proportionally.

> **Did You Know**
>
> Floating algae and suspended sediments quickly reduce the intensity of light and thus reduce color that reflects from underwater objects including your fly.

A major factor in color reduction in a lake is color absorption by the water. But not all colors are created equal. Each color has its own wavelength. Water intercepts and reduces the intensity of some wavelengths faster than other wavelengths according to their energy content. You can view the relative amounts of energy in the colors of light by viewing a rainbow after a rain shower. The colors are refracted from red, to orange, to yellow, to green, to blue and finally to violet. Sunlight passing through the raindrops is separated into its colors much the same a sunlight passing into water. As sunlight penetrates deeper into water, the colors are reduced to gray in the same sequence as the color you see in a rainbow.

Therefore, the color reflected from sunlight deeper in a lake is not proportional to the colors entering a lake. For example, at a depth of 12 feet in very clear water, only 4% of red colors remain while 93% of the blue colored light remains. Greens, blues and violets have the shortest wavelengths and are the last colors to be

Did You Know
The color of your fly above water will not be the same as your fly in the water. And that color difference is greater the deeper the fly settles into the lake.

filtered out of light in water. As a point of interest, that's the reason why deep, clear water appears blue (or greenish) in color. Other colors have been filtered out and only the greens or blues are reflected back to the viewer. Lakes that appear brown or other colors are probably reflecting the color of sediments or algae near the surface. Table 10 shows what happens to the five basic colors at different depths in two different water clarity situations.

Table 10 – Percent of Color Remaining By Depth and Water Clarity

Note – Applicable under conditions of bright sunlight with the sun directly overhead. Percents of color remaining will rapidly decrease as light intensity decreases.

Color of Light	Very Clear Water					Cloudy Water				
	Red	Orange	Yellow	Green	Blue	Red	Orange	Yellow	Green	Blue
Depth in Water	Percent of Color Light Remaining					Percent of Color Light Remaining				
3 Feet	44%	81%	91%	96%	98%	20%	36%	41%	43%	44%
6 Feet	19%	66%	83%	93%	97%	4%	13%	17%	18%	19%
9 Feet	9%	54%	75%	89%	95%	0.8%	5%	7%	8%	9%
12 Feet	4%	44%	68%	86%	93%	0.1%	1.7%	2.7%	3.4%	3.7%
15 Feet	1.6%	35%	62%	83%	91%	0.03%	0.6%	1.1%	1.5%	1.6%
18 Feet	0.7%	29%	58%	80%	89%	0.01%	0.2%	0.5%	0.6%	0.7%
21 Feet	0.3%	23%	52%	77%	88%	0.001%	0.08%	0.2%	0.3%	0.3%
24 Feet	0.1%	19%	47%	74%	87%		0.03%	0.08%	0.12%	0.14%
Wavelength in Nanometers	670	615	580	530	460	670	615	580	530	460

So how can the angler use this information? If we are "color aware", we can improve our odds of attracting a Rainbow to our fly. From Table 10 it should become obvious that the trout will view many of our flies or lures as various shades of gray to black as we fish them deeper in the water column. The color of your flies will only be of significance in shallow, clear water. So it may not be important to spend a lot of time getting a color that is just right when tying your flies. It is more important to make sure your flies are of the right size and shape to imitate a particular bug. My records show that black colored flies and those in the darker color range are the most consistently successful.

When discussing the visual trigger earlier in this section, we saw that movement physically excites the trout and they are visually alert to contrast. Putting ribbing or some other contrasting colors on a fly can be useful. I often use black and white as contrasting colors on my flies or black with a silver or gold wrap.

Besides flies, there are other ways you can use your awareness of color to improve your angling success. For example, I've had good success by retrieving black flies across light colored marl patches. The light color of marl provides a good background to contrast the fly and makes movement detection easier. Adjacent weed patches are darker and provide good camouflage for the trout to hide.

Rainbow Vision and the Angler

Since Rainbow vision is such an important consideration for the angler, it wouldn't hurt to review some of the aspects of vision affecting fishing.

> Rainbows are nearsighted but at short distances can see quite well under low light levels. This allows successful angling at night.
> Rainbows tend to be most active and feed most frequently during periods of low lighting. During bright sunny periods, these fish will often move into deeper water where the intensity of light has been filtered to lower levels of brightness.
> The angler will often have better success when the fly is presented above or to the side of the fish as opposed to below or behind the fish. This avoids the blind spots and puts the fly into the best line of vision.
> The silhouette of a fly including size and shape are more important to the angler and fish than the correct color of the fly.
> When the trout are surface feeding, the fly should be cast in front of the fish rather than be delivered directly into the trout's visual window.
> Trout are constantly alert to movement and contrast. The angler can entice the trout to a fly with these attributes.
> As water clarity declines, the distance at which the trout can view its food also declines. An angler should adjust fishing depth to match lighting levels.
> Especially in murky water, your fly should be retrieved slow enough that the trout doesn't loose sight of it.
> The trout become excited by movement and contrast. Try varying your retrieve and be prepared to try flies with lots of contrast when the fishing gets slow.

The Sense of Hearing in Rainbows

Sound waves and other vibrations in water may be more important to Rainbow Trout than vision. We know that light doesn't transmit very well in water. In low sunlight or murky water, the light intensity rapidly decreases with water depth and so does the trout's ability to see. Even though Rainbows can see well enough to feed at very low light levels there comes a point when they must rely on senses other than vision to obtain food.

Hearing and the lateral line are senses that trout rely on to supplement vision or even use instead of vision. Even though water doesn't transmit light very well, it is an excellent conductor of sound and pressure waves. Trout do have ears and an excellent sense of hearing. It is said that they can hear the sounds of an insect crawling or hatching. They can hear sounds that we cannot hear and that allows them to detect their prey from a distance.

A blind man improves his hearing and other senses to compensate for the lack of vision. Rainbows are often in water conditions that restrict or eliminate vision as an effective sensory tool. So like the blind man, the other senses of a Rainbow are well developed and can be used in conjunction with or in place of sight.

When something moves or pushes water, vibrations and pressure waves are formed. If there are enough vibrations per second, these water movements are detected as sound. A Rainbow requires a minimum of about 30 vibrations per second to detect and interpret those vibrations as hearing. The trout can detect pressure waves at frequencies of fewer than 30 vibrations per second but not as sound. The trout then uses the lateral line to detect these lower frequencies and pressure waves. The lateral line also picks up vibrations in water but we will be discussing it under a different section.

What is Sound?

Sound is a vibration. Hearing is impossible without sound vibrations. Sound is created when something vibrates and that vibration is transmitted from one location to another through a medium. If we drop something on our desk, energy is released when that object strikes the desk. The energy release causes the molecules in the desk and object to vibrate for a brief moment. The energy from those vibrations is transferred to the surrounding air molecules causing them to vibrate and they in turn cause the air molecules next to them to vibrate. This vibration "wave" continues through adjacent air molecules until it reaches our ear. Within our ear, the vibrating air molecules encounter our eardrum and make it vibrate. This vibration is passed through the hammer, anvil and stirrup into our inner ear where they finally set small hair-like nerve cells into motion. When these nerve cells move they release electric impulses that are transmitted to the brain and the brain interprets these signals as sound. That is a brief and concise explanation of hearing and the perception of sound but naturally, there is a little more to it than just that.

A very important property of sound is that a sound wave will pass through a medium of about the same density as the material through which it is traveling without releasing much energy. If the sound wave encounters something that is of higher or lower in density, the energy of the sound wave is then absorbed and/or reflected and energy is released. The human eardrum is made of flesh and tissue mostly composed of water. In an air environment, the human eardrum is denser than the air and captures the energy of the sound wave. If a human ear is under water and the sound is passing through water (about the same density) then there is little energy released at the eardrum. The human eardrum tends not to vibrate in water. Therefore, a person cannot hear worth a hoot under water.

The Ears of a Rainbow

Rainbow Trout have two ears. These are located within the head of the trout at approximately the same relative position as the inner ears of a human. The basic structure and functioning of the trout's inner ear is quite similar to the inner ear of a human. But there are also significant environmental differences that translate into differences in how the ears of each work.

The human ear transfers the vibrations of the eardrum (tympanic membrane) to the inner ear known as the Cochlea. The Cochlea contains about 20,000 cilia or hair cells known as "neuromasts". When moved by sound vibrations, the neuromasts translate sound waves into electrical impulses for the brain. At the lower limit of human hearing, a person can hear a sound vibration that is equivalent to about one billionth of an atmospheric pressure. The trout has modified this basic structure so that it works well in water.

The Rainbow Trout doesn't have an eardrum. To compensate, the trout and many other fish use their air bladder as an eardrum. The air bladder is less dense than the surrounding water. The density difference allows the air bladder to intercept the energy from a sound wave in water and vibrate much like a human eardrum. It is also much larger than a human eardrum and is hollow. Being hollow, sound waves reverberate within the air bladder. This resonance increases the amplitude of the sound waves and actually "amplifies" the sound. The result is an organ that captures and amplifies sound more efficiently than the human eardrum.

The human ear has the Ossicles (hammer, anvil, and stirrup) to transfer sound from the eardrum to the inner ear. Rainbows have a similar yet different arrangement. The trout have a modified version of the Ossicles that is called the Weberian Ossicles. These are modified vertebrae. The Weberian Ossicles are in contact with the air bladder on both sides of the fish's spine and these then connect directly with the trout's inner ear. They pick up the air bladder vibrations and pass these into the inner ear. This arrangement can be seen in Figure 18.

The innermost part of the trout's ear has a sac-like structure with two chambers called the saccule and the lagena. This structure contains the neuromasts that convert sound vibrations into electric pulses for the brain. However, the tissue of the neuromasts is close to the same density as water. In water, the trout's neuromasts would not vibrate and bend sufficiently well to generate strong electric signals. To compensate, the trout have a little something extra in their inner ear called an "otolith".

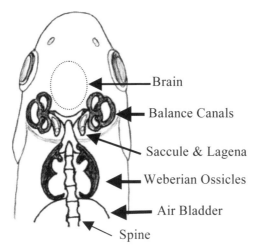

Figure 18 – A Rainbows Ear Structure

An otolith is an ear stone. The otolith is a hard piece of calcium (similar to bone) that is about three times denser than water. It is surrounded by and touching the neuromasts. Because they are denser than water, the otoliths pick up the energy vibrations of sound very well. The otoliths are in direct contact with the neuromasts. They pass the sound energy directly to the neuromasts causing them to move and thus generate the electric current needed for hearing. The otoliths have irregular shapes and that helps the trout to extend the range of frequencies it can detect. Otoliths act like amplifiers and can even respond to sonic vibrations.

Rainbows do not have an external ear. The trout's skeleton acts as its external ear. The bones of the fish are denser than the surrounding water and intercept sound waves very well. All the bones of the Rainbow connect to the spinal column. And the spinal column connects directly to the Weberian Ossicles and ears. The skull and skeleton serves the same purpose in the trout as the outer ear of a human. With the large surface area of the trout's skeleton, it is probably a much more efficient collector of sound than the outer ear of a human.

The Rainbows ears are not able to locate the source of a sound unless that sound is relatively close. The air bladder and skeleton of the fish are directly connected to the ear but the trout's ears have no way to distinguish if faint sounds are being received from the left, right, front or back side of the fish. Humans receive different sound levels in each ear to help us determine the direction to a sound. The trout rely on their lateral line to perform this task. The ears can only determine if a sound is becoming louder or fainter to determine direction.

That has all been a bit technical and my apologies. However, it was necessary to go into the technical stuff to understand the trout's ear. Additionally, much of this information also pertains to the trout's lateral line. We may as well present all the technicalities at the same time and get it finished.

Sound and Vibrations in Water

Sound and vibrations in water follows the same rules of physics as sound in air. However, fresh water is about 780 times denser than air. This environmental difference magnifies the properties of sound in water with results that we, who live in thin air, seldom consider.

Because water is denser than air, sound travels about five times faster in water than in air. If you bang your oar against the side of your boat, a trout in water and across the lake will hear that noise before an angler who is the same distance away. Sound will also travel faster in warm water than cold water. A sound wave in water that has the same amplitude (strength) and frequency (vibrations per second or Hertz) as a sound wave in air will have a longer wavelength. However, it will travel further and carry more energy than it would in an air environment. In turn, those factors affect how the trout hear, how sound behaves in water and how the angler approaches the trout as a prey.

A small book could probably be written about sound and vibrations in water. We haven't the time for that, so following is a quick summary that will help us to understand how these behave in water but without all the justifications and details.

➢ The intensity (strength) of a sound wave is about 3,340 times greater in water than the same sound wave in air. Trout can hear sounds significantly below our range of hearing.
➢ A sound wave in water is about 4.3 times longer than in air. Longer wavelengths tend to refract (bend) around obstacles and interference. These longer wavelengths will travel further. Trout hear longer wavelengths (lower frequencies) better than short wavelengths and from greater distances.
➢ Higher frequency sounds carry more energy but have shorter wavelengths. Short wavelengths are absorbed into rather than refracted around matter. That is probably why the Rainbows range of hearing doesn't extend into the higher frequencies.
➢ At the same amplitude, a low frequency sound has less power than high frequency. Below about 30 vibrations per second, the trout cannot detect this low power level as sound. However, the lateral line is capable of detecting these low frequencies. It will take over where the sense of hearing leaves off. Hearing and the lateral line work together in the trout to detect most vibrations in the water.
➢ As sound moves away from the source that created it, the sound wave becomes weaker and weaker. The distance for the energy from equal sound waves to dissipate is about 58 times further in water than in air. Expect a Rainbow to detect audible sounds from great distances.

➤ The strength of a sound signal weakens about six million times faster in dry air than it does in water. Thus, we expect the trout can hear weaker sounds from greater distances than we humans could possibly perceive.

➤ The speed of sound decreases in colder water. As we move down in the water column, water temperature drops and the speed of sound decreases. This temperature difference essentially bends and slows the sound wave. In general, the trout can detect sound better at the same depth and temperature as the depth of its origin. This can help the trout determine the location of a sound source such as an aquatic invertebrate.

➤ At the thermocline, water temperature rapidly changes. This rapid change acts like a density barrier and tends to reflect much of the sound energy. If a trout wants to escape the noisy upper layers of water, all it has to do is drop below the thermocline.

➤ The surface of a lake is also a density barrier. Less than 1% of sound generated above water will penetrate into the water. Likewise, very little of the sound generated under water will penetrate into the air environment. However, your aluminum boat is in contact with both mediums. It will pass along any vibrations created in either medium.

➤ Sound is reflected from the lake surface and from the thermocline. At these barriers, it merges with and reinforces the original sound waves. Thus, sound is amplified along these barriers. A trout that is near the lake surface or near the thermocline will be able to hear noises better in those locations.

➤ Inside hollow spaces, such as the trout's air bladder, sounds will reflect from the surrounding surfaces at the same frequency and produce louder sound. You may have had this demonstrated in school with a tuning fork and a hollow 'sound board'. This property of sound in water provides considerable improvement in the trout's ability to hear.

➤ "Decibels" are used to measure the intensity of sound. Decibels increase by factors of ten much like the Richter scale for earthquakes. For example, 60 decibels has ten times the sound intensity as 50 decibels. The decibel system uses different reference points in air than in water with water having a much lower starting point. To convert decibels in air to decibels in water, add 61 decibels to the air measurement (60 decibels in air equals 121 decibels in fresh water).

> Add 61 decibels to convert the intensity of sound in air to the intensity in water. And the "loudness" of sound doubles with every increase of ten decibels.

➤ Human hearing would perceive 60 decibels as being twice as loud as 50 decibels. The perceived "loudness" doubles with every increase of ten decibels. We can't be certain, but it would seem logical that a trout would perceive loudness in about the same way. Thus, underwater sounds will seem very loud to a trout.

➤ Because sound travels so well in water, there is a constant source of background noise. In a lake this background noise isn't as significant as in a creek or river but the trout in a lake must still contend with noises from wind and wave action, diving birds, motor boats, and anything else that generates more than about 30 vibrations per second. This constant background noise can interfere with the trout's ability to detect specific vibrations.

71

➤ In naval warfare, Sonar is used to locate submarines. Sonar is an extremely loud, low frequency vibration. The use of this type of sound is being linked to the deaths and beach stranding of whales and dolphins. It is probable that loud, low frequency sounds also affect the trout.

➤ Echolocation uses high frequency sound to locate schools of fish and other objects under water. Studies have shown that fish respond to and flee from these high frequencies even though it isn't likely that they actually 'hear' these vibrations. The otoliths or earstones probably vibrate under these high frequencies and this unusual sensation creates panic in the fish. If you use a fish finder with echolocation, it may actually be spooking the fish.

Put that all together and we can see that water transports vibrated energy much better than air. Trout also hear much better than humans do. Although few anglers are aware of these factors, sound has a considerable impact of the trout's daily way of life.

How Well Do Rainbows Hear

To test the hearing of a fish, researchers usually train small fish to respond in a given way to a sound. The loudness and pitch are then varied. If the fish responds when a sound is provided then there it is certainty that the fish heard the noise. If the fish doesn't respond it could be because it didn't hear the sound, or that the particular sound just didn't trigger the same response. So information provided on hearing is within a known range but not necessarily the only possibilities.

A secondary consideration regarding this research is that small fish are usually used for the testing. In larger fish, it is very probable that the larger size of the skull, skeleton and air bladder will intercept sound better and a larger air bladder will increase the resonance amplification. I strongly suspect that large trout have better hearing than the small trout normally used in testing.

It may be out there, but I haven't seen any research or reliable information on the decibel range that a Rainbow can hear. However, we can make an educated guess based on comparisons with the human ear. I won't provide the details, but going through the amplification factors of a trout and comparing those with the human ear, I calculate that the trout's hearing system would improve sound detection by about 50 or 60 decibels. Then, we use the rule-of-thumb that loudness doubles with every ten decibel increase.

Put it all together and if my calculations are in the ball park, it means that a Rainbow can probably detect sounds about 30 times better than the human ear. And that is without adding the 61 decibels to convert sound in air to sound in water.

> Please don't shout
> When trout are about.
> Yes, they have an ear
> And noises can hear.

Regardless of the precise numbers, the trout can hear extremely well. It gives them the ability to hear an insect hatch, detect swimming noises and hear other sounds that we can't imagine. Now that we have looked at all the technical stuff, let's see how this affects our angling.

Rainbow Hearing and the Angler

Because of the environmental differences, it is difficult for us humans to fathom the world of noise perceived by the Rainbow Trout. To compound the problem, there is overlap in how the trout uses its ears and lateral line to detect sound and pressure waves in the water. For a better understanding of these links, the reader should also reference the information about the lateral line. In our discussions, I will try to provide the applicable information where it "best fits" into the trout's world of sensory perceptions.

Invertebrate Noise

Insects and other aquatic invertebrates produce vibrations in the water. Usually we just think of those vibrations as the low frequency pressure waves created as a bug moves in water and most suitable for detection by the trout's lateral line. However, most of the invertebrates have hard chitinous shells that can be quite noisy when scraped or banged against their own chitin or other hard objects. Even the clank of hard mandibles or jaws when chewing or the banging together of legs while swimming can create audible sounds.

At close range, the trout can detect these faint noises. Some bugs even produce underwater sounds intentionally. Waterboatmen, for example, will rub their legs against their body to produce a mating song much like a cricket and that sound will carry a moderate distance in the water.

> **Did You Know**
> Most aquatic invertebrates make noise that the trout can detect. These sounds may be a factor in exciting the trout into a feed.

While the trout's ears don't locate the source of sounds very well, the lateral line does and is used to direct the trout to the source of these sounds.

Lures and plugs used by Bass anglers incorporate the use of sound and vibration. However, we fly fishers can't do much to improve the audibility of our flies. On occasion, it helps to get your fly to land with a splash to attract the attention of the trout. Even though we don't incorporate sound into our flies, we can put knowledge about sound to use. When the aquatic invertebrates are active, they will be producing noise. The more noise they produce, the greater the odds that those sounds will excite the trout into seeking food. We can't hear the noise made by those invertebrates but we can observe their activity. If you see lots of invertebrate activity in the lake then the chances of successful fishing are greatly improved.

Ambient Noise

We humans are constantly bombarded by noise and we tend to ignore most of it. The same happens with trout in their lake environment. The sounds from wind and wave action, other fish jumping, boating traffic, and so forth adds to the underwater noise levels. In the ocean, these ambient noises are recorded at about 81 decibels in water.

The level of underwater noise is probably ten or twenty decibels less on our lakes but still significant.

The fly fisher can make a pretty good guess as to how much ambient noise is being delivered to the trout by just being observant and applying a little common sense. On days with strong winds and large waves breaking against the shoreline, you can bet that underwater noise levels are high. Likewise, noise levels will be high on days with people swimming, lots of boat traffic, or just a little boat traffic with very noisy folks in those boats.

> **Did You Know**
> Wind and wave action increase the underwater noise levels and make it more difficult for trout to locate bugs.

Rainbows will frequently use their hearing and lateral line to detect and locate prey. If the level of ambient noise is low, this task becomes rather easy. However, if the level of background noise becomes too high it is difficult for the trout to hear the faint sounds of their prey (or your fly) and even more difficult to determine the direction to the source of those sounds. Here are some things you can do to improve fishing on days with high ambient noise levels.

If deciding on a lake for the day and it is windy, then choose a lake that has clear water. With high ambient noise levels, the trout are more likely to be locating their food through visual means rather than trying to follow faint vibrations to their source. Visual detection works much better in clear water than it does in murky water.

> **Fishing Tip**
> When ambient noise is high, try fishing deeper in the water column (with colder water) and perhaps with a larger fly that has a hackle.

If you are already on a lake and it becomes noisy you should try to remove yourself from the noise or reduce the impact. Get away from the noisy boaters or locate in a bay with reduced wind and wave action. In summer, there is another alternative. You can try fishing below the thermocline. Remember that the thermocline acts as a density barrier and much of the ambient noise will not penetrate this layer. Lastly, you can try using a larger fly or a fly with a hackle. These flies will provide more vibrations under water and make it easier for the trout to detect and locate with high levels of ambient noise.

As a side note, the ambient noise levels in a stream or river are very high. Trout in those environments don't use sound or the lateral line to locate food as much as trout in lakes. In streams and rivers, the trout learn to feed mostly by vision with hearing and the lateral line being used more for the detection of bigger noises such as an approaching predator.

Angler Noise

Most of us could probably reduce the amount of noise we make in a watercraft. Loud or unusual noises advertise our presence and can make the trout very cautious or even spook the trout. Be careful about dropping your beer can or tackle box in the bottom of an aluminum boat. Leave your radio, ghetto blaster and CD player back on shore.

Turn off that gasoline motor before you move onto a feeding shoal and oil the oar locks so they don't squeak.

A rubber belly-boat transmits less noise than a fiberglass canoe. A canoe transmits less noise than an aluminum boat. For the aluminum boat, place a rug, rubber mat or square of carpeting on the floor to reduce noise. Drop your anchor so the rope doesn't run over the boat gunwale and

> **Did You Know**
> A trout can probably detect the sound of your heart beating as its vibrations go through your boat and into the water.

the anchor contacts the lake bottom softly. If possible, align your boat when anchored so that there isn't a constant sound of waves against the side of the boat. Don't slap the water with every second false cast. Whooping and hollering when you hook a trout could make that the last trout taken for a while. Turn off the ratchet that makes the clicking noises on your fly reel. Avoid banging your landing net against the boat and try to release a fish in the water rather than bringing it onboard to thrash and flip across the boat bottom. It's also easier on the fish. And when you are ready to leave, remember the noise factor if there are still other anglers in the vicinity.

Trout Noise

Even though it isn't a vocalization, the trout do make noise in water. Their sound production is mostly associated with feeding and swimming. Sound is produced when they jump from the water, when they slurp a Caddis off the surface and when they swallow that large dragonfly nymph. Even though we can't hear it, the trout make noise by their body muscles and the

> **Did You Know**
> The sounds emitted by a few feeding fish is likely to stimulate other fish into the feeding mood. It is a part of the reason that many fish will feed at the same time.

movement of joints. The rapid sweep of a tail against water produces sound vibrations within the trout's auditory range. In addition, the trout seem to have the ability to distinguish normal swimming sounds from the sounds of movement to capture prey. Trout are stimulated by the sounds of another trout feeding. This often excites them into searching out their own food.

I wasn't going to discuss fishing as it relates to trout living in lakes with other species of fish. However, there is an important point to be mentioned as it relates to the sounds that fish make. In those mixed species lakes the trout will usually become a predator that feeds on the small bait fish in the lake. For protection, those fish normally travel in schools. The trout can hear the swimming noises from these schools and be attracted to a potential food source. Each bait fish produces its own individual swimming sounds. If there is one minnow in a school of a thousand that swims differently because it is sick or injured, the trout can detect and locate that individual through its swimming sounds. A predatory trout will target that minnow. A fly or lure mixed in with a school of bait fish will send out different sound vibrations than the minnows and thus become a target for the trout. That is why an angler is often successful even though the trout had a thousand potential victims from which to choose.

The Sense of Balance

Before we leave the Rainbow's hearing ability and move onto the lateral line, we should quickly mention the Rainbow's sense of balance. Only because the ability to determine up from down occurs within the trout's ears.

Balance isn't a true sense like sight, smell, taste, touch and hearing. I have always wondered why but I don't make the rules. Other than allowing the trout to perform those amazing fighting acrobatics, knowledge about the trout's sense of balance will not benefit the angler. However, it does help to round out our investigation into the trout.

Figure 18 showing the trout's ears shows three "semicircular canals" in the inner ear of the Rainbow that control balance. The human ear and trout ear are similar in how balance works with a major exception that I wanted to mention. The human ear uses fluid in these canals to determine balance. In a watery environment, this won't work. To compensate, once again the trout use an otolith or earstone. These little calcium spheres are in the semicircular canals and through gravity provide enough pressure on the neuromasts to let the trout determine down from up.

There is an interesting note about otoliths. As the trout grows, the ear and semicircular canals also grow. As a result, the otoliths must grow in size to maintain the same proportional relationship. Just like the rings of a tree or the rings on the scales of a fish, the otoliths form growth rings that can be used to determine the trout's age and growth rate.

The Lateral Line or "Distant Touch Perception"

Scientists have long known that fish can perceive objects in water without the use of their basic five senses. In a clean and spotless aquarium, for example, your goldfish will not bump into the transparent glass unless fleeing in panic. You or I might accidentally walk through a plate glass patio window. The goldfish would not make that same mistake. It would know there is a solid barrier in its way even if it couldn't see, taste, touch, smell or hear the glass. Scientists have systematically removed senses such as vision or hearing and the fish will still avoid the barrier. However, if the nerves to the lateral line are deadened the goldfish will bump into the glass.

The recognized name for this form of extra-sensory perception or ESP is "distant touch". This perception is extra-sensory because fish and a couple of amphibians are the only animals that possess this sensory capability. The lateral line is the organ responsible for this sensory perception and only these water dwelling animals have a lateral line.

What the Rainbow perceives through distant touch is much the same as what the name implies. It is believed that the trout can pretty well "feel" an object without coming in physical contact with it. If we close our eyes and someone places a marble in our hand, we can determine the size, shape, texture and temperature of the marble without seeing it. We aren't sure if the trout can detect the temperature or texture from a distance but it could perceive the other physical attributes if the marble or the trout were moving toward each other. Like many other things in the trout's perception of the world, this is made possible by the density of water.

What is the Lateral Line?

One string of scientific thinking suggests that ears of all vertebrates were evolved from the lateral line. The theory suggests that the lateral line neuromasts near the brain evolved into the ear and balance canals to improve sensory perception. The neuromasts of all three organs are essentially the same. Then, as the evolving ocean creatures left

Did You Know
It is possible that the ears of land dwellers are evolutionary remnants of the lateral line, left over from an aquatic existence.

their watery homes and crawled out onto the landmasses, their lateral lines became ineffective in an air environment. Evolution then eliminated the lateral lines of land creatures but they were left with the ears and balance canals. That is interesting stuff.

The basic sensory unit of the lateral line is the neuromast. The neuromasts are a bundle of sensory hairs or cilia that generate an electric pulse when moved. They are covered with a gelatinous cap called the Capula. These are much the same as the sensory organs in the ear and balance canals. However, a different part of the trout's brain receives the electrical impulses from the lateral line and interprets the information in a different way.

The lateral line is one of the main sensory organs of the Rainbow and serves a number of sensory functions. Some of these functions you probably already know but I'll bet there are one or two functions you don't know. Following are the basics functions.

➢ To detect low frequency vibrations – from about one Hertz to about 100 Hertz.
➢ To detect the source and size of a pressure wave generator. This gives the trout information on direction, distance and size of a moving object in water.
➢ To detect obstacles through pressure waves – such as the glass aquarium side.
➢ To avoid predatory attack – warns of approaching predators.
➢ To assist schooling behavior – allows co-coordinated turning with schooling partners.
➢ To detect water movement – helps determine river currents and migratory paths.
➢ To determine depth – through water pressure lets the trout know how deep it is.
➢ To detect and capture food – even a blind fish can feed via the lateral line system.

If you knew all those, give yourself a gold star. Some fish (and maybe the Rainbow) have additional sensory capabilities with the lateral line.

➢ To detect electricity in the water – a part of food detection and capture.
➢ To detect gravitational forces – aids with migratory navigation in the ocean.

I'll discuss these last two when we look at the possibility of other senses in the Rainbow Trout.

The design of the lateral line mechanism is relatively simple. Just under the skin of the trout is a lateral line canal. This canal contains a series of neuromasts. Every neuromast is connected to a lateral line nerve that transmits information to the brain. The lateral line canal also contains a series of lateral line pores that connect the canal to the surrounding water environment.

The lateral line pores allow any increases in water pressure or vibrations in the water to enter the canal and disturb the neuromasts. Increases in water pressure compress the Capula with its sensory hairs and that creates an electric signal to the brain. Moving water or vibrations in the water cause the Capula and sensory hairs to move or vibrate at different rates or intensities and send different electric signals. The lateral line nerve has a continuous flow of electricity that keeps the trout constantly informed of its surroundings. Figure 19 shows a pictorial representation of what I have just described.

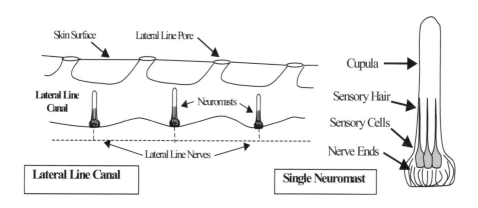

Figure 19 – Sensory Components of the Lateral Line

Where is the Lateral Line?

Most folks think of the lateral line as that single line extending from the Rainbow's tail to its head. That is the lateral line but it is only one branch of an entire network. There are actually eight components on each side of the trout plus some smaller branches in the network. In addition, there are scattered receptor cells called "free neuromasts". The

> **Did You Know**
> The lines extending down each side of the trout's body are only 2 parts of a 16 part lateral line system. Most of this system is located in the head of the trout.

entire network is called the Octavolateralis system (meaning eight page-like parts) or more simply just the "lateral line system".

While the actual lateral line traverses the body of the trout, the remaining parts of the lateral line system are in the head of the Rainbow. In Figure 20, I've shown the main parts of the lateral line system but should explain where the unlabeled canals are located to total up to eight.

1. **Lateral Line (trunk) canal** – from head to tail along the central torso of the body.
2. **Occipital canal** – across the top of the head.
3. **Supraorbital canal** – above the eye.
4. **Suborbital canal** – below the eye.
5. **Postosic canal** – between the supraorbital and occipital canals.
6. **Optic** (not shown) – fairly small, just behind the eye and joins the supra & suborbital.
7. **Hyomandibular canal** – down the gill plate and also known as the Preopecular.
8. **Mandibular canal** – along the lower jaw and joins the Hyomandibular.

Each of the eight main lateral line canals is repeated on each side of the trout's body for a total of sixteen main canals. That's probably a lot more than you expected. In addition, minor canals plus some free neuromasts are scattered about the head. The free neuromasts are individual sensor cells scattered in various locations around the head.

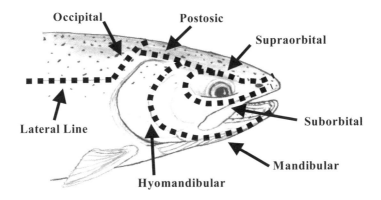

Figure 20 – Main Sensory Canals of the Lateral Line System

For many years, I wondered how a lateral line that is located behind the head and on the sides of the body could help a fish direct food into its mouth. Finding out that a good portion of the lateral line system is actually located in the head explained a lot. And from the placement of the canals, you can see that the system is well suited to help guide food items into the mouth.

When a bug wiggles, the neuromasts on the same side of the trout will pick up a strong sensory input. Those on the other side of the fish may pick up a weak signal. The trout will turn into the direction of the stronger signal and then move left, right, up or down to equalize the vibration signals from the bug. When the vibrations are of equal strength on both sides of the head, then the bug is directly in front. With neuromasts in the lower

Did You Know
The ears of the trout are very sensitive but do not locate the source of sound or pressure waves very well. Locating the source is a main function of the lateral line system.

jaw, nose and gill plates, the trout can feel the bug (distant touch) right up to the point that it enters the mouth. With sensors on both sides of the trout's head, the system works much the same way as binocular vision.

Sensitivity of the Lateral Line System

The neuromasts of the lateral line system are particularly good at detecting disturbances in the water. Those disturbances create changes in water pressure. As we saw when discussing the trout's hearing, even sound waves create small changes in water pressure. The neuromasts in the ears of the trout are more attuned to picking up high frequency sound vibrations (from 30 Hz to 3,000 Hz). Conversely, the neuromasts in the lateral line system are more attuned to picking up low frequency vibrations (1 to 100 Hz). The lateral line system will even pick up changes in water pressure that are too slow (< 1 Hz) to be considered as sound vibrations. For example, the lateral line system will pick up pressure waves from objects that are stationary but in the path of the swimming fish.

As the trout swims, it builds up a pressure wave in front of itself. If that pressure wave encounters something more or less dense than the water, it causes a change in this pressure wave. The trout can detect these variances and probably the size, shape and density of the object. Detection through these pressure waves is different from sound vibrations but the trout can still detect these through the lateral line.

So just how sensitive is the lateral line system? The short and blunt answer is that we don't know.

The latest opinion of the scientific community is that the lateral line is used for "near field" detection and the ears are for "far field" detection. In other words, they

Because of their larger surface and reception area, it is likely that bigger fish have a more sensitive lateral line system than smaller fish.

think that the lateral line only works up close (within a few feet or less) and long-range detection is done through the ears.

My personal opinion disagrees with that assessment but I'll caution you to remember that I'm only an amateur. I have read a number of the research papers on lateral line sensitivity. All are cautious to make statements such as "this does not necessarily mean that the sensory system cannot be used to detect prey from somewhat greater distances". In addition, all the research that I've reviewed also has a basic flaw in the experimental design.

To test the lateral line sensitivity, small fish are always put into glass or metal tanks with something that vibrates at low frequency to attract the fish. The fish are trained in advance to know that the vibrations are a food source. Other senses are incapacitated and the fish are

When it's night
Trout don't rely on sight.
The lateral line
Locates flies just fine.

allowed to try and locate that vibration. The design flaw of these experiments is the placement of fish into a walled tank. If we remember our discussions on sound, vibrations will reflect off the walls of the tank. Vibrations will then reflect from the aquarium walls and come at the fish from all angles. A fish would need to be fairly close to the vibrating source to determine its direction from the strength of the vibrations. The comparison would be similar to placing a person in a large echo chamber, turning off the lights and expecting the person to find, by sound alone, a radio that is playing somewhere in the room. Until the person is very close to the radio, they couldn't tell its location from the direction of the sound.

In open water, I have watched trout go directly to a fly from over 100 feet away. The distance is too far for sight or smell and it ears couldn't locate the source even if the vibrations from the fly were of a high enough frequency to be considered sound. In my opinion, the only plausible way the trout knew the exact location of that fly was through low frequency vibrations (water pressure changes) that were detected with the lateral line system. I have talked with other knowledgeable anglers who have the same opinion.

There is also a second consideration in regards to the potential sensitivity of the lateral line system. When discussing sound, we saw that it was the low frequency, long wavelength sound waves that were best carried through water. The whales, for example, use low frequency sounds to communicate at distances over 100 miles. The lateral line system is designed to detect these low frequency sounds.

Whales use low frequency sounds (vibrations) to transmit their songs over more than 100 miles. The trout's lateral line also detects low frequency vibrations.

On the other hand, the ears are designed to detect higher frequency sounds that don't carry as well in the water. To me, the physics and logic would indicate that the lateral line system is capable of detecting small vibrations at distances greater than a few feet.

So the sensitivity of the lateral line is in doubt. It is my opinion that the ears will be the first to detect a bug. Then, the lateral line system will be used to locate the bug. And I expect that the movement of a bug or your fly can be detected and located from more than 100 feet away under good conditions. The trout probably uses a combination of these senses for locating food. However, the current scientific thinking is that the system may only be capable of locating movement from a few feet and maybe less. For now, consider your own observations and make up your own mind on the lateral line sensitivity. Hopefully we will have verification at some time in the near future.

Determining the Size and Source of Objects

If we have our eyes closed and someone hands us an object, we can determine some of its basic attributes by feeling the object. Through its lateral line system, the trout can determine some of the basic attributes of an object generating a pressure wave. Things such as basic size, shape, speed and location are "felt" by the neuromasts in the lateral line. Thus, the term "distant touch perception" has been applied to this ability.

The 16 main canals of the lateral line system are strategically placed on both sides of the trout's body in such a manner that the direction of a source creating a sound or pressure wave can easily be determined. If a pressure wave is generated on the left side of the fish, then the neuromasts on that side of the fish will receive the pressure wave much stronger than on the opposite side of the fish. Also, if the neuromasts at the tail of the fish receive a pressure signal before the neuromasts near the head of the fish, then the trout knows that the signal original from behind.

Direction to a vibrating source can be determined from the time lapse in different neuromasts receiving the vibrations. For comparison, the human ear also determines direction because one ear hears sound fractions of a second before the other ear. In addition, the size of the object creating vibrations gives off different pressure waves that the trout can feel and interpret. Most of the time the trout can tell if something large (a predatory diving bird) or something small (an insect) has created a pressure wave even if the amplitudes are relatively similar.

> **Did You Know**
>
> Through its lateral line system, a Rainbow Trout can actually "feel" bugs, flies and other objects from a distance. It can also determine where the object is and how fast it is moving.

In the dark of night, in murky water and at other times when hunting by sight isn't efficient, the trout will rely on the lateral line system as a primary senses for locating prey, escaping predators and avoiding obstacles.

An angler can use a number of tactics to improve their success when underwater visibility is limited. Bass anglers will often use a lure that sends out lots of vibrations duplicating swimming motion and frequently the lure will rattle or send out sound. The lure is rapidly pulled a short distance to create the vibrations and noise but then stopped for a second to let the bass find it. Not many of our flies will create noise or vibrations similar to the motion of swimming. However, in poor visibility, it does pay to retrieve the fly fast enough to generate a pressure wave and then to let it sit

> Some fish live in caves and are totally blind. Other fish live on the deepest ocean floors that are devoid of light. All these fish can freely move about and capture prey via their lateral line system.

for a second or two to allow the trout time to locate the fly. It doesn't pay to retrieve the fly so fast that it is always one pull away from the fish.

Another thing that helps under poor visibility conditions is to use a fly that has a hackle or legs or something else that will increase the vibrations and pressure waves emitted from the fly. I have watched trout go after a strike indicator rather than the fly a short distance away presumably because the indicator gave off more or at least more interesting vibrations than the fly. And lastly, a larger fly will send out more signals and be easier for the trout to find than a smaller fly. I would suggest larger flies under conditions of poor visibility and smaller flies when vision is relatively good.

Lateral Line Uses

At the beginning of this section, we saw some of the functions of the lateral line system. Several of those can have a direct impact on angler success. An angler should be aware of the other functions just as a matter of better understanding their prey. Here are some of the ways lateral lines are used and where applicable I have added the angler implications.

Angler Generated Vibrations

The lateral line system will detect changes in water pressure including low frequency sound vibrations in the range of 1 to 100 Hertz (or vibrations per second). The ear is designed to detect vibrations in the range of 30 to 3000 Hz. There is some overlap but the lateral line is the main organ for detecting vibrations that are below the trout's ability to hear.

Even as a kid, my dad taught me to approach a pool in a stream very quietly because a noisy approach could spook the trout. I later learned that the vibrations of my footsteps were transmitted through the ground, into the water and received by the trout. In the still waters of a lake, there are less background vibrations and the trout will perceive these more readily than in a stream. When fishing on a lake, your boat is in direct contact with the water and often made of aluminum. Metal in contact with water is a good transmitter of vibrations.

The trout will perceive bumps and clanks that we make in the boat even if those vibrations are below our own threshold of hearing. It is quite probable that the trout can even perceive your heart beating as those vibrations are carried into the water through your boat.

Fishing Tip
A hassle-free trout will feed more readily than one being cautious because of unusual vibrations in the water. Soundproof your boat to put the trout at ease.

We simply can't avoid most of the low frequency vibrations we create in a boat. Sitting on a soft cushion and placing a rug or some other sound muffler on the floor of the boat will help. My canoe is made of fiberglass that doesn't transmit vibrations as well as aluminum and the rubber of a belly-boat doesn't transmit vibrations well at all. Most of the time the trout become accustomed to the various vibrations transmitted into the water by humans and these don't seem to affect the trout. However, on several occasions it has appeared that anglers in fiberglass and rubber watercraft were more successful than nearby anglers in aluminum boats. This may have been my imagination working over-time but it is a factor worth considering. I would suggest that precaution is a good policy. We should always try to avoid any unnecessary vibrations in our watercraft.

Food Detection and Capture

If an aquatic invertebrate is moving and sending out low frequency vibrations, it is likely that a Rainbow will detect the bug with its ears or lateral line system before anything else. Even in relatively clear water with reasonable lighting conditions, there is a good possibility that a Rainbow will visually miss an aquatic invertebrate unless it was first detected with the lateral line. In addition, many of the movements of a bug will not generate enough vibrations per second to be detected as sound by the trout's ears. Smell is generally not directional enough to help the trout and the senses of taste and touch are usually employed after the bug has been located. In most cases, we can pretty well say that initial detection of food occurs through the lateral line. The role of the other sensory perceptions increases after initial detection of a prey.

> **Did You Know**
> Many aquatic invertebrates also use vibrations in the water to detect an approaching predator such as a Rainbow.

Aquatic invertebrates are not totally vulnerable to detection by the trout's lateral line. Many of the aquatic bugs and crustaceans are also able to detect vibrations and pressure waves in the water. Furthermore, smaller critters are more likely to detect larger critters before the larger animal detects them. When an aquatic invertebrate detects an approaching Rainbow or other predator, the instinctive reaction is to seek shelter or cease movement. Those that don't avoid detection or don't make it to shelter quick enough are destined to become a meal. There are also times when a bug can do little to avoid detection or reach shelter. When an insect has left the lake bottom and is on its way to the lake surface to hatch it is totally exposed and vulnerable. This bug vulnerability is one of the reasons the trout will often feed during a hatch.

The fly fisher should remember that the trout's initial detection of a bug, crustacean or fly is likely to be through the lateral line system. Initial detection isn't always through vision. The odds of success are improved when the fly is periodically creating low frequency vibrations.

> Your fly should match
> The bugs that hatch.
> Copy movement and size
> To present your flies.

I have watched anglers using a Chironomid and dry line and they just let their fly sit motionless in the same location for long periods. Eventually a trout will come along that visually detects the fly and the angler gets a fish. I would suggest that if the angler imparted a little motion to the fly, it would improve their success. A little motion will create low frequency vibrations that allow the trout to become aware of the fly even before visual detection. The trout will then actively search for the fly.

The necessary motion can be created by letting the dry line drift with the wind, or using a very slow retrieve or by giving the fly a twitch (one or two inch pull) every minute or so.

The success of a fly fisher can also be improved if the vibrations from the fly resemble those of the invertebrate as close as possible. The best way to mimic the particular signal of an invertebrate is have a fly of the same size that is retrieved at the same speed as the critter it is supposed to imitate.

Obstacle Avoidance

As a fish swims, it displaces water and generates a pressure wave in front of itself. Whenever the fish is swimming this pressure wave is always there and the neuromasts in the fish's head are constantly feeling the pressure from this wave. When the fish approaches an object, such as a glass aquarium wall, the force returning from this pressure wave is increased and the fish knows that an object is in front of it even if it can't see the obstacle. At slow speeds, this pressure wave is only sensitive for a short distance. At faster speeds, the fish will detect differences in the pressure wave for much greater distances.

This sensory input has a value to the trout. It helps to keep them from bumping into submerged logs, weed patches, and so forth in poor visibility conditions. However, there is little application to the angler in terms of improving your catch. There is an interesting side note though. If you have ever had a fish jump into your boat, it was likely because of this obstacle avoidance ability of the fish. The probable cause was that the fish was rapidly swimming toward your boat, detected it as an obstacle and immediately had to decide on a direction in which to turn. If it decided to avoid your boat by taking the upward direction, it would jump out of the water near your boat. Since it was swimming toward your boat, its forward direction would most likely place the landing location at your feet or in your lap.

> Because of its forward pressure wave and lateral line, it isn't likely that you will see your Goldfish bump into the glass wall of its aquarium unless fleeing in panic.

Predator Detection

In the early stages of evolution, the detection of predators was probably a primary reason for the development of a lateral line. Large objects can be detected easier with the lateral line than smaller objects. A small fish could detect the approach of a large predatory fish before the predator could detect the smaller fish. Over the eons the system has improved and today's trout can probably tell if an approaching predator is another fish, diving bird or mammal from the type of vibrations and pressure waves emitted. Each will have its own characteristic set of vibrations and pressure waves created from the swimming motions or the splash of an Osprey diving into the water.

When predators are active in a fishing area, the trout will be on alert and more cautious about feeding. If the fishing seems to slow down because of predator activity, try fishing where the fish shelter and feel more secure. Deeper water, underwater weed beds, submerged logs and similar shelters offer protection and the fish are more likely to remain active in those areas. Once the predator leaves the area, the trout usually resume normal feeding activity within about 15 minutes.

> If a Loon, Osprey, Otter or other fish predator is active in your fishing area, be patient. The fish should resume feeding within about 15 minutes of the predator's departure.

Schooling Behavior

You have probably watched a nature show on television where large schools of fish swim and turn in unison. The main reason these fish are able to perform those maneuvers is because of their lateral line system. As a fish pushes through the water, it creates a pressure wave in front of it. Body undulations and thrusts with the tail also create pressure waves and low frequency vibrations to the sides of the fish. The lateral lines of adjacent fish are in constant contact, can immediately detect any signal changes and then adjust their own location to keep the same distance from nearby fish.

Young Rainbows and small bait fish will school as a defense mechanism. The school is larger and easier to detect from a distance than an individual fish but the combined vibrations from a school make it harder for a predator to single out an individual. The

> Via their lateral line system, trout can detect each other as well as prey or predators in their environment.

exception is a wounded, hurt or sick individual that sends out a different set of vibrations than the rest of the school. Through its hearing and lateral line, a predatory fish can zero in on that individual. In a lake with bait fish, an angler can put this knowledge to work.

Detecting Water Movement

In a gentle flowing stream, water movement tends to be more of an "ebb & flow" with differing water pressure. The neuromasts in the lateral line canal will gently sway and compress with these differences. In a rapidly flowing stream, sound vibrations can also be generated. The combination of swaying, compression and vibrations in the neuromasts can direct the trout to the line of least resistance when navigating a waterway.

> **Did You Know**
> Under the right wind, water and temperature conditions a lake will sometimes develop a "flow" of moving water. When this happens, the trout will often face into this water flow to feed. If you see this flow, try to present your fly so that it drifts with this slight current.

The detection of water flow will also inform the trout which current pathway is most likely to bring food.

In our lakes, wind action combined with temperature changes will create minor currents in what is generally considered still water. If you watch submerged algae or other matter suspended in the water column, you can determine the direction of flow within the lake. Water flowing over the lateral line system of a Rainbow will also detect these small currents. Frequently trout will orient their body so they are facing or swimming into this small current. Most of the time current direction makes little difference to an angler fishing in a lake. On rare occasions, particularly when a very slow retrieve is needed, the trout will become fussy and want their foods (or a fly) to drift in the same direction as the current. A fly fisher should be aware of this for those few times it is needed to improve success.

Depth Detection

Compression of the neuromasts alerts the trout to changes in water pressure. The degree of compression will inform the trout as to how deep it has gone in the water. Air bladder inflation and other physiological adjustments can then be made. Changes in barometric or atmospheric pressure will also cause slight changes in the water pressure. It is possible that these slight changes can be detected by the lateral line neuromasts as they are compressed. Later, we will take a closer look at barometric pressure. For the angler, the ability of a trout to determine its depth in the water has little application to catching a fish.

Lateral Line Summary

The lateral line system supplements a trout's hearing by detecting the lower frequency vibrations in water. These vibrations travel further than sound waves. While we are not sure about the sensitivity of the system, we know that it allows trout and other fish to move about and catch prey under the total absence of vision. This sense is called the "distant touch perception". It is believed that trout can actually feel (like the sense of touch) what is causing pressure waves in the water. All this is made possible by the density of water. It allows trout to feel their environment to a degree beyond the comprehension of us air breathers.

The Rainbows Sense of Touch

In general, we humans rely on our sense of touch to a greater degree than the Rainbow Trout. Gravity keeps us on the solid surface of our world with our feet and other bodily parts constantly coming in direct contact with our surroundings. If we were suspended in water, our need to feel our environment would be greatly reduced. In that case, Mother Nature would probably diminish our tactile senses through evolution. This seems to be what has happened to the trout. The trout's need for "touch" or direct contact with its world is not as important and thus not as acute as a person's sense of touch. The trout have come to rely more on their indirect sense of touch through the lateral line system. That type of touch is more important to the trout than physical contact.

We gather most of our conscious tactile sensations through our hands, feet, mouth and sexual organs. It seems that a Rainbow is most sensitive to tactile sensations in these same areas with hands and feet replaced by fins. Touch allows us to feel the shape, size, hardness, texture and temperature of whatever we are touching. Most of that doesn't affect the everyday life of a Rainbow. However, there are two important exceptions. The trout uses its mouth to feel the food it is ingesting and it uses the tactile sensors over its entire body to determine water temperature.

Temperature Perception

Rainbows are cold blooded and thus many aspects of their life are regulated by water temperature. Temperature affects water density, the ability of water to hold oxygen, the trout's metabolic processes, digestion rates and most other things in the trout's life. It behooves the trout to monitor water temperature.

> If the water is hot,
> Then the fishing's not.
> Fish water that's cool,
> Is the golden rule.

Rainbows are able to detect water temperature changes of about 0.02°F. That's a much higher degree of sensitivity to temperature change than humans are able to detect. A trout will use this ability to change its water depth to a temperature that best suits its needs at a particular point in time. It also helps to explain why trout are so fussy about the temperature of the water they inhabit.

> A trout will know
> When the bugs will show
> On the shoal it will wait
> At just the right date.

Many hatches of aquatic insects are triggered by a combination of temperature, light and moon position. Water temperature doesn't normally change very rapidly in a lake and differences in the range of 0.02°F may be all that is necessary for a certain bug to pupate. After a couple of year's experience, trout learn to predict when a certain insect is going to hatch and at what water depth. The trout don't always wait for a hatch to begin. With their sensitivity to light and temperature, they are often on the shoal waiting for those first individuals of a hatch to show.

Pain Perception

I have had people criticize my fishing because of the pain I was inflicting on the trout. For a long time I was bothered about that aspect of my fishing. I'm one of those people who refuse to kill a housefly until it exceeds a critical point in my ability to tolerate its nasty habits.

> It is likely that trout do not have the mental development to interpret an injury as pain. The primitive brain will not process concepts that complex. It is sort of like the trout is always on pain killers.

Recently I read a paper by a James D. Rose who is a professor with the Department of Psychology and the Department of Zoology and Physiology at the University of Wyoming in Laramie. In that paper Professor Rose provides the reasons why I don't need to worry about the "pain" a trout may experience by having a hook in the mouth or the trauma a trout may have trying to throw my fly. He says "fish do not have the brain development that is necessary for the psychological experience of pain or any other type of awareness".

Professor Rose systematically explains that pain is a psychological experience that requires a certain degree of development in the cerebral hemispheres of the brain. The cerebral hemispheres in fish are primitive and are the simplest types of brains of any of the vertebrates. The "brainstem" of the fish dominates its existence. The fish will detect injury but that is not translated into the conscious and unpleasant experience we call pain. The regions of the brain responsible for fear and pain are not present in a fish. The 'fight and flee' responses to being hooked are simply protective measures. Humans can take aspirin or other pain killers to reduce the amount of perceived pain from, for example, a headache. That wouldn't be necessary in a fish. They simply wouldn't have a headache although they may perceive that something is physically wrong.

Mouthing the Prey

When a trout closes its mouth over a morsel of food to eat, it must be able to feel that prey. Before anything else, the trout will usually 'feel' the prey with its mouth to make sure there isn't something wrong with its meal, such as the presence of a hook. If the food item is very small, such as a tiny Chironomid, the trout won't be able to feel the prey very well and may just swallow before it escapes. For bigger food items, the trout will usually give the prey a quick roll around the mouth to feel it and then clamp the mouth closed to kill or stun the prey so that it doesn't escape. The trout doesn't want to squash all the nutritious stuffing out of the prey or fail to stun the bug. So the trout needs

> **Did You Know**
> A trout will "mouth" your fly for a second or two before detecting the hook and spitting it back out. You only have a short while in which to set the hook.

the ability to feel the pressure applied. For bigger food items, the trout will also want to swallow the prey lengthwise. The trout needs to feel the prey to make this adjustment. These are the most likely reasons that a trout retains its sensitivity to touch perception in the mouth area.

Implications to the Angler

An angler should be aware that trout use their sense of touch to adjust to temperature changes and use temperature to forecast insect hatches. The angler must also be aware of that momentary pause when a trout first engulfs a food item and mouths the prey. It is during that pause when the hook must be set.

When the trout feeds, it is inevitably moving to capture the prey. The prey is sucked in, mouthed and tasted by the trout as it continues to swim. That is the moment when the line tightens or the strike indicator dips. If a fly fisher is too slow the trout will feel or taste the 'wrongness' of the prey (or fly) and spit it out. It only takes a second or two for the trout to feel something is wrong and spit out an intended meal.

Many fish species are not as cautious or as quick to reject a fly as a Rainbow. An angler that is asleep at the switch will miss many strikes or not even be aware that they had a strike, particularly when using a dry line. Even experienced fly fishers will miss about 40% of their strikes with Rainbows and lose another 10% because the hook wasn't properly set. Watch the line or strike indicator for the slightest movement and don't hesitate to set the hook when it moves. When Rainbows are foraging the strike will often be soft and subtle.

The Rainbows Sense of Taste

Taste is the perception of differences between sweet, sour, bitter and salt. Different combinations of these are all that our taste buds distinguish. Those different combinations are registered in our brain as different tastes. Taste begins as chemicals are dissolved in a solution such as our saliva or in water. Taste cannot be achieved unless chemical compounds are dissolved. When we chew our food, it is mechanically ground into pieces fine enough to dissolve in our saliva and that is when taste is first perceived. Our drinks already have dissolved chemicals that we can taste. While in solution, the chemicals bind with the receptor cells in our taste buds. The receptor cells depolarize the chemical molecule and that sends a signal to the brain as taste.

We will never be able to perceive taste from the trout's perspective. However, we must assume that their brain receives the sense of taste in pretty much the same way. We also know of some similarities and differences between a trout's sense of taste and a person's that are of importance to the angler.

In people the sense of taste and smell are closely linked. How a bit of food tastes is often more smell related than taste related. There is a direct connection at the back of our throat to our nasal chamber. The nasal chamber is where smells are detected. As we chew, odors are released that are carried by air into our nasal chamber and that greatly affects how we perceive our food. Trout do not have a direct connection from their mouth to their nasal chamber. In that respect, the trout's sense of smell and taste are distinctly separate.

Taste in a Water Environment

Like a human, the trout have different sensory organs for taste and smell. The parts of the brain that process these chemical signals are also different. For taste perception in a human, the food must be dissolved and in direct contact with the taste buds in our mouth. We can smell something from a few feet away but we cannot taste it. The same doesn't hold true for the trout.

> **Did You Know**
> A Rainbow can taste and smell its food even before it enters the mouth. So be careful about what is on your fingers before you handle your fly.

Trout live in a watery world and any chemical compounds to be tasted are in solution before delivery to the trout. Even if a trout bites down on a bug to release its chemicals, the molecules are delivered to the fish through water rather than something like saliva. The taste molecules are dissolved in water before reaching the trout's taste buds. These molecules can travel to the trout from significant distances. In effect, the trout have a sense of "distant taste". They can taste something from a distance like we can smell something from a distance. The trout doesn't need to place something in its mouth to perceive the taste.

Mother Nature made some modifications in the Rainbow to take advantage of this ability to taste things from a distance. Because saliva isn't needed to form a solution, taste buds don't need to be restricted to the inside the trout's mouth. With this open window of opportunity, Mother Nature gave the trout some additional taste buds.

> Smell and taste are closely related. In a water environment the differences are even less distinct.

The trout have taste buds scattered around their body rather than just localized in their mouth. Trout and other Salmonids have a few taste buds in their tail, fins, gills and facial nerves as well as their mouth. They can taste and thus reject something before it is ingested. They can taste something near their tail and turn to grab it without any other sensory perception of its presence.

In humans, taste discerns the differences between sweet, sour, bitter and salt. Trout can taste sweets about 500 times better than people can. They can taste salt about 200 times better. They seem indifferent to things that taste bitter to a human and I don't have any reliable information on how they perceive sour tastes.

> **Did You Know**
> Rainbows are 200 to 500 times better than humans at tasting certain items.

Implications to the Angler

Sometimes a Rainbow's rejection of a certain fly isn't the specific pattern you using. It may be that a foul taste that has gotten onto the fly. If you let something get on your fly that tastes "different" or bad to the Rainbow, it may reject the fly even before it enters the trout's mouth. Before each season begins, I sometimes soak my flies in salt water and then rinse them in hot water to remove the salt that will rust the hooks. The combination of salt and hot water seems to remove any unwanted tastes and any remaining residue seems not to affect the trout.

I would also suggest that you keep anything with a taste away from your fly box, fly gear or your hands. While the trout may like the taste of the chocolate from your candy bar, there is just as much chance (or more) that they will reject it because they don't like the taste or it isn't what they expected from a Chironomid or Caddis.

While the Rainbow's sense of taste and smell are distinctly different, they are still closely related. Therefore, I wanted to keep the sections on both senses in sequence in this book. When we are discussing smell, it should be noted that many of the same principles would also apply to taste. The reason is that both taste and smell are delivered to the Rainbows through the medium of water.

The Rainbows Sense of Smell

With humans, airborne molecules stimulate the olfactory organs. The source of the odor doesn't need to come into direct contact with a person to be perceived. With Rainbows, both smell and taste can be detected from a distance. The distinction between the two senses is somewhat obscure in Rainbows because they use essentially the same chemical cues. It's hard to tell where one sense ends and the other takes over. Between smell and taste, smell seems to be more important and possibly much more sensitive in the trout.

The Nose of a Rainbow

Smells are delivered to a Rainbow through its nostrils or nose. As shown in Figure 2 the two nostril openings are located just in front of the eyes and above the mouth. If you look close, you will find that the Rainbow actually has four nostrils rather than two. Each nostril opening has a small flap that divides the opening into two parts. I'll warn you in advance that these flaps are hard to find on a dead trout. They are much easier to see on a live trout as the nostrils function. Trout, salmon and other fish with this four-nostril system are known to have a very sensitive sense of smell.

Did You Know
A Rainbow actually has four nostril openings rather than two. This type of system is very sensitive to smell.

It is believed that the four-nostril system is so much better than a two-nostril system because it increases the pumping action and therefore the amount of water flowing over the organs that detect smell.

The nostrils on each side of the trout's snout lead to separate olfactory (smell) organs. With the intake of water, the nostril flaps are open in one direction and the water flows through a short channel to the olfactory organ. That organ has more than a half million olfactory or smell cells per square inch of surface area. In addition, the nasal chamber is "wrinkled" or folded to increase the amount of surface area. The water is then returned through a different channel to the nostril opening. When the water is expelled, the nostril flaps are open in the opposite direction from the intake. This allows a circular flow of water that permits more water to be pumped over the smell cells than systems that pump water in and out through the same channels. As more water is pumped through the olfactory chamber, the sense of smell is significantly increased.

Trout constantly pump water through the gills by expanding and closing their gill plates. This movement also expands and contracts the nasal chamber. That helps to increase water circulation over the smell cells. As the trout swims, water pressure over the nostrils increases. This added water circulation into the nasal chambers also improves the trout's ability to detect smells.

The smell cells that line the nasal chamber are designed to detect the presence of chemicals in the water. These sensory cells bind with and then depolarize the odor molecules and that is how smells are sensed. Each chemical combination has its own special signature and

when sent to the trout's brain is translated as a different smell. The concentration of those chemical compounds provides the trout with clues regarding intensity or the distance to the source of the smell (or taste).

In humans, the nasal openings merge into one nasal chamber and that is connected to the throat. That is why our sense of taste and smell are so closely linked. In trout, the two separate nasal chambers are not connected to the throat. That arrangement allows the trout to distinguish the difference between chemical concentrations in one nasal chamber versus the other and thus provides the ability to determine the direction to the source of a smell. Through a systematic search pattern, the trout can locate the source of a certain smell (or taste). Mind you, locating a source via smell will take some time.

How Well Can Rainbows Smell?

As mammals, we often think of the champion 'smeller' as something like the Bloodhound. We have mental pictures of this dog following an escaped criminal through swamps and bogs and doing so entirely by the sense of smell. While the Bloodhound may have that ability, most fish can detect smell far better than this dog. Among fish, Rainbows are counted as one of the better sniffers.

Some eels, catfish, sharks and a few other fish that are very reliant on smells have developed a better sense of smell than Rainbows. However, the Rainbow still has a much better sense of smell than a Bloodhound and many other fish. The sense of smell is so important to the Rainbow that a large portion of its brain is devoted to doing nothing but interpreting smells.

After 4 or 5 years, salmon and trout use their sense of smell to navigate back to their birthplace in a particular stream.

Salmon and trout (as steelhead) use smell to navigate back to their place of birth. The odor of their home river is imprinted on the fish. These fish can then tell which fork of a river or stream to take by the smells carried into the water from the land surrounding their birth site. Tests have shown that about half the fish will take the wrong fork if their ability to smell is removed and they are placed back into the river somewhere downstream of the fork. Fish with their smell left intact all returned to their spawning beds.

Just like humans, Rainbows have different thresholds for detecting different smells. If we squash a shrimp and drop it in the water, the trout can detect the smell to levels of about one part in 100 million.

L-serine is a substance found in the skin of mammals including humans and bears. Trout are very sensitive to this substance. They can detect L-serine to levels of about one part in 100 billion. This is a greater degree of sensitivity than most scientific instruments. For an analogy, this is equivalent to all trout in a lake detecting one drop of L-serine (after dispersion) in a lake if that lake has a surface area of 75 acres, a maximum depth of 25 feet and holding about 2,000,000 gallons of water. It would take about 2.5 fluid ounces of squashed shrimp to provide the same levels of smell detection in this lake.

The Role of Smell

Trout are able to discriminate between the odors of thousands of different chemical compounds. Science doesn't have a good understanding of how this sensory perception works but has examined some of the quirks associated with the process in trout.

➤ When the trout are first exposed to an odor, they are able to detect the odor much better than after they have been exposed to it over time.

➤ Hungry trout are able to detect odors better than a trout that has just finished a meal.

➤ A frightened or injured trout will become alarmed and produce an alarm substance (called Schreckstoff) that other trout can smell. When the other trout smell this odor, they will flee or go into hiding for a while.

➤ Even without being frightened or injured, the trout can smell each other. It is possible that trout can recognize a specific individual by its smell.

➤ The trout can smell the differences between underwater plants. Through these specific plant odors, a trout can navigate around a lake and then return to its home territory.

> Different bugs contain different amino acids that the trout need at certain times of the year. The trout can smell these amino acids and seek out that specific invertebrate.

➤ To a degree, trout can smell invertebrates in the lake. Injured invertebrates expel bodily fluids and are then easier to smell.

➤ Smell plays an important role in mating. Odor is used to indicate sexual readiness and plays a part in sexual arousal.

➤ Because of water density, it takes longer for odor to disperse from its source than in air. However, this factor combined with two separate smell organs help the trout to locate the source of the smell.

➤ Some smells, such as particular amino acids in bugs, attract the trout while other smells repel the trout and some smells the trout just don't seem to react to or notice. Surprisingly, human urine is a smell the trout seem not to notice.

For years, I heard stories about commercial fishermen using bulk oil to coat their lures to increase their fishing success. I related this information to a friend who had access to a lab that tested commercial fish attractants. He offered to have this tested and I asked him to have a few other substances tested at the same time. The results were that the bulk oil has large molecules that tend to mask the smell of other odors with smaller molecules. While the oil didn't attract the fish, it did hide other smells that might repel the fish.

> **Did You Know**
>
> Many anglers are beginning to use certain smells on their flies or lures to entice the fish. These range from home concoctions of squashed bugs to commercial attractants. One favourite that has been in use a long time is Anise Oil that has a licorice flavour.

The other substances tested were suntan oil, insect sprays and nicotine from cigarettes. The fish had a definite dislike for all three of these smells. Insect spray will wreck fly lines and you don't want it on your flies. I would suggest you don't even keep insect sprays or suntan oil near your fly gear.

My fishing buddy wasn't catching fish over several trips even though I did all right. I even gave him some of my flies and we fished side by side. Come to find out, he is sensitive to the sun and had been placing suntan oil on his nose. I suggested that perhaps the suntan oil might be the problem. He then started cleaning his hands 'very' thoroughly before

> If you use suntan oil,
> The fishing you spoil,
> And put away,
> That sticky bug spray.

handling any of his fly gear. His catch improved significantly and now he is always careful with the oil. As for nicotine, I smoke and will just say to rinse your hands before changing flies. Besides, it provides me with a legitimate excuse if someone else has a much better day of fishing.

The Smell of an Angler

As far as the Rainbows are concerned, you and I stink. The trout can easily detect the substance L-serine from our skin and they don't especially seem to like that odor. Just rinsing our hands in a stream will cause the downstream trout to flee, even at a considerable distance. If you don't take precautions, such as rinsing your hands before tying on a fly, you will undoubtedly rub some L-serine onto your fly from your

> **Fishing Tip**
>
> If you tie your own flies, I would suggest that you wash your hands before starting this task. Otherwise, L-serine from your hands will most likely get on the flies and could cause the fish to reject that fly. Also rinse your hands in a lake prior to fishing.

fingers. If this substance gets onto your fly, you will likely find that it takes about a half dozen casts or more before the substance rinses off and you start to catch fish even when the fish are actively feeding. I would even suggest that you wash your hands before tying flies at home.

I can't be sure but I suspect that L-serine will have different odors depending on a person's particular body chemistry. Undoubtedly, you have had days when you catch lots of fish and no one else can or it's reversed and everyone is catching fish but you. My theory is that it might be what you had for dinner the night before or for breakfast that morning. You are

> The trout can smell
> Extremely well
> And they won't bite
> If the smell isn't right.

what you eat and the L-serine odor may change from bad to terrible or from bad to appealing depending on a recent meal. I also use this theory to explain away those people who can catch fish out of a rain barrel. Some people are consistently successful even though they don't know squat about fishing and are doing everything wrong. Maybe I'm just appeasing my ego but I like to think it's because of their particular body chemistry. This might be a good subject for some researcher to undertake.

The Schreckstoff Factor

Schreckstoff is the alarm substance given off by fish when they are injured or otherwise alarmed. Other Rainbows in the vicinity can smell this alarm substance and will flee or hide. On occasion, they will come to investigate. I have watched other Rainbows follow a fish I had on the line. It is possible that the Schreckstoff smell can communicate different degrees of trouble or different types of problems.

If Schreckstoff is given off by each trout that we hook, it can affect how we angle. Other trout may become alarmed by the presence of Schreckstoff in the water and flee. A lot of their reactions will depend on how much Schreckstoff is given off by the hooked fish, how interested the other trout are in feeding and how much risk they are willing to accept to continue feeding.

Fishing Tip

Rainbows give of an alarm substance, called Schreckstoff, which other trout can smell. If fishing declines, try moving a casting distance or two away from your starting point. This should remove your casts from the area that has an accumulation of the Schreckstoff factor.

When the trout are interested in feeding, it doesn't seem to matter if you hook several fish in one location. They will continue to feed in that spot. But when they are selective, they often stop taking a fly after several fish are hooked. I suspect the amount of Schreckstoff given off by hooked fish finally reaches a critical point that warns other trout to stay away for a while. I call this the Schreckstoff factor.

By lifting anchor and moving one or two casting distances further along the shoal, I can usually get back into good fishing for a while. If the fish are cautiously feeding, it may only take one or two hooked fish to warn the other fish to avoid this location. If you have hooked a couple of fish and then get nothing, move down the shoal a short distance and then try the same fly and presentation. After several moves, you can return to the original location and probably get a couple more fish.

Invertebrate Smells

Each species of aquatic invertebrate has its own particular set of amino acids and thus its own smell. I'm reasonably certain that a Rainbow can tell one species of Chironomid, for example, from others by the specific odor it gives off.

With smell and taste closely linked, I even suspect that trout develop a preference for one species of bug over another based on its amino acid signature. The trout demand certain amino acids at specific times and of the year. Their body will demand a certain type of amino acid and they will find a particular species of bug that satisfies this need. Sort of like when we get a craving for a certain type of food.

> **Did You Know**
>
> Each and every bug in a lake has its own amino acid "signature" at a given time of year. The trout will key on those bugs that provide the amino acids necessary for that particular time. This isn't conscious thought by the Rainbows but more of a "craving" for certain food types.

Most invertebrates in the lakes have hard chitinous outer shells. With its shell intact, I doubt that the odoriferous signals given off by those bugs are very strong. However, there are probably times when the smells of these invertebrates are stronger and easier for the trout to locate. The most obvious time is when an invertebrate is injured and its bodily fluids enter the water. The second occurrence is when it expels bodily fluids through defecation or urination. The less obvious time for detection, but probably the most important, is when the bugs are pupating.

During pupation, the bugs' body goes through major chemical changes. Compounds of chemicals are released into the water that the trout can detect. Many insects, such as Caddis and Chironomid, also pupate within a closed shell or casing. When the pupal case opens, the chemical compounds are released into the water and it doesn't take long before every Rainbow in the neighborhood knows that a hatch is occurring.

Other invertebrates, such as the Waterboatman, have intentionally developed smells that the trout find offensive. These bad smells seem to protect those particular bugs. In the case of the Waterboatman, their bad odor protects them throughout the summer months but it doesn't prevent Rainbows from feeding on them during the spring or fall mating season. Most likely, the bad smell and taste of the bug during the summer has changed chemical signature as the bug matures into an adult. As the bad smell diminishes, the bug becomes a favorite food source.

> **Fishing Tip**
>
> A fly fisher needs to key on flies that imitate a specific bug when those bugs are hatching, pupating, molting, or mating. At those times their smells are most noticeable.

Another time when invertebrates exude more odors is when they shed their hard chitinous shells and replace them with a larger version. When a shrimp or dragonfly, for example, molts its old shell for a new shell, the body is exposed and gives off the chemicals of smell. If you see discarded invertebrate shells floating on the surface of the lake, the owners of those shells might be the prime bugs to imitate with a fly.

97

There is a good chance that those particular bugs can be smelled by the trout and are the target of a Rainbow feed.

Commercial Attractants

I have to admit that I haven't really tried any of the commercial attractants that are designed to bring fish to your fly through smell. I keep promising myself to give these a try but so far haven't taken the plunge. It is reasonable that the right odor placed on a fly at the right time of year will entice a Rainbow. I'm not yet convinced that one odor will work at all times. As the trout go through the season, their requirements for

> As an alternative to using commercial attractants, try putting a fly in your mouth prior to a cast. I have found several sources that claim Rainbows are attracted to human saliva.

amino acids and other chemical compounds will change. The trout will probably seek smells that match seasonal nutritional requirements.

There is a word of caution about using chemical attractants on your fly. Check your local fishing regulations prior to using these substances. A number of lakes I fish have a "bait ban" imposed through the regulations. On closer investigation, I find that our regulations define bait as follows; "Any substance which attracts fish by scent and/or flavor". Bait includes artificial lures and flies to which scent or flavoring has been added as well as roe, worms and all other edible substances". On local lakes that have bait bans, I would be breaking the law by using a commercial attractant.

The Rainbows Sense of Rhythm

Natural cycles or rhythms have been known since the caveman days. Major weather patterns are cyclic, many animal populations are cyclic, and even sunspot activity is cyclic. A lot of scientific effort has gone into studying cycles but our understanding is still somewhat rudimentary.

Most creatures possess a sense of rhythm. We are not talking about their musical abilities but rather the ability to detect the passage of time. Humans have come to rely on clocks and calendars to tell us when upcoming events will be happening. In nature, the animals also need to foretell upcoming events such as the onset of winter. However, wild creatures must rely on environmental signals to their biological processes to prepare for these upcoming events.

Having "biological clocks" is the term most often applied to critters keeping track of time through natural cues. These processes are genetically controlled in everything from bacteria, to plants, to aquatic invertebrates, to trout, to humans. All have a form of biological time keeping. An example for humans would be the menstrual cycle in women.

Biological clocks seem to serve two different purposes. The first is simply to mark the passage of time. The clock ticks away until enough time has lapsed that genetic materials are activated that cause a certain reaction. Salmon return to home rivers for spawning every four years for example. They only do this once in their life. But their biological clocks have ticked off enough time that genetic material is activated, the body becomes sexually mature and all the salmon of the same age return to their home river at the same time. This is a genetic controlled event. The cycle repeats for the species but not for the individual salmon.

The second purpose of the biological clock is to denote cyclic events. Cycles can be species specific, such as returning salmon, or cyclic within an individual's lifetime. Cycles within a lifetime would include things such as a bear preparing for hibernation, Caribou migrations, sea turtles returning to breed and so forth. As anglers we are going to be mostly concerned with cycles occurring within the lifetime of an individual Rainbow.

> Most things in life occur in cycles. If you know the cycles you will be successful.

How Biological Clocks Work

We know that living organisms have biological clocks and we can see the results of these timepieces in action. However, our understanding of how critters track time and determine cycles is very basic. It seems that there are three primary driving forces that run the biological clock. These are:

> ➤ **The Passage of Seasons**; the seasonal cycles of summer and winter are tracked by the biological clock. Spring equinox along with day length, sun angle, temperature changes and so forth seem to be detected by the biological clock.
> ➤ **The Passage of the Moon**; the moon is a well documented source for triggering the biological clock. Exactly how isn't well documented. The light from full moons and the gravitational or tidal effect are the most likely causes.
> ➤ **The Passage of the Sun**; the alternating day to night cycle every 24 hours seems to be a major force driving biological clocks. These day–night cycles are called circadian rhythms and are the most studied of the three influences. We do have a basic understanding of how these work in animals.

For the circadian rhythms, specialized cells in the hypothalamus portion of the brain detect the day-night cycles. In addition, proteins called cryptochromes are located throughout the body and are used to detect these light cycles. So far nine genes governing the periodicity of circadian rhythms have been found and more are expected. In response to the day-night cycle, these genes are stimulated into the release of four regulatory proteins into the animals system. These proteins control such things as heart rate, body temperature, fluid balance, rest and activity periods, oxygen consumption, enzyme production, endocrine secretions, and hormone production. Those in turn affect the behaviour of the animal.

Circadian time keeping is simply a matter of turning "on" or turning "off" the appropriate genes in response to light. In response to detecting light, two regulatory proteins start being released. These proteins turn "on" the genes influencing bodily functions. As these proteins are released they combine to produce another two regulatory proteins. Over time, these accumulate until they reach a point where they turn "off" the influencing genes. When that happens, the whole process starts over again and we have a daily cycle. In turn, each daily cycle seems to trigger a similar response on a grander scale. The effects seem to be cumulative and stored into the trout's memory banks.

If you are interested or considering doing more research on the topic, it is worth noting the Pineal Gland probably plays an important role in this process. This gland is located in the upper portion of the trout's brain and is very sensitive to changing light levels or light angles. It controls the retracting or protruding of the rod cells in the trout's eye through the release of melatonin. In turn, melatonin controls other bodily functions such as the oxygen content in the blood.

The lunar and seasonal rhythms are thought to work in much the same way as circadian rhythms. Seasonal rhythms, for example, help trigger the release of hormones that start the spawning cycle. Numerous studies have also demonstrated that moon position has affects on the bodily functions and behaviour patterns of trout. These patterns have even been demonstrated under laboratory conditions without the moon being visible.

Before we move on, there is a last note about Rainbow Trout and the Biological Clock. The clock keeps track of time very well and triggers certain cyclic events in the trout. However, some of the cyclic activity in a lake must be learned by the trout. The cyclic occurrence of insect

> Certain cyclic events in a lake (such as hatches) are not instinctive and must be learned by the trout after a couple of repeated occurrences.

hatches, for example, is not an instinctive part of the trout's genetic makeup. But it seems that the Biological Clock will store into the trout's memory banks the environmental conditions around a point in time. If the trout experiences a good hatch, for instance, the information on the sun, moon, temperature and other pertinent data are noted. When those conditions are repeated the trout's memory banks are jarred. After one or two such cyclic events, the trout will learn to anticipate another when similar conditions are repeated.

Lunar Cycles

The effect of the moon on aquatic critters has fascinated me for many years. The moon is one of the more important factors affecting natural cycles but the underlying causes are not well understood. In our oceans, the tidal forces of the moon have long been known to affect fishing. In pristine lakes, there is little documented information. But over the years, I have gathered data and made some of my own interpretations.

We will keep our study of the moon and its influence on fishing to the short side. However, a few basics need to be presented. Let's start by looking at the moon in relation to the sun and earth.

Paul Kollerer

➤ The moon is one of the three most important factors affecting natural cycles and probably the least understood. The moon takes 27.3 days to complete one orbit around the earth (relative to the sun). However, it takes 29.5 days between moon "phases", such as Full moon, because phase is determined by lighting from the sun rather than orbital time. See Figure 21.

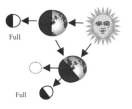

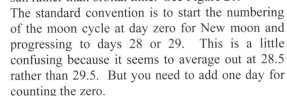

Figure 21 – Moon Orbit Versus Phase

➤ The standard convention is to start the numbering of the moon cycle at day zero for New moon and progressing to days 28 or 29. This is a little confusing because it seems to average out at 28.5 rather than 29.5. But you need to add one day for counting the zero.

➤ Moon phases are most important to the angler because of the combined gravitation effects of moon and sun alignment. These effects are strongest during the Full and New moon phases. Indeed Earth's ocean tides rise and fall to the greatest extend during Full and New moon. The gravitational effects are weakest during First and Third Quarter phases because these lack alignment with the sun. See Figure 22 and imagine viewing the moon from the earth.

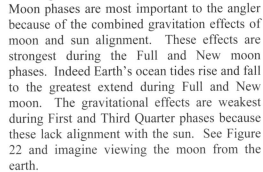

Figure 22 - Moon Phases

➤ While the moon slowly completes an orbit, the Earth is rotating every 24 hours. At some time each day the moon will be directly overhead. This is the "Moon's Southing" and when the moon's gravitation pull is strongest. In Earth's oceans the water actually bulges toward the moon creating high tides. As the earth rotates, this bulge remains facing the moon. A similar high tide bulge also happens on the side of Earth facing away from the moon. Low tides would be at 90 degrees from the high tides on each side of the Earth.

➤ The gravitational pull of the moon causes the ocean tides to rise and fall by 9 to 12 feet twice each day and the mean elevation of continental land masses to rise and fall by 9 to 12 inches each day. Anglers who fish the oceans know that fishing is best as the tides are changing.

Figure 23 – Tidal Bulge or High Tides at Arrows

➤ Hunting and Fishing Tables that provide the best times to go are usually providing the Moons Southing or else the time of a high tide if it were to occur inland. I have tried over the years but am unable to find any statistical correlation between these "Best Fishing Times" and the numbers of fish actually caught at those times of the day.

➤ There is, however, good correlation between the phase of the moon and fishing success. Figure 24 shows the average success rate for each day of the moon. Note that the best fishing occurs around the First Quarter phase of the moon while the worst fishing occurs around the Third Quarter.

101

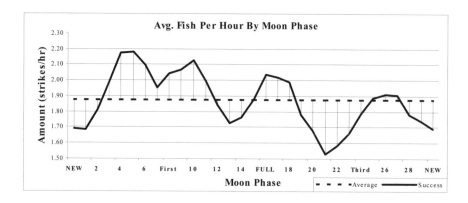

Figure 24 – Average Fishing Success by Day of the Moon

> Annual insect hatches seem to vary by $\pm$ two weeks each year even though environmental conditions appear to be the same. Likely, this is because the insects are adjusting their hatch to coincide with a particular moon phase which can vary by a couple of weeks from one year to the next.

> An important discovery I made is that each type of aquatic invertebrate is more active during certain moon phases and thus becomes a primary food of the Rainbow Trout during that specific period of the moon. The trout, for example, feed on Chironomids most frequently from the New to First Quarter moon while they feed on freshwater shrimp around the Full moon. I will be providing that information with each bug as we discuss the food of the Rainbows.

> Contrary to popular opinion, fishing for Rainbows in the evening or after dark is not especially good during the Full moon. The Full moon produces much better daytime fishing while the First Quarter (see Fig 24) produces the best consistently good fishing either day or evening.

> Moon in first quarter
> Good fishing's in order.
> Third quarter moon
> Good fishing will ruin.

> While I haven't yet confirmed the numbers, it appears that fishing success is above average when the moon is low on the horizon. That is, just before or just after the moon rises or sets for the day (see Appendix 8).

> The proportion of larger fish is highest just after the New moon. The proportion of smaller fish is highest during and around the Full moon.

Rhythmic Cycles and the Angler

The Rainbow Trout's sense of timing and cyclic rhythms is mostly centered on the cycles of the aquatic invertebrates upon which they feed. These invertebrates also have biological clocks that are tuned into the season, moon and daily light levels. In

102

turn, their cycles are governed by the things upon which they feed. The whole process is intertwined and very complex.

Many of these cyclic events in a lake are poorly understood and some we haven't yet discovered. If we fully understood the biological clock and its effects, we could probably predict the best day and hour to go fishing. As it is, we must keep our discussion to those we know. Following are a few tips that may help the angler.

➤ Trout are individuals and the biological clocks in some individuals will work better than for other individuals.

➤ Be aware of the seasonal cycles. Ice-off can be a short lived time of Rainbow activity prior to turn-over. Turn-over can be a poor time to fish. After turn-over, the fishing steadily improves as bugs become available. By mid July, most insects have hatched and the trout's food pantry is diminished. Warmer water also means the trout will be in deep water that is cooler. By fall, new broods of insects are available but remember that most of these will be small.

> Things that are just becoming available are in more demand than those that have been around for a while.

➤ Aquatic invertebrates are governed by their biological clocks. Mating, hatches, migrations and other invertebrate activities become cyclic. If the fly fisher knows when to expect these hatches and cycles it will undoubtedly improve their success.

➤ Insects that hatch follow a rhythm. They go from egg to small larva or nymph and grow until they become a large nymph or pupa just prior to hatching. After the hatch the insects mate and lay eggs and the cycle restarts. The eggs and very small bugs have limited value as trout food. It isn't until they grow, near maturity, or hatch that these insects are a primary food source. Anglers should concentrate on fishing imitations of these insects just prior to and during their hatch.

> Make your flies
> Match bug size,
> And in the fall
> The bugs are small.

➤ Insects that live a year or more will hibernate in deep water. This means they will migrate to and from the deep water in the spring and in the fall.

➤ The trout can tell time and seasonal variance well enough to know when a cyclic hatch is due. Rainbows will often gather over a shoal at the beginning or even in advance of a particularly important hatch.

➤ Rainbows are more active and thus feed more frequently at sunrise and sunset. Rainbows feeding on aquatic invertebrates are more likely to be active at sunset while those feeding on prey fish are more likely to be active at sunrise.

➤ The cyclic timing of sunrise and sunset changes as we move north and as the season progresses. The longest days, longest twilight and shortest nights will occur in late June (see Appendix 10).

➤ Trout and many bugs are more active when oxygen levels are best. Oxygen content is cyclic. Oxygen content reaches a daily peak in the evening and a seasonal peak in the fall.

103

➢ Because of their various rhythms, different types of bugs are more active at different times of the day. Damselflies, for example, are primarily daytime active while Dragonflies are primarily evening or night active.

➢ In Table 6 we discussed feeding intervals of Rainbows. This is a cyclic activity and undoubtedly links with the next major hatch or other food availability period. And that will frequently link to a moon position.

> When the ice first breaks
> The Dragonfly wakes
> And migrations start
> Especially at dark.

➢ The amount of sunlight entering the lake and affecting the trout's eyes is highest in mid summer. The trout are more likely to be feeding in the shallows during the spring and fall when the sun angle is lower.

Do Rainbows Have Other Senses?

We have discussed the Rainbows sense of vision, hearing, balance, distant touch, touch, taste, smell and their sense of timing and rhythm. Do trout have any other sensory capabilities?

There is still a lot about the entire animal kingdom that we don't understand. Every year some new marvel is added to our knowledge base. In years past, a lot of this new knowledge would have been considered as fantasy, science fiction or simply impossible. I'm confident that in the years to come there will be additional discoveries about the trout's senses.

In addition, there are three sensory possibilities that we have not discussed. There is reason to believe that Rainbows can detect electricity in the water, gravitational forces generated by the earth, and sonic vibrations. To my knowledge, the Rainbows ability to perceive these forces has not been confirmed, denied or otherwise categorized. To round out our discussions on the sensory abilities of the Rainbow we should at least have a quick look at these but I caution the angler to remember that these sensory perceptions have not been verified.

Electroreception

Electroreception is the ability to detect electric currents. We know that water is an excellent conductor of electricity. Even a small electric current, such as that generated by the movement of animal muscle, will travel a great distance in water. Sharks are one of the animals known to possess electroreception. The small electric signal generated by muscle movement is one of the ways that sharks detect their prey. It is estimated that a shark can electrically detect a human sized prey from distances over 300 miles if there is a lack of interference from other sources.

All Elasmobranches (cartilaginous skeletons including sharks) and a variety of Teleosts (bony fish of which trout are a member) have the ability to detect electric signals. However, I have yet to see confirmation that Rainbows and most of our freshwater sport fish are included on the list of fish with electroreception. The list does include all sharks, rays, eels, paddlefish, sturgeon, and so on. As a note of interest, even the platypus is known to detect electric signals in water.

The organs responsible for electroreception are known as the "ampullae of Lorenzini". The platypus has these in its bill. In fish, these are usually associated with the lateral line system. These organs are essentially the same as the neuromasts of the lateral line and ear of the trout. The ampullae of Lorenzini are receptor cells in contact with a gel conductive to electricity that detects low frequency AC or DC currents generated by prey. Reception of electric signals is not to be confused with the ability to generate electric fields such the electric eel does. That ability is done with tuberous cells that generate high frequency DC current.

When we looked at the lateral line system of Rainbows, we found that the neuromast is the basic sensory organ for detecting vibrations in water. Each neuromast is covered with a gelatinous cap called the Cupula (see Figure 19). If the Cupula is electrically conductive, and I strongly suspect it is, then there is a high probability that Rainbows have electroreception abilities. If Rainbows are able to detect electric current, then a whole new dimension of perception is added to the sensitivity of the trout's lateral line system.

If we assume that Rainbows have electroreception, we will have to look at other fish species to assess the potential implications to our fishing. Fish that have electroreception are able to detect electric fields as low as one microvolt from a distance of one kilometer. This is roughly equivalent to detecting the energy from one D-Cell battery from a distance of 950 miles. Fish with electroreception can detect the electric pulses released from the heart muscle, respiratory functions and swimming motions of other fish or the movements of small aquatic invertebrates. The retrieval of metal lures generates sufficient electric fields for detection by fish with electroreception abilities. In the ocean, tides generate electric fields that can be detected. Electroreception is a very sensitive form of perception. And as we will see in the next section, the ability to detect electricity will even allow fish to detect the earth's magnetic field.

Magnetic Field Detection

As the earth spins on its axis, it generates a geomagnetic field. When a compass points north, it is using this field. A magnetic field is essentially an electric field. Strong magnets can be used to generate electric currents for example. Fish with electroreception abilities are also sensitive to magnetic fields for those reasons.

I recently watched a Nature show on television that was attempting to explain how stingrays (with electroreception abilities) used the earths magnetic field to migrate vast distances across the ocean to their spawning grounds. A lot was conjecture but it is reasonably certain that geomagnetism and electroreception are the forces that allow this type of navigation. Fish and other critters that migrate or navigate to specific locations across the oceans probably need this type of perception to achieve the pinpoint accuracy needed. It seems unlikely that sun angles, smell detection, or other similar theories of navigation would allow the level of precision necessary to arrive at a specific location. Salmon and Rainbows (as Steelhead) navigate the oceans, then return to their home river and then to the original gravel bed where they hatched. To me, that is another reason to believe that these fish possess electroreception.

Fish that possess electroreception can detect disturbances in the geomagnetic field. If invertebrates or other fish swim through the magnetic field, it creates a magnetic disturbance that can be perceived. I'm not sure how well the disturbance can be detected (size, shape, distance?) but the fish will be aware of another creature's presence. If Rainbows possess electroreception abilities, using geomagnetism is another probable way for these fish to locate food.

Detection of Ultrasonics

In previous discussions, we have seen that the lateral line system of a Rainbow can pick up low frequency vibrations (below 100 Hz) and the trout's ear can detect sound vibrations in the range of 30 to 3000 Hz. Can the trout detect vibrations at frequencies above its range of hearing? These high frequency vibrations above the range of hearing are usually referred to as ultrasonic vibrations.

In humans, the range of hearing goes up to about 20,000 Hz. Ultrasonic vibrations would be above that level. The Rainbow can't hear into those high frequencies. To them ultrasonics would include anything over about 3,000 Hz. It has just been assumed that trout can't detect vibrations over that level. However, commercial fishermen have observed ocean fish fleeing when high frequency echo sounders were turned on to locate the schools of fish. Subsequent investigations showed shad, herring and sardines definitely responded to ultrasonics between 25,000 and 130,000 Hz. It is quite conceivable that Rainbows are also able to detect ultrasonic vibrations.

Dolphins generate ultrasonic vibrations up to 150,000 Hz to locate prey through echolocation and they sometimes emit powerful bursts to stun their prey. It is reasonably certain that Rainbows can't generate ultrasonic vibrations or use echolocation. However, that doesn't mean that they are unable to perceive these high frequencies. In our previous discussions, we found that Rainbows had otoliths or earstones within their ears to detect vibrations. They also use the skeletal bones and their air bladders to detect vibrations. It is very probable that one or more of these organs will vibrate to ultrasonics and the trout will detect those vibrations even if it isn't in the form of sound and hearing.

The main application of this information is for those anglers who use fish finders. It is possible fish will panic and flee because of high frequency vibrations being emitted by the fish finder. By the same token, I suspect that the trout would soon learn that those strange vibrations do not pose a threat and subsequently ignore the sensations.

5

Rainbow Behavior

What motivates a Rainbow Trout to actively feed one day at a certain location and not feed the next day or feed at an entirely different location? Would you say that your fishing success could be greatly improved if you knew the answer to that question? I don't have all the answers but we do know what motivates the Bows behavior on many occasions. Being able to predict the cyclic rhythm of these patterns is the tricky part.

In part, we want to look at the psychology of a Rainbow Trout. More specifically, since the trout have little conscious thought, we are looking at the psychobiology of the Bows. Given a certain set of conditions, trout will normally be motivated into a typical set of actions or reactions. However, an individual trout may exhibit behavior that is different than a normal behavior pattern. At this point it is probably best to provide a reference to the terms being used.

➢ **Behavior:** Ones actions or mode of conduct and usually as it relates to some standard of normal.
➢ **Behavior Pattern:** Consistent and typical actions or reactions by an individual or group to a given set of circumstances.
➢ **Motivation** (or motive): A causal agent, stimulant or inducement that gives rise to certain behavior or behavior patterns.

In this chapter we want to examine typical behavior patterns of Rainbow Trout under motivational factors that the angler can detect or estimate. Some of the motives such as the visual trigger and the Schreckstoff factor have already been discussed in Chapter 4. Now let's examine why the trout behave as they do.

The Rainbow Motivational Hierarchy

A fellow named Abraham Maslow developed a theory to explain how unsatisfied needs motivate human behavior. The basic premise in *"Maslow's Hierarchy of Needs"* is that the lower or primary needs must be satisfied before an individual is motivated into satisfying the higher or secondary needs. For example, personal survival and safety needs must be satisfied before a person can be motivated into becoming a contributing member of society or an artist or even a fly fisher. Naturally there are numerous interactions between the levels of need and what motivates people. However, the theory is well accepted and provides a working model of motivation and behavior.

Maslow's hierarchy was developed to explain complex human behavior and we can't directly use it to explain the relatively simple needs of fish. Trout, for example, rely heavily on instinct and Maslow doesn't include that in his hierarchy. He also includes self-esteem and actualization, which are unlikely attributes in the trout's world. However, we can modify Maslow's hierarchy to suit the world of Rainbows and to explain some of their behavior. Figure 25 shows a schematic tailored to suit fish behavior based on their simplified motivational needs.

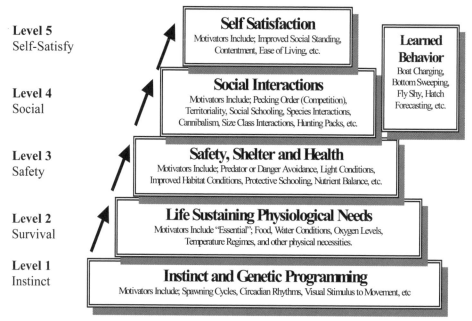

Figure 25 – The Rainbow Hierarchy of Needs That Stimulate Behavior.

In this schematic the bottom line or Level 1 needs are the most basic. These needs must be satisfied before trout are motivated to satisfy the needs in Level 2. Then Level 2 needs must essentially be satisfied before Level 3 and so forth up the pyramid.

From this hierarchy we can see that the basis of Rainbow behavior is instinct and genetic programming. At this level the trout have virtually no control over their behavior patterns. If their genes say it is time for the spawning cycle, for example, then they enter the spawning cycle even if it means certain death. The basic progression of trout behavior goes from instinct to survival and then through safety, social interactions and self-satisfaction.

Within this hierarchy there are 'offsetting factors' and 'degrees of motivation'. Within Level 2, for example, the need to feed may be offset by high water temperatures or low oxygen levels that reduce or cease trout feeding. If the trout are stressed by these adverse environmental conditions then they are unlikely to feed even when starving. Additionally, the degree of motivation will play a role in the behavior of the trout. As a rule-of-thumb the most immediate and pressing need seems to be the motivator that determines the current behavior pattern.

Let's take a moment to look at the 'degree of motivation'. The degree of hunger, for instance, affects trout behavior. Table 11 provides a good example of how hunger motivates the trout and their subsequent behavior. In this example, motivation moves up a level in the hierarchy with each decrease in the hunger level. If we ignore offsetting factors, Table 11 actually provides a good guideline to the typical behavior patterns of Rainbows in our pristine trout lakes.

Table 11 – Typical Rainbow Behavior Resulting from Different Hunger Levels

Circumstance	No Food 1 Month	No Food 1 Week	No Food 1 Day	Just Fed
Motivator	Starvation	Hunger	Appetite	No Appetite
Behavior Level	Survival Level 2	Health & Safety Level 3	Social Level 4	Self Satisfy Level 5
Feeding Behavior	Aggressively feeds on most anything at anytime	Cautiously feeds on most available foods	Opportunistic feed on preferred foods	Seldom feeds but may attack
Feeding Time	Anytime and ignores bright sunlight	Mostly when preferred foods are available	When light levels are low & preferred foods available.	Only feeds if choice foods are available
Danger Response	Ignores Danger	Aware of Danger	Very Cautious	Spooks Easily
Response to Brightness	Level of sunlight not a concern	May chance bright light to get food	Most activity in dim to low light.	Most activity in low light conditions
General Location in Clear Water	Shallow feeding shoals or anywhere food is available	Primarily over shoal and secondly at drop-off	Primarily at drop-off & secondly over shoal or deep water	Usually in deeper water near the thermocline
Territorial Behavior	Ignores territorial boundaries	May cross territorial boundary	Stays within and protects territory	May travel and seek new turf
Protective Shelter	Shelter not usually a concern	May venture away from shelter	Stays in or very near sheltered areas	Stays in water offering protection
Environmental Conditions	Ignores most adverse conditions	Will avoid adverse conditions	Sensitive to minor adverse conditions	Feeds only under best conditions

The typical eutrophic lake generally has an abundance of food and good environmental conditions for most of the year. In those conditions trout will generally behave as described in the last two columns (Levels 4 or 5) of Table 11. Therefore, we fly fishers are usually dealing with contented and cautious Rainbows and even minor changes in environmental conditions can bring on or stop feeding. In a large, deep oligotrophic lake the conditions are generally less favourable. That type of habitat isn't usually as good and the trout may be operating at Level 3 of the hierarchy. They will be less cautious, more aggressive, and may take on social deviations such as cannibalism.

Since we have already modified *"Maslow's Hierarchy of Needs"* to suit Rainbows, we also took the liberty of adding an extra box that Maslow didn't include. The box entitled 'Learned Behavior' is also useful in assessing the behavior of Rainbows. A trout in a stream environment, for example, will behave differently than a trout in a lake environment even at the same motivational level. Conditions are different and trout "learn" to cope with the particular environment in which they live. Trout can learn and adapt. The ability to deal with different habitats is not something that is genetically programmed in the fish. Trout also learn other behavior patterns that affect how we stalk our prey.

Have you ever noticed that advice to the angler always includes something to the effect that you should observe the lake conditions, insect hatches, other anglers and what is generally happening on the lake? Does anyone ever ask why or how that helps?

> As its stomach fills, a Rainbow becomes exponentially more cautious about what it eats.

Although rarely stated, the purpose is to determine the conditions likely to be motivating the trout. We then assess their probable behavioural response and then tailor the presentation of our fly to take advantage of that expected behavior. At least now you know why the reason is seldom explained.

With this basic background in motivation and behavior (cause and effect) we want to take the remainder of this chapter to look at more specific behavior patterns and what they mean for the angler. Since food and hunger are so important to the angler we will concentrate on these at each level of the hierarchy. Other motivators of importance to the angler will also be looked at within their specific tier of the hierarchy.

Level 1 - Instinct and Genetic Programming

This title is perhaps a little misleading. Instinct is a genetically programmed behavior. Instinct is an individual's inborn response or natural inclination because of its genetic makeup. If another individual doesn't have the same gene then it won't necessarily react in the same manner. An individual has very little control over this genetic programming.

Instinct develops through natural selection over thousands of generations. If, for example, an individual has a gene that triggers it to quickly react to motion (the visual trigger) then it is likely to obtain more feed, avoid more predators and generally survive better than an

> A trout lacks the ability for logical thought. Virtually all actions are instinctive reactions to current conditions and motivators.

individual without this gene. This same gene is then passed along to its offspring. They also survive in greater numbers than others without the gene. Eventually the entire population has this gene and it is instinctive to quickly react to motion.

It can be argued that the general behavior of Bows is instinctive. In general that's probably a fair statement. The small brain of Bows does not allow for much creative thought and most of their actions are instinctive. However, these instinctive reactions follow the behavior hierarchy. It is instinctive for Bows to be picky about food when they are well fed for example. Trout don't simply "decide" to be more cautious about feeding when the tummy is full. The important thing for the angler to remember is that we are examining "cause and effect". The full tummy is a motivator that causes cautious feeding behavior.

Instinct and genetic programming is the most basic level of motivation affecting the trout's behavior. These carry on regardless of anything else in the trout's environment. Most don't affect the trout's feeding or our angling but I would like to take a quick look at three of the most basic instincts.

The Spawning Instinct

The Rainbows biological clock keeps ticking until the cyclic triggers begin to release hormones and cause chemical changes indicating the trout has sexually matured. Individuals are genetically programmed to go into the spawning cycle at about the same time of year to increase their likelihood of finding a mate. When the spawning instinct kicks in, it is the primary motivator of the trout. Little else matters. In pristine lakes, spawning isn't likely to be successful but trout will gather in areas that 'best' satisfy their spawning drive. Anglers can find spawning trout gathered in these semi-suitable locations from spring through early summer.

Spawners may occasionally feed but are much more interested in their spawning rituals and chasing away intruders. An intruder may be a non-spawning fish or an insect or a fly that passes through the selected spawning grounds. Because of the instinct to chase away an intruding fly by nipping at it, spawners are not difficult to catch once you find their spawning location.

As previously stated, spawners are not good to eat. They are in a weakened state and may die, even with proper catch and release tactics. If you are fishing a specific spot and start to catch a batch of spawners then consider moving. Also note that sometimes non-spawning trout are interested in joining the spawning group but are chased out. These fish are often large and hang around the outskirts of the spawning area.

The Biological Clock as a Motivator

Biological clocks are genetically programmed into Rainbows from the time of their conception. They cannot control or ignore the workings of the rhythmic cycles the clock relays to the Bows body. We discussed these workings in Chapter 4 and mentioned that biological clocks are poorly understood. We know that trout anticipate and await certain events such as specific insect hatches. However we don't know how much of this behavior is via the biological clock, how much is learned or what combinations of genetics and learning motivate the trout.

111

We know that biological clocks are sensitive to circadian rhythms (day and night), lunar cycles, seasons, and so on. Insects use their biological clocks combined with environmental conditions to time and co-ordinate their mass hatches. When the season is right, with the proper lunar cycle and sun angle the insects will hatch as a group. Even then, certain insects may briefly postpone a hatch because of foul weather or incorrect water temperatures. We aren't sure how the insects know the weather is bad. It

> **Did You Know**
> Some insects can briefly postpone hatching if conditions above the lake surface are not to their liking.

may be a low barometric pressure or perhaps they can hear raindrops hitting the lake surface. Either way, the whole group is genetically programmed to await the right conditions and then hatch en-masse with their brood mates.

The biological clock of a Rainbow gets this same cyclic data as the invertebrates. The question is, does the trout's clock genetically "know" when the hatch will occur or does it learn this from experiencing previous hatches? The trout that gather on a shoal prior to a hatch may have learned the factors leading up to the hatch.

Regardless of how it happens, we know that Rainbows can anticipate certain cyclic events of aquatic invertebrates. It isn't likely that the trout are aware of WHY they have gathered over a shoal awaiting a specific hatch. It is just a behavior pattern they follow because of their genetic programming. Their biological clocks also trigger other behavior patterns in Rainbows.

> Full light of moon,
> Then fish at noon.
> Moon with small light,
> Then fish at night.

- ➢ In the late fall the trout are motivated into active feeding prior to the arrival of winter and the covering of ice on the lake. I doubt they are aware of winter's approach so much as feeling an urgency to feed.
- ➢ Trout seem able to anticipate a relative food shortage from mid July through August and thus eat enough during June to carry them through this shortage.
- ➢ Due to the Circadian Rhythms of the biological clock, trout are typically more active at sunrise and sunset. When trout are active they tend to feed.
- ➢ Trout have different behavior patterns depending upon the moons location. Around the Full moon the trout are most active during the day rather than the evening. Around the Third Quarter moon the trout tend to be fairly lethargic and not feed. During the First Quarter moon, the trout are most active and evening fishing tends to be especially good.

The Visual Trigger

As discussed in Chapter 4, the "visual trigger" is a behavior genetically programmed into Rainbow Trout. The trout receive the equivalent of an adrenaline rush from movement or contrast in their environment. This is not something the trout can control. It is a basic instinct in the fish.

This is something we fly fishers can use to our advantage. When trout aren't actively feeding we can use flies with lots of contrast and/or vary our retrieve to stimulate the visual trigger. It's sort of like pulling a string with a playful cat. When done right the cat or the fish just can't resist the urge to pounce. Like every other technique, it doesn't always work and I tend to save it for those times when the fishing is otherwise slow. This tends to be when the trout are near the top of the motivational hierarchy. That's a good time to appeal to one of their most basic instincts.

> You should know,
> If fishing is slow,
> An attractor fly,
> Is worth a try.

Level 2 - Survival Behavior

Obtaining the essential life sustaining needs is one of the most basic motivations in the animal kingdom. Survival is an instinct. However, the behavioural responses will vary depending on what limiting factor is jeopardizing the trout's survival. A trout suffering oxygen deprivation will not exhibit the same behavior as a trout that is starving for example.

In the previous level of the motivational hierarchy the trout could not control the onset of the spawning cycle or stop the biological clock or prevent the adrenaline rush of a visual trigger. At this level of the

Did You Know
Survival is instinctive but trout react differently depending on what danger is threatening their life.

hierarchy the trout has some very strong motivators but it also has options on how it will behave to resolve its survival needs.

Survival Feeding Behavior

A starving trout usually lacks caution and is very aggressive. Protective shelter and most dangerous conditions are ignored as the trout cruises in search of food. It will even venture into shallow, clear water in the brightest of sunlight while seeking food. It will eat most anything that appears edible. Biting and stinging aquatic invertebrates that are not usually on the menu become fair game. Cannibalism is likely to occur if given the opportunity. Social niceties such as territories and pecking orders become meaningless. Oxygen deficiencies and excessively warm temperatures (discussed below) are about the only two things that stop a starving trout from feeding.

Fishing Tip
If you want to catch a lot of fish, even if they are small, then try a lake that has more fish than the food chain can comfortably support.

If an angler can find very hungry Rainbows they aren't usually difficult to catch. In a large body of water, finding the fish can sometimes be more complicated than catching the fish. If food isn't concentrated on one part of the lake, the trout will usually scatter to optimize their chance of finding food. That makes finding the fish difficult. When the fish are concentrated, you can expect to catch a fish with almost every cast. This sometimes happens in lakes with too many fish for the food supply.

113

Sometimes even productive eutrophic lakes will experience periods in which food is not readily available. This often happens in the late summer to early fall when many of the aquatic invertebrates have emerged and the new brood of eggs haven't hatched. As fall progresses the very hungry trout will come into very shallow water in search of essential food. Watch for the signs and take advantage of these aggressive trout.

Low Oxygen Impacts – (Spring Turnover)

Adequate oxygen is a survival requirement for trout. The most common time for dangerously low oxygen levels is during spring turnover. Oxygen is a more immediate and pressing need than food. Even a starving trout will quit feeding when breathing becomes difficult and laboured. Under these stressed conditions the trout become lethargic. They tend to locate the most suitable areas for obtaining oxygen and then remain stationary gasping for breath.

As the oxygen levels begin to decline, the trout's first response will be to seek areas where it is easier to breathe. If turnover is gradual the trout will be able to do that. Turnover will occur in shallow water before it begins in the deeper water. To cope, the trout will simply move out to the deeper water. By the time turnover is occurring in the deeper water there may be more oxygen in the shallows. The trout then move back into the shallows. Even so, oxygen content throughout the lake is likely to be reduced from its pre-turnover levels and it is probable that the trout will discontinue feeding. If the rate of turnover is rapid then there will be little difference between shallow and deep water and the trout will simply become inactive and stop feeding to conserve oxygen.

> **Fishing Tip**
> When lake oxygen levels are low, try fishing during or just after a windy day when oxygen has been somewhat replenished.

The angler should seek locations where oxygen levels are highest. Since the underwater plants are not yet growing, a good source of oxygen will be from wind activity. Strong wind and whitecaps will replenish oxygen near the water surface. A dry line with a short leader and the fly kept near the surface may produce fish anywhere on the lake. However, the best wind oxygenated location will be where the waves are breaking against a shoreline with a water depth sufficient to hold fish. The surging action of the waves and the mixing action as they break will provide the needed oxygen. Also watch for locations where streams or other running water enters the lake. This running water typically has good oxygen content. If oxygen is sufficient the trout may be feeding in those locations.

High Water Temperatures – (Summer Downers)

We have already discussed some of the Rainbows behavior in various water temperatures. They behave normally in water temperatures around 48°F to 55°F (9°C to 13°C). The trout are typically inactive in higher water temperatures. In warm water (60°F to 70°F), the trout can become stressed and water over 70°F will often

114

kill the trout. A Rainbow needs about fifty percent more oxygen in water at 68°F than it does in water that is 43°F and we have already seen that warm water holds less oxygen than cold. Oxygen depravation is one of the stressing factors in high water temperatures. Thus the trout react much the same as discussed under low oxygen impacts.

High water temperatures mainly occur in the late summer. Many anglers use the term "summer doldrums" to describe this period of warmer water. They insist that this is not a good time to fly fish. I disagree. And I use the term "summer downers" for reference to this period because it better describes what is happening.

As water temperature warms, trout become uncomfortable. Similar to turnover, the trout's first reaction is to find water in which the problem does not exist. Their solution is simply to go into the deeper and cooler water of the lake. Remember that colder water sinks below warmer water. If the lake is deep enough they will find water cool enough to relieve the stress and resume normal activity. The key for the angler is knowledge that the fish will go "down" in depth to find suitable or better water temperatures. That's why I call this period the summer downers. Some fish will still make forays into the shallows where there is more food but most just stay in the deeper water during this period.

> **Fishing Tip**
> During hot weather with warming water, try to select deeper lakes and/or the deeper portions of any lake you are fishing. Then get your fly at least 20 feet down in the water column.

The summer downers can sometimes produce excellent fishing for the angler willing to adapt. Try a sinking line and wait for it to sink to a depth where the water is adequately cool. A line that sinks faster will get you down to the fish sooner but is more likely to hang up on the bottom. A line that sinks slower means that you wait longer to get the line down but you can utilize a slower retrieve and keep your line in the fish zone longer. A sinking tip line is often the best compromise.

The behavior of the trout during summer downers will depend on the specific conditions of the lake in which they live. In a shallow eutrophic lake the trout may not be able to find water sufficiently deep and cool to meet their preference. In warmer water their metabolism rate and need for food increases. In these conditions the trout may go into a period of inactive dormancy with just enough trips onto the feeding grounds to keep them from starving until such time as the water temperatures improve. Oxygen is not normally a limiting factor with warm surface temperatures unless alga blooms also create problems. Each and every lake will be different and the fly fisher will need to assess the specific conditions of the lake they have chosen to fish.

Toxins and Foul Water

On rare occasions (hopefully) you will find an area where toxins or other pollutants are in the water. The trout can easily detect the presence of toxins and will seek other areas to live and feed. If you get these substances on your fly or line it can also affect your future fishing success. Toxins can be something as simple as gas or oil slicks around a marina or wharf. Since these float the trout wouldn't immediately react to their presence. However, the first time a Rainbow comes to the surface to take a dry Caddis or Mayfly and gets a mouth full of gasoline, it would be aware of the contaminant and leave. Floating substances will also affect your flies and lines more readily than substances that dissolve in water. These also interfere with insect hatches. If you see pollutants entering the water, fish somewhere else and please report the circumstances to the appropriate authorities as soon as possible.

Sleeping Rainbows

In humans, sleep is considered a physiological necessity of life. Deprived of sleep a person will die sooner than they would from lack of food. Rainbows don't have eyelids and so can't close their eyes. That may mean that the trout don't sleep or at least not in the same way we think of sleep. There is very little literature regarding the subject of trout sleeping.

Active trout are more likely to feed than inactive trout. Folks have been known to throw rocks into the water or otherwise disturb the trout to make them easier to catch.

My personal opinion is that the trout go into a stupor that is very similar to sleep and I suspect that this only lasts for short periods of time much like a cat-nap. Normally a trout won't let your boat approach too close before it darts off. On occasion I have seen a trout resting near the bottom that seems totally unaware of my presence. A fly retrieved near the trout doesn't solicit a reaction. However, if you cast a shadow across the fish or make a noise in your boat the trout is immediately gone. I believe those fish were having their equivalent of a cat-nap. From the little experience I've had, you may as well forget about trying to entice a sleeping (?) fish into taking a fly.

Level 3 - Basic Safety, Health and Shelter

The next tier up in the motivational hierarchy is the level where trout behavior is guided by their needs for basic health, safety and shelter. In the previous tier, the trout might totally ignore dangerous conditions to satisfy food, oxygen or temperature requirements. Once those conditions are no longer an immediate threat, the trout become very "danger aware". Even though they may be hungry, it isn't imperative that they eat regardless of risk and the trout begin to seek conditions that improve their comfort level. Following are some of the important angling considerations at this level of the motivational hierarchy.

Feeding Behavior of Hungry Trout

As soon as a trout is hungry rather than starving, it begins to be cautious. Feeding is aggressive but high risks to danger are avoided. The trout will move into shallow waters to feed if it doesn't seem too dangerous and the food source is adequate. Most available foods are taken but the trout begins to be selective. Often the trout will tend to avoid those aquatic invertebrates that bite or sting and those that taste bad. The trout also learn to avoid aquatic bugs and beetles that don't digest very well.

Catching a hungry trout is almost as easy as catching a starving trout. However, the angler must take a few more precautions. Avoid making sharp noises in the boat, casting shadows over the trout's feeding area or doing anything else likely to spook the fish. Most fly patterns should work

> Hungry trout are cautiously aggressive and often feed in the shallows. In these conditions, the unobtrusive fly fisher will do best.

well unless a preferred hatch is due within a few days. If food is plentiful in the shallows, then that is where you will find these hungry trout.

Light Sensitive Rainbows

Rainbow Trout and most other fish consider bright lighting conditions as dangerous. As brightness increases, the trout are more susceptible to predation from Ospreys, Eagles, Loons, Bears and other animals relying on vision. Their fear of bright conditions is instinctive. A trout that is starving must ignore the danger. A hungry trout may choose to avoid the light or it may chance the danger if the food is plentiful and the reward is adequate. As hunger abates, the trout will tend to avoid bright light.

> A trout feeding in the shallows during bright sunlight is either hungry or else has found a food that makes it worth the risk.

At this level of the hierarchy, cautious behavior can generally be expected. The method of being cautious will vary with the particular habitat and water conditions. In a stream, the trout will seek deep pools or the shade of trees or bank vegetation. In a deep lake with clear water, the trout will simply go down deeper where the sunlight is filtered. If the water is not clear, the sunlight is filtered much faster and the trout can remain in the shallows to feed. In all cases, the trout also have the option of feeding at sunrise, sunset, after dark, during cloudy periods or at other times when the sunlight is dim. The best advice to the angler is to assume the trout are "light cautious" even if hungry.

Loons, Diving Birds and Other Predators

The presence of a predator can create stress conditions in the trout. The presence of a Loon or the shadow of an Osprey or Eagle flying overhead and any number of other signals can send the trout into hiding in the weed beds or deep water. Usually the stressful condition is eliminated or reduced shortly after the predator is gone and the trout return to their normal foraging. On

> Fish stealing Loons will instinctively know when you are catching fish.

occasion however, the predator will persist in the area you are fishing and the trout will stay hidden and remain very cautious. I'm not suggesting that you bring out the

117

12-gauge or throw a beer can at these predators. Just be aware that the trout have probably changed their behavior and you may have to adjust your tactics to be successful. Consider fishing next to a weed bed or in deeper water if you suspect the trout have been spooked and are seeking shelter.

> **Fishing Tip**
>
> It's the business of a Loon to know where the trout are. If the fishing is agonizingly slow, you may want to try where the Loons are hanging out but be aware that fish in that area will be very cautious.

This is probably a good place to briefly mention Loons. These magnificent birds are becoming very adept at removing a trout from an angler's line and the size of the fish doesn't seem to matter. If the Loon sees a fish in distress it will instinctively give chase even if the fish is much too big for the Loon to swallow. Too frequently the results are that the angler looses a nice fish and the Loon doesn't get a meal either. If you have a fish on the line and a Loon is giving chase, then land the fish as quickly as possible. If you intend to release the fish, and you don't really want to give the Loon a free meal or want it to pester a big fish to death, make sure the trout is fully recovered before the release. Try to avoid releasing the trout if the Loon is within 200 feet. If you keep the fish in the water and in your dip net long enough the Loon will sometimes give up and go in search of other prey.

Protective Schooling

Many species of ocean fish school for protection from predators. Young Rainbows will school in much the same way. Small Rainbows will usually stay in close contact with other fish of the same size class. When very small they will form tightly packed schools and swim together. As a rule-of-thumb, the smaller the fish, the more tightly packed will be their school.

As they grow in size the average distance between fish steadily increases. By the time these young fish are about ten inches in length they are no longer a school but more like a "group" of fish that hang out together. By the time they are about 16 inches in length the group may consist of two to five fish. Big Rainbows are often solitary but may tolerate one or two other Rainbows as hunting partners.

The reason that small fish school or group is for protection from predators. The odds of a minnow surviving are much better in a school than individually even if it means more competition with the other members of the school. There is even scientific evidence that trout exude a chemical to warn other fish in the group of danger or an approaching predator (the Schreckstoff factor).

> As a rule,
> Small fish school.
> Then they compete
> For what they eat.

Naturally, with many individuals of a school or group sharing the same territory, there is a high degree of competition for the available food. We will be looking at this competitive behavior when discussing the social interactions of the Rainbows.

Many interior lakes are stocked with harvestable trout.
ART LINGREN PHOTO

Wooden row boats, like this yellow one, were fashionable on interior lakes during Bill Nation's day.

ART LINGREN PHOTO

Pristine lakes can offer a tranquil setting.
BILL GRAEPLER PHOTO

Flippers and bows.
PAT HARRISON PHOTO

Fly fishers casting away on a
productive interior lake.

Let a big bow have a lot of line.

Some interior lake sunsets are spectacular

Rainbow trout congregate at lake outlets and inlets so they can reproduce in flowing water.
Art Lingren photo

Pontoon boats are popular in interior lakes.
ART LINGREN PHOTO

A variety of water depths are
usually found in pristine lakes.
BILL GRAEPLER PHOTO

The colors of a rainbow are beautiful.
RON NEWMAN PHOTO

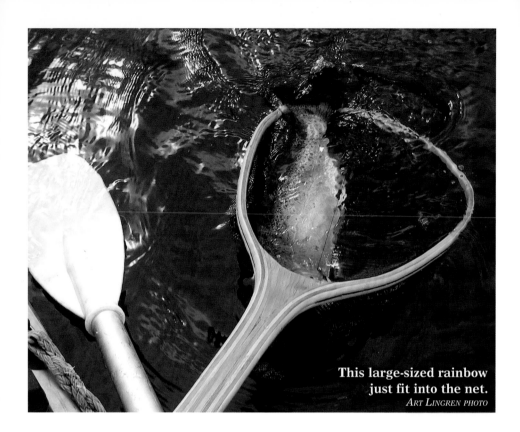

This large-sized rainbow
just fit into the net.
ART LINGREN PHOTO

In June when the damsel nymphs hatch the
trout feed on them greedily.
ART LINGREN PHOTO

Cool weather can be productive.
RON NEWMAN PHOTO

May can be a good time to fish interior lakes but every now and then the weather can turn foul.
ART LINGREN PHOTO

Kamloops rainbows are often short and fat.
PAT HARRISON PHOTO

Because of the small average size of individual Rainbows in a school or group, most anglers aren't too interested in stalking these as prey. However, the loose groups of ten to twelve inch Rainbows offer an excellent opportunity for the kids or novice to hone up on angling skills. When you find one of these schools, you can usually be very successful.

Often, schools of smaller Rainbows are found at times or places not preferred by the larger trout. When larger Rainbows aren't feeding, these schools are often found on the prime feeding shoals. Watch for the surface activity of these smaller fish. As larger Rainbows move onto a shoal, they often chase away the smaller trout. The school of less dominant fish then move into the very shallow water of the same shoal, or into deeper water just off the shoal. They may even be driven onto a nearby shoal that is not generally considered a prime feeding territory. Because of sunlight conditions, mid-day is not usually a preferred time for larger Rainbows. That's often when the younger Rainbows are found on the prime feeding shoals.

Fishing Tip

When you find a school of fish, the odds are that you will be in for some action. Expect most fish to be 13 inches or smaller. However, sometimes large fish are found in the company of these schools. Be prepared.

Naturally, there are exceptions to what I've just said. The sounds and vibrations from the feeding activity of a school of small fish may attract larger trout into the area to investigate. Rather than chase away the smaller trout, these bigger Bows will sometimes join into the feeding activity if they find the food of suitable quality and quantity.

Protective Shelter and Safe Water

As soon as Rainbows begin to satisfy their physiological needs and become "danger aware", they seek water that is considered safe. Actually the trout are trying to find locations that provide a good balance between safety and adequate food. The food is found on the prime feeding shoals. Safety is obtained in areas that have deep water and/or protective shelter near the feeding shoal. Deep water is almost always considered as "safe water" by the Rainbows. Predators can't normally pursue the trout into deep water, they are protected from sunlight, oxygen and temperature are usually good and deep water is a permanent structure. This safe water is usually where the trout will rest and digest their latest meal. As an added feature, a drop-off usually separates the feeding shoal from the deep water and offers an additional level for safely feeding under varying circumstances.

When a Rainbow takes a fly, it is usually because of action and reaction. The behavior of a trout is usually because of cause and effect. The wise angler should assess what is motivating the trout at any given time.

119

By protective shelter I am predominantly referring to weed beds and other structures that hide or help camouflage the trout while along the drop-off or on the feeding shoal. Other structures includes things such as old docks, submerged logs, beaver dams, sharp drop-offs, lake bottoms of a darker color and so on. These areas allow the trout to temporarily seek shelter and thus safety while in shallower water.

Fishing Tip

I have found that Bows tend to seek the protective shelter of weed beds more from late summer thru fall than they do at most any other time of year. I often search out weeds beds at this time of year.

An ideal habitat for a Rainbow is an area of the lake offering a productive feeding shoal, protective shelter and the safety of deep water, all within a short distance. You often hear advice suggesting you look for "structure" in a lake. Too often those offering the advice are just referring to the protective shelter. It is much better to look for areas that also offer the feeding grounds and safe water. As a bonus, the dominant larger trout tend to claim this type of prime habitat as a part of their territory.

The angler should be aware of these basic habitat components and tailor their fishing to the specific circumstances of the day. If there is no apparent trout activity on a feeding shoal then an angler is probably wise to fish near areas offering protective shelter or even into the safe water. You would probably see Rainbow surface activity in the shallows but not necessarily around the protective shelter or deep water.

Traffic Stress

A healthy Rainbow will almost always swim away from an approaching watercraft. Even a stealthy approach in a canoe will cause the trout to scamper away. Each approaching watercraft is a potential danger and easily detected by the trout. The potential of danger creates stress in the trout. In areas with heavy traffic, the amount of stress increases proportionally and can cause behavioural

Being bombarded by the noise of motorboats every few minutes would even cause stress in a meditating monk.

changes in the trout. Areas of heavy traffic are typically in front of a marina, resort or campsite where boats are launched and return after a day of fishing. Other areas may include narrow channels between two main portions of the lake or it could even be a frequently used fishing shoal. Rainbows may use and feed in these areas but how they behave in these areas can be different than on other parts of the lake.

If there is a prime feeding shoal in a high traffic area, the trout will try to avoid the perceived danger as much as possible. They can't stop the boat traffic but they can change when and where they feed on the shoal. The trout may learn to feed at times when the amount of traffic is reduced. They might begin to frequent this high traffic area after dark or on weekdays when the traffic isn't as heavy. The trout may also find places on the feeding shoal where the effects of the traffic are reduced. This could be in water too shallow for the boats or perhaps on a side of the shoal not in the lane of traffic.

One of my favourite shoals is located a short distance in front of a fishing resort. The shoal is large and shallow, with deep-water on two sides and the shore on the other two sides. The boat traffic from the resort must use the deep-water channel on one side of the shoal to gain access to the rest of the lake. On weekends and other busy times the trout seldom feed along the side of the shoal with ongoing traffic. Instead they move around the corner of the shoal to the drop off with little traffic. However, on weekdays or at other times when there isn't much traffic the trout tend to reverse the process. In this way they avoid much of the traffic stress and get full utilization of the feeding shoal. Each set of traffic conditions will be different and the fly fisher should try to assess if there is a problem and if so, how the fish react to minimize the danger.

Nutrient Balance

Hunger is a motivator. The hungrier a trout becomes the more it is motivated to eat. Earlier in this chapter (Table 11), we examined some of the behaviors resulting from different levels of hunger. At that time, we didn't mention anything about a well balanced diet or the nutritional values. Trout can be well fed and still lack some of the essential dietary requirements to be healthy. The same happens to people who constantly eat junk food. Unlike people, the trout doesn't have a dietician or a mother to tell it what foods and how much of each are needed for a well balanced diet. Instead, the trout's body will inform it about the foods that are needed to get a proper balance of nutrients.

> Trout can get a "craving" for certain foods much like a pregnant woman craving pickles and ice cream.

When the trout are starving or very hungry, they will eat most anything that is available. The hunger pangs in the trout's belly tell the fish to eat anything it can find. These hunger pangs have "signaled" the trout to eat. The trout's body has told it what to do because it was lacking a needed ingredient to sustain a healthy life.

After the trout gets enough food to quell the immediate hunger pangs, they start getting picky about what they eat. Similar to the hunger pangs it experienced, the trout's body will begin to signal the fish that certain types of food are needed. The trout doesn't consciously know what foods are needed. However, the trout's body develops "cravings" for specific foods. Unconsciously the trout is being guided into the selection of certain foods at certain times. These bodily instructions are probably much like a pregnant woman craving pickles and ice cream. These instructions become a behavior pattern that guides the fish.

As the trout's body consumes certain proteins and amino acids, these need to be replaced. The body begins to crave certain nutrients to satisfy these requirements. One type of aquatic invertebrate may contain an abundance of the protein or amino acid lacking in the trout's diet while another doesn't. Without the trout's knowledge, its body is directing it to feed on certain types of food at certain times to obtain a specific nutrient balance. These bodily instructions may go so far as to direct the trout to feed on one species of Chironomid, for example, in preference to another.

121

These dietary instructions from the trout's body are constantly changing throughout the season. The Bows body often requires different nutrients at different times of the year. What the trout's body needs in early Spring isn't necessarily the same as what it needs in late Fall. Additionally, many species of invertebrates are only available at certain times of the year. Over a season or two, I suspect the trout learn when specific invertebrates are available that supply the nutrients craved by the trout at that specific time. Undoubtedly, the trout will take advantage of that nutritional source while the supply lasts. These changing bodily requirements and bug availabilities keep the trout seeking different foods through the year. The trout begin to seek one type of food in preference to another at different times. In fact, the trout develop certain food preferences based on nutrient requirements. We will be discussing this in more detail under Rainbow Food Preferences in Chapter 6.

> **Fishing Tip**
> Keeping fishing records of when, where and what was successful can significantly increase your odds of having better success in subsequent years.

Level 4 - Social Interactions

Once Rainbows have overcome their basic instincts and drives for survival and danger avoidance, they become concerned with social interactions. Essentially, trout are social animals. They have a social hierarchy as well as a motivational hierarchy. The behavior patterns exhibited by a Rainbow, depends on its social standing within the community. And a Rainbows place within the social hierarchy usually depends on size. As you grow bigger, you move up the social ladder. In short, the behavior of a Rainbow is directly proportional to its size.

A pristine lake is usually eutrophic with an abundant supply of food, favorable habitat and has a population of fish in balance with the food supply. Seldom do the trout need to worry about basic survival. This is great for the trout, but it means an angler must consider many factors for consistent success.

Typically, the angler is faced with trout that are contented and that makes them much harder to catch. We want to look at some of the Rainbow social interactions in this section. In turn, those interactions sometimes affect how we angle for Rainbows of different sizes.

Cannibalism

It isn't nice to eat your brother unless you are very hungry. If you must eat another fish then try another species first. That seems to be one of the basic social rules governing Rainbows.

You can find some strange things in the stomach samples of Rainbows. It sometimes seems they will eat almost anything at least once. Each year our lakes are stocked with many small Rainbows that would make an easy meal for larger trout. However, don't expect to find these young Rainbows in the stomach samples of the larger trout. As long as the populations of aquatic invertebrates are sufficient to sustain the

Rainbow population, these fish seem to avoid cannibalism. Rainbows are not naturally cannibalistic. If food becomes scarce, trout will revert to cannibalism as a last resort but it doesn't seem to be their preferred way of feeding.

Catching a minnow isn't easy. It takes a lot of energy with more misses than catches. Rainbows are naturally lazy and would prefer to just swim around sucking in bugs that are easy to catch. If there isn't much choice, Rainbows begin to feed on minnows. In the large deep oligotrophic lakes the quantity of aquatic invertebrates is usually low and trout then feed on minnows. Rainbows will also begin to feed on minnows in the smaller lakes where other species of fish are introduced. Most of these other fish species are better foragers than the ever-cautious Rainbow. Often bug populations will quickly decline. To compensate, Rainbows will soon start feeding on the minnows. Even then, Rainbows will target other fish species rather than the young of its own kind. In return, other species will often target the young Rainbows.

Did You Know
Insectivorous Rainbows in a pristine lake will only resort to cannibalism as a last resort for survival. In lakes that aren't pristine, the trout will usually begin to feed on bait fish when the Bows are about 15 inches in length.

An angler should be knowledgeable about the water body being fished. Does it have adequate supplies of aquatic invertebrates and are other species of fish present? If the lake has lots of invertebrates and doesn't have other fish species, then flies representing invertebrates are recommended over flies that imitate minnows. Flies that represent minnows will still be taken as "attractor flies" with strikes occurring as a result of movement and stimulation of the Visual Trigger. If invertebrates are scarce or if other species of fish are present, then a lure or fly to represent minnows will be taken by the larger trout (over 15 inches). Adjust your fishing techniques accordingly.

Competitive Behavior

A constant social interaction among Rainbow Trout is competition. Rainbows in a lake constantly compete for food, dominance and territory. Competition differs between size classes and differs by fish within the same size class. The levels of competition even vary by season and time of day. In one form or another, almost every aspect of a trout's life is driven by competitive factors.

In the Rainbow's world, bigger fish are higher in the pecking orders, higher in social standing and thus seize the best times and places to feed.

Size is the most important consideration in regards to competition among trout. By definition, larger Bows are bigger, stronger, and higher in the pecking order than a smaller fish. The bigger fish are dominant and thus have the right to bully smaller fish. A truer form of competition exists among fish in the same size class. How a fish competes within a size class takes on different rules than competition between size classes. In this section, let's look at competitive behavior among the trout and relate that to angling strategies.

Competition Between Size Classes

As we saw in Chapter 3, within a lake there are a number of Rainbow size classes. Fish stocked at the same time generally grow at about the same rate and form a size class. However, as they mature, the more aggressive fish will grow faster than the timid fish. Eventually size classes will overlap. For now, we will just consider that there are bigger and smaller size classes.

> **Did You Know**
> Larger or more aggressive Rainbows will chase and nip at the smaller or timid trout to drive them away from a territory or feeding ground.

Small Rainbows are the most competitive. Proportional to their body mass, it takes more food for a small trout to survive and grow than it does for a larger trout. However, small fish are low in the pecking order and thus relegated to the worst feeding periods or locations. To maintain a steady influx of required food, small fish will feed at most any opportunity offered under reasonably favorable conditions. Small trout are the most aggressive.

Even though highly competitive, small Rainbows usually stay in close contact with other fish of the same size class. When discussing level 3 of the hierarchy, we saw that small Rainbows school for protection. The protection advantages offered by a school seem to be more important than the disadvantages of competition required with this living arrangement.

Because Rainbows live about five years, there are about five size classes in a lake. As the fish move from one size class the next, the number of fish in a school or group steadily decreases while the distance between fish steadily increases. Two year old fish tend to form loose groups while fish or three years and older may maintain small

> Large Rainbow's feed when they choose. Small Rainbow's feed when the opportunity arises.

hunting packs. These hunting packs seem to be a hold-over of the schooling instinct. When you see a larger trout, you may not even be aware that it is part of a hunting pack. Sometimes the individuals in these packs travel in close proximity to their partners but just as often, they are yards apart. Far enough to avoid direct competition with a partner but close enough to share predatory warnings.

> Large fish are prone
> To swim alone
> Small fish they chase
> From their home base.

Large Rainbows are not nearly as susceptible to predation as smaller Rainbows. That's part of the reason larger fish outgrow the need to school or group and tend to become more solitary. A large fish may become a "loner" but the more cautious fish will often travel together as a unit of two or three fish to help spot incoming predators. These small hunting packs are good at territorial protection and alerting one another to potential danger.

Because they are at or near the top of the pecking order, the size classes of larger Rainbows are the ones that feed at the best locations and during the "preferred activity periods". Generally, this is when the trout feel reasonably safe, food is relatively abundant and available, environmental conditions are satisfactory, food is a preferred food and the trout's body tells them it is time to feed. Larger fish are usually more active at the beginning of a hatch than near the end of a hatch. If the larger Rainbows have just finished a major feed, then it isn't likely they will feed again for a significant time.

And there is a last note about competition between size classes. The classes of larger Rainbows don't always exercise their right to chase away the smaller size classes. It isn't uncommon to see all size classes feeding at the same time in the same area. Why the bigger fish will chase away the smaller fish one day and not the next isn't clear. It probably has something to do with food availability, the type of food and the

> **Fishing Tip**
> If small fish are rising around the lake but you notice one good shoal lacking these, then stop and make it few casts over that shoal. It may be that larger trout have chased the smaller fish off the shoal. Also, note that large fish tend not to rise as frequently as small fish.

environmental conditions but I haven't yet found a consistent correlation. So it pays the angler to cast a fly anywhere there is feeding activity. If only small fish are being taken, you can always decide to try somewhere else on the lake.

Competition Within a Size Class

Most of the competition within a size class occurs when the younger trout school or group. That's because of their close proximity to one another. Larger trout remain apart even when in a hunting pack. Within these groups of smaller fish, there is probably more competition between individuals than there is between size classes. However, competition by Rainbows of about the same size is different from competition between size classes. Competition within a size class is motivated by the trout's aggressiveness and it doesn't usually involve chasing away another trout in the same size class. This aggressiveness is not generally directed at other fish. Rather, it is most frequently aimed at obtaining food.

> After a couple of years, an aggressive trout can potentially be double the size of a timid trout. But it also doubles its chances of being taken by an angler.

Within a size class, an individual may be aggressive, cautious or timid. An aggressive trout will be the first to dart out of the school and grab food. It may stray from its school and take other risky chances. Conversely, the timid trout is overly cautious. While it debates about taking an aquatic invertebrate, another fish has already eaten the tidbit. The majority of Rainbows are cautious and fit into the middle ground. Within its own size class, the aggressive trout tends to tolerate and feed with the timid trout. There doesn't seem to be much chasing and nipping by trout of the same size.

The degree of aggressiveness begins to manifest itself when the trout hatch. For a lack of better information, let's say that about 20% are aggressive, 20% timid and the other 60% are in the cautious category when they hatch. By the time the trout are four years old, probably fewer than 5% of the fish in the aggressive or timid categories are still around. So what happens to these fish because of their aggressive or timid behavior patterns?

The aggressive trout grows faster but with all the risks it takes, it is one of the first to fall prey to a predator or anglers fly. In opposition, the timid trout grows slowly and may lack food and essential nutrients. It will be one of the first to die from adverse environmental conditions or illness. The cautious but middle-of-the-road Rainbows are the ones who seem to fair best over the long term.

Rainbows that survive into the middle and large size classes have shown that they are able to compete and survive in their environment. As the trout grow larger, being aggressive or timid is less likely to be a competitive trait. Larger Rainbows are more likely to be cautious but efficient and effective hunters. These trout won't waste a lot of energy hunting when food is scarce. They hunt at prime times but prime times are not necessarily during hatches. These fish become good at foraging in the weeds and along the lake bottom. When food is abundant and conditions are right, you can bet that some of these larger fish will be over the primary feeding shoals but they won't totally rely on the main hatches for a meal.

> Typically, large Rainbows are efficient and effective foragers that are cautious and vigilant.

Seasonal Competition

The degree of competition for food changes with the seasons. At different times of the year, there are greater or lesser amounts of food. The degree of competition changes proportionally. When food is seasonally plentiful, the degree of competition is low. In times of plenty, the larger fish are more likely to share their time and space with the smaller fish because all can obtain adequate food in a short period and then leave the feeding grounds for the next shift of hungry fish.

When food is seasonally scarce, the larger fish are more likely to drive competitors away from the feeding grounds prior to a feed. It will take longer for them to quench their hunger and thus they will tie up the feeding grounds for longer periods. Under these conditions, the smaller fish will be forced to feed at times not normally considered desirable. All the trout tend to become more aggressive and competitive. Seasonal periods of scarcity can actually prove good times for the angler to be on the lake and casting a fly.

> The most dangerous time for a trout is when the demand for aquatic food is high and the supply of aquatic food is low.

From the Seasonal Food Availability graph (Fig. 26), we can get an idea of how food availability affects the seasonal feeding behavior of trout. This graph shows all the "available" food sources for Rainbow Trout throughout the ice-free season. This includes all elevations, all times of day and all types of food. The line for "fishing" is angling success superimposed on the same scale as feed. The purpose of the graph is to show the seasonal trends of food abundance and when the Rainbows are more likely to be competitive and aggressive.

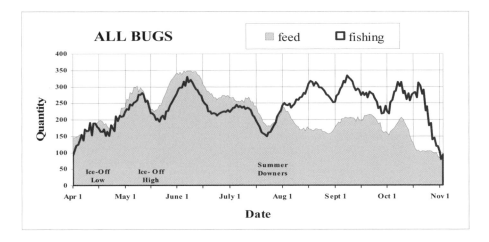

Figure 26 – Seasonal Food Availability with Angling Success Overlay

During the first half of the season, food is relatively abundant. Trout are less competitive and are more likely to be cautious about eating something not exactly right such as your fly. During the second half of the season, many bugs have already hatched and their replacements are still in the egg stage or are too small to be considered a primary food. Rainbow food sources are less available in the late season, but as we see in Figure 26, the fishing is probably better at that time than it is in the first half of the season. The trout have become more competitive and aggressive late in the year. They are more likely to take a fly even if it does appear a little strange.

Knowledge of the seasonal competition factors gives the angler an overview of trout behavior and general trends. However, on any given day the behavior of the trout can vary from these generalities.

Daily Competition

The availability of food and thus the degree of competition changes within a 24-hour day. Each day has peaks and troughs of food availability. When these occur is strongly linked to the season and what type of aquatic invertebrates are available. Some invertebrates are more active or hatch in the morning, others at mid-day and still others in the evening or after dark. Trout activity tends to follow the activity of their preferred foods. In addition, trout have "preferred activity periods" that are strongly related to light intensity. The larger trout are more likely to feed during the preferred activity periods and the smaller trout are often relegated to the "not so good" activity periods. This sets the stage for daily competition among the Rainbows.

127

Rainbows in the larger size classes get to pick when they feed. They usually try to pick times when preferred foods are available and that coincide with a time of day that is preferred by the Rainbows. However, the invertebrates don't always co-operate and may only be available at a time that is less than desirable. These big fish will then select the 'best' conditions. If the daily conditions aren't just right, the larger trout may even wait a few days for conditions to improve.

Fortunately, for fish in the smaller size classes, larger fish may not feed for long periods. When they do feed, these larger fish will likely tolerate smaller fish if the supply of food is abundant. If the amount of food is limited, large fish will often chase away fish of the smaller size classes.

> Big fish rise at night,
> To the fishers delight.
> Small fish rise at day,
> To the fishers dismay.
> (But not always)

Following are some general guidelines to help determine preferred activity periods on a daily basis from the trout's perspective. An angler won't necessarily prefer these same periods.

➢ When low light levels are optimized is the best time of day. This is usually at sunrise or sunset in clear waters and mid-day in murky waters. Cloudy to overcast days will also reduce light and bring the trout into shallower waters.
➢ Best fishing occurs when oxygen levels are at their best. On a daily basis, this is generally at sunset.
➢ Best fishing occurs when the water temperature over the shoals is most suitable. Although there is little daily change in average water temperature it is slightly cooler at sunrise and slightly warmer at sunset. In mid summer (warm water) go for sunrise and in the spring or late fall (cold water) the best time is likely to be near sunset or even mid-day.
➢ During the full moon phase, trout feed better in the daytime than during the evening. At other moon phases, evening fishing is generally better.
➢ Bugs that prefer bright light levels are usually more active and hatch more frequently from 9:30 a.m. to 2:30 p.m. than at other times of the day. If that bug is a preferred food at the time, the trout are likely to be active but of course it will also depend on the other environmental conditions.
➢ Bugs that prefer low light levels are usually more active and hatch more frequently between sunset and midnight. If that bug is a preferred food, the trout are likely to also be active at the same time. Also note that some bugs hatch just prior to sunrise and use the early morning sun to dry their newly developed wings.

Competition is a big factor affecting the social interactions and behavior of Rainbows. The knowledgeable angler should be aware of these behavior patterns to help assess where, when and how to fish for these cautious Rainbows. It's good to remember that in the Bows world, the biggest fish get to choose the best conditions.

Rainbow Territories

Rainbows are very territorial. It is instinctive. While all trout have these territorial drives, the behavior patterns in regards to territory changes with the type of habitat in which the trout lives. The territory a trout defends in a stream or river, for example, is different from how trout will behave in a lake.

In a stream, the trout's feeding and resting grounds are usually the same parcel of topography. The largest trout will claim the best territory by driving away intruders. The best territory is usually a hole or riffle with lower lighting conditions near the primary currents channeling in the best supply of food. Depending on the degree of competition, this territory may be small or large. It may even be shared with

> By shallow weeds
> The big trout feeds,
> Near water that's deep
> Where cool they keep.

other Rainbows if conditions allow. A trout will generally stay within and protect that piece of turf until it feels there is opportunity to claim a better territory or else changing currents force it to seek new territory. However, trout in a stream are often stationary within their territory for extended periods. The angler simply has to look for the best holding water to find the trout. These types of behavior patterns are not applicable in most lakes.

Did You Know
In a lake, the Rainbows often move and the territory they defend is usually the area they currently occupy.

In a pristine lake, the trout's feeding and resting grounds are usually in different locations. The best feeding locations are the shoals or drop-offs. The best holding or resting areas are usually in deep water. So in a lake, a trout does a lot of traveling. And it can't defend an area of its territory that it doesn't currently occupy. Additionally, in pristine lakes the Rainbows frequently change the location of their territory. One day a group or young Rainbows or a hunting pack of larger Rainbows will be in a specific location and the next day they may be somewhere else. While the Rainbows in a stream defend a particular piece of underwater turf and only move when forced to, the Rainbows in a lake frequently move and only tend to defend the area they currently occupy. Both have the territorial instinct but their behavioral patterns differ with the type of water they live in.

The area defended by a trout in a lake may be a radius of 100 feet or smaller depending on the numbers of fish in competition. And remember that Bows of the same size class tend to tolerate each other. Often the schools, groups or hunting packs of the same size class will share the same territory and work together to chase off intruders even if they are

> If you are fishing in water not currently occupied by the trout, it will be difficult to get a fish to take your fly.

somewhat larger. A bunch of small trout can effectively annoy a large trout into leaving.

With these trout frequently on the move, the job of the angler is to locate the territory the trout are currently calling home turf. When you get onto the lake, watch for trout rising to the surface. In clear water, you may even be able to see the trout swimming along a shoal or drop-off. If you're fishing in water not currently occupied by the trout it's going to be difficult to get one to take your fly.

129

Rainbow Social Orders

We have seen that Rainbows in a pristine lake have a crazy kind of social order based on competition. Food and territorial instincts are two of the main motivators for this competition. Fish size and aggressiveness are the two main factors determining where an individual trout fits into this society. The biggest fish are at the top of the pecking order and get first choice on feeding times and territories. However, if food or other environmental factors begin to lack, the trout may resort to behavior patterns that are lower on the motivational hierarchy. Often this means that the social order among the trout begins to deteriorate and the fish resort to satisfying personal needs and possibly free-for-all tactics.

Level 5 - Contented Rainbows

We have looked at some progressive behavior patterns of Rainbows. From those Bows that are starving and on up the motivational hierarchy to those that have most of their needs satisfied. Now it's time to look at the uppermost level of the hierarchy that I've labeled as "self satisfaction". At this level, the trout are well fed and living in a good environment with good water conditions. In short, these fish are fat, lazy and contented. There aren't a lot of external factors to motivate these trout.

Many pristine lakes provide the trout with ample food and generally good environmental conditions through most of the year. Rainbows that are well fed and satisfied are the hardest for an angler to catch. And often that's what we anglers face, contented Rainbows that have little motivation to take our fly.

Contented Rainbows will feed whenever they get the urge. They don't usually need to worry about food being available. They tend to select the best conditions to feed and then only on foods that are highly preferred. If anything looks amiss, they will simply ignore your fly and move on to the next food morsel. The success of a fly fisher may

A fly can't compete
If trout have lots to eat.
If a meal is in doubt
Your fly will catch trout.

depend on simple things such as wind direction or barometric pressure. But we will discuss those factors later.

If you have a dog or cat that is well fed then you know what they do. Their biggest ambition is to laze around digesting their latest meal. When the mood strikes they may socialize, carouse or play. Contented Rainbows have about the same motivations and behave in much the same way. Naturally, the trout's actions are tailored to their watery environment.

When not totally bloated with food, contented trout may cruise into the waters of the neighboring territory to check out food supplies and to see if the Chironomids really are greener over there. If it likes what it finds, the trout may even change its territory.

There may be territorial challenges with trout that already live there. For a trout, this is the type of socializing and carousing that it will find interesting.

For a trout, playfulness might be something as simple as jumping out of the water just to see what is there or chasing smaller fish just for the thrill of the chase. To the consternation of a dry fly angler, a trout may even swamp and drown Caddis or Mayflies at the surface with no intention of feeding on the insects. Contended Rainbows might even become curious. They have been known to approach an anchored boat, for example, and watch an angler. It is quite possible that a lot of the learning about their particular habitat occurs during these contented periods.

> **Fishing Tip**
> If the trout are well fed and content then try appealing to their sense of playfulness rather than their sense of hunger.

For success, we anglers appeal to the trout's need for food. When the trout are already well fed and content it is difficult to get them interested in another bit of food. However, there is one thing the fly fisher can do. Try appealing to the trout's sense of playfulness. Sometimes they playfully chase and nip at things including each other. Via your fly, try enticing the trout much like you would pull a string to play with a cat. This response is a part of the Visual Trigger. Simply let the fly sit on the bottom for a while and then give it a couple of short twitches to attract the attention and curiosity of nearby trout. Let it sit for another short time as trout approach to investigate. Then rapidly retrieve the fly. The trout's Visual Trigger will often kick in and the fish will take the fly even though they have little intention of feeding on it. Try various such retrieves to see what may entice the trout to chase and nip at the fly. The process is very similar to enticing a cat to pounce on a string. But since the trout is only playing with your fly, expect to miss a lot of strikes.

Learned Behavior

In Figure 25, we provided the hierarchy of motivations that stimulate behavior patterns in Rainbows. Learned behavior was set off to the side because it can affect how trout behave at any level of the hierarchy. We should take a moment to examine some of the specific behaviors that trout learn.

Laboratory experiments have shown that Rainbows have the ability to learn. They can be taught to perform certain tasks. Most often this teaching/learning relationship involves food as a reward. Other than food, few things seem to offer the Rainbow enough incentive to actually do what a researcher is trying to teach. For food the Rainbows will go to a certain color to feed, push a button to deliver food, go to a buzzer and perform other neat little tricks for a meal. These conditioned responses are not instinctive. The trout must learn these feats and the common theme around this learning seems to be food.

It seems obvious that trout in the wild will also learn certain behaviours. However, food won't be the only motivator through which wild trout learn. These fish will also learn from motivators such as fear, stress, and curiosity or simply by observing other trout.

Most of the daily activities of a Rainbow are instinctive. By instinctive we mean that a certain physical condition will elicit a given response even if it has never previously experienced the condition. For example, if the mid-summer water temperature gets too warm the trout will instinctively seek cooler water. However, they had to learn that water is

<table>
<tr><td>Did You Know</td></tr>
<tr><td>Rainbows have the ability to learn. Most learning is thru trial and error but some learning occurs from observing other fish.</td></tr>
</table>

cooler deeper down in the lake. Trout moving into a lake from a stream would not instinctively know this fact. The first time the trout encountered warm water conditions, it found the cooler water by trial and error or perhaps it observed other fish going deeper and followed their example. However, the following summer when the water got too warm, that particular fish will have "learned" where to go to be comfortable.

Trout can and do learn. Sometimes it isn't easy to distinguish instinct from learned behavior. However, as long as an angler knows what to expect from the fish it doesn't really matter whether that behavior is learned or instinctive. Let's have a look at a few behavior patterns that I suspect the Rainbows have learned.

Motor Wise

The sound of an electric or gasoline motor and the under water vibrations of the propeller will instinctively trigger a predator alert in the trout and it will flee. Instinct will tell the trout to stay a safe distance away. However, on a lake with a moderate amount of motorized traffic the fish will soon learn that these sounds and vibrations are not predatory. They will move out of the way of an approaching boat but return to their feeding shoal after the motor noise has stopped and things have settled down. However, they may shy away from the boat location for up to a half hour. That can be a long time for an angler to be fishing unproductive water, especially when a rise is on and the fish are actively feeding.

An angler should be aware of this learned behavior. If you are fishing on a lake that sees very little motorized traffic then don't roar up to your intended fishing spot with the motor at full throttle. In this type of lake the trout probably haven't learned the boat and the noises made by the angler isn't a predatory threat. They may

<table>
<tr><td>Fishing Tip</td></tr>
<tr><td>It is always a good idea to shut off your boat motor and row the last 200 feet or so onto a shoal or other area you intend to fish.</td></tr>
</table>

stay away for extended periods.   Turn off your motor before reaching the feeding shoal and row that last hundred yards or so. Oarlocks should be oiled to prevent loud squeaks, the anchor should be gently lowered and try to avoid any noise in the boat while fishing. Throw an old piece of carpet or rug into the bottom of the boat to help muffle any noise. On lakes that have lots of motorized traffic these precautions become less important. Personally I try to follow those rules even on busy lakes.

Fly Shy

In most of our fishing lakes, larger trout have probably been caught and released at least once and most likely several times. Each time that fish is caught it learns to be very cautious about feeding on the type of bug that caused it grief. If the trout was caught on a fly representing a Chironomid then it will learn to always approach Chironomids with caution. If that Chironomid isn't just exactly right, and a fly never is, then the trout will reject the offering and go in search of a different food morsel. I refer to fish that have learned this behavior as being "Fly Shy". A Rainbow that has become Fly Shy can still be caught but probably not on a fly pattern that even closely resembles something that previously caused it discomfort.

> Big fish are wise
> And won't take flies
> That they once took
> And felt the hook.

I offer this Fly Shy learning behavior as an explanation for why certain popular fly patterns loose their effectiveness over time. Someone develops a fly pattern that is really good and shares that knowledge with other fly fishers. Soon there are many fly fishers using that same pattern. Lots of fish are caught and released over the course of a year or two. Those fish become Fly Shy when it comes to that fly pattern and are not likely to make the same mistake twice. It may even be possible that other fish observing a territorial partner rejecting that fly will also become cautious of that particular offering. Over the course of several years that fly pattern will loose its effectiveness. Sure it will still catch fish but not as many and fewer large trout than when its use first began.

Fishing Tip

Rainbows can become overly cautious of some fly patterns. If your standard patterns aren't working then try something atypical or a little unusual.

Most of the bigger Rainbows I catch are taken on fly patterns that aren't considered typical or popular. I usually keep a few of the currently popular patterns in my fly box but I also have a significant number of flies that are probably fairly unique. I recently developed a little fly that I call an SBS and it has proven to be a very effective fish catcher. To make sure that it remains effective, I don't share the pattern with other fly fishers. Most anglers will not divulge any information regarding their "secret lake". I tend do the same with my best flies because I want them to remain effective.

If you are after big Rainbows in a likely looking spot and not having success with your typical fly patterns, then it might be worth while to try some of your more unusual patterns. It is quite possible that a lack of success is because the trout have become Fly Shy.

Boat Charging

Sometimes a Rainbow is hooked and escapes the dip net by making a full speed charge directly at the angler. The angler has little control and often looses a fish running straight at them. The first time this happens is undoubtedly just a matter of

133

chance. The fish has arbitrarily chosen that particular direction to make its escape attempt. However, through this random choice of direction the trout has learned a lesson. The next time it is hooked you can be fairly certain that it will again try a run or two directly at the angler.

I call this learned behavior "boat charging". The incidence of boat charging used to be fairly rare but now seems to be on the increase. Last year I had three fish pull this tactic on the same day. I suspect that the increased use of barbless hooks plays a part in the trout learning this escape tactic. Having a fish run directly at you is one of the few instances when a barbless hook is a disadvantage. The fish will

> Rainbows that have been hooked and escape, will likely try that same escape tactic the next time they are hooked

often throw the fly and in the process learn to try this same approach the next time they are hooked. I can't offer any suggestions to foil this tactic except to restore tension between the fish and your rod as soon as possible.

Hatch Forecasting

During its first year in a lake, a young Rainbow doesn't know when a particular invertebrate is going to hatch or otherwise become available. The trout's genes don't have this information stored as instinct because food availability changes by water type and elevation. Through their first year, these young fish feed whenever the opportunity arises. From that first year's experience, however, they learn when food is abundant or scarce and when a particularly tasty food is available. This information is stored in their memory banks and then co-ordinated through the Rainbows biological clock. During their second year, more data is added and their original data is reinforced. By their third year, the trout can pretty well predict the location and time when particular food items are going to become available. Sometimes the trout will postpone a regularly scheduled feeding interval in anticipation of a preferred food that will soon become available.

> **Did You Know**
> It takes stocked Rainbows a year or two to learn the conditions and cycles of the lake in which they are placed.

> **Fishing Tip**
> For the best fishing, be on a lake at the start of a hatch rather than at the end of a hatch.

I keep detailed records and know when hatches are expected on the lakes. Often I go to a lake on a certain date expecting a specific hatch to be just beginning and anticipating that the big Rainbows will be claiming the first feeding rights. Several times I have arrived at the lake to find absolutely no sign of the expected hatch. For some reason the hatch is later than expected. I have learned to fish as if the hatch were in progress. Frequently the big Rainbows are there and awaiting the hatch. Eagerly waiting fish, no real bugs to distract the trout and your fly representing the first of an expected major hatch can produce some of the best fly fishing conditions you are likely to encounter. The trout have learned to know when hatches are likely to occur. If a fly fisher has this same timetable it can significantly improve your odds of a great day of fishing.

134

Bottom Sweepers

A trait that Rainbows have probably learned from watching other trout is what I call "bottom sweeping". When a trout detects slight movement in the mud or silt of the lake bottom, it will sweep its tail at that location to stir up whatever was there. The fish will then circle back through the suspended muck to feed on aquatic invertebrates that were swept out of the silt. I have only seen this action a couple of times but suspect it happens more frequently than we might expect. If you have ever foul hooked a Rainbow in the side or near the tail it is possible that the trout was performing this manoeuvre. It is possible that the trout detected your fly moving through the lightly suspended bottom sediments. As it swept its tail it also encountered your leader causing the hook to embed in the fish.

> **Did You Know**
> Rainbows that are efficient and effective feeders learn ways to find food even when it seems to be scarce.

Intentionally fishing a fly in the bottom silts can produce some good success particularly in the late summer and fall months. However, be prepared for foul hooks or bumps that are the trout's tail striking your leader. If fishing this way, wait for a good solid take before setting the hook. Otherwise you are likely to set the hook on a false take and remove the fly from the trout's search area.

Trout Trails

Wolf, cougars, bear and many other animals have set routes they use to patrol and mark their territory. Many animals also have a path or route to and from favourite feeding grounds (game trails). I'm not sure if the trout "mark" their territory in the traditional sense but they do have established routes that they use over and over again. These pathways may change with the daily and seasonal conditions but they do exist. An angler who places a fly along one of these routes will increase their odds for success.

> **Did You Know**
> In the late evening and at night the Rainbows will often cruise right next to the shore in search of bugs. This tactic is too risky during the daytime.

Finding one of these trout trails can be difficult, especially in water that is less than clear. Since the trout are suspended in the water they don't often leave a visible mark on the lake bottom to mark its location. You pretty well have to see the trout cruising back and forth in a certain location to detect one of these trails. However, there is an exception.

The next time you are on a trout lake, have a look at the area where the reeds are poking out of water but anchored on the lake bottom. If the water is two to four feet deep the odds are that you will find a strip paralleling the reeds that is devoid of bottom dwelling plants. That's a trout trail. The trout will cruise right next to the reeds after dark. You seldom see them there during daylight hours because it is so shallow and exposed. After dark the trout feel safe and frequent that particular stretch of shallows because of its abundance in aquatic invertebrates. In the shallow water the swimming motion of the trout will continually disturb the bottom and limit plant growth. Thus you can see the trout trail. Casting a fly right next to those weeds after dark is an excellent place to fish.

Miscellaneous Behavior Traits

There are a few aspects about trout behavior that haven't previously been mentioned or else just mentioned in passing. These behavioural traits just don't seem to properly fit anywhere else in our discussions so I've created this miscellaneous category. It is worthwhile for the fly fisher to be aware these.

Synchronised Rises

Numerous times I've been on a lake without a single fish rising and then within fifteen minutes there are fish rising all over the lake. How is this change in behavior synchronised? The answer may be a "sound trigger". With the visual trigger we saw that movement and contrast in their environment instinctively excite trout. It is also likely that the sound of a fish feeding can excite other trout into feeding.

The process of a synchronised rise may work something like this. The trout are not feeding. They are all placidly resting when two mating Mayflies fall into the water. An observant trout sees them and slurps down the first and then the second. A nearby trout hears the slurp of food being eaten. It thinks about food and becomes excited.   It mistakes a leaf floating on the surface for a tid-bit of food and rises for the leaf.

Did You Know
As if given a secret signal, the bulk of fish in a lake will begin to engage in the same activity at the same time. How this works is a mystery but likely links to their sensory perceptions and/or environmental conditions.

Another slurp and other trout become excited.   They too rise to anything that resembles food on the surface. Soon trout all over the lake are rising to the surface even if surface food isn't very abundant.

This seems to be the best explanation for synchronised rises. It seems to happen more frequently among the small opportunistic trout than the larger more experienced trout. However, they too will become involved if a food source is indeed available. When a synchronised rise starts an angler should consider using a dry line and a fly on or near the surface.

Hi Jumpers

On occasion you can observe Rainbows that aren't rising but are jumping out of the water. This generally happens when the fishing is poor and you swear that the only way you will get a fish is with a shotgun. It's sort of like the trout are jumping up to say "hi" to the anglers and taunt them. That's the reason I apply the term "hi" jumpers to this behavioural trait.

Over the years, I have been told by someone who heard it from someone that this trait is caused by trout shaking lice from their gills. Numerous times I have looked and looked for any sign of lice or another parasite in the gills or elsewhere on the fish that would verify this phenomenon. I have found internal parasites but no sign of anything external that would explain this jumping. So I have developed my own theory about this behavior.

When the trout are hi jumping the fishing is generally poor. It often happens during turnover or at times with rapid weather or water changes. To me this is an indication that changing conditions are causing some sort of stressful condition for the fish. When we discussed the anatomy of the trout we mentioned that they fill their air bladder by gulping air from the surface.

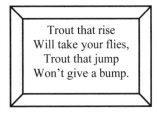

Trout that rise
Will take your flies,
Trout that jump
Won't give a bump.

I suspect that the changing conditions cause an unbalanced equilibrium in the air bladder and the trout are jumping to quickly expel or inhale air for their air bladder. In my humble opinion, this theory makes as much sense as trout trying to shake invisible lice.

Rise Lines

The range of water, light and feeding conditions that trout find preferable is fairly limited. Parts of a lake may have good feeding conditions while other parts won't. As a result, feeding trout tend to congregate in these preferred locations. Trout in other parts of the lake with unsuitable conditions simply won't feed.

Did You Know

Suitable conditions for Rainbow feeding may occur within limited areas of the lake and not at other locations. The main clue given to the angler is the sign of fish rising in these areas and not others.

An observant angler can often determine where these areas are located. Watch for signs of rising fish even if there are only a few of them. Keep track of where you see these rises. They sometimes form a "line" parallel to a certain water depth that is providing the preferred conditions. I call that string of rising fish a "rise line" but it won't necessarily follow a precise line. You may find the rises are over certain shoals, or at certain depths, or at a certain distance from a drop-off. These rise lines can come in many shapes and sizes.

Especially when fishing is slow, it helps to mark exactly where you see an occasional fish rise or jump. After a few observations you may be able to deduce if these are random or if they form a rise line. If you detect a pattern then change your location to one that allows you to cast a fly along the line of rising fish. If possible, retrieve through the rise line rather than across it. That generally means you will be casting parallel to a given water depth rather than across changing water depth. More specifically, place your fly in the water that seems to be meeting the conditions that the trout find most favourable as indicated by the pattern of rises. You may have to experiment with different lines, flies and retrieve styles until you find the right combination, but you are probably in the best location. On slow days, fishing the rise line is a good way to improve your catch odds.

Rainbow Behavior and the Angler

In this chapter we have examined what motivates Rainbows and typical behavior patterns that can be expected from the trout. The task of an angler is to assess the status of the trout and their environment, determine how that will affect the behavior of the trout and then apply this knowledge to improving your catch. It isn't an easy task but most fly fishers unconsciously do this every time they go fishing.

As a rule-of-thumb, the angler should begin an assessment by looking for the most severe or most limiting factor that is likely to affect fishing. On pristine lakes the availability of food is seldom a major limiting factor. Even if you don't see food on the surface there is usually abundant food below the surface. And trout that are well fed are usually operating fairly high up the motivational hierarchy. This means that food preference, lighting conditions, wind, water and weather conditions are more likely to be motivating the trout. After assessing the most limiting or stressful conditions, an angler can often adjust fishing techniques to compensate for those conditions based on how we expect the fish to behave. On some days we will just have to live with the fact that fishing isn't going to be good. My words of wisdom are to be observant, watch the trout, try to determine what is happening and adjust how you stalk your prey accordingly. Often it's the little things that make the difference.

6

Rainbow Feeding Considerations

Hunger is a primary motivational factor which we anglers rely on to catch fish. As fly fishers, we imitate aquatic invertebrates in the Rainbow's environment and present these to the trout and hope they are hungry. With this method of stalking our prey we intend to fool their fantastic sensory abilities and make the trout believe our fly is part of the current smorgasbord. An understanding of our prey would be far from complete without a closer look at the trout's food and some of its feeding considerations. After all, this is the most direct link between the angler and trout.

Rainbows don't instinctively know about the foods they will eat. Trout need to learn about the foods and food chain of the particular environment in which they are raised. Rainbows in lakes, for example, won't need to learn about Stoneflies or Hellgrammites since these are only found in

> **Did You Know**
> Through trial and error, a young Rainbow recently stocked into a lake must learn what to eat and what to avoid.

running water. In pristine lakes, the young trout need to learn what aquatic invertebrates are edible, which ones to avoid and which are only seasonally available. For survival, it is imperative that the trout quickly learn about all the items on the menu for its particular lake.

Like the trout, a fly fisher needs to learn about the foods and food chains of the lakes being fished. After all, a fly fisher is an angler who uses false bugs. Our flies are made to look like an aquatic invertebrate and the retrieve is designed to imitate the movement of that

> A fly fisher is an angler who uses false bugs (flies) to fool those elusive Rainbows.

invertebrate. True, we don't need to know all the details about food chains and the aquatics to catch Rainbows but a basic understanding helps. Indeed, many fly fishers are content to just throw on their favourite fly or simply look in the water and then put on any fly that looks something like an invertebrate they see on that particular day. These methods work but they fall short of optimising the potential for success. To me this approach even seems to be something a little less than fly-fishing.

Being "consistently" successful is difficult without an understanding of food chains, aquatic invertebrates and how Rainbows interact with these. As an angler of false bugs we need to understand the relationship between those bugs and the trout. In this chapter we want touch on the usual basics and then provide information you won't likely find anywhere else. Since every food chain is different, we can only provide general trends and then it's up to the angler to apply these to their specific lakes. I'm sure you will find that this chapter offers more than a basic course in aquatic entomology.

Invertebrates in Pristine Lakes

A young Rainbow that has just been stocked into a pristine lake isn't sure what to do or where its next meal is coming from. Everything is different from the fish hatchery where it was raised. After a short period of adjustment to its new surroundings the small fish develop an appetite and thus a need to feed. It won't find any of the food pellets that it received in the hatchery. The only thing that seems edible is a variety of small creatures either swimming in the water or crawling on the lake bottom. Tentatively the young trout begins to try a few of these. Through trial and error it soon learns what tastes good, what doesn't and what bites back. It is learning about the aquatic food chain and discovering which aquatic invertebrates are on the Rainbow's menu.

The Aquatic Food Chain

We covered the food chain basics near the end of Chapter 2. However, now that we are getting into the invertebrates of pristine lakes, it would be a good time to review some information regarding food chains.

➤ A food chain looks at what an organism eats and then who eats that organism.

➤ Aquatic plants only require sunlight, water and nutrients to survive. These are the primary producers and everything higher in the food chain depends on plants.

> A food chain examines what an organism eats and then who eats that organism.

➤ Grazers are critters that eat plants. Scavengers eat dead plants, grazers and other things that settle to the lake bottom. Predators hunt and eat the grazers, scavengers and other predators. Some critters fill more than one niche.

➤ Grazers live near plants which are usually found on the shoal or at the drop-off. Scavengers can live in the shallow water or in deep water if enough food settles to the lake bottom. Predators are found where sufficient quantities of grazers or scavengers are found.

➤ Algae and non-rooted plants live in the photic zone (light penetration zone) which may extend over deep water. Rooted plants, on the other hand, only live in the littoral zone. About 80% of the life in a lake occurs in the littoral zone which encompasses the shoal and drop-off.

➢ In pristine lakes, Rainbow Trout are at the top of the food chain. They feed on the grazers, scavengers and invertebrate predators. Because the vast majority of these bugs live in the littoral zone, that's where the trout go to feed.

➢ While the food chain of a lake is unique, similar lakes have similar chains. Rainbows stocked into a lake must learn about the food chain of their new home. This isn't instinctive knowledge.

➢ A Rainbow can only eat items that are smaller than about 6% of their own size. Therefore, large trout can eat large or small bugs while small trout are limited to small bugs.

Did You Know
Typically, small fish eat small bugs, in part because they are not able to swallow the bigger bugs unless they can rip it apart first.

As we begin to look at bugs and Rainbow feeding considerations, those are some of the important things to remember about food chains.

Invertebrate Life Cycles

Aquatic invertebrates go through various developmental stages in their life. For most invertebrates, Rainbows feed more readily on certain stages of the life cycle than the same bug in other stages. The eggs of invertebrates, for example, are rarely on the trout menu. The eggs of most invertebrates are just too small to be of interest to all but the smallest of newly stocked trout. However, to begin our discussions we should first have a look at what metamorphic stages of invertebrates are available to the trout.

Table 12 - Metamorphosis of Some Important Invertebrates

Invertebrate	Metamorphosis	Developmental Stages
Shrimp, Leech, Snails (non insects)	None	Egg - Immature - Sexually Mature Adult (young look like the adult)
Insects		
Dragonflies, Damselflies, Waterboatmen	Incomplete	Egg - Small Nymph - Large Nymph - Winged Adult
Chironomid, Caddis, Chaoborus, Most Terrestrials	Complete	Egg - Larva - Pupa - Winged Adult
Mayflies	Complete	Egg - Larva - Sub-Imago (Winged Pupa), and Imago (or Winged Adult)

Aquatic invertebrates typically start life as an egg. Any similarity stops after that. Some invertebrates hatch and look like a small version of their parents. The "true insects" go through stages in which they are totally unrecognizable from their parents. These changes are called metamorphosis. Metamorphosis is defined as a change of physical form, structure or substance with striking alteration of appearance, character or circumstance. The egg develops into something and that something develops into something else we call an adult. Fortunately we can categorize metamorphosis of

141

invertebrates by the way they develop. Table 12 provides the quick overview of invertebrate life cycles and how these morph from egg to adult.

Shrimp, Leech and Snails are not "insects" and do not go through metamorphosis. They hatch from an egg looking like a small version of a sexually mature adult. The fly tier can simply tie larger or smaller flies to represent the various life stages. All the rest of the important invertebrates are insects and will eventually become winged adults that generally look very different than the aquatic stages of their life cycle.

Those insects with incomplete metamorphosis hatch from the egg as a nymph. Nymphs grow larger but otherwise look much the same from the time they hatch up to the time they transform into winged adults. Again, the fly tier can simply tie larger or smaller flies to represent the nymphet stages. However, the adult stage usually looks much different than the nymph and the fly tier will need a different pattern for those. Insects with incomplete metamorphosis will swim to the water surface or shoreline weeds to emerge into adults. Waterboatmen tend to be an exception to these last two statements but this will be discussed later in more detail.

For insects with complete metamorphosis, the process is different again. When these insects hatch from an egg, they look much like a small worm and it is called a larva. The larva feeds and grows in size until it is ready to transform into an adult. At that point the general process is to

Did You Know
Aquatic invertebrates that are true insects hatch into some form of winged adult. Those that aren't insects do not.

enclose itself inside a capsule while it transforms into a pupa. The pupa is the life stage that emerges into a winged adult. The pupa most frequently looks different from either the larva or the winged adult. Transformation into adults almost always occurs at the surface of the lake rather than the shoreline weeds. For insects with complete metamorphosis the fly tier will need to tie flies representing the larva, the pupa and the adult for use at different times through the season.

That's the very quick and short entomology lesson on invertebrate life cycles. I expect that most intermediate to advanced anglers know these basics but I needed to introduce the terms for later reference. Some of these stages in the life cycle of an invertebrate will not be of importance to the angler while other will be very important.

Invertebrate Protective Mechanisms

Invertebrates are anything without a spine or backbone. In a lake, the majority of invertebrates are insects. But a lake holds many critters that are potential trout food and are not insects. There are Crustaceans such as shrimp and crayfish. There are aquatic earthworms and leeches. There are mollusks such as the clams, snails and limpets. The water mites are related to spiders and there are even spiders that live underwater. And there are a whole variety of terrestrial invertebrates that fall into a lake to become a potential meal for the trout. I frequently refer to all the combined food items of the trout as "bugs". The dictionary tells me that bugs are insects. So from a scientific perspective my use of the term "bug" is sometimes wrong.

The newly stocked Rainbow is learning what bugs to eat through a process of trial and error. It may feed on a particular item only once, but often it will eat almost anything just to see if it's edible. I have found sticks, stones, cigarette butts and a variety of critters in the stomachs of trout that aren't a normal part of their diet. The young trout will learn what to eat as well as what not to eat but it has to try a sampling first.

> **Did You Know**
> A Rainbow may only eat an item once, but at one time or another it may eat almost anything from small sticks and stones to cigarette butts.

While trout feed on almost anything at least once, they won't continuously feed on all invertebrates in the food chain. As a matter of survival, many of the invertebrates have methods to protect themselves from predation by trout. These protective mechanisms are either designed to make the invertebrate unavailable or to discourage the trout from feeding on their species.

> **Did You Know**
> Many bugs have protective mechanisms designed to protect them from predation by fish. Some of these tactics are only used during certain stages of metamorphosis.

I haven't yet provided a list of invertebrates nor the metamorphic stages that are of importance to Rainbows in pristine lakes. That is coming shortly. First, let's have a look at some of the reasons to take certain bugs off the list that's important to fly fishers. Sometimes these reasons are only applicable during certain stages of a bug's life while other reasons are only applicable to certain invertebrates. This discussion will show why we eliminate some invertebrates from the Rainbow's menu and consider others to be of limited importance or availability.

➢ **Not In The Lake** - Some invertebrates are not available to Rainbows because they are not found in lakes or in certain pristine lakes. One of my pet peeves is a fly fisher who talks about using a fly that imitates a mosquito. The mosquito must obtain its oxygen from the atmosphere through a siphon tube that extends through the surface tension of the water. Wave action swamps this process and is the reason these insects are restricted to marshes, ponds, swamps, puddles and pools with very little wave action. Mosquito larvae are not found in water with significant wave action and that includes the trout lakes. Conversely, some invertebrates such as Stoneflies, Hellgrammites, many Mayfly species and some Caddis species require the higher oxygen content provided by flowing water. They too are not found in the trout lakes. And certain lakes provide conditions for certain invertebrates that another lake won't provide. For example, freshwater shrimp tend to be found in lakes that are not acidic while water

> Many critters in a food chain are just too small to be considered important. Bugs should be about a quarter inch long before they are important to the fly fisher.

striders tend to be found in lakes that are slightly acidic.

➢ **Size** - Some invertebrates or life stages just aren't big enough to be an important food to even the smallest of trout. I have already mentioned that we aren't considering microscopic invertebrates or the eggs of any invertebrates. They are too small to be of importance. We can also eliminate Copepods, Daphnia, Cyclops and Water Mites from the list of invertebrates important to the fly fisher. The trout feed on these but it is virtually impossible to tie a fly small enough to represent these food items. Thousands of these in the trout's stomach will only look like mush.

➢ **Biting and Stinging** - Some aquatic invertebrates have mouth structures that allow them to inflict a painful bite or sting. All the true water bugs (Hemiptera) except for Waterboatman have this ability. Most of the water beetles (Coleoptera) and the hellgrammite type insects (Megaloptera) are also biters and stingers. If you have ever seen a Giant Water Bug or a Dytiscus Beetle or a true Hellgrammite you will understand why these ferocious invertebrates are not on the list of the Rainbows preferred food items. After being bitten or stung a time or two, the young trout avoid that same type of bug in the future. As a back-up protective mechanism, virtually all of these invertebrates are very hard for the trout to digest. The

> **Did You Know**
> Unless it's very hungry, a trout will not continue to feed on Backswimmers or other stinging bugs after it has tried one or two and been stung. Waterboatmen, however, do not sting and are a primary food source.

list of stinging bugs includes the Backswimmer, Giant Water Bug, Water Strider, Dytiscus beetle, Alderflies, Fishflies, and Dobsonflies. The fly fisher using flies that resemble these types of invertebrates may have hungry trout reject the offering. These bugs are occasionally found in Rainbow stomach samples but not on a regular basis unless the trout are very hungry.

➢ **Bad Taste** - If something tastes really bad it isn't likely that the trout regularly feed on it unless food is becoming scarce. We don't have any reliable documentation on what tastes good or bad to a Rainbow. But we do know that some invertebrates are preferred and thus eaten more frequently than other invertebrates. Taste is undoubtedly one of the factors in determining a trout's preference for certain invertebrates. We also know that some invertebrates intentionally exude substances to make them

> Many critters in the animal kingdom exude substances that repel predators. We don't have documentation on which aquatic invertebrates do this but it is probable that some do.

taste bad and thus avoid predation. The terrestrial Stinkbug is a good example. I'm convinced Waterboatman nymphs use this technique to avoid predation. During the summer, when the population consists almost exclusively of nymphs, the trout seldom feed on Boatmen. Either the adult Boatmen don't have this ability or the trout ignore the bad taste when the adults are available in the Spring and Fall.

Adult Dragonflies and Damselflies are rarely found in the feeding samples of Rainbows even though they frequently fall into the water. I can't be sure but I suspect that the chemical change that occurs during pupation makes these adults taste bad. I also suspect a similar process happens with leeches. The vast majority of leeches found in trout feeding samples are small and undoubtedly immature. Adult leeches are rarely found in the feeding samples. Taste and smell may be the reason that certain species of an invertebrate are preferred over other species of that same invertebrate. I realize that I'm doing some speculating and assuming in this section but it does explain the results from many stomach samples. As a suggestion, use flies to represent species of invertebrates that you regularly find in feeding samples.

➢ **Camouflage** - Most aquatic invertebrates employ camouflage as a form of protection. The most basic form is having coloration that is dark on the upper side of the body and light color on the underside. The dark blends with the dark surroundings below them when viewed from above. The lighter color on

> Not all bugs in the aquatic ecosystem are on the menu of Rainbow Trout.

the underside blends with the sky when viewed from below. Some invertebrates take camouflage a step further. Freshwater shrimp are semi-transparent and take on the coloration of what they have eaten. What they have eaten is usually the same color as the surrounding vegetation. When choosing a fly to represent a shrimp try one that closely matches the color of the nearby underwater vegetation. The Glassworm has taken camouflage transparency to the extreme. As the name implies the Chaoborus larva is almost impossible to see except in certain lighting conditions. However, as the larva transforms into a pupa, this transparency is lost and the fly fisher can imitate Chaoborus pupa the same as a Chironomid pupa. Camouflage will make an invertebrate less available to fish but not remove it from the list of invertebrates important to the fly fisher.

➢ **Concealment** - Not being noticed seems to be one of the best protection strategies afforded to all the invertebrates. When not on the move to emerge, migrate or feed, most invertebrates will stay well hidden. Areas of concealment are places that make it difficult for the trout to detect the invertebrate. Hiding under rocks and submerged logs, within the bottom substrates and among the underwater vegetation provides very good protection.

> If a trout can't find a bug then it can't feed on it.

Once I even pulled up a tangle of monofilament that contained about a hundred small Damselfly nymphs. The tangled fishing line was ideal for protection from the trout while still allowing the nymphs to feed. Wide-bodied Dragonfly nymphs will burrow into the lake bottom mud for concealment while waiting for a meal to chance by. During the summer months, Bloodworms will burrow into the stems of aquatic vegetation. Aquatic worms are usually so far buried in the mud that they are impossible for the trout find. Seldom will the invertebrates venture too far from their hiding areas.

➤ **Protective Housing** - Except for Mayflies, the insects with complete metamorphosis will build a casing or some sort of housing for protection during pupation. The Caddis and Chironomid also use protective housing during their larva stage. The casings built by the Caddis larvae are probably the best known among anglers. The type of casing can even be used to determine the species of Caddis.   In a stream environment the Caddis casing seems to offer little protection. If the Caddis is dislodged and floats downstream the trout will eat the Caddis including the casing. The same doesn't often happen in a lake environment. Seldom do the trout feed on Caddis larva within their casing in the trout lakes.

> **Did You Know**
> The larval stages of many insects build casings, tubes or other types of housing for protection from feeding fish.

Chironomid and Chaoborus also build protective housing. The larvae of most Chironomid species build mud tubes in the lake bottom. These seldom leave the mud tubes and are effectively protected from trout predation by this practice. The larva of Chaoborus will also build mud tubes in the lake bottom when it's time to pupate. The Chaoborus, Chironomid and Caddis will all seal their protective housing while pupating and are generally unavailable to the trout at these times. Other types of protective housing that the fly fisher seldom thinks about are the hard shells of clams, snails and limpets. The hard shells of some are virtually indigestible by the trout. However, some species have shells soft enough for the trout to crunch and digest. Those are the ones showing up in trout feeding samples. In pristine lakes, the fly fisher is seldom successful presenting flies that imitate invertebrates within protective housing.

> When the lighting is low, a man can expect more action.

➤ **Sensory Perception** - Water density provides many of the invertebrates with the same fine-tuned sensory abilities as Rainbow Trout (refer to Chapter 4). The hair-like structures on the legs of many aquatic invertebrates are very similar to the neuromasts of the trout's ear and lateral line. These allow the bugs to hear through their legs. Fortunately, for the trout and fly fisher, the invertebrates aren't very smart and often ignore the perception of an approaching predator. If they do respond it will often involve remaining motionless until the threat disappears or by trying to seek shelter before the predator's arrival. Either seems to offer good protection against the trout's sensory abilities.

> Bugs can detect the vibrations of an approaching predator and then seek shelter.

That provides a quick overview of typical protective mechanisms used by aquatic invertebrates. Some of these tactics effectively remove a number of critters from the trout's diet and put others on a limited availability status. Now that we have eliminated a variety of bugs that aren't "generally" of interest to the fly fisher, it's time to look at what the trout does eat.

Invertebrates On the Rainbow's Menu

Fortunately for the fly fisher, the list of important invertebrates normally on the trout's menu isn't very long. There may be many species involved but the basic types of food are somewhat limited. Table 13 provides a quick look at the basic food types that are classically found in Rainbow feeding samples over the course of a year.

Table 13 - Basic Rainbow Foods in Feeding Samples

Type of Invertebrate	Importance to the Angler	Quantity of Food in Samples	Frequency of Times in Samples
Freshwater Shrimp (or Crayfish?)	Yes	30.9%	27.7%
Chironomid (Larva, pupa or adult)	Yes	22.7%	25.0%
Caddis (Pupa or Adult)	Yes	11.5%	11.6%
Dragonfly Nymphs	Yes	6.6%	5.5%
Damselfly Nymphs	Yes	3.4%	4.1%
Waterboatmen (Adult)	Yes	5.3%	5.2%
Chaoborus (Glassworms)	Maybe	5.0%	3.2%
Mayflies (all stages)	Yes	2.7%	2.5%
Copepods, Daphnia, Cyclops and Mites	No	4.5%	4.8%
Snails & Limpets	No	3.4%	3.9%
Leeches	Maybe	1.1%	1.6%
Terrestrials	Maybe	0.5%	1.1%
All Others	Maybe	0.6%	1.1%
No Food in Trout	?	0.0%	2.5%
Baitfish	NA	None	None

The information provided in Table 13 is based on about 30 years of data and is applicable to a cross section of pristine lakes in the southern interior of British Columbia. I expect that the same general trends can be anticipated in most pristine lakes throughout North America. However, as we already said, each food chain is different and the relative quantity or frequency of these invertebrates may differ on lakes that you fish. Remember, pristine lakes don't contain baitfish.

> While the proportions may vary, pristine lakes tend to support the same basic types of aquatic invertebrates.

Most of the pristine lakes I fish contain populations of freshwater shrimp (Gammarus Shrimp) but do not contain crayfish or fairy shrimp. In lakes with crayfish or fairy shrimp, these will probably take on an importance similar to Gammarus shrimp. Also note that the abundance of Mayflies is somewhat limited in my local lakes. As we move east and away from the Pacific Coast, the importance of Mayflies becomes much greater. Many British Columbia lakes do not have the big Mayflies or the abundance of Mayfly hatches found to our east. I'm sure there are other differences throughout North America, but the percentages in Table 13 accurately reflect Rainbow feeding around the Kamloops area.

I have differentiated between the 'quantity' of food found in Rainbow feeding samples and the 'frequency' of times that food was found. A trout can feed heavily on a food item but not very often OR it can feed frequently on a food but only nibble each time. Each option could return different percentages of the trout's diet. Therefore, both are presented and for the most part are fairly consistent over a long period of time.

Another point to notice from Table 13 is that the list of invertebrates important to fly fishing in pristine lakes is not as big as you might expect. We have narrowed the Rainbows feeding list down to those given in the table and of those only seven basic types are important to the angler.

The Seven Primary Invertebrates

The seven primary foods for Rainbow Trout in pristine lakes are freshwater Shrimp, Chironomids (including bloodworms), Caddis, Dragonflies, Damselflies, Mayflies, and Waterboatmen. These seven encompass more than 80% of the trout's diet. All other foods in the Rainbows world are secondary to the angler. However, we know that a trout will eat virtually anything at various times.

> The Seven Primary Invertebrates for Fly Fishers Include:
>
> Freshwater Shrimp, Chironomid, Caddis (Sedge), Dragonfly, Damselfly, Mayfly & Waterboatman.

While Rainbows feed more frequently and in greater quantities on the seven primary invertebrates, it doesn't mean they won't feed on other foods as demonstrated in Table 13. Rainbows in a pristine lake will occasionally feed on terrestrials, for example, but they are not a primary food. A stream angler might tie a variety of flies representing different terrestrial insects because of their importance in a stream habitat. Seldom would we do the same for fishing a pristine lake. A few dry fly patterns to cover the most common terrestrials will generally suffice.

It is also worth mentioning that freshwater Shrimp, Chironomids and Caddis make up more than 65% of a trout's diet. A fly fisher that simply had flies representing the various stages and sizes of these three bugs would do pretty well on most days. It isn't a bad idea to tailor your fly box to an assortment of flies that reflect the relative portions of the primary seven and then throw in some attractor flies to cover the bases.

In the next chapter, we will examine these seven primary invertebrates in more detail including the various stages in their life cycle that are important. Before we do that, there are other considerations about the trout's menu that we have yet to examine.

The Availability of Aquatic Invertebrates

A specific species of bug may not be on the Rainbows menu throughout the ice free period even if it is one of the seven primary invertebrates. We have mentioned some of the protective mechanisms and other reasons that trout won't feed on certain bugs at certain times. But there is more to it, especially among the true insects.

Each bug on the trout's menu is "available" to greater or lesser degrees throughout the season depending on a number of factors. By availability, I mean subject to predation by the trout and thus of importance to the fly fisher. Let's quickly examine some of these.

<u>Size</u> – We have already mentioned that very small invertebrates aren't important to the trout or the angler. However, there is an opposite side to that. The larger the invertebrate, the more likely it is to become a meal for the trout. Large invertebrates create larger vibrations in the water making them

> A few big bugs will fill a trout much faster than many small bugs.

easier for detection by the Bow's lateral line. Also, bigger bugs can't hide as well within the vegetation making them easier to see. As invertebrates grow in size, they become more available and subject to predation by the trout.

<u>Numbers</u> – The number of eggs laid by a species of aquatic invertebrate are in the thousands if not millions. Most manage to hatch into young bugs too small for the trout but still a food source for other predatory invertebrates. With each passing day, they grow in size but there are fewer and fewer of the original brood due to predation and natural mortality. In terms of availability, the greater the quantity of individuals, the greater the availability to the trout and the more likely it is that the trout will feed on that bug. The very small Daphnia, for example, are usually ignored by the trout. However, in late summer, Daphnia are sometimes in a lake by the billions and the trout will actively feed on these because of their high population density and sometimes because other foods are scarce at that time of year.

> **Fishing Tip**
> Examine the lake for aquatics and select flies that represent currently available bugs. The availability of an invertebrate can change daily and sometimes hourly.

<u>Hibernation</u> – Many aquatic invertebrates hibernate through the winter months when ice is on the lake. They typically burrow into the lake bottom muck in deeper water and aren't available as a trout food at that time. Different bugs go into or come out of hibernation at different times. This means they will be available earlier or later in the spring or fall.

<u>Sheltering</u> – Throughout the season, various bugs are not available to the trout because they are hiding in places where the trout are unable to locate them. Wide-bodied dragonfly nymphs generally hide in the lake bottom muck except when migrating. Many species of Chironomid larva build mud tubes in the lake bottom

muck where they feed and grow. Other species of Chironomid larva (typically Bloodworms) burrow into the stems of underwater plants. In both cases these larva are not available to the trout at that time. The Caddis larva builds a casing that trout seem to avoid in pristine lakes. And most aquatic invertebrates tend to hide within weeds and debris unless they need to leave for feeding, mating, migrating or some other reason. When sheltering, invertebrates are not readily available to the trout.

Hibernation Migrations – Some invertebrates, such as Dragonflies and Damselflies, migrate to deep water in the fall to hibernate and then migrate from the deep water to the shallows in the spring after they awake from hibernation. These migrations often involve large numbers of individuals and that attracts the attention of the fish. Since they must leave their hiding places to make these treks, invertebrates are easy prey during migrations.

Hatch Migrations – Some aquatics will migrate from their locations on the shoal or drop-off into the shoreline weeds to hatch into adults. Damselflies make this trip en masse while Dragonflies tend to spread this migration over several weeks. In both cases, the bugs are exposed and more available to predation. Waterboatmen, Mayflies and Caddis will often gather in localized areas prior to a hatch or swarming flight. This isn't really a migration so much as congregating for a common purpose. However, the bugs are more obvious and thus more available to the trout at these times.

> **Fishing Tip**
> Hatch migrations and hatches are when bugs are most vulnerable to predation and when the trout prefer to feed. These are usually good times for the fly fisher. However, in very large hatches the anglers fly can become lost among so many actual bugs and fishing can be difficult.

Hatches – Those invertebrates with complete metamorphosis need to get from the lake bottom to the water surface to transform into adults. They float or swim upward and leave their protective shelter. They are totally exposed in the water column at this time and individual bugs are as big as they are going to get. This makes them an easy target for predatory trout. Once on the surface, these bugs must sit for a while until they shed their pupal skin and transform into an adult. Again, they are an easy target for trout. During hatches, insects are very available and become a preferred item on the trout's menu.

Mating – Naturally, insects that become winged adults and mate outside the water aren't available to the trout unless they fall into the lake. However, freshwater Shrimp and Waterboatmen mate within the lake. To increase the likelihood of finding a mate, these bugs tend to gather in specific locations. The concentrations of bugs attract the trout and make predation easy. The Shrimp leave their hiding

> **Did You Know**
> In pristine lakes, dry flies usually represent insects emerging into adults, those that are laying eggs or bugs that have fallen into the water.

places and swim in tandem providing the trout a two-for-one meal. For the fly fisher, unfortunately, it won't take long before the trout have eaten their fill under these conditions.

Egg Laying – Several types of aquatic invertebrate lay eggs on the water surface after mating. They are somewhat available to the trout during this process. I say somewhat because they tend to rapidly travel across the water surface while dropping eggs and the trout must be in a good location to get the bug into its visual window. Caddis and Chironomids are most known for this. Mayflies tend to drop their eggs while in flight above the water and are not available. However, the Mayflies will die within hours of laying eggs and their bodies will float on the surface providing an easy target for foraging trout.

Molting – Most aquatic invertebrates have hard chitinous shells that must be shed and replaced periodically through their life. Without these shells, the bug is highly susceptible to predation by other bugs. As the shells are shed, the chemical smells of a bug are transmitted into the water alerting the trout of a nearby meal. Instinctively knowing their vulnerability, invertebrates seek secure hiding places to molt. Molting occurs at much the same time for invertebrates of the same age and species. If a molting bug is well hidden, it isn't available to the trout. However, if the bug picked a poor hiding place, the trout can locate the bug through smell and enjoy a meal.

Moon Cycles – Many factors regarding the availability of specific aquatics are controlled by the life span and the season. However, fine tuning of this timing and availability is often linked to a phase of the moon. Migrations, hatches, mating, egg laying and molting are some of the things that the bug's biological clock may link to specific lunar phases to increase it's chance of survival. Thus, the moon often plays a part in the availability of food for the trout.

Time of Day – Invertebrates have different times of day in which they are active. The active time of day changes with the type of bug, time of year and stage in the life cycle. An active bug is more likely to be in open water and thus available to the trout. Times of day preferences for the primary invertebrates are provided in Chapter 7.

Life Span – The timing of an invertebrate's availability through the various conditions described above will largely depend on the life span of a given species. As a rule-of-thumb, the bigger the bug the longer it must live to attain that size. Small Chironomids, for example, will typically have several generations through the season while the large Chironomids may only have one or two generations. Most Damselflies, Caddis and Waterboatmen will have one generation in a season. The flat-bodied Dragonflies tend to live a couple of years in the lake while the large

> As a rule-of-thumb, the larger the bug, the longer it lives.

Darner Dragonflies will live about four years as an aquatic nymph. These varieties in life spans make different critters available to the trout over different time frames.

That provides a quick run down on some of the factors affecting the availability of Rainbow foods. I would like to show this for one species and will use a Damselfly with a one season life span for the example as shown in Figure 27.

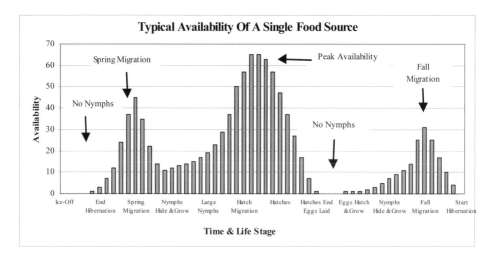

Figure 27 - Typical Food Source Availability During a Season

In this example, the Damselfly is not available during the winter. Young nymphs hibernate through this period and are out of reach of predators. After ice-off the water begins to warm, the nymphs come out of hibernation in deep water and migrate toward the shallows. At this time their population is plentiful and they are exposed as they migrate. Trout will readily feed on the nymphs even though they are fairly small. As they reach the shallows, they hide in the weeds limiting their availability. As they grow in size they become more noticeable. The trout eat more and more of a population that is steadily being reduced. Just prior to emerging into an adult, the nymphs are at their maximum size and they must swim to the shoreline weeds to hatch. It is at this

> **Did You Know**
> Most aquatic insects hatch, lay eggs and die in the spring to mid-summer. That leaves a period in the late summer when numerous aquatics are in the egg to new hatchling stage. Trout food becomes a little scare and the timing coincides with the period known as the summer downers.

time that the population reaches its peak availability as a trout food. As the nymphs emerge over several days or weeks, their numbers rapidly decline and the trout do not feed on the Damselfly adults. By the time the last nymph emerges many eggs have been laid but those are too small to be available to the trout. At this point the graph shows the Damselflies are not an available food. Eggs hatch and new nymphs emerge but are generally too small to be of importance. Just before fall hibernation, the

> Don't plan your evening meal around a fish you haven't yet caught.

Damselfly nymphs migrate to deep water in great numbers. They have grown in size and during migration have left their protective shelter. This provides the trout with one last chance to feed on Damselflies for the season.

Figure 27 shows this simple version of invertebrate availability to trout predation. If we added a second species of Damselfly to the graph that had two generations per year and a different number of individuals in the brood, you can imagine how the graph could change. The peaks, troughs and timing could be totally different. Graphs containing multiple species tend to average between the species or types of bugs. Remember this point when examining graphs presented in this text.

Artificial Flies as Invertebrates

There is something else in the lake that trout take as food. We haven't yet mentioned the "pseudo-bugs" or as most people call them, artificial flies. Naturally, these aren't real bugs but the trout consider them as food.

Through this text I have mentioned imitator and attractor fly patterns. Before we get too much further, we should discuss a little bit about these. We often think a fly is supposed to duplicate or give the impression of being one particular type of invertebrate. Often, we fish and retrieve a fly to imitate one of the seven primary invertebrates. However, many very productive flies are not designed to imitate. Some are designed to attract the fish and can be fished in a variety of ways. Essentially, there are two basic designs of flies used on pristine lakes. Following are quick definitions.

> Ten minutes per fly
> Then give another a try.
> If the fly was right,
> Your line would be tight.

➤ **Imitator Flies** – Those flies designed to duplicate or give an impression of being one particular aquatic invertebrate. Examples are flies that look like a Chironomid Pupa, Shrimp or Caddis Adult.

➤ **Attractor Flies** – Those flies that don't look like a specific bug. They may look like two or more invertebrates (examples: Half Back, Idaho Nymph, Doc Spratley) or they may not resemble an invertebrate (examples: Royal Coachman, Leech or Wooley Worm).

Each type of fly can produce excellent results and satisfies a specific fishing need. Imitator flies are best when the trout are actively feeding and you have identified the particular invertebrate being eaten. An imitator fly fools the trout into thinking it's another one of those bugs currently on the menu. The trout usually inhale these bits of food and the angler experiences very soft strikes.

> If what you are trying isn't working, then try something else.

Attractor flies that look "buggy" are sometimes called Representational Flies. They can represent several types of bugs. The Half Back, for example, can represent a Mayfly Nymph, a Caddis Pupa, a dark Damselfly Nymph, a small Dragonfly Nymph or even a Chironomid if retrieved as such. The fly looks enough like each of these bugs that the trout will key in on the aspects it is looking for and assume your fly is that particular bug. With representational attractor flies, the trout fools itself into

153

thinking it is the bug currently on the menu. Strikes on representational flies are often soft like imitator flies.

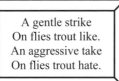

A gentle strike
On flies trout like.
An aggressive take
On flies trout hate.

Attractor flies that don't especially look like a bug are often good when the trout are fairly inactive or when the fishing is slow. These flies tend to stimulate the trout into a strike via their visual trigger. The Royal Coachman, for example, doesn't look like a bug but provides visual contrast enticing the trout to investigate and strike. Leech patterns are usually large and create a wake in the water. Especially with rapid movement, this fly stimulates the trout's visual trigger. Leech patterns do not look or move anything like a leech. Some folks would say that a Wooley Worm imitates a Caddis larva but these larvae seldom leave their protective casing. Actually the hackles around this fly create vibrations in the water that the trout investigate and are then stimulated to strike. When trout strike attractor flies it is often a hard aggressive strike.

Using imitator flies to catch fish is probably the most satisfying and rewarding method. However, if you choose the wrong bug to imitate, you may go for long periods between strikes. If a specific bug is desired, the same thing can happen if you choose an attractor fly that doesn't look like a bug. Frequently the most successful flies are those that represent two

Fishing Tip
When the Bows are feeding, many types of flies will catch fish. When they aren't, most flies are rejected. It's the in between times that an angler must choose just the right fly.

or more types of invertebrates. If your fly has a key visual component of a bug the trout are after, they will usually take the attractor fly.

De-barb your fly before trying it on as en earring or catching a fish you intend to release.

Over the last five years, two-thirds of my fish have been taken on representational flies. I have found that a fly that represents two or more bugs is often more effective than putting on the wrong imitator fly. It isn't always possible to determine what to imitate. Some folks use Chironomid patterns consistently and often have good success because the trout so frequently feed on Chironomids. However they could probably improve their success by trying other imitations, representations or attractor flies as conditions dictate.

Many fly tiers will meticulously try to match the color of a bug being imitated. However, when we discussed the Rainbow's vision and what happens to color in water, we found that color changes with depth and water clarity. Except for Shrimp, Bloodworms and dry flies, most of my flies are black or very dark in color. I gave up trying to match color a number of years ago and it hasn't affected my success rate. As a note of interest, over the last five years, 86% of my Rainbows have been taken on black or very dark flies. If you think about it, Boatmen, Mayflies, Chironomid, Dragonfly nymphs and many types of Caddis are either black or mostly dark in color.

Frequently, flies must be presented on or near the bottom in order to get the trout interested. However, my favourite line is a dry line because it allows for a very slow retrieve. In water that is even moderately deep it can take a long time to get a fly down to depth on the floating line. I tend to get impatient and so I tie most of my flies with weighting on the hook. A few wraps of thin stainless steel wire around the hook before tying the fly is usually all it takes to get the fly and leader to sink without waiting forever. I would suggest that you keep weighted flies separate from flies that aren't weighted. It helps to know what type of fly you are putting on which type of fly line.

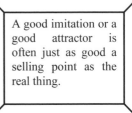

A good imitation or a good attractor is often just as good a selling point as the real thing.

That's a very quick overview of pseudo-bugs. It quickly explains what we are talking about when mentioning attractor versus imitator flies or flies that are weighted.

Rainbow Feeding Patterns

In this section, I would like to examine a couple of specific points about Rainbow feeding. When discussing nutrient balance in Chapter 5, the concept of preferred foods was introduced. I would like to discuss that a little further. In addition, I would like to discuss how often a Rainbow eats assuming the lake has a plentiful supply of food.

Rainbow Food Preferences

Table 13 on page 147 provided us with the relative quantities of food that Rainbows eat over the course of a season. However, it isn't likely that a trout will eat those precise quantities over any given week. Food availability plays an important role in what the trout eat. If a food isn't available, it can't be eaten. But, trout also seem to prefer some foods to others when given a choice.

An angler first notices this preference when trout take one fly pattern and ignore another even though they represent the same invertebrate. The different fly patterns will be slightly different in size or shape and the trout will only be interested in that one particular pattern. The trout probably prefers that fly because it has the visual keys for a specific species of the invertebrate the trout are seeking. I have observed this happening during Chironomid and Caddis hatches more than most other invertebrates. Then again, those two types of bugs have numerous species in the lake.

Rainbows need certain proteins and amino acids that specific bugs provide at certain times of the year and trout unconsciously switch to those bugs.

Aquatic invertebrates are made up of various types and combinations of proteins and amino acids. These combinations will change from one species of bug to the next.

155

Even as a bug goes through different developmental stages, the protein and amino acid mixture can change. It seems likely that these different combinations produce bugs of a different flavor. We like or dislike certain tastes and prefer one flavor of ice cream to another. Why shouldn't Rainbows also have likes, dislikes or preferences?

Similar to the bugs, Rainbows are made up of various combinations of proteins and amino acids. The trout's body can produce some of these regardless of what the trout

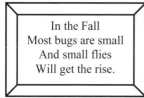

In the Fall
Most bugs are small
And small flies
Will get the rise.

is eating but others are obtained directly from the trout's food. If a trout is lacking certain chemicals, it may get a craving to eat a particular type of food high in the proteins or amino acids needed. Much like a pregnant woman, the trout will seek out specific foods to satisfy the craving.

Food preference isn't a constant. As discussed in Chapter 5, the Rainbows will follow behavior patterns depending on the degree of hunger. As feeding conditions improve, Rainbows will follow a sequential process in determining which invertebrates get on their "preferred list". Following is a quick look at how this process works and progresses from difficult times to times of plenty.

1. In difficult times the trout will feed on almost anything.
2. As conditions improve, the trout will feed on invertebrates that don't have protective mechanisms that actively repel the trout such as those that sting or taste bad.
3. Then, trout feed on invertebrates that are easily available. In other words, anything that can be located, provides a good meal and isn't too hard to catch.
4. As food becomes more abundant, trout tend to seek out those invertebrates that are larger. The bigger invertebrates fill the stomach quicker with less energy consumption and are targeted by the trout.
5. Finally, as food becomes plentiful, the trout will target invertebrates that have the particular taste, proteins and amino acids that the trout are seeking, especially if these have previously been in short supply.

As we move from step 1 through step 5, angling success becomes harder. The trout are becoming more selective and eventually they only feed on invertebrates that are preferred.   However,   there   are   complex interactions in the process just like we find with the entire food chain. For example, the trout may be seeking a specific species of Chironomid for its chemical content even though it is smaller or relatively scarce compared to other Chironomids emerging at the same time. If the trout is lacking the proteins or amino acids offered by the smaller Chironomid, then it will probably target that

Fishing Tip
Watch for minor components of the food chain that are currently available and be prepared to switch to those if the main food items aren't of interest to the trout.

species. A fly fisher should watch for these less abundant species in a hatch and try a fly to imitate those if imitations to match the main hatch aren't working.

Invertebrate size is often a consideration in getting on the trout's preferred list. The bigger bugs tend to be preferred over the smaller bugs. For example, you and I tend to select the bigger grapefruit from the supermarket bin in preference to the smaller ones. Rainbows tend to do the same thing. The trout also tend to prefer those invertebrates that are the easiest to find and catch. If a Shrimp is hidden within the weeds and a Chironomid is slowly drifting part way up the water column, the trout will most likely take the Chironomid. It is easiest to find and catch.

If the trout have been feeding on a particular invertebrate for a long time, it tends not to be on the trout's preferred list. After extensive feeding on one type of bug, the trout get tired of it. They will happily switch to another type of bug to vary their diet. The angler should watch for new sources of food as they come on the menu. The trout are likely to switch to this new food as soon as it becomes available, but gradual transitions sometimes occur. The wise angler will always watch for new and different foods.

Rainbows seem to prefer items that have recently been added to the menu. Discard that old saying of "Match the Hatch" and replace it with "Match the New Hatch".

Feeding Intervals

Near the end of Chapter 3, we discussed the growth of Rainbows. We said that the average growth rate of a trout is around one pound per year in typical pristine lakes. We examined metabolic rates, weight gain ratios and we found out how much a trout's stomach can hold. With that kind of information, can we determine how frequently a trout must feed for body maintenance plus average growth?

I consulted the internet, various texts and research journals to see if I could find something on trout feeding intervals. I ran into my same old malaise with research information. Researchers have a fixation for using small trout under artificial conditions to do their research. The reports tended to indicate that all fish fed at least once per day and needed to eat about 2% of their body weight for typical growth. But the information was generally based on studies involving fish of 100 grams (3.5 ounces) or less in size. When I projected that information into larger size categories of trout, it just didn't make sense. The information might be applicable to fry but certainly couldn't be used for large fish. So I began to develop my own information based on any reliable data I could find.

Following are some of the reliable factors we know regarding the feeding intervals of Rainbows.

- ➤ We know that large trout feed less frequently than a small trout.
- ➤ We know that the stomach of a large trout is most often empty when that trout first begins a major feed.
- ➤ If a preferred food is available and abundant, the trout will usually eat as much as it can. That amounts to about 6% of its body weight.

➤ If food is scarce or hard to catch, the trout will feed to something less than its maximum capacity.

➤ When finished feeding, the trout will find someplace to rest while it digests the meal. These resting-places are most frequently in cool deep water and in the summer that will be near or below the thermocline.

➤ In cool water, the metabolism and digestion rate of trout is slowed. In water near freezing, it will take a small trout about nine days to digest its food. At optimum temperature levels, digestion takes one or two days. Digestion proportionally speeds up with increasing water temperature.

➤ Because it is cold-blooded, a trout does not need to maintain a minimum core body temperature like warm-blooded animals. Allowing the body temperature to fluctuate with the surrounding environment allows more food energy to be directed toward growth in the trout.

> **Did You Know**
> When a Steelhead migrates upriver to spawn, it may go for six months or more without a meal and still survive to return to the ocean.

➤ Small quantities of food, such as in the stomach of a small trout, will be processed faster than large quantities of food.

➤ A small trout must eat about three ounces of food to gain one ounce in weight (food to weight gain ratio of 3:1). A large trout must eat about 5 ounces of food, to put on that same ounce in weight (food to weight gain ratio of 5:1). This is because the larger body mass of big Rainbows requires more energy for maintenance.

➤ Especially while inactive, a slow digestion rate will allow the trout to maintain bodily functions as well as grow in size.

➤ Shortly after all the food has been digested, the trout will return to its feeding grounds to obtain another meal and repeat the process.

➤ The interval of time between feeds will be directly proportional to fish size and water temperature. If the period between feeds is too long, all the energy goes into maintaining the trout and nothing is left over for growth.

➤ The feeding cycle might be interrupted by an opportunity to feed that the trout just can't pass up but the trout is more likely to be lured out of the cycle when the stomach or intestines are nearly empty rather than just after a major feeding event.

Those are just some of the considerations needed to estimate the feeding intervals of Rainbow Trout. I have merged the feeding process outlined above with some of the research data to come up with the following table on feeding intervals. Naturally, we can't predict precisely when the trout will

> **Did You Know**
> Rainbow of a quarter pound will likely feed at least once a day while Rainbows over five pounds may go several weeks between feeds.

feed. To a large degree, it depends on when a previous feeding event occurred and how much food was consumed at that time. However, we can provide some general trends based on the size of the Rainbows. If you observe a certain size class of trout feeding, you may be able to estimate when those same fish are due for their next major feeding event. My estimates of feeding intervals are provided in Table 14.

Table 14 – Feeding Interval Trends for Rainbow Trout

Trout Size	Trout Size	Maximum Stomach Content 6%	Food to Weight Ratio*	Feeding Interval If Previous at 100% of Maximum	Feeding Interval If Previous at 67% of Maximum	Feeding Interval If Previous at 33% of Maximum
Pounds	Ounces	Food Ounces	X oz to 1 oz	Days	Days	Days
0.125	2	0.12	2.89	0.9	0.6	**0.3**
0.25	4	0.24	3.01	1.8	1.2	**0.6**
0.50	8	0.48	3.23	3.4	2.3	**1.1**
0.75	12	0.72	3.42	4.8	3.2	**1.6**
1.0	16	0.96	3.57	6.1	**4.1**	**2.0**
1.5	24	1.44	3.82	8.6	**5.8**	2.8
2.0	32	1.92	4.02	10.9	**7.3**	3.6
2.5	40	2.40	4.18	13.1	**8.8**	4.3
3.0	48	2.88	4.30	15.3	**10.2**	5.0
3.5	56	3.36	4.41	**17.4**	**11.6**	5.7
4.0	64	3.84	4.50	**19.5**	**13.0**	6.4
4.5	72	4.32	4.57	**21.5**	14.4	7.1
5.0	80	4.80	4.64	**23.6**	15.8	7.8
6.0	96	5.76	4.75	**27.7**	18.5	9.1
7.0	112	6.72	4.83	**31.7**	21.2	10.5
8.0	128	7.68	4.90	**35.7**	23.9	11.8

* The number of ounces of food needed to gain one ounce of weight.

For Table 14, if the fish you observe feeding are gorging themselves (filling their tummy to maximum) then they are feeding at the 100% of maximum level. If these fish were about three pounds then we estimate their next major feed would occur in about 15.3 days. If the fish are about one pound and nibbling at their food (33% of maximum?) then we estimate their next major feed would occur in about 2.0 days. The shaded areas show the most likely trends since small trout are more likely to feed sporadically while the large trout are more likely to feed to maximum capacity and then rest for long periods.

> **Did You Know**
>
> Rainbows that have a small head in relation to their body size are growing fast. Rainbows that have a large head proportional to body size are being deprived of food and are slow growing.

This table is not likely to allow you to pinpoint the next major feed. That's partially because we don't usually know consumption rates and partially because these are only estimates during typical summer conditions. While this information is not precise, it is important for the angler to realize some of the implications.

159

Knowing when key feeding events are happening on a lake will help you to succeed. Since these larger fish need more food to fill their tummy, they tend to target specific hatches or prime times of invertebrate availability. Often, big trout target large insects, especially when there are lots of them. Some of the pertinent information about specific bugs is provided in Chapter 7. However, it's a good idea for the knowledgeable fly fisher to keep records of approximately when certain hatches occur on specific lakes.

Environmental Influences on Rainbow Feeding

As long as we're examining factors affecting Rainbow feeding, we should look at some of the environmental influences such as weather and water conditions. Anyone who has angled for awhile knows that weather and water conditions play a role in fish feeding and thus catching fish.

> If you upgrade to equipment that is more expensive you will find your success decreases proportional to the cost of that equipment.

The data used in the following is based on my fishing records since 1976. The data includes information for all pristine lakes I fish, at all elevations and for the entire fishing season. That means it's an average and typical of what you can expect. However, when we discuss the specific bugs in Chapter 7, you will see that preferences for weather and water conditions will differ among the invertebrates. In turn, that will affect when the trout feed on each.

Seasonal Influences

The time of year affects Rainbow feeding. Early Spring is about the worst time of year for fishing even though many folks complain about the summer downers. In the Spring, various lakes are going into turnover which forces trout into physical stress and inhibits their feeding activities. The graph on the right side of Figure 28 shows the frequency of fishing success with April and May being below average. The number of hours with strikes isn't very good. However, the quantity of fish, as shown in the left side graph, is about average in the spring. That tells us that we can angle for a number of days in the Spring without success but when we do have success, the fish are usually plentiful.

> Fishing success is getting a strike, not necessarily landing the fish.

By way of explanation, I count "success" as having a strike, not necessarily landing the fish. If I'm able to get the trout interested enough to take a fly, it shows the fish was interested in feeding and it's probably my fault if I didn't land it. You may also be interested to know that 50% of all strikes result in a landed fish. If my daily average drops below that, then I'm doing something wrong.

But getting back to seasonal feeding trends, the graphs also show that fishing in the Fall is more productive than average. The number of strikes per hour (quantity) and the number of hours with strikes (frequency) is generally better than other times of the year. What the graphs don't tell you is that the proportion of small fish (less than a pound) is much higher in the fall. I won't show another graph for this. But when the numbers of small fish are graphed, their numbers are proportionally higher after September 1st. This makes sense because the fingerlings stocked in the spring are growing large enough to take a fly by Fall.

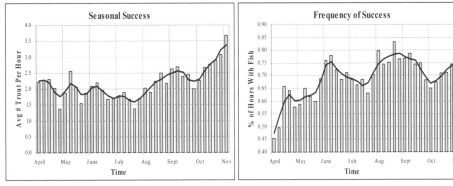

Figure 28 – Seasonal Angling Success

Lunar Influences

The moon plays a big part in Rainbow feeding. Most folks aren't aware of the influence the moon has on Rainbows and invertebrates. I'm not talking about Moon Tables or the Sol-lunar Tables you see in magazines or pamphlets that provide the time of day to fish. For pristine lakes, I haven't found any correlation between the moon's place and the time of day that fish are feeding or active. But there are days during the moon's cycle that bugs and fish are more or less active. Some of this activity can be narrowed down to daytime or evening but not down to 10:57am, for example.

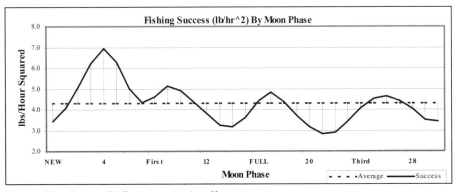

Figure 29 – Lunar Influences on Angling

Figure 29 shows fishing success by day of the moon. The best all around angling occurs from moon days 2 through 11. The Old Farmer's Almanac also lists this period around the First Quarter moon as the best fishing. It's nice to have someone confirm my information. There is a word of caution about the success shown just after the Full moon and before the New moon in this graph. Small fish often feed just after the full moon or before the new moon. That places more importance on those two periods than is actually justified. The best overall fishing is around the First Quarter moon.

Again, I'm not going to show the additional graphs but there are a couple of more points about the moon's influence on Rainbow feeding. The larger trout (over 2 lbs.) follow much the same pattern as Figure 29. The best fishing for bigger fish occurs from moon day 1 thru 10. This is also the prime time for Chironomids. Conversely, the most abundant insect hatches occur around the new moon from moon days 25 thru 5. Many aquatics prefer the dark of the moon to hatch.

Time of Day Influences

As plants photosynthesize, the oxygen content in a lake steadily increases over the day. With a minor exception, that general trend is reflected in the fishing success during a day. Fishing is generally poor in the morning compared with the afternoon and evening.

Figure 30 shows fishing success by time of day. The average line is like a rolling regression line and considers the number of hours fished for each time of day. The number of hours fished after 11pm are somewhat low and that's why the

> At night don't stay
> If fishing is good in the day.
> At night you should go
> If daytime fishing is slow.

average line drops well below the calculated bar graph. I'm not an early morning angler so the graph only starts at 8am. My guess is that fishing success would increase around sunrise but probably not to the same levels as mid afternoon.

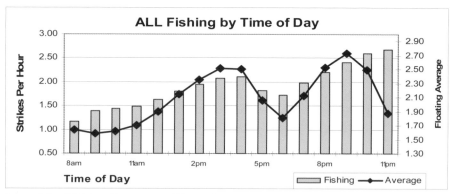

Figure 30 – Fishing Success by Time of Day

Fishing success is about 30% better in the evening (after 7pm) than it is for the rest of the day. I'm at a loss to explain why success decreases from 5 to 7 pm. However, that decline shows for each month graphed except April and May. Maybe it's just a lull as the daytime fish are changing shifts with the evening fish.

I've also noticed that when fishing is good during the day, it is often poor in the evening. And it works in reverse. When daytime fishing is poor then evening fishing is often good.

The Influence of Wind Direction

One day I was thinking about that old saying "wind from the east and fishing is least but wind from the west and fishing is best", so I decided to check it out. A very strong graph emerged from my computer that strongly reinforces that old saying.

As shown in Figure 31, fishing is far better when the wind is blowing from the westerly or southerly quadrants than when it's blowing from the easterly or northerly quadrants. The two bars at the right side of the graph are for winds that are "variable" in direction (frequently changing) or when the wind is calm (no wind).

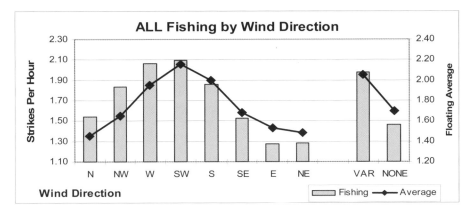

Figure 31 – Fishing Success by Wind Direction

Rainbows and bugs shouldn't be influenced by wind direction. From their underwater world, the direction of surface waves would be their only clue to wind direction. And that shouldn't have an underwater impact. I have tried to find reliable or even reasonable explanations for this phenomenon without success. Even more puzzling is that virtually every one of the seven primary invertebrates shows the same general trend.

Wind direction is determined by the counter clockwise movement of passing weather systems. As a system approaches, the winds would usually be from the south. After the center of the system passes, the winds would be from the north. It also makes a difference whether the center of the system is north or south of your location. But it's the same system. None of this explains to me why wind direction has such a significant impact on trout and the bugs they feed on.

The Influence of Wind Strength

How strong the wind blows is another factor affecting Rainbow feeding. Fishing can be difficult when the wind is calm. A smooth surface on the lake allows sunlight to penetrate full force. Ripples and waves on the lake surface will interrupt the sunlight and reduce the light intensity.   We already know that Rainbows and many invertebrates prefer lower light levels. Winds also cause water movement that may stir some food up off the lake bottom.

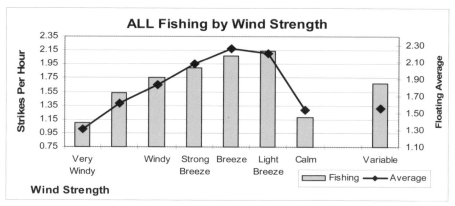

Figure 32 – Wind Strength and Fishing

Fishing tends to be reasonably good with winds ranging from a light breeze through windy conditions.   When it gets very windy, fishing success drops off, partly because of the fly fisher's inability to place and then control the fly under those conditions. In strong winds, boats turn and fly lines drift. But in fairness to the graph, many

> A mild to strong breeze
> And trout feed with ease.
> But wind calm or strong,
> They won't feed for long.

of the insects that hatch on the lake surface are reluctant to do so in certain adverse weather conditions. For a limited time they can postpone a hatch and can detect wind strength through wave vibrations transmitted into the water. Freshwater Shrimp and Dragonfly nymphs tend to fish better than most other aquatics in very windy conditions.

Air Temperature Effects

Figure 33 shows the influence of air temperature on fishing. As you might expect, fishing success decreases as the weather gets warmer. Warm to hot days are typically associated with mid-summer and the summer downers along with cloudless days with lots of sunlight. Warm days also mean warming water temperatures. All these factors can result in poorer fishing and the air temperature graph confirms that. Of interest in this graph is the decreased success as we go from cool to cold days. Fewer bugs are available on cold days than might be found on days that are cool to mild. Even then, cold days often produce better fishing than hot days. Mayflies are the most notable exception to this graph. They fish well in hot weather with cool water.

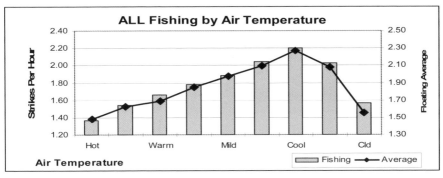

Figure 33 – Air Temperature and Fishing

The Influence of Clouds

We said at the start of this section that these graphs show the average for all fishing. The graph for fishing by cloud cover (Figure 34) demonstrates how this averaging can eliminate or miss some important trends.

> The chance of rain is increased by 90% if you forgot to take your rain coat.

Because this graph includes all fishing, the trend line is almost flat indicating that cloud cover is of little importance. However, the same graph for each of the seven primary invertebrates shows something different. Waterboatmen, Mayflies, Damselflies and Leech patterns fish well when the skies are clear or have a light cloud cover. Caddis, Bloodworms and Dragonflies fish better when the skies are cloudy. Chironomids fish best under skies that are partially cloudy. The averaged result shows little difference. Other considerations being equal, an experienced fly fisher might even consider selecting flies based on the level of cloud cover.

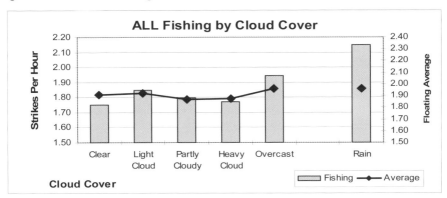

Figure 34 – The Influence of Cloud Cover

An interesting point emerges from the cloud cover graph. Fishing is good on days with rain. The data includes the time fished before and/or after a rain. The rain is typically light or of short duration. Even I won't fish in a heavy rainstorm.

Barometric Pressure and Fishing

I've always heard it said that you should fish a high or rising barometer and that fishing is poor when the barometer is low or falling. I haven't found that to be true. However, there is a word of caution about the data in Figure 35. I use visual indicators to determine what the barometer is doing rather than

> An angler's best success is often in the absence of any witnesses.

actual readings of barometric pressure. Indicators such as leaves on trees turning over, sunny skies, clouds, rain and winds were all used. It was the best I could obtain under the circumstances. So don't rule out barometric pressure as an influence.

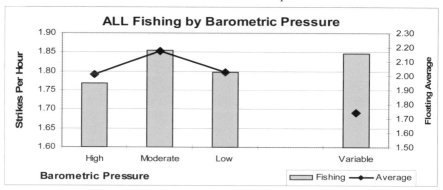

Figure 35 – Fishing by Barometric Indicators

Some averaging has once again occurred in this graph. Shrimp, for example, seem to be a bigger item on the trout's menu under low barometric conditions while Boatmen definitely prefer a high barometer. A changing or variable barometer seems to produce good fishing whether it was rising or falling.

Water Temperature Influences

Trout are cold blooded and don't like warm water. When I sample water temperature, it is just at the lake surface. Trout can usually go deep to find temperatures cool enough but even the surface temperature affects trout feeding. Trout mostly feed over the shoals and those are shallow enough to be affected by warm surface water temperatures.

Most aquatic bugs live on the shoals and are cold blooded critters. They can't easily move into the thermocline to find suitable water. Warm surface temperatures probably affect the aquatic invertebrates to a larger degree than the trout. The

> Flashlight batteries only die after you decide to fish after dark.

only bug consistently on the trout's menu in warmer water is the Caddis. Mayflies, Boatmen and Bloodworms are barely on the trout's menu in warm water.

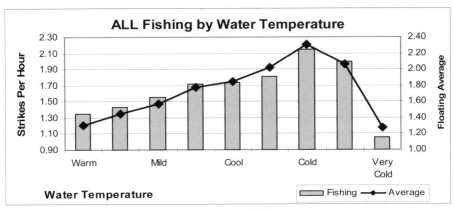

Figure 36 – Water Temperature Affects on Fishing

Water temperature is very cold just before ice-over and just after ice-off. At these temperatures, lots of bugs are going into hibernation or, conversely, may not have come out of hibernation. Many invertebrates aren't readily available and this affects the fishing under very cold water conditions.

The Influence of Water Clarity

The effects of water clarity on Rainbow feeding and fishing activity is shown in Figure 37. Very clear water makes fishing difficult. Rainbows become very cautious under these conditions and I suspect the aquatic invertebrates do as well. Very clear water allows more sunlight penetration into the water and may hurt the Rainbow's eyes. Trout will tend to forage deep in the water column and often move onto the shoals after dark or other times of lower light levels.

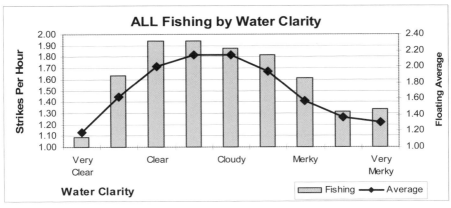

Figure 37 – The Influence of Water Clarity

Very murky water is only slightly better fishing. Under these conditions, the trout cannot see further than a foot or two. They must rely on their lateral line system and other sensory perceptions to locate food. It works but isn't the most efficient way to

167

feed. Aquatic bugs can detect the underwater vibrations of an approaching trout long before the trout sees the bug. The trout may have detected the movement of the bug but it is often well hidden before the trout can pinpoint its location. Trout feed best in water ranging from slightly murky to clear.

> In clear water, fish deep. In murky water, fish shallow.

Lake Water Levels and Fishing

The water level in a lake tends to be high in the spring with snow melt and spring runoff. Many pristine lakes are also licensed for water consumption. With water withdrawals and evaporation, lake levels tend to be low in the fall. That's the rule-of-

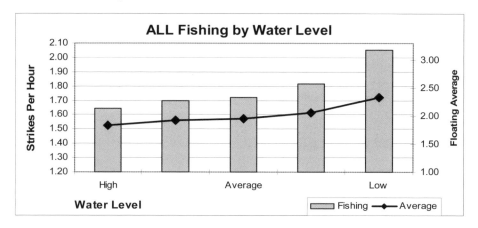

Figure 38 – The Influence of Water Levels on Fishing

thumb but I have seen a number of years almost opposite to that trend. Sometimes snow packs are low giving low water levels in the Spring. And heavy Summer rains can sometimes produce high water levels in the Fall. With this in mind, Figure 38 shows the usual fishing success by lake water levels.

Rainbow feeding and thus angling success is better in low water conditions. The graph shows improving success as water levels drop. This may be because water levels tend to be lower in the Fall and fishing is usually better in the late season than other times of the year.

Numbers of Bugs and Angling Success

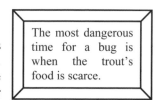

The average angler would probably think that fishing is better when lots of bugs are observed in or on the water. Actually, the reverse happens. Fishing tends to be better when bugs are relatively scarce. Your fly never duplicates a bug's looks or movement exactly. As more

> The most dangerous time for a bug is when the trout's food is scarce.

bugs become available, trout tend to become more selective about which one they choose. In times of plenty, the slightest flaw in presentation can mean that the trout will move on to another bug rather than take your fly.

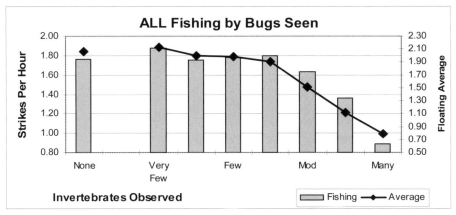

Figure 39 – Numbers of Bugs and Angling Success

The above graph shows how rapidly the fishing will decline as moderate to many bugs are seen in the water. If you have ever been on the lake when Chironomids are everywhere or there are thousands of Damselflies migrating to the shore then you have probably experienced the decrease in fishing success at these times. You can usually expect better success when you haven't seen a single bug. With the possible exception of trout feeding on Mayflies, this trend seems to hold for the other six primary invertebrates.

Rising Fish and Angler Success

Looking across a lake and seeing how many fish are rising is a good indication of how many fish you might expect to catch that day. Figure 40 shows angling success by the number of trout rises observed.

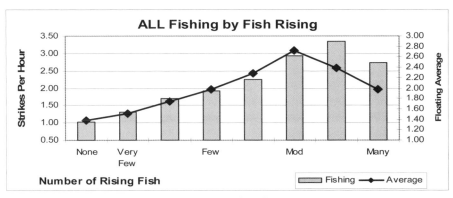

Figure 40 – Angler Success by Numbers of Rising Fish

169

When Rainbows are active, they tend to feed and that's when the fly fisher is most successful. A sure sign of active trout is when you see them rising to the surface. Rising fish are not necessarily feeding on the surface. But you can bet they are likely feeding somewhere in the water column. For some reason, active fish often come up to the lake surface and you can see the rise rings of their passing.

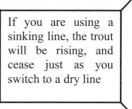

If you are using a sinking line, the trout will be rising, and cease just as you switch to a dry line

Figure 40 shows a slight decrease when many fish are rising. This may link with Figure 39 and the numbers of bugs seen. When there are lots of insects on the surface, lots of trout may be surface feeding. If so, your chance of success among so many natural bugs is somewhat limited even though the trout are active.

Water Depth and Fishing

I've regularly said that fishing is best in the shallow water over the shoals. Figure 41 shows the graphical representation of this tendency.

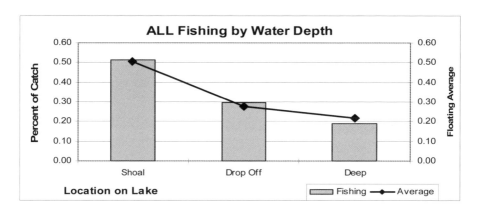

Figure 41 – Fishing Success by Water Depth

Rather than strikes per hour, I've used percent of catch for this graph. About 50% of my catch has been over the shoals. Rainbows primarily feed over the shoals in the Spring, Fall, and during hatches. However, during July and August the proportion of fish taken in deep water is typically high. By deep water, I'm referring to the open water beyond the shoal or drop off. Depth often ranges from 20 to 30 feet. Since your fly should often be fished within a few feet of bottom, it is difficult to fly fish depths much greater than 25 feet. Even in the middle of summer, the thermocline is often about 12 to 15 feet below the surface. That's usually deep enough to get into water sufficiently cool for the Rainbows. However, as a rule-of-thumb, you can expect about 80% of your fish to be taken over the shoal or at the drop-off.

End Notes

When young Rainbows are stocked into a pristine lake, they must learn what they can eat through a process of trial and error. They can't simply ask an older trout "what's good for dinner today". We anglers have the advantage of sharing knowledge. Through experience, we learn what, how, where and when the trout eat. We can share that information with novice anglers and discuss details with more experienced anglers to improve our own understanding.

In previous chapters, we have examined the Rainbow's habitats, the physical and sensory abilities and its behavior patterns. In this chapter, we have discussed some feeding considerations about this fish. These discussions tended to revolve around aquatic invertebrates but with good reason. The trout need to learn about these invertebrates to be efficient and effective predators. Likewise, we need to know about those same bugs to understand the trout's feeding patterns. After all, the Rainbow's feeding activities and foods are the only direct link between angler and fish.

In the next chapter, we will delve into more details about the primary aquatic foods of the Rainbow. But first, let's rehash the more important points from this chapter.

> ➤ Through trial and error, a newly stocked Rainbow will learn what is on the aquatic menu. Not all aquatic invertebrates are food items.

> ➤ While there are many species involved, only about seven basic foods are important to the fly fisher of pristine lakes. These are freshwater Shrimp, Chironomids (including Bloodworms), Caddis, Dragonfly and Damselfly nymphs, Mayflies and Waterboatmen.

> ➤ The basic foods are not always "available" to the trout. Protective mechanisms in the various life stages of these bugs will make them available at certain times and not at other times.

> ➤ The trout learn when hatches will occur and their biological clock will alert them to a pending meal. They may also feed according to their dominance in the pecking order.

> ➤ As trout grow and mature, their feeding patterns change. Young trout need to eat frequently to maintain their bodily functions and put on growth. The older and larger trout will eat more but feed less frequently. These big fish may go for extended periods between meals.

> ➤ As Rainbows learn what is edible in the lake, they sometimes develop a preference for specific foods. They may also develop cravings for specific proteins and/or amino acids that are abundant in one invertebrate and not another.

> ➤ Rainbows will feed more actively in some weather and water conditions than others. You may see bugs readily available and the trout simply not interested because of these environmental factors.

➢ Aquatic invertebrates can also detect weather and water changes. Hatches, migrations or other bug activities may be temporarily postponed because of these factors. Naturally, if the invertebrates aren't available, that will affect trout feeding.

➢ The trout feed and thus take your fly better when there are lots of fish rising to the lake surface. Conversely, if lots of bugs are seen, your chances of success are diminished. In these circumstances, the trout will often reject your fly which is a less than perfect imitation of the aquatic.

Those are the chapter highlights. Now it's time to examine the main Rainbow foods in detail.

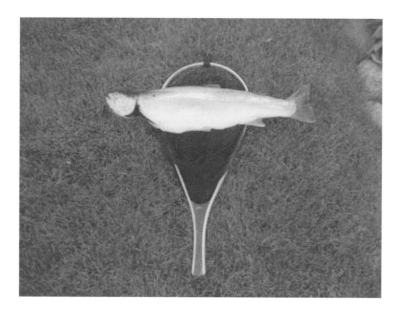

7

Rainbow Foods in Pristine Lakes

Any fly can catch a Rainbow at any time on any type of retrieve. However, using the right fly at the right time with the proper retrieve can significantly improve your odds of success. Some flies appeal to the trout's visual trigger while others imitate one of the seven primary invertebrates.

In this chapter, we want to examine the seven primary invertebrates in detail plus provide a little information on the other bugs. We will concentrate on these seven because they are the most important to the fly fisher. Snails and Limpets, for example, are major food items but it's impractical and/or inefficient for the angler to fish with flies to represent these. So we are going to stick to the main seven. However, Bloodworms will be split from Chironomids because they are significantly different. Because so many anglers are enthralled with Leeches, I'll even include some information on these and a few other minor food sources.

Details on the Major Aquatic Invertebrates

Since this book is directed at the intermediate to advanced angler, I won't waste time on lots of entomology details. Instead, an entomology data sheet is provided for each invertebrate. This data sheet provides the entomology basics. Discussions will concentrate on topics that affect the angler's use of flies to represent specific bugs. I'm sure you will find discussions on the timing, rhythmic cycles, bug availability and Rainbow preferences for specific invertebrates to be of use.

The Visual Key

Rainbows quickly examine a bug before making it a meal. In that short glance, key characteristics of the bug are identified. The trout quickly examines the bug or your fly for size, shape, movement and other key factors before eating it. I call this quick identification for key characteristics the "visual key". Your fly should have the key characteristics of the bug being imitated. Through this chapter, I will mention what I believe are the visual keys for each type of invertebrate (fly) being discussed.

NOTE: Seasonal and lunar availability (hatch) graphs are presented for each invertebrate. These are for the southern interior of British Columbia but are likely to be applicable to other areas. These graphs present the availability of the specified aquatic as a Rainbow food source. Feeding samples and the success of flies to imitate specific bugs provide the base data of these graphs.

Freshwater Shrimp

The freshwater Shrimp of interest is the Gammarus Shrimp and to a lesser extent, the Hyella Shrimp. Both are found in the majority of pristine lakes. Adult Hyella Shrimp never grow longer than about a quarter inch which means they are about the minimum to be of interest to the fly fisher. The Gammarus will sometimes exceed three quarters of an inch in length and is of prime importance to the angler. Therefore, discussions are centered on Gammarus Shrimp. We are not discussing Crayfish or Fairy Shrimp but they could be important in some pristine lakes.

Shrimp Basics

Gammarus shrimp aren't insects and don't morph from one form to another. They aren't found in all pristine lakes. They need good quantities of calcium to replace their exoskeletons. This makes life difficult if the lake is on the acidic side. Fortunately, most pristine lakes are eutrophic or in the late mesotrophic stages and acidity isn't a problem. Even then, a lake may never have produced a population of shrimp. These critters are unable to move from one body of water to another unless there is a direct water connection. Because of their importance to Rainbows, some lakes have been artificially stocked with shrimp. If you are unsure if a lake has shrimp, walk along the shoreline, look carefully in the water or even flip over some loose rocks and check underneath.

> **Did You Know**
> Shrimp have 11 body segments and 16 legs (2 grasping pair, 5 walking pair & one pair of hind legs) plus 3 pair of swimmers, 2 antenna and 2 tail protrusions.

In lakes that contain shrimp, they are usually the Rainbow's number one food item. Stomach samples from trout in pristine lakes show about 31% of all food consists of shrimp. Naturally, this rate isn't consistent throughout the open water season or on all lakes. And since they don't hibernate, shrimp are probably an important food source during the winter months under the ice.

Shrimp live about a year but may have slightly longer or shorter life spans. A female produces about three broods of offspring during her life. About 50 eggs are carried in an internal egg pouch. Young hatch within the pouch and are then expelled into the water. New hatchlings are almost microscopic in size but look essentially the same as an adult. It takes several weeks to grow to a size of interest to the fly fisher. Mating Shrimp are frequently seen in mid-summer. In the Fall, most Shrimp are young and fairly small.

These invertebrates are primarily scavengers that feed on plant and animal materials settling to the lake bottom. They may live and feed in deep water but most seem to prefer the shallows. Shrimp have been known to form packs that attack, kill and eat other invertebrates but this is not their normal feeding process. Favorite foods are zooplankton, Copepods and algae.

174

Shrimp are translucent. What they eat often provides their coloration. Shrimp like to eat blue-green algae and that often gives them a blue-green coloration. They also come in various shades of green, gray and reddish browns. Their color usually matches the surrounding vegetation or a muddy lake bottom. These aquatics can change color within a short period. For example, by the time I netted a shrimp, placed it in a water dish and focused my camera, it had changed from a bluish color to a typical yellow-green color. When shrimp die, they turn a dull orange color, so don't rely on feeding samples to determine the color of a fly to use.

Table 14 – Base Data for Gammarus Shrimp

Freshwater Shrimp

Gammarus Shrimp, Scuds, Shrimp, Side Swimmers

Class: Crustacea
Order: Amphipoda
Family: Gammaridae

APPEARANCE	LIFE AND HABITAT	Relatives	
Laterally compressed body	**Water**	Hyella Shrimp	
Eleven body segments	Prefer alkaline waters	Fairy Shrimp	
Eight pair of legs	Need calcium for skeleton	Clam Shrimp	
Three pair of swimmerets	**Shelter**	Lobsters, Crayfish	
Head has two pair of antenna	Lake bottom weeds		
Tail has two tail protrusions	**Protection**		
Chitinous exo-skeleton	Camouflage & Hiding		
Two small dark eyes	**Diet**		
Semi-transparent body	Mostly a Scavenger		
Curled when resting	Occasionally a hunter		
Elongated when swimming	Most deleterious materials		
SIZE	Prefers blue-green algae		
Up to 3/4 inch in length	**Breathing**		
Usually less than 1/2 an inch	Gills near tail		
Generally small in fall	**Metamorphosis**		
COLOR	None		
Upper darker than underside	**Life Cycle**		
Various greens to blues	Internal egg pouch	**Flies**	**Fishing & Retrieve**
to reddish-browns	50+ young hatch in pouch	Best in sizes 18 to 12	Retrieve slowly
Take on color of surroundings	Grow till sexually mature	Weighted or Unweighted	5-10 inches & stop
Egg sac is orange & visible	Mate while swimming	Tie in swimming position	Fly near bottom in day
MOVEMENT	Approx one year life span	Show many legs	Keep fly higher at night
Swims 5-10 inches & rests	3 broods per female	Make fly translucent	Adjust fly line to depth
Usually on or near bottom	Shrimp DO NOT hatch	Smooth upper surface	Keep fly near weeds
Seasonal Fishing	**Daily Fishing**	**Visual Keys for Rainbow**	**Rainbow Preferences**
Good any time of year	Good day or evening	Body shape & legs	Not available in all lakes
Best mid July & after Sept 15	Slightly better in evenings	Translucent body	#1 food where available
Good shortly after iceoff	Fish deep in daylight	Movement	Shrimp are the staple food
Try when other foods scarce	Good fly for foul weather		when other foods scarce

Shrimp are found from the shoreline to deep water. Most of the time they are found within one or two feet of the lake bottom but can swim to the lake surface when they choose. They use their legs for swimming and movement is fairly slow. After swimming a short distance, a Shrimp will stop to rest in a curled position as it settles toward the bottom. While swimming the Shrimp's body is extended. Flies to represent shrimp are usually tied in this extended position.

Shrimp Availability and Active Periods

Shrimp live and die in the waters of a lake and are available at all times of the year. Whenever other foods are hard to find, trout can always fall back to feeding on Shrimp. As winter's ice disappears in April, other foods are still scarce and the trout continue to feed on Shrimp. As other foods become available, Rainbows will generally develop a preference for those even though Shrimp are still present.

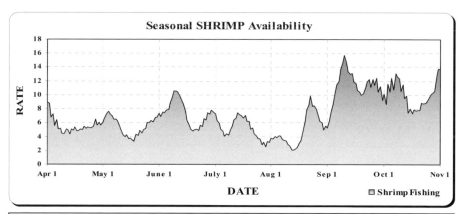

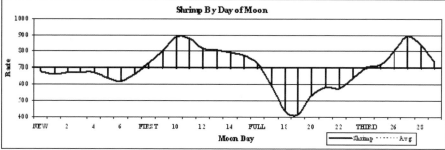

Figure 28 – Seasonal and Lunar Availability of Gammarus Shrimp

The top graph in Figure 28 shows the seasonal availability of freshwater Shrimp. Notice from this graph that the quantity of Shrimp in feeding samples is significantly greater through September and October than at other times of the year. Fall is the prime time to fish Shrimp patterns. The poorest time is from mid-July through mid-August. That coincides with the summer downers and is the poorest time for most of the seven primary invertebrates. If I showed seasonal graphs for some of the secondary invertebrates, such as snails, leeches, zooplankton and terrestrials we would find they tend to be more abundant during the summer downers and take

> **Fishing Tip**
> Seasonal hatches and bug availability often vary by a couple of weeks from one year to the next. Weather and water conditions are sometimes the cause but often the moon's position can make the difference. Try fine tuning your seasonal estimates by using the lunar availability information.

176

the place of the primary invertebrates. Even though the quantity of Shrimp appears limited during this period, they are still an effective fly when other foods are scarce.

The dips in the graph during April and May are because the lower and then the higher elevation lakes are going into turnover. Both are averaged on the graph. If only one lake or elevation were graphed, the feeding drop during turnover would show much more clearly. The bumps and dips

> The relative abundance of "available" critters, affects their abundance in feeding samples.

through June and July are different broods becoming available to the trout. With female Shrimp producing three broods per year, these periodically reach a size, quantity or condition that is of interest to the trout.

The second graph in Figure 28 provides the availability of freshwater Shrimp by day of the moon. It shows trout actively feed on Shrimp from the First Quarter moon, until the Full moon (moon days 8 – 16). Then a secondary period occurs for a few days before the New moon (moon days 25 – 29). The worst period is from Full moon until Third Quarter moon. This graph shows how rapidly Rainbows can stop feeding on a particular source of food due to lunar effects.

> If you aren't sure what the moon day is, try an almanac or even a calendar that shows moon phases. New moon is day zero and then count the days after.

I have found documentation to help explain this graph. Shrimp often feed on Zooplankton and Copepods which are sensitive to moon phase and the light cast by the moon. On dark nights, these critters migrate from the lake bottom toward the surface to feed. The Shrimp follow the zooplankton to feed on them. Naturally the trout will then feed on the Shrimp. When the moon is overhead and bright, the Zooplankton and Copepods do not make this migration. The Full moon rises at sunset and then rises about an hour later each night. Thus, the amount of bright, night time moonlight is greatest just after Full moon. This stalls the upward zooplankton migration and partially explains why the trout aren't readily feeding on Shrimp just after the Full moon. The process sets up a cyclic rhythm and the trout seem to know the routine. It shows the affect of the moon on many critters at the same time.

In higher elevation lakes, Shrimp are a larger part of the trout's diet than in lower elevation lakes. For local lakes, I generally consider low elevation to mean that ice-off usually occurs before May 1. When I first ran this data I questioned these results. I have seen lots of

> 62% of all Shrimp found in feeding samples were from higher elevation lakes.

lower elevation feeding samples with Shrimp. But the data isn't saying that Shrimp aren't important at lower elevations. What the data tells us is that Shrimp play a 'bigger role' in the total food chain of higher elevation lakes. Other invertebrates (particularly Waterboatmen, Dragonflies, and Damselflies) have bigger populations and contribute more to the lower elevation food chains. That means the relative proportion of Shrimp is greater at the higher elevations. When the selection of a fly pattern becomes difficult, the fly fisher is more likely to have success with a Shrimp on the higher elevation lakes than lower elevations, simply due to the relative abundance of other foods.

Shrimp leave their hiding places and are more active at night. Of all Shrimp found in Rainbow feeding samples, 53% were from fish taken in the evening or night. Thus, they are slightly more available at night. For data summary purposes, I consider "night" to be an hour before sunset and lasting until about midnight. What this statistic doesn't tell us is that a good portion of the daytime Shrimp samples were obtained

> Your fly should appeal to the trout's appetite rather than its appreciation for aesthetics and beauty. Too many flies are tied for the angler rather than the fish.

on cloudy to overcast days. On bright sunny days, Shrimp will often stay hidden in the bottom weeds, under rocks and in other hiding places. These critters prefer low light levels much the same as Rainbow Trout.

Environmental Factors and Shrimp Fishing

In Chapter 6 we examined the affects of environmental factors. However, that was an overall average for all bugs. When we look at a specific bug, a few of the environmental factors are likely to be different. The environmental factors affecting Shrimp are summarized in Table 15.

Shrimp prefer low light levels. This means the angler should fish Shrimp in deeper water on clear, sunny days since light levels are reduced with water depth. I tend to automatically adjust fishing depth to light levels and that partially explains why cloud cover doesn't show significant benefits to fishing Shrimp imitations on cloudy days.

> Keep weighted flies separate or distinguishable from unweighted flies in your fly box so you know which are best suited for a dry line.

Moon position seems to be a main factor in determining the success of fishing Shrimp patterns. While the period from First Quarter to Full Moon is best, it should be noted that the period from New Moon to First Quarter is about average. Since Shrimp are the number one food of Rainbows, average fishing success with these bugs should be considered as fairly good.

Shrimp seem to be fairly sensitive to water temperature and wind direction. A good time to fish Shrimp would be when the moon is between the First Quarter and Full Moon with cold water temperatures and winds from the southwest or south. Probably the worst time would be just after full moon with warm water and winds from the east or northeast.

Table 15 – Environmental Factors Affecting Shrimp

FRESHWATER SHRIMP - Environmental Factors	
Factor	**Best or Worst Fishing Times by Factor**
Season	Good throughout the year but best in the Fall after Aug. 15 when most other invertebrates are somewhat scarce.
Day of Moon	Worst after Full moon (days 17 to 23). Best before Full moon (days 8 to 16) with a secondary period before New moon (days 25 to 29).
Time of Day	Fishing Shrimp is poorest during the mourning hours. Afternoon thru evening is the better time to fish Shrimp.
Wind Direction	Fairly good when winds are from most directions except E, NE & N.
Wind Strength	Worst when wind calm (no wind). Otherwise wind isn't too important. Fishing can remain good even under very windy conditions.
Air Temperature	Best with cool air temperatures such as in the Spring or Fall.
Cloud Cover	No significant differences but slightly better in overcast skies. Also good in clear skies when fished deep. Worst when raining.
Barometer	Generally best with a low to moderate barometer and worst when the baromoter is changing.
Water Temperature	Cold water (such as Spring or Fall) is best, especially over shoals. As water warms, fish Shrimp deeper in the water where it is cooler.
Water Clarity	Fishing Shrimp is poor when the water is either very clear or else very merky. Cloudy to slightly merky water is best.
Water Level	Not significantly important but best when water levels are low such as in the Fall.
# Bugs Seen	Worst Shrimp fishing when lots of other bugs are seen. Good fishing when other bugs are scarce or not seen.
# Fish Rising	While trout don't "rise" to Shrimp, fishing this bug is best when moderate numbers of trout are rising and thus active and thus feeding.
Location	Best over the shoal and near the weeds but fishing Shrimp over the drop-off is more productive than most other fly patterns.
Miscellaneous	Best fishing is on or near the lake bottom and next to aquatic vegetation.
Any fly can catch a fish at any time. Success is improved by using the right fly at the right time.	

Flies To Represent Shrimp

When feeding on a particular invertebrate, trout won't spend a lot of time examining the details. If your fly gives the right visual keys for the food of choice, the trout will simply inhale your offering as it continues the search for more of the same. For Shrimp, I believe the visual key to provide the right impression is a fly with a smooth back, the impression of many legs, a translucent appearance and light in color. Beyond that I don't spend a lot of time trying to make a fly look pretty. Too many flies are tied for the angler rather than the fish.

Shrimp patterns can be tied weighted for use with a dry line. For a sinking line they can be unweighted or even buoyant. Cellophane or other shiny materials can be added over the back to provide the dorsal sheen on the Shrimp. Also try to provide the impression of a small tail that can be seen on the Shrimp. Shrimp patterns can be tied in the extended swimming position or in the curled resting position. Dubbing provides the translucence desired in the fly. Good imitations of legs are difficult and can be anything that gives the correct general impression. The dubbing material can be extended from the body to give the impression of legs.

Visual Keys for Shrimp
Translucent, lots of legs, light in color with smooth upper surface. It's usually tied in the swimming position.

Shrimp often come in light greens to greenish-blues and those are the colours that transmit best under water. For that reason, you should be more careful with color selection for Shrimp patterns than most other flies. A light coloration is probably one of the main visual keys for the trout. Some of the Shrimp patterns I tie are almost white in color with a hint of green.

Fishing Shrimp Fly Patterns

Whether you use a sinking line or a weighted fly on a dry line, you should probably fish a Shrimp pattern on or near the lake bottom. When it comes time to feed on Shrimp, trout will usually expect to find them near the bottom as opposed to higher in the water column. Shrimp will venture over muddy bottoms but prefer the protection and food offered around weedy areas.

Shrimp patterns are good day or night and from the early spring through late fall. Often, it is best to cast into deep water on a bright sunny day but over shallow water in the evening or during cloudy periods. As a rule-of-thumb, large or small Shrimp patterns can be used throughout the first part of the season. However, after early August, small Shrimp patterns (#18 to #14) should be the

When imitating a bug, how you retrieve a fly is often as important and sometimes more important than the fly itself.

fly of preference. By that time, the bulk of the Shrimp population will be small and immature. As water temperature cools in the fall the trout will often move into very shallow water seeking these invertebrates.

Whether you are fishing over the shoal or in water that is 30 feet deep, wait for the fly to get near the bottom before starting the retrieve. If your fly represents a Shrimp in the curled resting position, lift it up and let it settle toward the bottom. The lifting is liable to attract the trout and the strike often occurs while the fly is settling back toward the bottom. Alternately, a series of very short pulls will work when fishing with the resting Shrimp pattern.

With a fly representing the Shrimp in the extended swimming position, the retrieve can be slow and steady. Progress of the retrieve should be no more than ten or twenty feet per minute and slower works just fine. With that kind of slow progress, sinking lines often snag into bottom weeds. One way to help avoid bottom snags on a sinking line is to use a fly that is somewhat buoyant and tends to float above the weeds.

Chironomids (Pupa & Adult)

Chironomids are abundant around the world, found in almost any type of water and available at most times of year the water isn't frozen. Chironomids are an insect and go through the larva, pupa and adult stages. Each stage is of importance to the fly fisher but each stage has significantly different attributes and implications for the angler. I will cover the Chironomid pupa and adult in this section but the larval stage will be covered in the next section (Bloodworms). There are over 2,000 species of Chironomid in North America. The Chaoborus and mosquito are close relatives to Chironomids but those aren't really important to the angler. Chaoborus larvae are transparent. Chaoborus pupa and adults fish the same as Chironomids. Mosquitoes are found in ponds rather than lakes. In lakes without populations of Shrimp, Chironomids are usually the number one food of Rainbow Trout. Even in lakes with Shrimp, the Chironomids come in a close second.

Chironomid Basics

Adult Chironomids swarm and mate in flight. The pregnant female returns to the lake to drop eggs while flying virtually "on" the water surface. The eggs settle to the bottom and hatch into larvae that look much like a small grub or worm. The larva seeks shelter from predation by burrowing into the stems of aquatic plants or building mud tubes. Most species build mud tubes for pupation. The mud tubes are sealed, pupation occurs and the pupa breaks the seal to migrate to the surface to emerge into an adult.

> After extensive analysis, you will find the trout are feeding on the one single fly not in your fly box.

Many species of Chironomid share a pristine lake. Depending on the species, they may have one, two or multiple generations per year. As a rule-of-thumb, larger Chironomid species have fewer generations per year. If you see a hatch with large individuals, it probably has a life span of one generation per year and the same species will most likely emerge about the same time next year. By large, we are talking about individuals up to about in inch in length. Small species can be so tiny that you can't imitate them with a fly.

Chironomids are numerous in most lakes, ponds and other water bodies. Chironomids even live in the sediment ponds of pulp mills. A square meter (or a square yard) of lake bottom will sometimes house up to 50,000 small Chironomid larvae or up

> **Did You Know**
> A square meter of marl shoal can contain up to 50,000 individual Chironomids.

to 10,000 large larvae. These population densities have an interesting impact on the lake. The Chironomid mud tubes combined with the calciferous shells of dead invertebrates and are the primary materials of 'Marl Shoals'. Frequently, those shoals are excellent places to cast a fly. As a side note, the Marl Shoals are the main ingredients of oil forming shale. Chironomid populations from a million years ago are providing the oil and gas that allows you to drive to the lake.

If an adult Chironomid lands on you, don't worry because it won't draw blood like its cousin the mosquito. In fact, Chironomid adults and pupa don't eat at all. Chironomids in the pupal stage are only availably to the trout for as long as it takes to get from the lake bottom to the surface. That trip can be in shallow or deep water so time-lines vary. In part because the pupa fills a floatation sac with air to slowly drift to the surface. The longer the trip takes, the higher the risk of predation by trout.

Table 16 – Base Data for Chironomid (Pupa & Adult)

Chironomid Pupa
and Adults
Chironomid, Midges, Gnats

Class: Insecta
Order: Diptera
Family: Chironomidae

APPEARANCE	LIFE AND HABITAT	Relatives	
Adult	**Water**	Mosquitoes	
Looks like a mosquitoe	Lives in all water types	Houseflies	
Has fuzzy antenna	**Shelter**	Chaoborus (glassworms)	
Pupa	None as floating to surface	All two winged flies	
White gill tufts on head	**Protection**		
Bulbous head/thorax	None as floating to surface		
Tapered tubular abdomen	**Diet**		
Larva	Only feeds as a larva		
See Bloodworm	See Bloodworm		
SIZE	**Breathing**		
Up to 1 1/4 inch in length	Gills on head		
Usually less than 1/2 an inch	**Metamorphosis**		
COLOR	Complete		
White gill tufts	**Life Cycle**		
Dark head/thorax	Eggs laid on water surface	**Flies**	**Fishing & Retrieve**
Black to reddish-brown	Eggs hatch on lake bottom	Best in sizes 18 to 12	Use floating line
Color is seldom critical	Larva live in plant stems or	Need to be weighted	Slow to still retrieve
MOVEMENT	in mud tubes in sediment.	Gills & tail optional	Try drifting with the wind
Fills internal air sack	Pupa float to surface	Slim tapered abdomen	Suspend fly in water
Floats, wiggles and kicks	Hatch into adults	Bulbous head/thorax	Strike indicator helpful
on way to surface.	Adults swarm & mate	**As Adults**	**As Adults**
Adults skim water surface	Life span from several	Tie adults as dry flies	Fish adults as dry flies
LOCATION	weeks to one year.	Small & mosquitoe-like	Still or "S" retrieve
Anywhere in water column	Large species longest lived		Usually over shoals
Seasonal Fishing	**Daily Fishing**	**Visual Keys for Rainbow**	**Rainbow Preferences**
Good any time of year	Best hatches mid-morning	Body shape & movement	Available ice free period
Best in spring months	through late afternoon.	Size of preferred species	#2 trout food source
Small flies in the fall	Best over shoals & drops	Location in water column	Certain Chironomid species
Watch for hatches	Best during cloudy periods		are preferred over others.

After emerging, adult Chironomid will live as two-winged flies for a short while as they swarm, mate and lay eggs. The process of laying eggs is important to the angler. As the adult skims over the water surface laying eggs, they sometimes become a food source for the Rainbows. The ones of importance are usually the larger species. Even so, it requires a relatively small dry fly to represent an adult Chironomid.

Chironomid Availability and Active Periods

Chironomids emerge throughout the ice-free period. On flowing rivers that didn't freeze, I have seen small Chironomids flying just above the water surface in February when the air temperature a few inches higher is well below freezing. On the lakes, Chironomids are a little more selective about when they emerge. If conditions are right they may start to emerge the same day as ice off or they may wait for better conditions to arrive.

Chironomid larvae are available in the Spring and Fall. These will be discussed in the next section. Some Chironomid species will be in the final stages of pupation and ready to emerge into adults immediately after ice-off. The numbers of these bugs steadily increase until early May

| Did You Know |
| Chironomids have been found at water depths of 500 feet. |

and remain abundant through mid-June. Populations then steadily decrease until November. In October, there is a minor resurgence of small Chironomids that is important to the trout as they feed prior to ice-over.

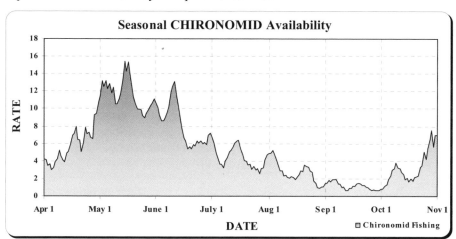

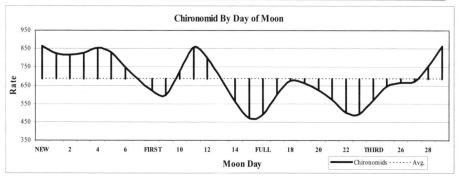

Figure 29 – Seasonal and Lunar Availability of Chironomid (pupa & adult)

Figure 29 shows the seasonal and lunar availability of Chironomid pupa and adults. The series of small peaks in the seasonal graph are likely different hatches as various species of importance are taken by the trout. Interestingly, these hatches or peaks seem to occur about every two weeks.

From the lunar graph, we can see that most species of Chironomid hatch and become trout food from the New moon through the First Quarter moon (days 27 thru 7). The increased angling success around day 11 of the moon is probably due to a hatch of a different but important species. The same thing seems to be happening around the 18th day of the moon but with species that isn't nearly as important. The worst Chironomid fishing is during the few days of the Full moon and then again during the Third Quarter moon.

> Your best dry flies won't float as soon as the trout are actively feeding on the surface.

> Have you ever tried fishing a Chironomid pattern at or after dark? It may be worth trying a dry line, short leader and a Chironomid at this time of day.

Chironomids hatch at all times of the day or night. However, I was a little surprised to find that 40% of the Chironomids from feeding samples were obtained from fish caught after sunset. This rate might be inflated. The samples may have contained Chironomid that were not "fresh" and possibly eaten during the daytime hours. As far as we anglers are concerned, I think it is safe to say that Chironomids are a daytime bug. The abundance of hatching Chironomids steadily increases through the day and peaks at about 4 pm. The data shows a secondary peak in the evening between 9 and 11 pm. This could be an interesting time to try Chironomid fishing.

On lower elevation lakes, Chironomids are a big portion of the food chain and thus are slightly more important. About 57% of the Chironomids in feeding samples were from low elevation lakes. Lower elevation lakes have a longer season, generally more plant life and provide better habitat for the larvae. But

> **Did You Know**
> Columns of mating Chironomid can reach heights of several hundred feet and get so dense that folks have been known to suffocate in the middle of a swarm.

don't let this statistic discourage you. There are plenty of Chironomids in the higher elevation lakes as well.

Environmental Factors and Chironomid Fishing

The environmental conditions best suited to Chironomids seem to be slightly cloudy skies in the mid afternoon, with a breeze from the West in the cool to cold water over a shoal. With these conditions, Chironomids pupate and are readily available to the Rainbow trout.

The same basic conditions that suit Chironomids seem to be conditions that Rainbows like when feeding. Maybe that partly explains why Chironomids are a preferred item on the Rainbow's menu. Murky water is about the only situation that Rainbows don't feed well on Chironomids. Perhaps this is because an individual pupa doesn't cause many vibrations in the water and the trout has trouble locating an individual by eyesight alone.

Table 17 – Environmental Factors for Chironomid Pupa (and adults)

CHIRONOMID (Pupa & Adult) - Environmental Factors	
Factor	**Best or Worst Fishing Times by Factor**
Season	Chironomids are good throughout the year (ice off till ice on). The peak occurs in late May and gradually declines thereafter.
Day of Moon	Best from the New Moon thru First Quarter (days 27 to 7) with a secondary on days 10 to 12. Worst from moon days 14 thru 25.
Time of Day	Starting about 9am, the quantity of Chironomid steadily increases and peaks at about 4pm. May be good from 9 to 11pm for those willing to try. Worst in the early morning or late evening.
Wind Direction	Best from the westerly quadrants but still good from other directions except SE, E & NE. Generally poor when wind is calm.
Wind Strength	Poorest fishing when winds are calm or strong. Best under breezy conditions.
Air Temperature	Poorest in hot weather conditions but that is still better than most other bugs. Can be good at most air temperatures.
Cloud Cover	Best under light cloud or partly cloudy skies but still good under most other cloud conditions including rain.
Barometer	The worst Chironomid fishing is when the barometer is high.
Water Temperature	Chironomid fishing is good over a wide range of water temperatures but worst in very cold water and poor in warm water conditions.
Water Clarity	Worst in murky to very murky water and better than most bugs in very clear water. Clear to slightly cloudy is often the best fishing.
Water Level	Worst Chironomid fishing is in high water conditions and steadily improves as water levels drop. Best in low water conditions.
# Bugs Seen	If you don't seen any bugs, try a Chrionomid. Success with Chironomids gradually decreases as more bugs are seen.
# Fish Rising	Worst when fish aren't rising and steadily improves as numbers of rising fish increases but drops when many are rising.
Location	Best (55%) over the shoal. Chironomid success is about the same over the drop off and in deep water.
Miscellaneous	Chironomid patterns are often successful in conditions when other flies aren't producing but it requires patience.
Any fly can catch a fish at any time. Success is improved by using the right fly at the right time.	

Flies To Represent Chironomid

You can tie flies to imitate Chironomid pupae in almost any natural color and on any hook less than about an inch in length. Once again I'll say that I tie my flies as simple as possible as long as they still catch fish. Following that philosophy, I seldom put gills, a tail or ribbing onto my Chironomid patterns. I do keep a few fancier Chironomid patterns in the fly box in case the trout get very selective. However, the visual key for Chironomids seems to be no more than something of the right size and shape. But, there is one thing I do with all my Chironomid patterns. I weight them. Whether you choose a bead head or place wire under the thorax, the weight will help

185

the fly to sit correctly in the water, keep the leader straight and get it down to a good fishing depth with the minimum of wasted time.

> The longer it takes to tie a fly, the greater the chance that it will unravel on the first fish it hooks.

My most productive Chironomid pattern is simply peacock herle for the abdomen that has all the fuzz removed (stripped) with a thicker thorax of unstripped peacock herle. The stripped peacock seems to have all the necessary color tones to represent most any Chironomid species. Another nice thing about a Chironomid pupa is that it is about the only fly that allows you to totally camouflage the hook. Tie the pattern to look like the bend in the hook is the curled tail of the pupa. For adult Chironomid, most any small dry midge pattern will do when the trout are taking those on the surface.

Fishing Chironomid Fly Patterns

The most conventional way to fish imitations of Chironomid pupa is with a dry line and a leader length that has been adjusted to a suitable fishing depth. Rainbows can be very choosy about where in the water column they will feed on Chironomids. I was once fishing a Chironomid pattern on a 20-foot leader without success even though there were lots of signs of the trout taking these near the surface. Finally a light bulb went on over my head. I shortened my leader to about 18 inches and started catching numerous fish. The fish can be just as choosy about only taking Chironomids over a shoal or only in deep water.

> The likelihood of a strike is inversely proportional to the amount of attention you are devoting to your fly.

These days, many folks use a strike indicator to adjust fishing depth. I'm old fashioned and find the strike indicator a little harder to cast. I stick to physically changing the length of my leader as the need arises. Also, you should make sure the leader is straight when fishing Chironomids. Many of the commercial leaders have a memory and will retain coils from being on the reel. Those coils must be removed otherwise they act like a spring. With coils in the leader, they stretch and you can have a soft strike without realizing a strike has occurred.

> Rainbows may selectively feed on one species of Chironomid and not another. Be prepared to try different sizes of flies to match what the trout are after.

After casting a Chironomid, the fly fisher must wait for it to sink to a proper depth and then have the patience to retrieve the fly "very" slowly. If you think your retrieve is slow enough, then the general rule is to slow it down some more. A retrieve of one inch per second (or five feet per minute) is a fast enough retrieve for the Chironomid. The fly should stay at full leader depth rather than move upward during the retrieve. Women are often good Chironomid fishers because they have the patience for a very slow retrieve. Men tend to become impatient and the

186

speed of their retrieve increases proportional to their impatience. An effective way to maintain a slow retrieve is to cast perpendicular to the wind and let the wind drift your fly line. The slow but steady wind drift of your fly line is often slow enough to correctly fish a Chironomid pattern.

A less than conventional but effective method of fishing a Chironomid is with a fast sink line. If you are anchored in 30 feet of water, make a cast of 29 feet (including leader) and let the line sink until it is directly below your boat. The fly should be just above the bottom. Slow and gentle movements imparted to your rod tip will make the fly wiggle and thus attract the trout. This is a particularly effective method during the heat of the summer when the fish are down deep. However, I have to admit that this type of presentation requires more patience than I can usually muster.

Before leaving Chironomids we should mention techniques for fishing the adults. Adults are occasionally taken by the Rainbows immediately after emerging or when the female returns to the lake to drop eggs. When you see Rainbows feeding on Chironomid adults, almost any small dry fly should

Did You Know
Pulp mills often use Chironomids in their settling ponds to help clean the water.

produce results. If the adults are being taken while letting their wings dry after emerging, your dry fly should be fished still. Let it drift with the wind. If the adults are being taken while laying eggs then your dry fly should be moved with long and steady retrieves to imitate the insect skimming over the surface. If possible, try to prevent the leader from lying straight when cast. Get some bends in the leader so the fly moves in arches or an "S" shape when coming across the water surface. This is more typical of the adult movement while laying eggs.

Bloodworm (Chironomid Larva)

Bloodworm is the common name most frequently applied to Chironomid larva. All Bloodworms are Chironomid larvae but not all Chironomid larvae are Bloodworms. The name refers to the blood red coloration that certain larva will sometimes exhibit. At

certain times of the year, Bloodworms are a favoured food of Rainbows and can be successfully imitated. However, a large proportion of Chironomid larvae do not take on the blood color and many aren't available to the trout.

Bloodworm Basics

While the name implies that Bloodworms are always blood red, this is not the case. Chironomid larvae are frequently cream or green colored and sometimes found in shades of brown. Perhaps they should be called Creamworms or Greenworms. The red coloration only develops in larvae that live in an oxygen poor environment. Oxygen can be scarce within plants or when living under the lake bottom muck. Under those conditions, hemoglobin is used to store oxygen and that turns the larva red. It is much the same as hemoglobin turning human blood red. I have even seen individual Bloodworms that were partially red and partially cream colored.

Table 18 – Base Data for Chironomid Larvae (Bloodworms)

Bloodworm

or Chironomid Larva

Class: Insecta
Order: Diptera
Family: Chironomidae

APPEARANCE	LIFE AND HABITAT	Relatives		
Adult	**Water**	Mosquitoes		
See Chironomid	Lives in all water types	Houseflies		
Pupa	**Shelter**	Chaoborus (glassworms)		
See Chironomid	Mud tube in sediments,	All two winged flies		
Larva	within aquatic plant stems,			
Segmented & worm-like	or under logs & rocks.			
Small legs & gill tuft	**Protection**			
COLOR	Staying within shelter			
Often blood red but also	**Diet**			
brown to cream to green.	Blue-green algae			
Color depends on oxygen	Aquatic vegetation stems			
SIZE	Most deleterious materials			
Up to 1 1/4 inch in length	**Breathing**			
Usually longer than 1/2 inch	Gills on head			
MOVEMENT	**Metamorphosis**			
Stays within shelter or	Complete			
crawls on bottom.	**Life Cycle**	**Flies**		**Fishing & Retrieve**
Leaves shelter spring & fall	Eggs laid on water surface	Best in sizes 14 to 10		Keep fly on bottom
LOCATION	Eggs hatch on lake bottom	Weighted or unweighted		Slow to still retrieve
Not able to swim	Depending on species,	Usually tied blood red		Adjust line to fly weight
Only found on lake bottom	builds mud tube or	(but try other colors)		and to bottom depth.
NOTE	burrows into aquatic plant.	Tie to look like		Dry line with weighted fly
As trout food, mostly large	Larva grows & pupates	segmented worm or grub.		helps prevent hang-ups.
species that hibernate.	(then see Chironomid)			
Seasonal Fishing	**Daily Fishing**	**Visual Keys for Rainbow**		**Rainbow Preferences**
Good in the spring	Best in daylight hours	Body shape & movement		Prefer larger bloodworms
Best in the fall	Best in the shallows	Size of preferred species		Preferred in the daytime
Seldom a trout food	Seldom good at night	Trout search lake bottom		Prefer individuals that
during the summer months.		to feed on bloodworms.		venture away from shelter.

Bloodworms and other Chironomid larvae have an appearance similar to a small worm or grub. They have a small gill tuft at the tail plus a couple of pair of small graspers to help them move or anchor. Bloodworms are almost microscopic in size when they hatch from the egg. They grow and may reach sizes slightly larger than the pupa of their species. Large Bloodworms might reach a little more than an inch in length.

Fishing Tip

Many "Bloodworms" found in feeding samples are not red. Many are cream colored and some are even green. Try tying and fishing Bloodworm patterns that are cream or green colored.

Most of the time, Bloodworms will stay within their protective housing and thus are not available to Rainbows. When they leave this protection, they are only found on the bottom of the lake and don't move any faster than a worm. They cannot swim or propel themselves off the bottom.

Over winter, Chironomid larvae hibernate in mud tubes constructed from saliva and the surrounding lake bottom materials. In the spring some species remain in these mud tubes to pupate. Other species leave the mud tube and live inside the stems of aquatic plants to feed directly on the plant as opposed to vegetation that happens to settle near the mud tube.

> Unless you enjoy fishing in a crowd, don't advertise when the fishing is good.

The plant-dwelling larvae are the ones of primary importance to the angler. These species typically grow larger and are more available to the trout in the Spring and Fall. As the plants begin to grow, these larvae leave the protection of their hibernation mud tubes to find a suitable plant to call home. As they crawl across the muddy bottom in search of living plants, they are totally exposed and vulnerable to predation. Some species pupate within the plant stem with little chance of being eaten by the trout. In the Fall, the plants begin to die. The larva must evacuate the plant and find a suitable place to hibernate. They leave the plant community to crawl across a muddy bottom to deeper water and once again are exposed to trout predation. They construct a mud tube for winter hibernation.

Bloodworm Availability and Active Periods

Because of their treks to and from plants, Bloodworms are primarily available during the Spring as plants begin to grow and again in the Fall as plants begin to die. I have found them in feeding samples throughout the season but Spring and Fall are the best times. Occasionally, for unknown reasons, Chironomid larvae leave their plant stems or mud tubes during the summer and become a meal for the trout. But as shown on the Bloodworm graph (Figure 30) these invertebrates are not normally available during the summer months and imitations don't fish well.

> The worm of blood
> Lives in the mud
> And it will crawl
> Both Spring and Fall.

Bloodworms are one of those invertebrates that are more active during the daytime than near or after sunset. Flies can be successfully fished in the evening but for the best and most consistent results I would suggest mid-day.

> Your fly fishing vest will contain everything except the one item you really need.

As expected, the information regarding Bloodworms in feeding samples by elevation is almost identical to what we saw for Chironomid pupa. Bloodworms are a more important feeding consideration on the lower elevation lakes than the higher elevation lakes. But, as we mentioned for the pupa, that shouldn't discourage you from trying Bloodworm imitations on the upper lakes.

189

About the end of April, aquatic plants begin to grow in the lower elevation lakes. Figure 30 shows Bloodworm fishing success to be good during the same period. In October, aquatic plants are dying prior to the onset of winter. Bloodworms leave the plants and seek places to hibernate. That is also good time to fish Bloodworm flies.

Bloodworm availability has five peaks through the lunar cycle. I don't have a good explanation for this. Perhaps it is just different species of Chironomids showing up on the graph. However, it appears the New moon period is best and that matches with the lunar timing of the Chironomid pupa and adult.

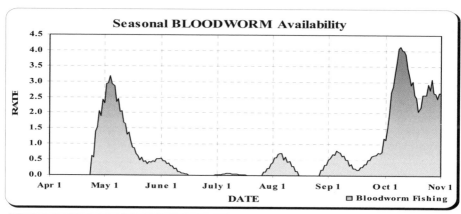

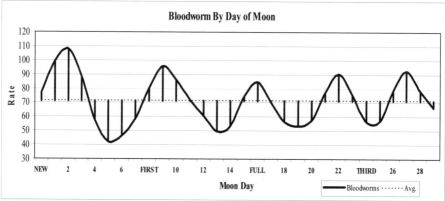

Figure 30 – Seasonal and Lunar Availability of Bloodworms

Environmental Factors and Bloodworm Fishing

Bloodworms fish better around noon than at other times of the day. They probably time their treks to and from plants during the midday hours. They also fish better over the shoals, in cloudy water that is cold. Days with heavy cloud cover, a breeze from the southwest and a variable barometer are preferred. Bloodworms are seldom on the trout's menu when water is very clear, very murky or with warm water temperatures.

Table 19 – Environmental Factors for Chironomid Larva

BLOODWORM (Chironomid Larva) - Environmental Factors	
Factor	**Best or Worst Fishing Times by Factor**
Season	Best in the Fall after Sept. 1 but also good in the Spring after ice off. Not very good through the Summer months.
Day of Moon	Best on moon days 26 to 3 with secondaries on days 8 to 11, 15 to 17 and 21 to 23. These cycles may be different species.
Time of Day	Best from 11am to 4pm with each hour after getting poorer. Worst in the morning or late evening.
Wind Direction	Significantly better with winds from the SW or S and worst with wind from the NW or SE or Calm.
Wind Strength	Worst in windy conditions but also poor when wind is calm. Best fished in a mild breeze.
Air Temperature	Best in colder water conditions such as Spring or Fall. Not very good with air temperatures from hot to warm.
Cloud Cover	Bloodworms fish best under cloudy conditions but not well in the rain. Bright summy days are worst.
Barometer	Worst with a high barometer and best with a changing barometer.
Water Temperature	Best in cold water but poor if the water gets very cold. Doesn't fish well in warm to cool water temperatures.
Water Clarity	Significantly better in cloudy water conditions. Poor in either murky water or clear water.
Water Level	For some reason, Bloodworms fish well in high water conditions and steadily decreases as water levels drop.
# Bugs Seen	Best when very few bugs are seen and steadily declines as more bugs are observed. Below average when no bugs are seen.
# Fish Rising	Good when there are few to moderate numbers of fish rising. Not so good when the fish aren't rising or when lots of fish are rising.
Location	More than 60% of success is over the shoal and less than 10% in deep water.
Miscellaneous	Bloodworms do not swim or float and should be fished right on the lake bottom. Also try fly patterns that aren't red.
Any fly can catch a fish at any time. Success is improved by using the right fly at the right time.	

Flies To Represent Bloodworms

I always tie Bloodworm patterns with weighting to ensure they get on the lake bottom. Most folks tie their Bloodworms with materials that are blood red. However, almost half of the Bloodworms in feeding samples are cream or green colored, even when they are the same species. Large numbers of these larvae lived in an environment that didn't need hemoglobin to store oxygen. Thus, they didn't turn red. You may want to try a few flies that are not red in color. These larvae have definite segmentation like a worm. Try to represent the segments in your flies. I sometimes use a red underbody wrapped with clear plastic tubing to show segmentation. The plastic helps the fly to sink. You can also use a waterproof ink marker to color the plastic.

191

Fishing Bloodworm Fly Patterns

When I fish Bloodworm patterns, I try to find an area with a muddy bottom that is between weed patches and deep water. I expect the larvae to be migrating to or from their winter hibernation grounds through these areas. The fly should be on the lake bottom and make sure your retrieve very slow like you would a pupa imitation. You can even fish this fly still on the bottom with an occasionally twitch to attract the trout's attention. The fly can be fished on a dry line or a slow sinking line. I prefer the slow sink line when over a muddy lake bottom. If I can't find a muddy bottom, I use a dry line over the weedy bottom. When feeding on Bloodworms, trout usually inhale the larvae and strikes are often soft and subtle. Set the hook even if you suspect a bottom snag. Sometimes you will be pleasantly surprised.

Caddis (Sedge)

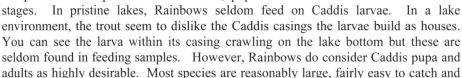

Another name for Caddis is Sedge. They go through complete metamorphosis with the larva, pupa and adult stages. In pristine lakes, Rainbows seldom feed on Caddis larvae. In a lake environment, the trout seem to dislike the Caddis casings the larvae build as houses. You can see the larva within its casing crawling on the lake bottom but these are seldom found in feeding samples. However, Rainbows do consider Caddis pupa and adults as highly desirable. Most species are reasonably large, fairly easy to catch and I suspect provide many of the proteins and/or amino acids the trout find necessary. Unfortunately, Sedges are only abundant from early June through mid-September. If they were available throughout the year, they might be the Rainbow's number one food source. Even with a limited season, they are the third most important food and the number one food at certain times of the year.

> **Did You Know**
> After pupation, a Sedge pupa will sometimes crawl around the lake bottom for a short period before swimming to the surface to hatch.

Caddis Basics

The adult female Caddis (or Sedge) generally lays eggs while skimming over the water surface near a shoreline in shallow water. Because of this trait, they are often called "Traveling Sedges". When the eggs hatch, the bug looks like a small grub. But these small worm-like creatures quickly build a casing to enclose their body and protect them from the trout. Each species of Caddis builds a different type of casing.

When the biological clock says it's time, the larva seals its casing and pupates within. Unknown by many fly fishers, after pupation the pupa will sometimes leave the larval case and crawl around the lake bottom for a short time before emerging into an adult. At this time, the pupa is extremely vulnerable to trout predation. After this short "crawl about", the pupa rapidly swims to the lake surface and splits open the pupal shell to emerge into an adult. The new adult quickly flies away and mating occurs in

192

the nearby forest or among the shoreline weeds. Most species of Caddis live about a year but the smaller species may have two or three generations in a year.

Table 20 – Base Data for Sedge Pupa and Adult

Caddis (Sedge)
Caddis, Caddisfly, Sedge,
Shadfly, Periwinkle, etc.

Class: Insecta
Order: Trichoptera
Family: Limnephilidae

APPEARANCE	LIFE AND HABITAT	Relatives	
Adult	**Water**	Aquatic cousin to the	
Moth-like	Prefer cool, shallow &	moths & butterflies	
Triangular cross section	well oxygenated water.		
Pupa	**Shelter**		
Long legs & antenna	Larval casing		
Obvious wing stubbels	None - Pupa & Adults		
Abdomen wide at tail	**Protection**		
Gills on sides of abdomen	Larval casing		
Larva	Rapid swimming or flying		
Worm-like in casing.	**Diet**		
Not normally consumed	Plant & animal material		
COLOR	**Breathing**		
Adult	Gills on sides of abdomen		
Greyish to reddish brown	**Metamorphosis**		
Often green abdomen	Complete		
Pupa	**Life Cycle**		
Greens to browns	Eggs laid while female	**Flies**	**Fishing & Retrieve**
Black gills & wing stubs	skims over water surface.	Best in sizes 16 to 10	Pupa - slow along bottom
SIZE	Larva forms cocoon casing	Pupa best weighted	or fairly rapid to surface.
Up to 1 1/4 inch in length	Pupates within casing	Show pupa legs/antenna	Adult - still in hatch or
MOVEMENT	Pupa swims to surface	Dubbing good for body	"S" retrieve at egg laying.
Adult skims water surface	Hatches at surface film	Make pupa wide at tail	Usually best over shoals
Pupa craws on bottom	Adult lives 2 wks to 2 mo	Adult as dry deerhair fly	Use fly slightly larger
before swim to surface.	Life span 3 mo to 1yr	Pyramid shape for adult	than the actual Caddis.
Seasonal Fishing	**Daily Fishing**	**Visual Keys for Rainbow**	**Rainbow Preferences**
Best in mid-summer	68% taken evening/night	Adult - triangular wings	Caddis a preferred food
Cinnamon sedge - Sept.	Best in the shallows	& type of surface motion	Prefer caddis in low light
Try pupa early June	Best at higher elevations	Pupa - legs, abdomen,	Prefer pupa on bottom
Watch for surface adults	Best in clean water	& type of movement.	just prior to main hatch.

The adults of many Caddis species look like a moth. The pupa looks like a Caddis adult without wings. The larva looks like a grub but isn't overly important to the fly fisher. Pupae are about the same size as the adult and range from about 0.3 inches to 1.4 inches in length. Adults may be moth-like with grey to cream colored wings but many smaller species have semi-transparent wings that are reddish brown in color. Neither the pupa nor the adult feed. The pupae have dark gills around the end of the abdomen. Caddis can fly between widely separated lakes. When a lake becomes overstocked with trout, the Caddis populations can suffer and possibly disappear.

> Try Caddis fly patterns just after the Full moon in June.

Caddis Availability and Active Periods

Sedges don't like the cold. The larvae hibernate over the winter. They are in the lake and become mobile after ice off but are not generally available until the weather and water warms. The first sign of trout feeding on Sedges begins in late May on the lower elevation lakes. The earliest Sedges are completing pupation by then. Some individuals will leave the larval casing and crawl around the lake bottom for a short time prior to emerging into an adult. This can be an excellent time to fish pupa imitations. By the end of June, hatches will peak and then steadily decline for the remainder of the season. A minor but important peak occurs in late August to early September. This secondary peak is the small reddish-brown Caddis commonly called "Cinnamon Sedge". For some reason the trout seem to really like this small Caddis. They tend to emerge in the evening. At this time of year, hatches progress from higher to lower elevation lakes. Even into October a few Caddis are still emerging.

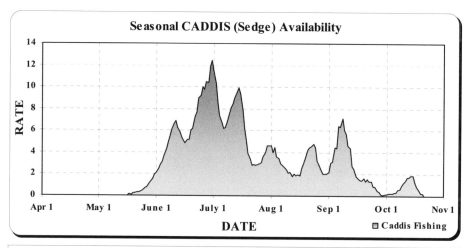

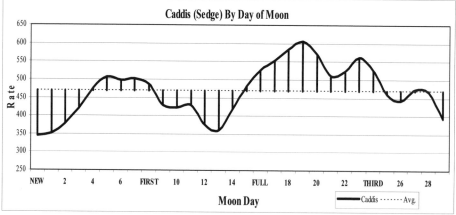

Figure 31 – Seasonal & Lunar Availability of Caddis

Sedges are more abundant in the evening and night than during the daylight hours. Evening hatches occur two times more often than daytime emergence. Also of interest, 70% of the Sedges found in feeding samples were from higher elevation lakes. These bugs are a bigger part of the food chain on upper elevation lakes than on lakes with ice-off occurring before May 1st. Both of these statistics are important to an angler interested in some serious fishing with either wet or dry Caddis patterns.

> The Caddis takes flight,
> Both day and night,
> And the trout know when
> Those hatches begin.

On the Rainbow's list of preferred foods, Caddis pupa and then Dragonfly nymphs, are probably at the top. Rainbows actively seek out these large bugs even when they are relatively scarce. Except during major hatches, a Caddis pattern is often more productive than the relative number of bugs available. Often this happens when Sedges are in the pupal stage and crawling on the lake bottom prior to emergence. It surprises me that so few anglers use a Caddis pupa except when they see a Caddis hatch in progress. Even then, many will fish adults as dry flies rather than pupae as wet flies.

Sedges are primarily available between the Full and Third Quarter moon. They seem to prefer the brighter moon light of this period. Sedges are one of the few bugs that are abundant during this moon phase. It is also worth noting that the quantities of Sedges are a little above average just before the First Quarter moon. The wise angler will keep an eye open for Caddis at that time.

Adult Sedges are only available when emerging from their pupal skin or returning to the lake to lay eggs. When emerging, the new adult will sit on the lake surface for a very short period to let its wings dry. At this time, a dry fly is best fished still or wind drifted. When laying eggs, the female will skim or skitter over the water surface and the dry fly should be retrieved at about the same speed. If in doubt, watch how the trout are taking adults and retrieve your fly accordingly.

Environmental Factors and Caddis Fishing

Sedges are not bugs that like cold weather or cold water conditions. These critters need warmer temperatures before they become active. If water temperature gets down to the cold category, Caddis activity dramatically drops. That's probably why they wait until so late in the year to begin their hatches. However, these bugs don't mind overcast or rainy conditions as long as the temperatures are suitable.

Fishing Tip
Most fly fishers will use dry flies and just imitate Caddis adults. With this approach, some great angling opportunities are missed. Feeding samples show that pupas are taken more frequently than adult Caddis.

Sedges continue to hatch in relatively strong winds but prefer winds from the southwest. Probably because of their typically large size, Caddis are taken better than many bugs in water that is murky to very murky. Low water levels in the lake seem to suit these bugs and most (60%) are taken over the shoals.

Like many bugs, Sedge pupae seem to be most successful when moderate numbers of fish are rising and only a few bugs are seen. Caddis pupa even work well when no bugs are seen. To fish Caddis adults successfully as a dry fly, it is better to see a few bugs on the surface.

Table 21 – Environmental Factors for Caddis

CADDIS (SEDGE) - Environmental Factors	
Factor	**Best or Worst Fishing Times by Factor**
Season	Caddis aren't often available until late May, peak by late June, fish well thru July and then decrease in the late summer.
Day of Moon	Good after the Full moon from days 15 to 25. Worst after the New moon from moon days 29 to 3.
Time of Day	Caddis are best in the evening and worst in the early morning.
Wind Direction	Good with winds from the W, SW, S and SE. Poor fishing with winds from other directions.
Wind Strength	Best in breezy conditions. Poor when the winds are very strong or calm. Also poor when wind strength significantly varies.
Air Temperature	Best with cool air temps. Poorest in hot or very cold air. Fishes better in warm temperatures than most bugs.
Cloud Cover	Best with overcast skies or heavy cloud and fishes well in the rain. Somewhat worse in clear skies to light cloud.
Barometer	Best with a low barometer, and little difference in other conditions.
Water Temperature	Not good in cold to very cold water, otherwise temp isn't important. Even fishes well in warm water temperatures.
Water Clarity	Fishes well in clear, cloudy or murky water. Worst in very clear or very murky water.
Water Level	Best in low water conditions and worst in high water conditions.
# Bugs Seen	Caddis pupa fish well when aquatic bugs aren't seen. Otherwise, Caddis fishing steadily declines as observed bugs increase.
# Fish Rising	Worst fishing when no fish or very few fish are rising. Best when moderate numbers of fish are rising.
Location	Far better over the shoal than elsewhere on the lake but the adults will drift into deeper water.
Miscellaneous	Caddis aren't just for dry fly fishing. Caddis pupa often fish well even when adults aren't seen on the surface.
Any fly can catch a fish at any time. Success is improved by using the right fly at the right time.	

Flies To Represent Caddis

Caddis larvae are not often eaten by the trout but on occasion a Caddis larva will leave its protective housing and be taken. Variations of the Wooly Worm are as good a fly as any to imitate the larval stage of a Caddis outside its casing.

As adults, Sedges no longer live in the water and are only available to the trout at the water surface. So the first requirement of a fly pattern to imitate the adult is for it to float. Deer hair floats well, has the basic color shades of many Caddis species and is the material frequently used to imitate adults. The basic shape of an adult, with its wings folded over its back, is pyramidal. Tie your fly in this basic pyramid shape and add some deer hair or other material to represent legs and antenna. That's about all that is needed to tie an adult imitation. I sometimes gob lots of deer hair on the hook and then trim it into the pyramid shape. Sort of like a Mouse's Ear is constructed. The advantage is durability and floatability.

Not many fly fishers tie imitations of Caddis pupa much less good imitations. These same anglers will go into extreme details on a number 16 Chironomid pattern but not even get the correct body shape of a large Caddis pupa. They tie some sort of streamer fly or something with hackles and call it a Caddis pupa.

The basic body shape of these pupae is often a long slim pyramid. Many species actually have a slightly bulbous tail. The wing-stubs aren't necessary but if added are short and lay next to the thorax. Add some pronounced legs to the underside and you have the basic form. Vary materials, color and size to suit the local species. I often weight my pupa imitations for use with a dry line but they can be effectively fished with a sinking line and not weighted. When weighted, put the weight at the tail of the hook. When retrieved toward the surface, this provides the proper balance for a fly that appears to be swimming upward.

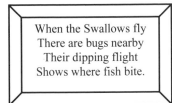

When the Swallows fly
There are bugs nearby
Their dipping flight
Shows where fish bite.

Fishing Caddis Fly Patterns

As dry flies, Caddis adults are fished with a dry line. However, there are two distinctly different approaches to fishing these dry flies. One method is to let the fly sit still and the other method is to retrieve the fly so that it skims across the water surface. When Sedges are emerging, they remain motionless to let their wings dry. Often the trout only take a motionless presentation during a hatch. If Sedges are laying eggs while skimming over the water surface, the trout will often insist that your fly be on the move. Watch for this difference in the insect and how the Rainbows are taking them.

Your longest cast will always be about 20 feet short of where the trout are feeding.

Fishing a Caddis pupa can be effective even if you don't see a hatch in progress. If you suspect a hatch will soon begin, it might be worth while to try a pupa imitation. At these times, imitations are most effective when fished right on the lake bottom. Use a weighted fly and fish it over the shoals. During a hatch I would suggest you watch to see how many Caddis are being taken on the surface. If conditions are good but there are only a few surface takes, it is quite possible that the majority of fish are feeding on the Caddis pupae on the bottom or as they swim to the surface to emerge. Let the fly sink to the bottom followed by a few short retrieves. Then rapidly retrieve the fly toward the surface.   Caddis swimming toward the surface move rapidly compared to most other invertebrates.   Your retrieve of a pupa swimming to the surface should also be fairly fast. In water that is cloudy to murky you may need to slow down the retrieve to provide ample opportunity for the trout to locate the prey.

Dragonfly (nymphs)

Dragonflies may emerge in one body of water and fly to another body of water to mate and lay eggs. There is even evidence that Dragonflies migrate over hundreds of miles but this aspect of their behavior is still not confirmed. With access to virtually all water, the types of Dragonflies in a lake can be quite varied. However, many species prefer certain types of water. Some species will stick to streams or ponds while others prefer lakes and so on. For the fly fisher the specific species isn't usually important.

For the angler, there are only two distinctions that need to be made between the types of Dragonflies. The long, cigar shaped Dragonfly nymphs of the Aeshnidae family (Darners) and the other Dragonfly nymphs that are short, flat, round and most frequently of the Libellula family (Skimmers). Because of their life style,

Did You Know
It takes about 25 large Chironomid pupae to provide the same amount of food for the Rainbow as one medium sized Dragonfly nymph.

the cigar shaped Darners are a much larger component of the trout's diet than the round-bodied nymphs. The short, flat and rounded bodies of the Skimmers, Gomphus and similar Dragonflies are shaped that way for a reason. They bury themselves in the lake bottom muck and lie in wait for their prey.   While thus concealed, they are virtually unavailable to the trout. The Darners are larger and actively search out prey. Thus, they are exposed to trout predation. The Darners also live longer making them available for greater periods of time. The following discussions are primarily aimed at the Darners but information on the Skimmers and similar families will be provided as applicable.

Even though they frequently fall in the water, it is very rare that an adult Dragonfly is found in a Rainbow feeding sample. In my literature reviews I haven't found a logical explanation for this. However, I suspect the chemical composition of an adult is different from a nymph. The chemical differences may repel the trout or cause an adult Dragonfly to taste bad. Conjecture on my part but a possible explanation why the trout don't often feed on adult Dragonflies.

Dragonfly Basics

Adult Dragonflies and adult Damselflies are often mistaken for one another. However, when at rest, the adult Dragonfly will always spread its wings away from the body while the adult Damselfly will always fold its wings together over its back.

As nymphs, it is easy to distinguish the cigar shaped Darners from the flat bodied Dragonflies. However, the species of Dragonflies within their group are difficult to tell apart. Most identifying characteristics are better determined after these insects become adults. Gomphus, for example, are called Clubtails because the tail of the adult has a distinctive widening at the tip that makes it look like a club. Many of our local anglers erroneously identify Libellula (Skimmers) as Gomphinea (Gomphus). Clubtails normally live in ponds rather than lakes. This mistake doesn't really matter but there is a lesson. Don't automatically assume something is correct just because lots of folks say it is so.

Table 22 – Base Data for Dragonfly Nymphs

Dragonflies

Dragonflies, Darners, Skimmers, Gomphus, etc.

Class: Insecta
Order: Odanata
Sub-Order: Anisoptera

APPEARANCE	LIFE AND HABITAT	Relatives	
Adult	**Water**	Damselflies	
Wings outstretched at rest	Darners - well oxygenated		
Not normally consumed	Skimmers - most any water		
Nymph	**Shelter**		
Darners - Cigar shaped	Darners - weeds & rocks		
Skimmers - Quite round	Skimmers - sediments		
Large head & eyes	**Protection**		
COLOR	Hiding & camouflage		
Black to grey or	**Diet**		
Dark green to light green	Predacious on invertebrates		
SIZE	**Breathing**		
Up to 2 1/4 inches in length	Internal gills		
MOVEMENT	**Metamorphosis**		
Darners - Crawl or use	Incomplete		
a form of jet propulsion.	**Life Cycle**		
Skimmers - Crawl or stay	Eggs deposited in water		
motionless in sediments.	and on submerged weeds.	**Flies**	**Fishing & Retrieve**
LOCATION	Eggs into small nymph	Best in sizes 12 to 6	Retrieve in short "spurts"
Darners - among weeds	Grow into large nymph	Show large head & eyes	of 6 to 18 inches then still.
Skimmers - burrows into	Crawls up weeds/shore to	Show prominent legs	Cast deep to shallow in
the bottom sediments.	hatch into adult.	Dubbed body can be	spring & opposite in fall.
NOTE	Hatches mostly after dark	trimmed to shape.	At drop-off during hatch
Term 'skimmers' used for	Life span of 2 to 4 years	Weighted or unweighted	Generally use sinking line
all the round bodied nymphs	Hibernate over winter	Beads make good eyes	
Seasonal Fishing	**Daily Fishing**	**Visual Keys for Rainbow**	**Rainbow Preferences**
Spring migrations best	Best fished evening/night	Large head & eyes	Trout actively seek out
July hatches second best	Good over shoals.	Body shape & size	in all seasons but preferred
Good fly to try all year	Best at shoal drop-off.	Spurt & still movement	during migrations.
Use small flies in fall	Fish deep in bright sun.		Large dragons preferred

Dragonflies have incomplete metamorphosis. They don't go through the larva and pupa stages. Instead, these are replaced by a nymph stage. When a nymph hatches from an egg, it is a very small version of the same nymph ready to emerge into an adult. While maturing, the nymph will go through a series of "instars" where the exoskeleton is shed and replaced with a larger version. Skimmers and similar families of Dragonflies will normally live for two years in the lake before emerging into an adult. The large Darners live about four years before emerging.

A newly hatched nymph is almost microscopic in size. When ready to emerge into an adult, Skimmers are about an inch in length and Darners can be about two inches in length. Skimmers are usually a dark olive-green while Darners are often black but sometimes light green. Both types move by jet propulsion. They inhale water and squirt it out through an anal opening. Thus, movement is a slow crawl or a series of rapid bursts through the water. Both types of Dragonflies are highly predacious and eat most other types of invertebrates in the lake. Because they are hunters, they are found near other invertebrates that can become a meal. Of course, that is usually over a shoal or drop-off. When it is time to emerge into an adult, the nymphs migrate to the shoreline weeds. Dragonflies don't normally synchronize emergence into adults. You don't often see large numbers of individuals transform into adults at the same time. It is more common for a few individuals to emerge on any given day and the majority of those transform into winged adults at night.

Dragonfly Availability and Active Periods

Dragonflies spend two to four years in the lake before emerging into an adult. Nymphs are generally available to the trout all year except during winter hibernation. Hibernation occurs in deep water. After hibernation, the nymphs migrate to the shallows in search of food and shelter. These spring migrations usually occur soon after the ice has come off the lake. The success of Dragonfly imitations is good after April ice-off on the lower elevation lakes and then again in early May as ice-off occurs on the upper elevation lakes. Spring migrations are a prime time to fish Dragonfly nymphs as shown in Figure 32. After spring migrations, the nymphs settle into their hunting and hiding places and are generally less available to the trout.

> Try Dragonflies, Damselflies and large attractor flies by the dark of the moon.

Before emerging into adults, the nymphs often congregate along the drop-off or at select places on the shoals. Gathering in these prime trout areas and their subsequent trip to shore makes them more available and vulnerable to predation. This availability is most pronounced from late June through mid July. That is the period when most of the Darners emerge into adults. The Skimmers tend to emerge a little later in the year. In Figure 32, that is shown as the minor increase in late August.

After the Summer emergence into adults, the number of large Dragonfly nymphs is much lower. The average nymph size is smaller and the general availability has been reduced. The Fall hibernation migration to deep water gets underway in early September. Stragglers and typically smaller nymphs

> **Fishing Tip**
> The best time for fishing Dragonfly nymphs is during the Spring and Fall migrations for hibernation. In the Spring this happens just after ice off. In Fall these are extended but mainly in September.

continue this migration until about mid October. The Fall migration is spread over a longer period of time than Spring migration and is more sporadic fishing for the fly fisher.

Dragonfly nymphs are more available to trout in the evening and at night than during the day. Most of the Dragonfly's food is also available during low light periods so that's when the Dragonfly hunts. However, hunting movement exposes the Dragonfly to predation by trout. Dragonflies are more important on the lower elevation lakes. Part of the explanation for this is simply a longer frost-free season at lower elevations. With a longer season, more individuals can successfully mate later into the fall and therefore provide a higher population density.

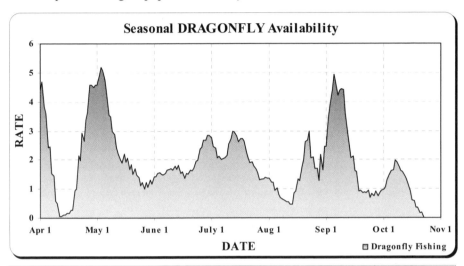

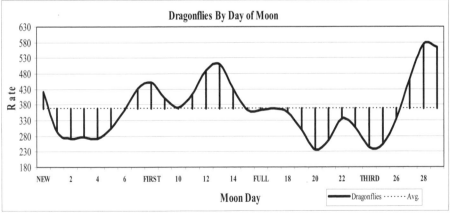

Figure 32 – Seasonal and Lunar Dragonfly Availability

The dark of the moon (New Moon) is the primary time for fishing Dragonfly nymphs. Most big flies fish well by the dark of the moon, including Dragonflies, Damselflies and large attractor flies. A secondary period for Dragonflies occurs before the Full moon (moon days 7 to 14). The worst times are after the Full moon (moon days 19 thru 26) and after the New moon (moon days 1 thru 5).

Environmental Factors and Dragonfly Fishing

Dragonflies fish best in overcast conditions with a low barometer and even in the rain. They prefer cool temperatures such as in the Spring or Fall. However, with their summer hatch migrations, Dragonflies fish better than most flies during the summer heat. Because many nymphs are large, they fish well in most water clarity situations except very clear water.

Dragonfly patterns are good during winds ranging from a strong to very strong. Wave action during these winds dissipates sunlight entering the lake and the Dragonfly nymphs feel safe enough to leave their shelter to hunt. They prefer winds from the Southwest but also fish well when the winds are calm or variable in strength. When winds are from the Northeast, Dragonfly patterns aren't overly successful.

Table 23 – Environmental Factors for Dragonflies

DRAGONFLY NYMPH - Environmental Factors	
Factor	**Best or Worst Fishing Times by Factor**
Season	Good just after ice-off (Spring Migration). Good around Sept. 1 and Oct. 1 (Fall Migrations) Also good from about June 21 to July 21 for main hatch migrations.
Day of Moon	Best around New moon (days 27 to 0) and secondary moon days 7 to 14. Worst around third quarter moon.
Time of Day	A good fly pattern for the evening. Worst in morning and average fishing in the afternoon.
Wind Direction	Best with winds from the NW, W, SW or S. Fairly good in variable winds or calm conditions. Worst with winds from N or E.
Wind Strength	Best from a strong breeze to windy conditions. Poor in light breezes or calm winds.
Air Temperature	Best in cool weather but above average in warm weather when hatch migrations are on. Worst when cold.
Cloud Cover	Not significantly different but steadily improves from clear skies to overcast skies. Good in the rain.
Barometer	Not significantly important but slightly better with low barometer.
Water Temperature	Best in cool water and worst when water gets very cold. Poor in warm water.
Water Clarity	Good in most water clarity situations but worst in very clear water.
Water Level	Best in average water levels. Worst when water is high and fairly poor in low water levels.
# Bugs Seen	Best when very few or no bugs seen. Steadily declines as number of bugs observed increases.
# Fish Rising	Follows the all fishing average. Best with moderate numbers of rises and worst when fish aren't rising.
Location	Best over the shoal, worst in deep water and average at drop-offs.
Miscellaneous	Most frequently available during migrations.
Any fly can catch a fish at any time. Success is improved by using the right fly at the right time.	

Flies To Represent Dragonflies

I believe the large bulbous eyes are one of the visual keys used by Rainbows for quick pre-strike identification of a Dragonfly nymph. I always tie my Dragonfly patterns with large eyes. To me, a Dragonfly pattern just isn't a good Dragonfly imitation without large eyes. As a test I once tied a set of eyes on a hook with nothing more than a dangling piece of black yarn behind the eyes. The fly worked and I kept the fish. Sure enough, the feeding sample contained small Dragonfly nymphs. That isn't conclusive proof but it sure reinforced my opinion that eyes are important on these imitations.

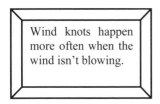

Wind knots happen more often when the wind isn't blowing.

Dragonfly patterns can be tied in almost any size up to about two inches in length. Eyes aren't necessary but I would recommend they be included. If included, the eyes are typically made of glass or plastic beads. The eyes should be attached so their weight is below the hook shank. If the weight of the eyes is above the centre of gravity, the fly will turn upside-down in the water. That isn't catastrophic but should be avoided to increase success. Imitations of Darners are easier to tie than the Skimmers and other flat-bodied nymphs. They also seem to be more successful on a consistent basis. I almost always use dubbing to tie the body of a Dragonfly nymph. The dubbing can be quite thick and then trimmed to the correct body shape. Trimming even works for the flat bodied Skimmer patterns. I always provide a wing case just behind the head. Add some heavy-duty legs and the fly is complete. Many Darners are black and I have found black to be more successful than the green versions.

Fishing Dragonfly Fly Patterns

Dragonfly patterns can be weighted and fished with a floating line. However, the more conventional method is with a sinking or sink-tip line. Imitations of the flat bodied nymphs should be fished on the lake bottom. Skimmers and other flat bodied nymphs seldom rise out of the bottom muck. You can fish them still, with an occasional twitch or use a short retrieve to attract the Rainbows attention. This is the best way to fish imitations of Skimmers. That's because these critters lie on the bottom and wait for their food. They don't move around much.

The cigar shaped Darners go in search of their food. They crawl or make a series of short squirts, using their jet propulsion to move around the lake. For this reason, Darner patterns can be retrieved in a variety of methods. With a dry or sink-tip line, use short pulls to bring the fly off the bottom and then allow it to settle back. With a full sink line, the distance of the retrieve can be long or short and the speed either fast or slow. However, the fly should stay within five feet of the lake bottom. Casting toward deep water and retrieving up the drop off is good in Spring. The reverse is good in the Fall. These retrieves follow the general direction of expected migrations. Casting and retrieving parallel to the drop-off works well in mid summer when the nymphs congregate prior to their hatch migration to shore. With Darner imitations

203

you can be quite flexible and try most any method that suits your fancy at the time. These are good searching patterns to find out where the trout are feeding.

Damselfly (nymph)

Like Dragonfly adults, Damselfly adults are rarely found in Rainbow feeding samples. Damselflies and Dragonflies are close relatives and the trout probably  don't feed on the adults of either for the same reasons discussed for the Dragonfly. Trout most frequently prey on Damselfly nymphs as they migrate to or from hibernation areas or as they migrate toward the shoreline weeds to emerge into adults. In pristine lakes, most species of Damselflies grow to about the same size and generally have one generation per year. They hibernate over winter but are available and a primary food of Rainbows through the open water season.

Table 24 – Damselfly Base Data

 Damselflies

Damselflies, Damsels, Narrow Wings, Bog Dancers, etc.

Class: Insecta
Order: Odanata
Sub-Order: Zygoptera

APPEARANCE	LIFE AND HABITAT	Relatives	
Adult	**Water**	Dragonflies	
Wings folded at rest	Shallow, clean water		
Not normally consumed	**Shelter**		
Nymph	Submerged weeds & rocks		
Tubular body/thorax	**Protection**		
Three-pronged tail (gills)	Hiding & camouflage		
Large head & eyes	**Diet**		
COLOR	Predacious on invertebrates		
Various greens to browns	**Breathing**		
Darkens as nymph matures	Broad gills on tail		
SIZE	**Metamorphosis**		
Up to 1 1/2 inches in length	Incomplete		
MOVEMENT	**Life Cycle**		
Crawls among vegetation	Eggs laid on submerged		
Swims like a fish	plants in shallow water.		
Progress is slow	Eggs into small nymph		
Migrates spring after	Grow into large nymph	**Flies**	**Fishing & Retrieve**
water warms and again in	Crawls up shorline weeds	Best in sizes 14 to 10	Use dry or sinking line
fall before too cold.	to hatch into adult.	Show large head & eyes	Best fished "still" since
LOCATION	Hatches at mid-day	Show prominent tail (gills)	nymph sweeps tail and
Hides among shoal weeds	Many individuals hatch at	Tube shaped abdomen	fly cannot duplicate.
Swims at most depths	same time on same day.	Weighted or unweighted	Best over shoals
Crawls up shoreline weeds	Life span of 1 year	Light colors for small flies	Better during migrations
to hatch.	Hibernate over winter	Darker colors for large.	rather than hatches.
Seasonal Fishing	**Daily Fishing**	**Visual Keys for Rainbow**	**Rainbow Preferences**
Best in June migrations	Migrations & hatches	Swimming motion OR	A preferred food during
Hatches in July / late Aug.	happen at mid-day.	tubular body & broad tail.	migrations & hatches.
Fall migrations in Oct.	Sunny days generally best	Large head & eyes.	Preferred in shallows
Use small flies in fall	Seldom good in low light.		

Damselfly Basics

An adult Damselfly will fold its wings over its back when at rest. Damselflies are dainty in comparison to a Dragonfly. Large Damselfly nymphs have a large head and eyes, like the Dragonfly, but they have a much slimmer and tubular abdomen. Small Damselfly nymphs do not have a head that is as well developed or pronounced. The tail of these nymphs is an identifying characteristic. The tail consists of three large and feathery looking flaps that are actually the gills.

Damselflies have incomplete metamorphosis and the angler is interested in the nymph stage. By the time a Damselfly nymph is ready to emerge into a winged adult, it will usually have grown to about 1.5 inches in length and lived in the lake for a year. As Damsel nymphs grow, they tend to darken in color. In the Fall, very young nymphs are often a pale yellowish-green to bluish green in color. By the following Spring, when they are ready to emerge, they are often a dirty olive-green to brown in color. Adult males are frequently a bright blue color while the females are a drab grey, brown or black color.

When moving, Damselfly nymphs normally crawl along the lake bottom or within the aquatic vegetation. When faster movement is required, these nymphs swim much like a fish. The entire abdomen and tail is swept back and forth to push the nymph through the water. This type of movement is almost impossible for the fly fisher to imitate. Damselflies migrate to and

> If you suspect Damselflies are hatching but haven't seen them in the water, then check the shoreline weeds. That's where they emerge into adults.

from hibernating areas and to the shoreline weeds to hatch. During migrations, these nymphs swim toward their destination anywhere in the water column but the majority are near the lake bottom.

Damselfly Availability and Active Periods

Migrations are the prime times for Rainbows to feed on Damselfly nymphs. Spring, hibernation migrations do not seem to be a major event with lots of individuals migrating at the same time. At lower elevations, these migrations occur around the beginning of May and around the beginning of June for the higher elevation lakes. In the Fall, small nymphs migrate back to their hibernating areas throughout October.

Emerging into adults occurs from late June through July but there is a secondary emergence near the end of August. These hatches can be seen graphically in Figure 33. The migrations associated with these hatches can sometimes be massive with thousands of individuals swimming toward the shore at the same time. The trout actively feed on these but can afford to become very selective. Your fly in the middle of such a migration becomes insignificant and isn't a likely target for feeding trout. The Fall migrations through October are probably more productive for the angler. At this time, the nymphs are smaller with a somewhat synchronized migration that isn't as massive as hatch migrations. This seems to provide a feeding incentive for the trout and allows the angler a chance for success since the individual nymphs are more scattered.

Unlike Dragonflies, the Damselfly nymphs are not generally active at night. A migration will typically start in mid morning, peak at midday and be over by mid afternoon. Trout may eat stragglers in the evening. Nymphs congregating for migration the following day may also be found by trout foraging in the evening. However, evening isn't the best time to fish Damselfly imitations. Like the Dragonflies, Damselflies are more important as a source of Rainbow food on the lower elevation lakes. Once again this is likely due to the longer season.

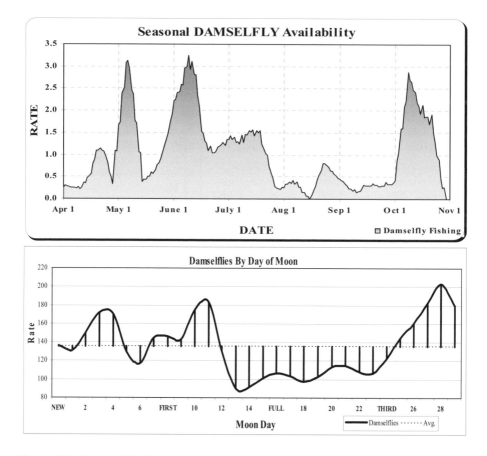

Figure 33 – Damselfly Seasonal and Lunar Availability

Damselflies, like Dragonflies, seem to prefer the New moon for coming out of hiding and being available to the trout. Around New moon (moon days 25 thru 4) seems to be the best. There is a secondary incidence of positive lunar effects just after the First Quarter moon. The worst time to fish Damselfly nymphs is when the Full thru Third Quarter moon is casting evening moonlight into the water. This occurs from moon days 13 thru 24.

Environmental Factors and Damselfly Fishing

When Damselflies begin to migrate, imitations fish well in the morning before too many individuals join the trek. Many of these nymphs start to migrate by eight o'clock in the morning. Often, numbers peak around 3 pm and by 6 pm the migration is finished. Imitations of Damselflies fish better when only a few individuals are seen. Success is usually poor when lots of individuals are seen. The angler should try to be fishing at the start of migrations to avoid large population densities.

These critters prefer clear, cold water on cloudless days with a mild temperature and a breeze blowing. They don't seem especially fond of rain or other foul weather conditions. I suspect this is because they want nice weather to migrate or dry their new wings when emerging into an adult. Damselflies like a breeze that is variable in direction or else from a southerly direction.

Table 25 – Environmental Factors for Damselfly Nymphs

DAMSELFLY NYMPH - Environmental Factors	
Factor	**Best or Worst Fishing Times by Factor**
Season	Best during migrations around early May, early June and again thru October. Main hatches are from mid June to mid July.
Day of Moon	Worst from moon days 13 to 24. Best before New moon (days 25 to 29). Secondary peaks around the 3rd and 10th days of the moon.
Time of Day	Fishes well in the morning as migrations start but is best in the mid afternoon. After 6pm is fairly poor for Damselfly fishing.
Wind Direction	Best with variable wind directions. Good with winds from the S and worst with calm winds.
Wind Strength	Worst when winds are calm or very strong. Best in breezy conditions.
Air Temperature	Best with mild temperatures. Worst on cold days. Can be successful on hot days when other flies aren't.
Cloud Cover	Best under clear skies. Otherwise no significant difference.
Barometer	Worst with a changing barometer and poor when moderate.
Water Temperature	Worst when water temps are very cold or else warm. Best in cool to cold water.
Water Clarity	Best in clear to cloudy water. Otherwise no significant difference.
Water Level	Worst in high water and significantly better in low water conditions.
# Bugs Seen	Damsels are often seen when migrating. Best when a few are seen and worst when many or else none are seen.
# Fish Rising	Best with moderate numbers of fish rising and fishes well when only a few are rising. Worst when no fish are rising.
Location	Best over shoals as Damsels migrate.
Miscellaneous	Damselflies swim like a fish and this movement is almost impossible to imitate so fishing this fly still is most effective.
Any fly can catch a fish at any time. Success is improved by using the right fly at the right time.	

Flies To Represent Damselflies

During the May and June hibernation migrations, the Damselfly nymphs are large. For the June and July hatch migrations, the nymphs are as large as they will get. For these larger nymphs, tie an imitation on a #10 or #8 long shank hook. Good

> A fly will not hang up in your vest, trousers or ear unless you forgot to bend down the barb.

imitations should have a bulbous head, eyes and a tubular abdomen ending in the three large tails (gills). These seem to be the Rainbows main visual keys for the large nymphs. The eyes don't need to be nearly as large as a Dragonfly nymph and are typically tied in olive green to brown materials. With these larger hooks I don't usually bother with weighting the fly. In fact, they tend to rest better on the underwater vegetation without the weighting.

In the fall, the recently hatched nymphs are small, light greenish-yellow in color and neither the tail nor head are nearly as pronounced. The visual keys are probably the small size, tubular shape and the light color tones. I usually tie these on a #14 or #16 hook and add the weighting to get the flies down in the water column. Your flies to imitate a Damselfly nymph should be tailored to fit the season.

Fishing Damselfly Fly Patterns

> ### Fishing Tip
> Rainbows seem to visually key on the swimming motion of Damselfly nymphs. Your fly cannot duplicate this movement. To sidestep this key, try fishing this fly without any forward motion.

Both large and small Damselfly nymphs swim like a fish during migrations. I have seen attempts to imitate that motion through different fly designs and different methods of retrieve, such as wiggling the rod tip during the retrieve. I haven't been impressed with the success of these attempts. I suggest you fish the fly still with a dry line. The trout tend to key on the swimming motion and this approach takes away that visual key. When the nymphs are swimming, it takes a lot of energy. They get tired and frequently stop for a rest while slowly settling toward the bottom. The trout show little sportsmanship and will take a resting Damsel as fast as a moving one. An imitation that is not retrieved but allowed to settle toward the bottom works well. Also, try fishing the fly right on the lake bottom or resting on the weeds. This seems to be an effective way to fish Damselfly patterns. The fly should be placed where you know the fish are actively feeding on Damselfly nymphs. Otherwise it could be a long wait before being discovered by a trout.

An important consideration on Damselfly fishing is when to use or not use an imitation. During the peak of a migration with 100,000 individuals, the odds of a trout taking your imitation, as opposed to a real nymph, are fairly limited. I sometimes think it best to lift anchor and go home when I see a major Damselfly event. However, if you can spot the first few Damselflies as an event is getting started, you can get some excellent fishing. The trout are pretty wise about knowing when an event will occur and there will likely be lots of fish waiting for it to happen. If you are lucky enough to present a Damselfly imitation when there are lots of fish waiting and only a few nymphs available, then you have the advantage. Any reasonable imitation is likely to be taken near the start of these migrations.

Mayflies

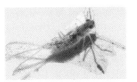

Mayflies require clean, unpolluted water. For this reason they are good indicators of lake health. As water becomes polluted, Mayflies are one of the first species of aquatic invertebrate to disappear. Even prolonged use of outboard motors with their slight discharge of oil will impact the Mayfly populations. I suspect this has happened to the Mayfly populations on the lakes I fish. Years of outboard motor use may have decreased the abundance of Mayflies. The hatches are small to moderate in size and we don't generally get those species with large individuals that attract the larger trout.

> The fish will always be more active upwind from where you are fishing.

My data for pristine lakes of the southern interior of BC shows only 2.5% of the Rainbows feeding samples consist of Mayflies. The relative abundance and importance of Mayflies is not as significant as on lakes found to our East. However, except for their abundance, I believe the data shows the general trends that can be expected for Mayflies on most pristine trout lakes.

Mayfly Basics

Mayflies have complete metamorphosis. However, the terms applied to this process are slightly different than the other bugs we have examined. When it hatches from an egg, the larva of a Mayfly isn't a worm-like critter similar to most species with complete metamorphosis. Instead the Mayfly larva has an abdomen, thorax, head, tail and legs. For this reason it is often referred to as a nymph. The larva or nymph transforms into a "sub-imago" when developed and those are what we see emerge from the larval shell during a hatch. The sub-imago isn't yet sexually mature. It takes a couple of days to a couple of weeks, depending on the species, for the sub-imago to transform into an "imago" or sexually mature adult. The stages of metamorphosis for a Mayfly are generally listed as egg, nymph, sub-imago and imago.

> All fly lines come with a guarantee that ensures they will wrap around anything in the bottom of your boat, including your feet.

Depending on the species, it's common for Mayflies to have one, two or three generations per year. The larger species have longer life spans and smaller species have shorter life spans. Mayflies have two or three longish tails visible through all their developmental stages. As nymphs, Mayflies have gills along the sides of their abdomen. This tends to give them a flattened appearance. The sub-imago sits on the water surface with its wings held upright over the body. This gives it a very triangular shape. I have seen winged Mayflies from east of the Rockies that are more than an inch in length without the tail. On the lakes I fish the average size is more like 0.6 inches including the tail and some species of half that size.

Mayflies come in a variety of colors. Reddish-brown to brown and slate grey are the most common colors. The wings are mostly transparent with veins. The nymphs burrow into substrates and crawl or cling to bottom plants. When faster movement is required, Mayflies in lakes swim like a fish. Swimming to the surface hatch is a fairly fast movement but not nearly as fast as the Caddis. When on the surface the sub-imago will sit motionless until it takes flight. The spent imagos may twitch or wiggle as they die and then, naturally, they remain motionless.

During swarming, mating and laying eggs, the imagos stay near the shoreline. Thus, most eggs are dropped in shallow to very shallow water. The nymphs continue to live in the shallows. Thus, most of the Mayflies life cycle is spent in the shallow waters near the shore. The winged stages may drift into deeper water, but the vast majority of Mayflies are found in very shallow water.

Table 26 – Mayfly Base Data

Mayflies

Mayflies, Mays, Upwings, Dippers, Fish Flies, etc.

Types of Mayflies: Swimmers, Crawlers, Burrowers & Clingers

Class: Insecta
Order: Ephemoroptera
Sub-Orders: Schistonota and Pannota

APPEARANCE	LIFE AND HABITAT	Relatives	
Pre-Adult & Adult	**Water**	Related to other Mayflies	
Called Sub-imago & Imago	Clean and well oxygenated.	12 Families of Schistonota	
Translucent upright wings	Cannot tolerate pollution	or "Splitbacks"	
2 or 3 long tails	**Shelter**	5 Families of Pannota	
Tubular tapered body	Weeds, mud, logs, etc.	or "Fusedbacks"	
Nymph	None - Imagos		
2 or 3 long tails	**Protection**		
Long narrow body with	Hiding in shelter and often		
gills on sides of abdomen.	staying in shallow water.		
Six thin legs	**Diet**		
COLOR	Organic bottom materials		
Browns, greys, greens, etc.	**Breathing**		
SIZE	Gills on sides of abdomen		
Up to 1 1/4 inch in length	**Life Cycle**		
Usually less than 3/4 inch	Swarm & mate in flight		
including tail.	Eggs dropped near shore		
Highly variable by species	Nymphs grow in shallows	**Flies**	**Fishing & Retrieve**
MOVEMENT	Nymph swims to surface	Best in sizes 18 to 12	Imagos best fished still
Imagos fly or sit on water	Hatches into sub-imago	Weighted or unweighted	as dry fly on surface.
Nymph crawls or sweeps	Sub-imago takes flight	Show sparse but long tails	Nymphs best fished over
tail to swim like a fish.	Develops into sexually	Tie imagos as dry flies &	shallows with long but
LOCATION	mature adult (Imago).	wings upright or on surface.	slow retrieve near bottom
Mostly over shoals and	Imagos die after mating	Halfback type flies good	with dry or sinking line.
often very close to shore.	Life span 3 mo to 1yr	to represent nymphs.	
Seasonal Fishing	**Daily Fishing**	**Visual Keys for Rainbow**	**Rainbow Preferences**
Available most of season	Best in evenings but also	Imago - on surface & wings	Imagos an easy prey and
Seasonal peak in June	good during daylight hours.	upright or outstretched.	preferred by smaller trout.
Good May & late July	Best in shallow clean water	Nymph - tails, body shape	Larger trout generally
Minor hatches into fall	Watch surface for Imagos	& speed of movement.	prefer Mayfly nymphs.

Mayfly Availability and Active Periods

Different species of Mayflies are available throughout the frost-free period. The seasonal peaks are in early May on lower elevation lakes and early June on the higher elevation lakes. Various hatches occur through the summer and even a couple of minor hatches occur in the fall. I suspect the position of the moon plays a more important role in the timing of the summer and fall hatches than it does for the early season hatches.

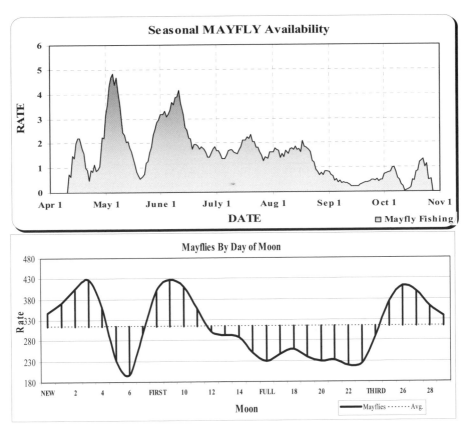

Figure 34 – Seasonal and Lunar Availability of Mayflies

Most Rainbows, and especially the larger ones, commonly feed on Mayflies during the evening hours. Hatches and mating flights tend to happen more frequently at this time of day. In addition, because Mayflies stay in shallow water, the more experienced fish will wait for low light levels to enter the shallows. During the day and bright light conditions, there are fewer hatches and fewer fish willing to enter the shallows. For the most part, those that do are the smaller and less experienced fish.

> Too often, the path of a hooked fish is directly at your anchor rope.

211

Mayflies are more important to the food chain of upper elevation lakes. Of the feeding samples containing Mayflies, 66% were from higher elevations lakes. Often, these lakes have cleaner water and thus a greater abundance of Mayflies.

Mayflies are primarily available during the dark of the moon (days 25 to 4 plus days 8 to 11). Mayflies tend not to hatch or become Rainbow food when strong moonlight is shining on the evening waters (days 12 thru 24). I'm not sure about the drop in Mayflies around the 6th day of the moon. Perhaps it's a data glitch or simply a lack of local Mayfly species with their biological clocks timed to that particular moon phase.

Environmental Factors and Mayfly Fishing

Mayflies prefer good weather conditions and that is when the trout are forced to feed on these critters. Mayflies like skies that are clear or have a light cloud cover. Even so, they sometimes fish well in rainy conditions. Some Mayflies like hot days while others prefer cool days. Very few, if any, seem to like cold days or warm water conditions.

Table 27 – Environmental Factors and Mayflies

MAYFLIES - Environmental Factors	
Factor	**Best or Worst Fishing Times by Factor**
Season	Peaks in early May and early June. Fairly consistent from mid June to Sept. Often poor after Sept. 1.
Day of Moon	Good from the 26th day of the moon thru the 11th except for the 5th & 6th. Poor from the 12th thru 24th moon days.
Time of Day	Best in the evening hours till 11pm. Poor in the early morning but steadily improves till mid afternoon.
Wind Direction	Best with variable wind directions and good with winds from the W, SW & S. Worst with winds from the north.
Wind Strength	Best in breezy winds but fishes well even in strong or variable winds. Worst in calm conditions.
Air Temperature	Good in hot or cool weather. Cold days are worst.
Cloud Cover	Good on clear days to days with light cloud. Also good in the rain. Worst with heavy cloud or overcast.
Barometer	Best with a moderater barometer. Worst with a variable barometr.
Water Temperature	Best in cold or very cold water. Worst in warm to mild water temps.
Water Clarity	Best in clear water. Worst in murky to very murky waters.
Water Level	Worst in high water and best at low water.
# Bugs Seen	Best when a few to moderate numbers of Mayflies are seen on the surface. Nymphs fish well when no bugs are seen.
# Fish Rising	Good when lots of fish are rising. Steadily gets poorer as numbers of rising fish declines. Worst when fish aren't rising.
Location	Best over the shoals and worst in deep water.
Miscellaneous	Hatches are usually in very shallow water in the afternoon with mating and egg laying in the evening.
Any fly can catch a fish at any time. Success is improved by using the right fly at the right time.	

Fishing dry flies to represent Mayfly sub-imagos and imagos is best when a few are seen on the water. However, none need be present for successful fishing of the Mayfly nymphs. The best place for fishing both is in the shallow water but when on the surface, these bugs often drift onto most parts of the lake.

Flies To Represent Mayflies

Flies to imitate Mayflies have been around since the dawn of fly fishing. I wouldn't be surprised if the first fly designed to actually look like a specific invertebrate was fashioned after the Mayfly. There is an abundance of good wet flies to imitate the Mayfly nymph and dry flies to imitate the terrestrial life stages of this insect.

For pristine lakes, an imitation of a Mayfly nymph should be small, slim-bodied with legs and have a sparse but longish tail. Small Halfbacks work as well as anything to represent Mayfly nymphs. These can be weighted or not and large flies would be a #12 hook. Dry flies to represent the terrestrial stages of a Mayfly should float well. Wings can be upright to imitate the sub-imago or lying on the water surface to represent a spent imago. Hackles are often used with these to assist with floatation. Dry flies should have two or three longish tails. The Rainbow's visual key to Mayflies, seems to be the general shape, size and a two or three pronged tail.

Fishing Mayfly Fly Patterns

Fishing Mayflies in pristine trout lakes differs from fishing Mayflies in a stream or river. For the most part, the species of Mayflies in flowing water are shaped differently, move differently and live differently from those in lakes. Thus, the trout in lakes have adopted slightly different approaches to capture Mayflies.

Small fish eat each day
And are easy prey.
Large fish have peaks
And may not feed for weeks.

During daytime hatches, you often see many smaller fish rising to Mayflies in the shallows. Smaller trout are opportunistic and will risk feeding in these conditions. Larger fish tend to avoid real shallow water in the daytime unless the water is murky and you won't likely find Mayflies in murky water. If larger fish are interested in a daytime hatch, they tend to feed at the drop-off on Mayflies drifting with the wind. Since I like to try for larger Rainbows, I often avoid these shallow water hatches unless I see an occasional larger fish participating in the feed. During these hatches the small fish are easy to catch and provide good experience for the beginning fly fisher but are not much of a challenge for the experienced angler.

The same is not true when the hatch is occurring at or after sunset. At that time, cast a nymph over the shallow feeding grounds. With the low light levels, large Rainbows frequently move into these areas even if they aren't taking dry flies. The big Rainbows will sometimes move into water that is

The biggest fish will always throw the hook just short of your landing net.

213

only two or three feet deep to feed on Mayfly nymphs. However, they seem to prefer the protection offered by a weedy bottom as opposed to marl or muddy bottom. A nymph fished on a dry line with nine to twelve feet of leader seems to provide a good presentation. An unweighted fly allows for a slower retrieve or presentation closer to the surface. Or the fly can be weighted for a faster retrieve or presentation closer to the bottom. You may have to experiment to find the right combination to suit the lighting and feeding conditions.

> The very big fish will never strike until just after a wind knot develops in your leader.

When a breeze blows Mayflies from the shallows into deeper water, dry fly fishing can be good, even in the daytime. Since Mayflies mostly hatch in the shallow water, there will be few nymphs out deeper. Larger fish that are hungry often wait for imagos or sub-imagos (dry flies) on the surface. The larger fish are likely to take dry flies in this deeper water at any time of day. If present, you should see these bigger fish coming to the surface. If you do, then it's time to place a dry Mayfly into their feeding zone. Remember not to cast the dry fly directly into the Rainbow's visual surface window.

Waterboatmen

Waterboatmen are not beetles (Order Coleoptera). They belong to the order of true waterbugs (Order Hemiptera). All waterbugs bite or sting except for the Waterboatman. For that reason, I don't include Backswimmers into this discussion. Backswimmers can inflict a nasty sting and I suggest you use caution if picking these up with your hands. Rainbows may feed on the occasional Backswimmer but you will usually find only one or two in a feeding sample. Only once have I had a confirmed report of a Rainbow eating its fill of Backswimmers. It must have been very hungry or masochistic to withstand more than a couple of Backswimmer stings.

Boatman Basics

> **Did You Know**
> Contrary to popular opinion, Boatmen flights aren't for mating. These swarming flights allow the Boatmen to expand their territory. In addition, these critters chirp like a cricket to attract a mate and mating occurs underwater.

Waterboatmen have incomplete metamorphosis but the nymph looks about the same as an adult. The nymph isn't sexually mature and doesn't have developed wings. Even when fully developed the membranous wings of an adult are covered by hard chitinous sheaths and are usually only visible during flight. It's difficult to tell a Boatman nymph from an adult.

Boatmen look something like a beetle, with a head as wide as the body. They have a pair of legs adapted as paddles or swimmers. Each swimmer has a hair tuft on the end to push against the water. The bug literally swims through the water with these paddles. Another pair of adapted legs, of about the same size, act as stabilizers and don't have the hair tufts. Swimming can be a chore because the Boatman carries an air bubble that supplies it with breathable air. These critters often place themselves under or cling to submerged vegetation to keep them from floating to the surface. When it's time, Boatmen will swim to the waters surface and grab a new bubble of fresh air.

When Boatmen reach sexual maturity, they attract a mate by chirping, much like a cricket but underwater. Mating occurs underwater and a short time later, many adults will congregate and then take flight. These swarming flights are not for mating. Instead, pregnant females accompanied by willing males are searching for new locations to lay their eggs. They may fly to somewhere else on the same lake or they may fly many miles in search of a new lake or pond. I have observed Boatmen bouncing off the hoods and roofs of parked cars. What they mistakenly thought was the reflection from water was shiny automobile paint.

Table 28 – Basic Information for Waterboatmen

Waterboatmen

Waterboatmen, Boatmen, Paddle Bugs

Class: Insecta
Order: Hemiptera
Family: Corixidae

APPEARANCE	LIFE AND HABITAT	Relatives	
Adult	**Water**	Backswimmer and	
Have wings, otherwise	Most types of water	all true water bugs.	
same as nymph.	**Shelter**	**NOTE**	
Nymph	Bottom vegetation	This is only water bug	
Large head & eyes	**Protection**	that doesn't bite or sting.	
No neck & Six legs -	Hiding in weedy areas		
2 swimmers with tufts,	Nymph has scent glands		
2 stabilizers & 2 graspers.	to give it a bad taste.		
Dorsally flattened body	**Diet**		
Oval shaped	Mostly algae & plant parts		
COLOR	**Breathing**		
Mottled brown - upper	Air - carries air bubble		
White to cream - lower	**Metamorphosis**		
Carries silvery air bubble	Incomplete		
SIZE	**Life Cycle**		
Up to 1/2 inch in length	Eggs on submerged plants		
MOVEMENT	Eggs into small nymph	**Flies**	**Fishing & Retrieve**
Adults fly & splash land	Grow into large nymph	Best in sizes 16 to 12	Best with sinking line
Swim with two paddles	Adult develops flight wings	Show 2 swimming paddles	and bouyant fly.
Swim to and from water	Chirp to attract mate	Give oval shape	Retrieve with short pulls
surface to get air.	Mate underwater, then fly	Best to show 2 stabilizers	to imitate paddling.
LOCATION	Have swarming flights and	Silver air bubble optional	Bring fly down, across &
Mostly in shallows near	travel to other lakes.	Best bouyant or unweighted	then up (up & down best)
bottom vegetation.	Life span about 1 year	Head/eyes are optional	Can be used on dry line
Seasonal Fishing	**Daily Fishing**	**Visual Keys for Rainbow**	**Rainbow Preferences**
Best in Fall (Oct/Nov)	Best when bright & sunny	Basic body with 2 paddles	Adults are preferred
Good in Spring	Best in middle of day	Up or down movement	Nymphs seldom taken
Seldom in mid-summer	Not for foul weather	Sometimes air bubble	due to foul taste.
Use largest flies in fall	Watch for "splash downs"		Best during swarm flights

After their swarming flight, Waterboatmen simply dive into the water and paddle towards the lake bottom. If the lake surface is relatively calm, you can see rings on the surface that look like rain drops hitting the water. Occasionally one will crash into your boat. They tend to land anywhere on the lake. Trout seem to become excited by the sound from these tiny splashes and actively begin to feed on Boatmen.

Boatmen nymphs don't 'hatch' into the adult stage. The process is a slow and gradual transformation. Depending on the species, Boatmen have one or two generations per year. Boatmen with two generations per year will mate and swarm in both the spring and fall. Those with one generation per year tend to swarm in the Fall. The net result is a greater number of individuals in the fall flights than the spring flights.

Boatman Availability and Active Periods

Only rarely do Rainbows feed on Waterboatmen during the summer months. The trout have a definite preference for adult Boatmen and these are only available in the Spring and Fall. From May through mid August, Boatmen are in the nymph stage and the trout seem to reject these. I suspect the nymphs emit a chemical repellant and the trout refuses to feed on that stage of their development.

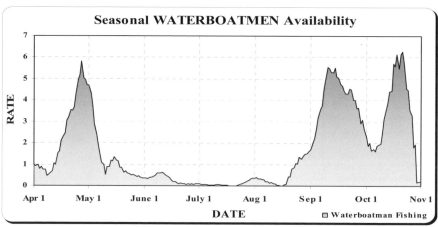

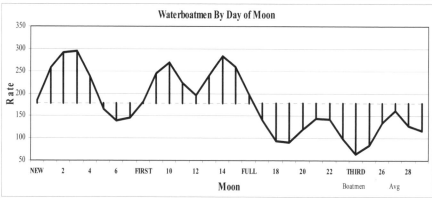

Figure 35 – Seasonal and Lunar Availability of Waterboatmen

Beginning in September is the primary time to fish Waterboatman fly patterns. All species of Boatmen have adults mating and swarming at that time. The species with

216

one generation per year are large individuals by that time and thus more attractive to the trout. The Spring period can also be good but this is a shorter cycle with smaller individuals. The majority of the species with two generations per year live in the lower elevation lakes. The result is Boatmen being slightly more important on lower elevation lakes with 55% of the Boatmen found in feeding samples. In addition, Boatmen aren't very active at night. Mating, swarming and other activities that make Boatmen available to Rainbows happen during the daytime.

Rainbows primarily feed on Waterboatmen from the New moon until the Full moon (moon days 0 to 16). An angler interested in being on a lake for Boatmen fishing, should plan their outings to coincide with these moon days. Fishing Boatman fly patterns is several times more successful after the New moon than it is after the Full moon.

Table 29 – Environmental Factors for Waterboatmen

WATERBOATMEN - Environmental Factors	
Factor	**Best or Worst Fishing Times by Factor**
Season	Best after Sept. 1st but also good on low elevation lakes just after ice-off in the Spring. Not good in the summer months.
Day of Moon	Good from the New moon (day 0) till the Full moon (day 16). Poor from moon day 17 thru 29.
Time of Day	Worst early morning or late evening. Poor during the evening hours. Best from noon to 6pm.
Wind Direction	Doesn't like winds from the N & NE. Best with winds from the W, SW & S. Variable wind directions also fairly good.
Wind Strength	Best with a light to moderate breeze. Worst in calm conditions.
Air Temperature	Prefers moderate air temps and not especially fond of hot or cold days..
Cloud Cover	Best on cloudless days or only a few clouds. No significant difference after that. Doesn't like rain.
Barometer	Significantly better with a high barometer. Poor with a low barometer and worst with a changing barometer.
Water Temperature	Boatmen like cold water but fishing drops off in very cold water. Worst conditions are warm to mild water temps.
Water Clarity	Clear to cloudy water best. Very clear water worst but also poor in murky to very murky water.
Water Level	Worst in high water and best in low water levels.
# Bugs Seen	Fish well when no bugs are seen or else bugs are very few to moderate in numbers. Poor when lots of bugs are observed.
# Fish Rising	Best when moderate number of fish are rising. Also fishes well with no rises or even when lots of fish are rising.
Location	Boatmen tend to land anywhere in the lake. No significant difference in location but slightly better at the drop-off.
Miscellaneous	Best fishing in the fall when Boatmen are dropping into the lake from their swarming flights.
Any fly can catch a fish at any time. Success is improved by using the right fly at the right time.	

Environmental Factors and Boatman Fishing

Waterboatmen are very picky about wind direction. They don't like winds that are coming in from the North or Northeast. These bugs like nice weather. They are not fond of any types of foul weather. They like clear skies, mild air temperatures and a light breeze with a high barometer.

Fishing flies to imitate Boatmen is best when a swarming flight is landing in the lake. However, these bugs don't seem to care where they splash down. They may land in the middle of the lake as often as over a shoal. Water conditions won't necessarily match the lake they left behind but they try to find water that is clear to slightly cloudy. Naturally, the water is typically cold in the Spring and Fall. Boatmen patterns are more successful when fished at midday than during the morning or evening. Details of the environmental factors affecting Waterboatmen are provided in Table 29.

> **Did You Know**
> Canada has more lakes than the rest of the world combined.

Flies To Represent Waterboatmen

The best Boatmen patterns are tied on size 16 to 12 hooks. The body should be oval shaped and dorsally flattened if possible. One of the main visual keys for this fly is the swimmers or paddles of the Waterboatman. They should be extended from the fly about half way down the body. Many folks like to make the paddles so they flex with a short pull on the line. This helps represent the swimming motion of the bug.

> If you are observant, it will improve your success as well as your enjoyment of the sport.

Boatman patterns are often tied with a black or dark brown wing case and a white or silvery underside. White is the color on the underside and silver is sometimes used to represent reflection from the air bubble the Boatman carries. I would suggest avoiding the use of yellows or pinks on the underside since the Boatman will start to look like a Backswimmer. I also suggest that Boatmen patterns not be weighted. These bugs don't sink while carrying their air bubble. If anything, they tend to rise in the water column. You may even consider tying Boatman patterns that float.

Recently I have started adding the stabilizer legs to my Boatman patterns. Those two legs are almost as prominent as the paddles. When these two legs are added, it seems to imitate the Waterboatman more accurately. I don't have confirmation yet, but I believe the pattern is more effective with the stabilizers than without.

> **Fishing Tip**
> Before and after their swarming flights, Boatmen can sometimes be seen on the surface gathering and diving with an air bubble. This is a sign for the angler to dig into the fly box for a Boatman pattern.

Fishing Boatman Fly Patterns

Even though Boatmen land most anywhere in a lake from a swarming flight, that doesn't mean the trout will be feeding on them in all locations. Watch for 'rise lines' to indicate the trout's location. For a variety of reasons, the trout may be selective in where they feed.

Boatmen spend most of their time near the lake bottom but swim to and from the surface for an air bubble. Therefore, the fly can be retrieved most anywhere in the water column. Trout will take these bugs on the surface one time and on the bottom at other times. A retrieve with short, jerky pulls that brings the fly straight up or down is a good fishing method. The short, jerky movement imitates the bugs paddling motion. Up or down is the general direction that Boatmen travel. Upward to get an air bubble and down with the bubble or after landing from a swarming flight. To get these directions, use a slow sink line with a buoyant Boatman pattern. Let the line sink while the fly floats. When the line pulls the fly under, start the jerky retrieve and that should pull your fly straight toward the bottom. The fly will then travel across the bottom and then vertically back up toward your boat. You are retrieving through a "U" shape that should locate any interested fish.

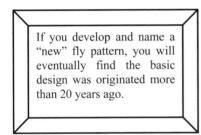

If you develop and name a "new" fly pattern, you will eventually find the basic design was originated more than 20 years ago.

Boatmen sometimes sit on the surface to rest when gathering an air bubble. I have watched many Boatmen taken by trout as they do this. You may want to try fishing the boatman as a dry fly. If it isn't taken within a short while, try the jerky retrieve to imitate the first part of a dive. Trout will sometimes be watching the floating Boatman and not take it till it moves.

Minor Rainbow Foods

Rainbow trout feed on bugs other than seven primary invertebrates we have just discussed. I consider these other foods to be of minor importance. Not necessarily because the trout seldom eat these, but because there are various reasons to limit their importance to the fly fisher.

Leeches

Many fly fishers tie and angle with fly patterns they call Leeches. These fly patterns are very successful. However, I'm convinced that Rainbows are taking these flies as an attractor fly rather than a fly to imitate a Leech.

Leeches are related to aquatic worms and belong to the class Hirudinea. They have 35 body segments with an anterior and posterior sucker. They can use these suckers to creep across the lake bottom like an inch-worm or they can swim like a fish or eel.

I've seen them up to five inches in length in our pristine lakes. Most are scavengers but some are predators seeking out snails and insect larvae. Leeches hatch from eggs and the young are small versions of the adult.

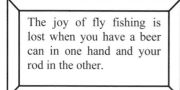

The joy of fly fishing is lost when you have a beer can in one hand and your rod in the other.

I have found Leeches in the feeding samples of Rainbows. The vast majority of these were small Leeches that were less than an inch in length. These amounted to 1.1% of the food found in Rainbow feeding samples. Rainbows most frequently feed on Leeches during the hot spells in Summer when other foods are scarce.

Fly patterns called "Leeches" do not look like a Leech and most are far bigger than the Leeches found in feeding samples. The fly patterns do not move like the invertebrate. Often they are retrieved or trolled much faster than the Leech can swim. This type of fly movement generally stimulates the trout's visual trigger rather than a desire to fill an empty stomach. Leeches are a limited item on the trout's menu and I'm convinced the Leech fly patterns are simply attractor flies. The visual keys on these flies could represent Dragonfly Nymphs or Caddis Pupa more readily than a Leech.

With all that said, the Leech is a very effective fly (but then, so is the Doc Spratley). Similar to most other attractor flies it can be fished in a variety of methods. The most common method is with a fast sinking line and a rapid retrieve. These flies fish well on the shoals or over the drop-offs. They do well most anytime of day and are a good searching pattern to find where the trout are located. They fish successfully throughout the season but do best when the primary Rainbow foods are scarce.

Snails and Limpets

The shell of a Limpet usually spirals in a cone shape. The shell of a true Snail usually has the shell spiral outward from a central point. The pristine trout lakes usually have both. Because they need calcium carbonate to form their shells, they are more abundant in the lower elevation lakes that have higher contents of calcium.

Both Snails and Limpets are on the trout's menu. Together they make up 3.4% of the Rainbows diet. They are eaten throughout the year but are most frequently taken by the trout during the hot summer periods. Sometimes trout that feed on these invertebrates will develop a muddy flavor. It is hard to tell which fish will have this muddy taste but it's typically associated with warm weather and certain lakes.

As fish swim by
To take your fly
Don't set the hook
Until it's took
But wait to long
And the fish is gone.

You could probably tie a good fly to imitate these invertebrates but it would require the patience of a saint to retrieve the pattern. Trout pick these critters off of aquatic weeds or from the lake bottom as they crawl along at a snails pace. You would need to let the fly sit on the bottom until a passing Rainbow decided your fly was more appetizing than the other snails. And that wouldn't likely happen.

Zooplankton (Daphnia and Copepods)

A number of organisms in the lake are almost microscopic in size and yet become food for the Rainbows. As a group, these small critters are called Zooplankton. They are too small to be duplicated with a fly pattern. If you find something that looks like tapioca pudding or mush in a trout's stomach, it is probably a type of Zooplankton. The most common types of Zooplankton found in feeding samples are Daphnia, Copepods, Water Mites and Cyclops. You can look these up if interested in more details on their entomology.

I mention these critters because they make up 4.5% of the Rainbow's diet in pristine lakes. They are primarily available during the Third Quarter of the moon when most other bugs are scarce. Trout feed on these through the season but heaviest in late Summer. When the trout are feeding on these, it is usually because they are available in great quantities. Rainbows don't need to search out individuals at those times. They simply swim through the Zooplankton soup with their mouth open and scoop in a meal. This process is similar to whales feeding on krill. If you see trout feeding when foods aren't apparent in the water, they may be feeding on Zooplankton.

Glassworms (and Chaoborus)

Chaoborus are two-winged flies and very closely related to Chironomids. The pupa and adult stages of this bug are virtually the same as the Chironomid. Rainbows feed on these the same as they feed on Chironomids. Use the data presented earlier for Chironomid to determine environmental factors, moon phase and seasonal times for Chaoborus. They are very similar in nature. About the only difference is that some species of Chaoborus pupa are bright green in color.

Chaoborus larvae are known as Glassworms and are not as important to anglers as Bloodworms (Chironomid larva). Glassworms usually float in the water column and are frequently near the water's surface. However, there could be thousands of them near your boat and you probably wouldn't see these critters. They are very transparent and impossible to duplicate with a fly.

My data shows about 5% of Rainbow feeding samples consists of Chaoborus and most of that are the Glassworm larvae. Many Chaoborus pupa are difficult to distinguish from Chironomid pupa and I may have included them with the Chironomid data. The same isn't true for Glassworms.

Glassworms are most frequently found in Rainbow feeding samples during the Third Quarter moon with a secondary peak around the First Quarter. Seasonally, these larvae are a significant food item in early May and early June with decreasing significance in late July and of minor importance in early September. The seasonal trend is very similar to the Chironomid.

Terrestrials

In pristine lakes, terrestrial bugs aren't a staple food of Rainbow Trout. However, on occasion they fall into the water and may be eaten. When moderate numbers fall into the lake, they can become important to the fly fisher. Over an angling season, certain terrestrials do this on a regular basis. The total of all terrestrials in Rainbow feeding samples amounts to 0.5%. This isn't significant in the scheme of things but can occasionally produce some good fishing.

<u>Flying Ants</u> – Each year, at least two flights of flying ants will have some individuals fall into the trout lakes. The two I see most often are the large, black Carpenter Ants and a smaller species of reddish colored ant.

In successful ant colonies, the queen lays a special batch of fertilized eggs. These are specially fed and tended by the worker ants. These eggs go through a pupa stage and develop wings for flight. When these pupae hatch, they take flight as fertile male drones and the future queens of new colonies. These are the flying ants you see landing in the lakes.

> What causes stress is different for fish than people but the reactions are often the same.

The large Carpenter Ants are most common from April through June (Spring) while the small red ants are more common from July through August (Summer). The trout usually take these bugs on the lake surface and a dry fly pattern is a good imitation. Ants don't swim or move so they are best fished still or drifting with the wind on a dry line.

<u>Moths and Butterflies</u> – Both moths and butterflies occasionally fall into the lake. Perhaps because of the large wings, butterflies are seldom eaten by the trout if other food sources are available. Moths, on the other hand, look much like a Caddis and the trout will often eat these thinking they are Caddis. Naturally, the angler should present flies to represent adult Caddis if trout are seen feeding on moths.

<u>Grasshoppers and Crickets</u> – The species of these critters that fly are most likely to fall into the deeper portions of the lake. Those that hop or crawl will usually be near the shore and many are able to struggle back to the shoreline weeds. Grasshoppers and crickets are more likely to be found at lower elevations and most abundant from July through August.

<u>Terrestrial Beetles</u> – Many species of terrestrial beetle fly and may end up falling into a lake. You may see Ladybugs, Bark Beetles, Ground Beetles

> **Did You Know**
> About 20% of all animal species on earth are beetles.

and other types of beetles on the lake surface. Most beetles are hard for the trout to digest. Older fish have usually learned this from previous encounters. It is typically the smaller trout that feed on surface beetles. If you see Rainbows taking beetles, the best fishing advice is to observe and imitate. Almost any shape, size or color is possible.

Miscellaneous Terrestrials – Spiders, bees, wasps, caterpillars, houseflies and other terrestrials are frequently falling into lakes and may be on the menu of Rainbow Trout. Usually, these are few in number and not of importance to the fly fisher. But be observant. I once saw a large batch of houseflies on the lake surface and sure enough, the trout were actively feeding on these. Naturally, I didn't have an artificial fly that even came close to imitating these. Critters like bees or wasps that sting probably wouldn't have received the same response.

Aquatic Bugs That Aren't Rainbow Food

A trout will eat almost anything at almost anytime. However, some bugs are not on the trout's menu while others may be a one time mistake. We should list a few of these with a brief explanation as to why.

➢ **Mosquito:** The mosquito is closely related to Chironomid. However, this bug doesn't have gills in the lava stage and must obtain oxygen via an air tube extended through the water surface film. If wave action occurs, it will swamp the mosquito's air tube and drown the larva. Mosquitoes are found in ponds and puddles but not in lakes with significant wave action.

➢ **Clams:** These are mollusks and are occasionally found in some pristine lakes. They typically bury themselves in the bottom muck and are not available to the trout. If the trout were able to dig up a few small individuals, they would not be digestible by the trout because of the hard shells.

➢ **Water Beetles:** Most water beetles prefer ponds and swamps but a few are found in pristine lakes. The Dytiscus beetle, Whirligig Beetles and small scavenger beetles are the main types. These aren't very digestible by the trout and the Dytiscus Beetle is a vicious predator with a large set of biting jaws. On a few rare occasions, I have found small scavenger beetles in feeding samples but I suspect these were experimentally ingested.

➢ **Hellgrammites:** Many anglers incorrectly identify the  larva of Caddis, Dytiscus Beetles and other aquatic invertebrates as Hellgrammites. True Hellgrammites live in streams, rivers and other running water. They are not found in pristine lakes.

➢ **Water Bugs:** The Waterboatman is a Water Bug but it is the only member of this  group that doesn't bite or sting.  Backswimmers are a Water Bug with a powerful sting. Trout occasionally feed on these but seldom more than one or two individuals (in a lifetime). Water Striders or Water Skaters bite and I suspect they also exude a chemical substance to prevent trout from feeding on them. Seldom are they found in Rainbow feeding samples. The Giant Water Bug can get up to two inches in length. The adult can sometimes be seen carrying up to 100 eggs on its back. It is a mean S.O.B. and has been know to attack and kill young ducklings. I have found a couple of Water Bugs half way through the digestive tract of trout. Not only were these bugs not digested, they were still alive.

➤ **Stoneflies:** These critters are a significant Rainbow food on streams and rivers. They require high oxygen levels such as provided in moving water. They are not found in pristine lakes.

Pseudo-Bugs as Rainbow Food

In this Chapter, we have provided details on angling with "imitator flies" for each of the primary invertebrates. That means we are still missing the details on attractor flies and dry flies, so let's have a quick overview.

In pristine lakes, about 90% of dry fly fishing is with flies that imitate Caddis adults. The other 10% is an assortment of Chironomid adults, Waterboatmen and various terrestrials. When I check my data for dry fly fishing, it almost mimics the Caddis data (see graph). Therefore, I won't spend any more time discussing dry fly fishing on pristine lakes.

That only leaves the details on attractor flies to discuss. There are differences between small attractor flies and large attractor flies. The trout visually key on these differently. By large I'm generally talking about long shank hooks of size 10 or larger such as might be used for large Leech or Doc Spratley patterns. By small, I'm referring to size 12 or smaller hooks. Typical fly patterns include the Half-Back, Full-Back, SBS, Idaho Nymph, Shady Lady and so on. I don't usually fish with flies that don't have visual keys for two or more bugs.

Large Attractor Flies

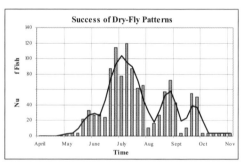

Large attractor flies do not represent a specific invertebrate. Often, Rainbows take these because motion or contrast has excited the visual trigger of the trout. With large flies, motion is the trigger more often than with smaller flies. These flies can set up low frequency vibrations in the water that trout can easily detect from a distance. When closer, large flies are easier to locate with eyesight. Leech patterns are good at sending out vibrations to attract the trout.

A large Doc Spratley and some other large attractors also provide contrast. The Spratley is usually black with silver or gold ribbing plus a white beard and tail to provide contrast. This contrast sometimes excites the trout into taking the fly. Large attractors are often good flies to use as 'search patterns' to help locate the fish.

Some flies, like the Doc Spratley, look like two or more bugs. The Spratley has visual keys that could represent a Dragonfly nymph, a large Caddis pupa, a Leech, a Damselfly nymph or even a very large Chironomid with some stretching of the imagination. A Rainbow feeding on one of those bugs could visually key on parts of the Spratley and assume it is the bug of choice. Often, the feeding samples from trout caught on large attractors will yield a large bug that could be mistaken for the large attractor fly.

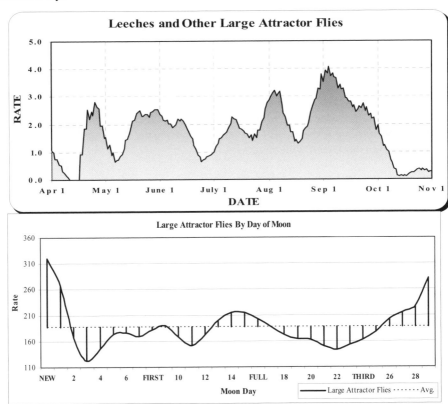

Figure 36 – Seasonal & Lunar Timing for Large Attractor Flies

I suspect that large attractor flies are often mistaken for Dragonfly nymphs. If you look at the seasonal and lunar timing graphs in Figure 36, you will find that they are similar to those presented for Dragonflies earlier in this chapter. Both are taken from shortly after ice-off through mid October. Both have peaks in September and May. That's when Dragonflies are typically migrating to or from hibernation. The biggest difference is in early August. Dragonfly nymphs aren't frequently taken at that time while large attractor flies are good. Many bugs are

225

scarce in August and I believe the Rainbows are enticed to large attractors at that time because of the relative scarcity of other foods.

> **Fishing Tip**
> As it is getting dark, try a Spratley on a dry line. Cast near the shore line weeds. Let the fly sit for about 20 seconds and then start a long but slow retrieve. Large fish often cruise into the shallows in low light levels seeking big bugs.

Dragonfly nymphs are primarily available around the New moon. This coincides with the best lunar time to fish large attractor flies. Both are significantly more productive around the New moon supporting the idea that large attractors are often taken as Dragonfly nymphs. The rest of the lunar timing doesn't have substantial peaks or troughs which would suggest the moon isn't playing an important role at those times. However, the minor peak just before Full moon comes close to matching that for Dragonfly nymphs.

Large attractor flies fish well over the shoals, drop-off or in deep water. They are frequently used with some type of sinking line when water depth permits. Retrieving the fly can be fast to create low frequency vibrations or slow to imitate a large bug. I would suggest retrieving these flies the same as you would a Dragonfly imitation. Variable retrieves work well with these.

Small Attractor Flies

Virtually all of my small attractor flies look buggy and are easy to tie. All have the visual keys to represent two or more bugs. I can't see much sense in tying a Royal Coachman or some other fly that doesn't really look like some sort of bug.

Like large attractor flies, small attractor flies can motivate the trout into striking because of the visual trigger or a visual key. Small attractors can excite the trout's visual trigger through contrast or movement but also do well by presenting several visual keys to fool the trout into thinking your fly is a specific bug. The black and white of the Idaho Nymph is a good example of contrast. The Shady Lady (pictured upper right) has hackles that send out underwater vibrations and provides some contrast.

The Halfback (pictured upper left) and similar nymph-like flies are excellent. They can provide the visual keys for Mayfly nymphs, small Dragonfly nymphs, Damselfly nymphs and Caddis pupae. Sometimes Rainbows will even key on the front half of the Halfback as a Waterboatman. Let it dangle on a dry line and it can be fished as a Chironomid. Anytime you can't determine which specific bug to imitate, try a small attractor fly such as the Halfback. The only problem with this fly is the Peacock Herle body. It doesn't last long. The herle tends to break and unravel after a few trout.

I usually tie small attractor flies on long shank hooks in sizes 12, 14 or 16. These days, most of my small attractors are weighted. Because color diminishes in water, my favorite body color is black. I typically add legs that lay along the side of the body or flow underneath the body. As long as the fly looks buggy, it should produce trout. Probably of more importance is how you fish these flies.

Many folks angle with small attractors on a sinking line. I prefer a dry line with a long leader and weighted fly. A sink-tip line also does well if the lake bottom isn't covered in weeds. The nice thing about small attractors is their versatility. After the cast, let the fly sink near the bottom and then begin a slow retrieve. With a dry line, the retrieve speed is almost as slow as you might retrieve a Chironomid pattern. The presentation of a small, slow moving bug along the lake bottom seems almost irresistible to the trout. If that isn't working, try varying the retrieve. Often, the trout don't seem to care what type of bug your fly represents.

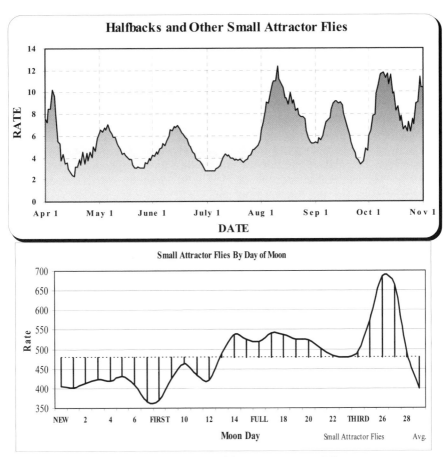

Figure 37 – Seasonal & Lunar Timing of Small Attractor Flies

Probably because they can represent so many bugs, small attractors are good through the entire fishing season. Starting in August, most of the bugs in a lake are small and small attractors are more successful in the second half of the season. Figure 37 shows the various peaks when angling with these types of flies. Many of these peaks equate to similar peaks of the seven primary invertebrates. The exception is during the hot summer downers. Small attractor flies seem to do better at this time than most other fly patterns.

The lunar timing for fishing small attractor flies shows the poorest time is from the New moon to just before the Full moon (moon days 0 thru 12). In contrast, many of the seven primary invertebrates are best fished around the First Quarter moon. I interpret this to mean that the trout are more interested in imitator flies around the First Quarter moon and more interested in small attractor flies around the Third Quarter moon. Possibly this happens because of the relative scarcity of real bugs during the Third Quarter moon phase.

End Notes

I wouldn't be surprised if you found something in this chapter to disagree with. Your memory probably tells you that seasonal availability, lunar timing or activity period by environmental factor is something other than what is shown in the graphs and tables. That's okay. Over the years, my memory has been tested and revised several times by good hard data. The memory just isn't as good at recording, retrieving and analyzing information as the computer.

There is a lot of invertebrate data in this chapter that you aren't likely to find anywhere else. The data to provide this information has been meticulously collected since 1976. My interpretation of the data could be wrong but the data is accurate. I encourage you to use this information and see if you can improve your angling success.

8

Rainbow Angling Strategies and Techniques

In the previous chapters, we discussed many strategies and techniques to catch those elusive Rainbow Trout in pristine lakes. In this, the last chapter, I would like to discuss a few topics that don't logically fit anywhere else. Let's take some time to discuss the generalities of fishing and fishing gear. I'll close with what I consider as the most important factors for fishing Rainbows.

Planning the Fishing Trip

The best time to go fishing is anytime you can. I'm able to go fishing on short notice but most folks don't have that luxury. Normally, the angler must set aside an advance date to go fishing. That means there is time to plan where to go and when. Sometimes these early planning choices can be significant in terms of fishing success.

Choice of Lakes

When a friend asks me to recommend a lake, I always ask a question. I ask if they are interested in catching lots of small fish, a few big fish or something in between. It makes a difference in which lake I recommend. I would suggest you ask yourself the same question and choose accordingly.

Most intermediate to advanced anglers will be familiar with their local lakes and know what to expect from each. However, some trips will be into unfamiliar territory or you may simply be new to the local area. If you're not sure which lake to choose, the fishing regulations can provide some clues.

> Any day you plan to go fishing and don't, will be the day that everyone got lots of big fish.

Fishery managers usually place heavy restrictions on small lakes with big fish in order to maintain the quality of the fishery. These restrictions may include restricted quotas (catch and release or a quota of 1 or 2 fish), gear restrictions (single barbless hook or fly only) and/or season closures (no ice fishing or time restrictions). When you see these types of regulations, there is a good chance the lake is being managed as a quality fishery for larger fish. Lakes without any special regulations are probably chocked full of smaller fish. Those are generally a better choice if you are taking your kids on a fishing trip.

If you're planning a wilderness trip with the guys, you may want to choose a lake with 4X4 access and really rough it. If the trip is a week long family outing, you may need to consider the facilities at the lake. Undoubtedly someone in the family will want a resort with breakfast served in bed. If so, you should probably consider going to

> The more time you spend planning a fishing trip, the greater the odds of forgetting something.

a lake that, at a minimum, has an outhouse or room to park your RV if you're lucky enough to own one. This won't directly improve your fishing success but you will be more relaxed and likely to enjoy the experience. And being relaxed does tend to improve your success. When relaxed, you are more likely to take the time to locate the fish and present a nice slow retrieve.

Once you become familiar with the lakes, you will become familiar with factors such as water clarity and elevation. These can be important considerations at different times of year or in various weather conditions.

In the middle of summer when you expect hot temperatures and lots of sunshine, you probably want to select a lake that is higher in elevation and thus cooler. You may also want to avoid lakes that are crystal clear. In the expected bright sunshine, a lake with cloudy water is more likely to produce good fishing. In the Spring, you will do better avoiding lakes that are in turn-over. Knowing the elevation will help you select lakes that haven't yet started into turn-over or have finished turn-over.

> Your first trip of the season will be the first time in years that you are checked for a fishing license. Of course, you will find that you forgot to buy a new one.

Lake selection is just as important on a last minute day trip as a trip planned well in advance. For example, if you are heading out for the day and it's windy, you will probably do better to select a lake that offers bays or islands where you can seek shelter from the wind. Or, if the season and moon are just right for Mayfly hatches, then you will want to select a lake with clean, clear water since that's what Mayflies prefer.

Think back over the factors presented in this book to help with the selection. One lake can have good fishing on a particular day while other lakes are poor. Select a lake that offers you the best chances of success. Which lake you choose can be an important decision.

Choice of Times

There isn't a bad time to go fishing but some times are better than others. If your schedule is busy and you must carefully select your fishing dates, then the time to go will depend on how you like to fish. If you like dry flies to imitate Caddis your selection will be different than if you like to fish Waterboatmen patterns. You aren't likely to get both at the same time. On day trips, you may have the choice of going in the morning, mid-day or evening but not all day. Which should you choose? Just like seasonal fishing, the time of day to go will depend on the type of fishing you prefer.

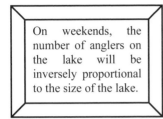

On weekends, the number of anglers on the lake will be inversely proportional to the size of the lake.

I have provided you with the tools to make informed decisions on the best times for each type of invertebrate. The seasonal graphs will key you into the most likely time of season to fish a particular bug. The lunar graphs refine that time down to a few days. Other information I've provided gives you the conditions a particular bug prefers along with the time of day that is most suitable. Unfortunately, I can't predict the weather and other environmental factors. I never guarantee success but with the provided information you can target the most likely times for success.

Some Tips on Fly Fishing Gear

In this section I would like to offer a few points on fly fishing gear that you may or may not know. I don't intend to provide you with the latest and greatest information on fancy new equipment. I only buy new fishing gear when it is needed. My fly rods and much of my gear is about 30 years old. As long as it remains functional, I keep using it. But there are a few points about fishing gear that should be mentioned.

It takes more than expensive equipment to be proficient at what you are doing.

Fly Rods

Today's fly rods are marvels of scientific engineering. These are meticulously designed for weight, strength, flexibility, balance and carrying capacity. This wasn't always the case. Some of the earliest fly rods were nothing more than a length of bamboo or stick with the handmade line attached to the pointy end.

Fishing Tip

Fly rods typically come in two or more sections. If these sections are coming apart when casting, try rubbing the male portion of the connection with bees wax.

The modern fly rod is flexible but not too flexible. Flexibility is used to impart energy to the fly line for casting and is used to provide spring action when landing a fish. If the rod is too stiff, it's like fishing with a broom stick. You can cast a fly line with a broom stick but you won't get much distance and the lack of flexibility could result in many fish breaking the leader. If the rod is too limp, it won't impart any energy to the cast and won't provide the spring action for playing the trout.

With modern materials, today's fly rods are very light weight and strong. They typically come in lengths of 7.5 to 10 feet with the longer and stiffer rods generally providing longer casting distances. Each rod has a specific strength and carrying capacity. This is designed to match with a specific weight of fly line. A number 7 rod, for example, should be used with a number 7 line. If these don't match the rod will be over loaded or under loaded and not cast well. The larger numbers are stronger rods and typically designed to handle larger fish. The smaller numbers are considered lighter tackle and generally designed for smaller fish.

When a novice asks what fly rod to buy for the pristine lakes, I usually suggest they get started with a rod that isn't too expensive. After learning how to use the gear they can make an informed decision on a more expensive outfit. With today's fly rods, inexpensive doesn't necessarily mean poor quality or hard to cast.

Don't plan your evening meal around a trout you haven't yet landed.

Because stiffer and longer rods cast further, I usually suggest the novice get a graphite rod of about 9 feet (8.5 to 9.5) in length. This combination is generally good for those larger trout likely to be encounter on our pristine lakes. The longer length also provides more spring action to prevent leader breaks. I suggest the rod has at least one guide for every foot in length and that the rod has a hook retainer near the handle.

The trend by local anglers has been to use lighter weight rods. Lately, more folks are showing up on the lakes with number 4, 5 or 6 weight rods because they think it to be more sporting. I find these lighter rod/line combinations are just too light for effective casting in windy conditions. The lighter rods also mean it takes longer to land the fish and thus increase the odds a trout won't survive being released. I would suggest a number 7 or number 8 rod provides the least problems with casting in a wind and landing the fish. These rods are still sensitive enough to feel a very soft strike while strong enough to land a ten pound Rainbow.

Fly Reels

Most of the time, your fly reel is just a place to store fly line when not in use. It should be light weight, have good bearings and an adjustable drag system. The reel should comfortably hold all of your fly line, leader and about 150 yards of 20 pound nylon

Fishing Tip
When a Rainbow is stripping line from your reel, never grab the backing to try to stop or slow down the fish. That can result in a nasty friction burn.

backing. The spool and casing of the reel should fit together snugly. There shouldn't be a gap between these wide enough to ensnare your fly line. The spool should be exposed (not enclosed) to allow "palming" or braking the reel by pressing a hand against the spool.

Most fish are landed by retrieving the fly line with hands and rod rather than "reeling in" the fish with the reel. For retrieving fly line with a fish on, the index finger of the rod hand can push the line against the rod to serve as a brake. Meanwhile the other hand strips or retrieves whatever line the trout will allow whenever you release the brake. For most trout, this system works just fine.

When you need the reel to do more than just hold line is probably the most important of times. The reel must perform efficiently and reliably when you hook into that very large Rainbow that has removed about 70% of the "backing" from your reel. Backing is the back-up line between the fly line and fly reel. Unlike the fly line, it isn't easy to retrieve this line by hand, it doesn't coil well in the bottom of the boat and if the fish runs while you are holding the backing, it can result in a nasty friction burn. Whenever a trout gets well into the backing is a time to start reeling in the fish with the reel. At least until you get back onto your fly line.

Fly Lines

I was just looking at a brochure and Cortland tells me that they "offer more than 500 lines in every conceivable taper design and every price range". Naturally I'm not going to try to explain them all. We will stick to the basic implications to fly fishing.

> **Did You Know**
>
> The American Fishing Tackle Manufacturers Association (AFTMA) ensures consistency of products so that the number on a fly line always matches the same rod number. A number 7 line is designed for casting with a number 7 rod.

The most important consideration is to ensure the weight of your fly line matches with your fly rod. Rather than give actual weights (weight in grains over the first 30 feet of the fly line) the weights are provided in AFTMA codes. A number 7 fly line (AFTMA code 7 at 185 grains) is designed to be used with a number 7 fly rod. Without getting into the specialty products, fly lines range from number 1 thru 12. As mentioned under fly rods, I would suggest a number 7 rod/line system is generally best for the windy conditions often experienced on pristine lakes. Characteristically, these lines come in lengths of 30 to 35 yards.

Various Line Codes	
Name	**Code**
Level	L
Double Taper	DT
Weight Forward	WF
Shooting Taper	ST
Floating	F
Sinking	S
Intermediate	I
Sinking Tip	F/S

After the weight of the fly line, we should consider taper. Without considering the salt water lines or the specialty tapers, we are talking about tapers that are level, double taper or rocket taper (weight forward). The level or non-tapered lines don't generally allow for a delicate fly presentation. The double taper allows you to reverse which end of the fly line attaches to the reel and theoretically extend the life of the fly line. On pristine lakes this isn't usually the case. Usually, you are casting more than 50% of the fly line with most of the line wear coming at the middle of the line when you accidentally step on it in your boat. So the line life isn't extended. I would recommend the lines that are weight forward with a rocket taper. They are a little easier to cast in the wind than the double taper.

Now we need to decide if we want a line that floats or sinks. The floating or dry line is probably the most versatile on pristine lakes and is my favourite. It's the only line to use for dry flies and a good line for wet fly presentations. With long leaders, you can fish a dry line with wet flies to depths of about 20 to 25 feet. Normally, Chironomid pupae are presented with a dry line. In shallow water, the dry line is the best line for keeping the fly from hanging up in weed patches.

Table 30 – Typical Descent Rates for Sinking Lines

Type of Sinking Line	Name	Sink Rate	Sink Rate
(Cortland Brand)	(Cortland Brand)	(in./sec)	(ft./min)
Type 1	Intermediate Sink	1.5	7.5
Type 2	Fast Sink	2.75	14
Type 3	Extra Fast Sink	3.75	19
Type 4	Super Sink	4.66	23
Type 5	Super Fast Sink	5.66	28
Type 6	Extra Super Sinker	6.66	33

For sinking lines we need to determine how fast the line should sink and how much of the line. With "sinking tip" lines, the forward 5 to 15 feet of the line will sink while the remainder of the line floats. With full sinking lines, the entire fly line sinks. The typical rate at which the sinking portion of the fly line will sink is provided in Table 30. Note that sink rates will vary by brand. The example is for Cortland fly lines.

> Being patient has its rewards as long as you are willing to wait for it.

Locally, most folks tend to use Type 2 or 3 sinking or sinking tip lines. Personally, I prefer the Type 1 Intermediate Sink (which should probably be called a slow sink). That's because the faster a line sinks, the faster you must retrieve the line to keep it from hanging up in the lake bottom weeds. Bugs don't move very fast in the water. Watch the bugs sometime to get an idea of how slow they move. If you are tying to imitate that bug, your retrieve will need to be just as slow. Fishing the Type 1 line takes a little patience but allows the fly to be presented with realistic speed and movement. I find the rewards worth while. If fishing in 15 feet of water, I'm willing to wait an extra minute for the line to sink to proper depth. I also recommend Type 1 for Sinking Tip lines.

> **Fishing Tip**
> Never let bug repellant or suntan oil get near your fly line. These can wreck your fly line and the smell may repel the trout.

There are numerous knots for attaching backing and leaders to the fly line. I often have trouble tying these various knots so I'm not a big fan of these methods. To compensate, I have developed a simplified method that works well for both leaders and backing. I buy Cortland fly lines because they have a braided string core. At both ends of the fly line I strip the coating off this core for about two inches. Electrical wire strippers are good for removing the coating. I tie a slip knot in the core string with a small loop very close to the coated line. Then a granny knot goes behind (next to the coated fly line) to keep the slip knot from slipping. Trim off the excess core string. Between the loop and coated fly line, I cover the granny knot with a small amount of bathroom tile grout. This is flexible, waterproof and provides a smooth transition between the small loop and the fly line. I can now attach a leader or backing to the fly line with a

> **Fishing Tip**
> Keep your fly lines clean. Otherwise, your dry lines won't float and sinking lines won't sink as fast as they should.

standard fisherman's knot. Except for the tile grout, this can be done in your boat and the system is simple and strong. I've landed Steelhead with this setup and never had a problem.

Leaders

Leaders are monofilament line that provides a transition between the fly line and the fly. It wouldn't be practical to attach the fly directly to the thick fly line. The leader provides a somewhat invisible connection, is small enough for tying a knot to hold the fly and breaks long before the expensive fly line. Normally, leaders are tapered with the heavier and stronger butt section attached to the fly line. The thin end of the leader

> **Fishing Tip**
> Even with a dry fly, you usually want your leaders to sink. If they don't, keep a small bar of soap in your fish bag to run the leader across. The soap will break the surface tension of the water, allow the leader to sink and the smell doesn't seem to affect the trout.

attaches to the fly. With this configuration, leader breaks are near the fly so the whole leader doesn't need to be replaced, just the fly. The taper in leaders is also helpful for casting the fly. Essentially it forms a continuing taper of the fly line and lays out better than an abrupt change in line thickness.

Most experienced anglers tie their own tapered leaders rather than buy the commercially packaged leaders. This allows the angler to choose their own rate of taper, size of butt section, preferred brand of leader, leader length and size of tippet. I find the commercially packaged leaders have very large butt sections that retain the "memory" of being coiled in the package. It seems almost impossible to get these commercial leaders to lay straight without the coils. Because these coils act like springs, unstraightened leaders can result in many missed strikes or you may not even be aware you had a strike.

> Never tie two leader sections together that are more than two pound test different (i.e.: 8 lb to 5 lb test). With that difference in size, the connections are liable to break.

To form a tapered leader, I usually tie about 18 inches of 12 lb. test monofilament to the loop in my fly line. The fisherman's knot to join these isn't very large and flows through the guides of the rod easily. The 12 pound test is followed by joining various lengths of 10 lb, 8 lb and 6 lb test monofilament. I tie the joins with a modified surgeons knot. These knots do not tighten on themselves and thus cut the leader or weaken leader strength. With various lengths, I can quickly build a short leader or a long leader that still casts well.

> **Fishing Tip**
> To remove coils from your leader, stretch the leader over your trousers a couple of times or keep an old shammy cloth or piece of leather in your fishing bag and stretch the leader over that to remove coils.

In most pristine lakes, the Rainbows aren't overly leader shy. A 6 lb tippet is usually small enough to prevent leader shyness and strong enough to land most Rainbows. When I'm expecting really large Rainbows, I use an 8 lb test tippet and seldom are the trout reluctant to take a fly using this larger leader. But there are always exceptions. Sometimes, in very clear water you need to go to 5 or 4 lb test to get the fish interested. This lighter leader is sometimes needed if the trout are especially timid. Because Rainbows are so strong in pristine lakes, I refuse to go finer than a 4 lb test tippet.

Leaders sometimes get unwanted knots. The knots you use to tie leader segments together for a tapered leader are designed to maintain leader strength. The casting knot or wind knot weakens the leader. This knot is made when your fly passes through a loop in your leader and then cinches shut. These types of knots cut across your leader and significantly reduce strength. Unless you don't care about landing that

> A "birds nest" in your leader is ten times more likely to happen when the fish are biting than when they aren't.

big fish, check your leader for these knots about every 10 to 15 casts and twice as often in windy conditions. If you find a casting knot, a sharp pull should break your leader at the knot. Then replace as much leader as needed.

Flies

For pristine lakes, flies are usually tied on hooks ranging from size # 18 through # 6. Anything larger than a #6 hook may spook the trout. Even a size 6 hook is getting a bit large. Smaller than a # 18 hook is OK for getting strikes but I normally expect to land 50% of my strikes. With hooks of size 18 or less, the ratio of landed fish steadily declines. Rainbows in lakes are able to throw small hooks unless they set just right in the jaw.

> **Fishing Tip**
> If you get impatient for a weighted fly to sink on a dry line, then try something like "Deep Soft Weight". It is like putty that you roll onto the knots in your hand-made tapered leader. The extra weight sinks the flies in a hurry.

Rainbows may take the fly most anywhere in the water column. However, the most frequent strike zone is within a couple of feet of the lake bottom that is over a shoal or near a drop-off. To get flies near the lake bottom, I suggest tying weighted flies. I probably tie 90% of my wet flies with weighting.

As for what flies go into your fly box, I suggest about 40% attractor flies and about 10% dry flies. Of the remaining 50% for imitator flies, you should probably have about the same proportions as the quantity of bugs provided in Table 13. Shrimp, Chironomid and Caddis should make up the bulk of imitator flies with a scattering of Dragonflies, Damselflies, Mayflies and Waterboatmen. Many anglers underestimate the importance of attractor flies and may find my estimate on the high side. However, I think a good variety of buggy attractor flies will prove more than useful to any angler.

For anyone who has ever lost the last of an effective fly pattern and then forgot exactly how it was tied, try tying at least 3 flies of each pattern. Fish with two of those flies until you determine if they are successful, but keep the third as a pattern to copy in case it works really well. Several times, I have lost the last of a successful fly and then kicked myself because I couldn't remember exactly how it was tied.

And lastly on this subject, wash your hands before tying flies, keep weighted flies separate from those not weighted in your fly box and make your patterns in various sizes, especially attractor flies. Bend down the barb on all your flies or else buy barbless hooks. Tie attractor flies to create vibrations or consider having contrast in these types of flies. Remember to tie in Visual Keys for attractor flies.

Watercraft

Your "boat" can be anything from a float tube, punt or canoe to an aluminum boat. Whatever you have, it should suit your needs for getting you around the lake, be environmentally friendly and not spook the trout by transmitting noise.

Aluminum and fiberglass boats hold lots of gear and passengers. They are good for speed and getting around when a motor is attached. However, aluminum boats are the worst watercraft for transmitting noise likely to spook the Rainbows. This noise can be muffled by placing carpet on the floor, sitting on a seat cushion and remaining quiet while fishing. Avoid banging anything hard against the aluminum. I would also suggest that you keep any loose gear in canvas bags rather than metal or plastic tackle boxes. It's just one more way to keep the noise level down.

> Whenever the fish are skittish is the precise time you will drop your fly rod or flashlight into the bottom of your aluminum boat.

Boat motors can scare the trout, especially in lakes with a low volume of angler traffic. The simple solution is to turn off the motor short of your intended fishing spot and row onto an intended fishing shoal. Because of physical inabilities, some folks need the motor and can't row that last bit into their fishing spot. For those cases, try using the wind to drift over your intended fishing ground before dropping anchor. If that isn't possible, then motor on in. Be a little patient and the trout will return to a good feeding area after a short while. Be sure to keep your motor well maintained. Gas and oil leaking into the water will kill invertebrates and that isn't the best thing for the trout and ecosystem.

> If there is a novice in the boat, they will catch the biggest and/or most fish.

Float tubes or "belly boats" are about the quietest watercraft but won't get you around the lake very fast nor allow you to carry lots of gear or passengers. They are great for getting into tight spots where it's difficult to launch other watercraft. They are easily transported and handled by one person. After buying waders, flippers and other accessories, I didn't find a belly boat much cheaper than some other watercraft. I found myself getting leg and feet cramps after using the flippers for an hour or two. It isn't easy getting back to the shore with only one flipper. And if you are a long way from shore and develop a sudden urge to pee, then good luck. Belly boats are ideal for some, but those are probably folks of the younger generation.

Personally, I use a 14 foot fiberglass canoe. It seems to be a happy compromise between a belly boat and an aluminum boat. I can load and launch this watercraft by myself; it is quieter than aluminum and offers more room and speed than a belly boat. However, a canoe isn't recommended for someone who needs to stand to cast a fly or a person who has trouble

> The wind will always blow from the direction you intend to go on the lake and then reverse as you return from fishing.

maintaining balance. Every person needs to find a watercraft that is just right for his or her own purposes. Watercraft can be expensive so choose carefully.

Miscellaneous Fishing Gear

Following are some considerations about the miscellaneous fishing gear that folks tend to take fishing. As a suggestion, don't take any more in your watercraft than you really need.

➤ **Personal Floatation Device (PFD)**: every angler should have and wear something to keep them afloat in case they fall overboard or the boat sinks. I find most life vests are too bulky for comfortable fly casting. I use a fishing vest that can be inflated manually or with a CO_2 cartridge. It doesn't breathe and gets a little warm during the hot summer months but is still more comfortable than the standard life vest. Whatever PFD you choose, be sure to wear it.

➤ **Landing Net**: as implied, a landing net is needed to land the fish. Whether you intend to keep or release your fish, you will need to control it for hook removal. The net should have a fine mesh that is made from material that

> You never discover a hole in your waders until after you enter the water.

doesn't harm the fish. Those nylon dip nets tend to be harmful to fish because they remove excessive amounts of fish slime. Soft cotton mesh is better. For releasing the fish, keep the fish in the net and in the water for removing the fly. Then keep it there long enough to ensure the fish is ready to swim away.

➤ **Rod Case**: your rod needs to be protected from breakage while getting to or from the lake. There is a good selection of types from which to choose. I'm not keen on leaving my reel attached during transport so I don't use the type of case that includes the reel. I like the aluminum tube that holds the rod. The fly rod is normally placed inside a cloth protector before inserting into the tube to avoid contact with the metal. I watched a pickup truck accidentally back over one of these tubes without any damage to the rod or case.

➤ **Hat**: an angler should wear a hat while fishing. A hat will protect you from the sun in hot weather and help keep your head warm in the rain or cold weather. The hat should have a brim to help shade or shelter the face, ears and back of the neck. The brim will also help protect you from being hooked by the fly if you have a bad cast or if the wind should change and blow the fly directly at you.

➢ **Sunglasses**: if you have ever had your eyes sunburned from glare off the water, you will appreciate the need for sunglasses. Polaroid glasses are best. They not only cut the suns glare but filter out some of the suns harmful rays. Sunglasses cut the surface glare on the water and make it possible to see into the water. You can sometime spot trout or shoals with sunglasses that you might otherwise miss without them. As an added benefit, sunglasses could protect your eyes from a wayward fly caught by the wind.

> **Fishing Tip**
> Whether you wear sunglasses or prescription glasses, use a chain or string to keep them around your neck rather than on the lake bottom if they fall off.

➢ **Fishing Vests**: these are handy but not essential unless your vest is also a PFD. The fishing vest has lots of pockets for storing items but those same items can be stored in a fishing bag that goes in your boat. Vests are nearly essential to someone wading a river but not for someone in a boat on a lake.

➢ **Fishing Bag**: I've seen some knowledgeable folks recommend a tackle box for your boat. These are usually plastic or metal and tend to create a lot of noise in a boat. I would suggest a canvas fishing bag with various size pockets. Small plastic boxes can be kept inside the main pouch for storage of similar items. Keep your spare reels, fly boxes and other gear in the bag for easy access. The canvas bag is handy and tends to muffle noise.

➢ **Fly Box**: you will need one or more fly boxes depending on how many flies you have and the size of the box. There are many good choices but I suggest you don't get a box with a foam rubber interior to hold your flies. Foam rubber holds water. Flies that are inserted wet into this material will rust. However, some other types of foam board do not retain water and are good for fly storage. That's what I use rather than metal clips or keeping flies loose in compartmentalized boxes. I prefer one large box (9"X12") for my main flies and have a couple of smaller boxes for miscellaneous and specialty flies. The foam board in my large box allows me to place flies up and down or cross-ways to separate weighted from unweighted flies. A tidy well-organized box comes in handy when the fish are biting and you need to find the right fly.

> **Fishing Tip**
> With a permanent marker, measure and mark off five foot intervals on your anchor rope as an easy way to determine the water depth.

➢ **Anchor**: your anchor should be heavy enough that a strong breeze doesn't drag your anchor across the lake bottom. This can ruin underwater habitat. The anchor shape should be designed so that it doesn't hang up on underwater rocks or logs. Attached to the anchor you will need about 40 or 50 feet of strong rope, which is small in diameter. Make sure the rope is securely attached to the anchor. You don't want a knot coming untied and your anchor remaining on the bottom. Some folks use an anchor on each end of the boat with a latch release system. It's a handy system but doesn't always leave you casting with the wind.

> **Rain Gear**: some form of protection from the rain should be taken to the lake with you. If it's hot and sunny, you can always leave it in the car. A rain jacket is good but doesn't protect your legs as well as a rain slicker. If you get stuck without proper rain gear, you can always use a large, plastic garbage bag with holes cut for the head and arms.

> **Oars or Paddles**: always have an emergency propulsion system. Oars for a boat with motor or an extra paddle in a canoe. However, I'm not sure that an extra flipper for a belly boat would help. I once lost my paddle overboard while landing a fish and was sure glad for that extra paddle I keep in the front of the canoe.

> **Fish Storage**: If you intend to keep any fish, you should have somewhere cool to store them out of the heat until you get home. Do not use a live-stringer. Those things are a means to torture the fish and should be outlawed. A cooler, preferably with ice, is about the best method. I don't have a lot of room in my canoe for even a small cooler so I use a gunny sack. Wet the gunny sack when you place a fish in it, keep it in a shaded portion of the boat and water evaporating from the sack will keep the fish cool. If the sack starts to dry, dip it in the lake again to restart the process. I would suggest keeping a gunny sack in the boat even if you don't intend to keep fish. Occasionally, a fish isn't going to survive release and you may as well keep it.

> **Flashlight**: at some time or another, you will be on a lake after dark, either intentionally or unintentionally. You will find a flashlight handy if you need to tie on another fly or signal an approaching watercraft of your presence. A small

> If you try to add 10 feet to your casting distance, the fly will fall about 30 feet short of your normal cast.

flashlight will easily fit into your fishing bag. Occasionally check the batteries to ensure they are functional.

> **Pliers**: pliers are often handy, and I suggest needle-nose pliers. Sometimes they are essential for gently removing the fly from a fish you don't want to harm. They can be used to bend down the barb on a hook or to assist with minor equipment repairs. I always have a pair with me while fishing.

> **Nail Clippers**: I find a pair of strong nail clippers better than a small pair of scissors for trimming leader ends after tying a tapered leader or placing your fly onto the leader. The clippers can trim loose leader ends very close with little difficulty. If you decide to use these, I would suggest you tie them to your fly vest or equipment bag with a longish piece of string. They are easily dropped overboard.

➢ **Knife**: I carry a large fold-up hunting knife that fits in a case. I carry it primarily for emergences but it is an effective fish "bonker" for those trout intended for the dinner table. With this knife, I don't need to bring along something else to dispatch a fish.

➢ **Two-Way Radio**: if you are fishing with friends in separate boats, two-way radios are handy for keeping in touch. Two or three anglers can scout a lake better than one. The radios allow you to communicate what the fish are taking or where. These certainly aren't essential equipment but can be an asset.

➢ **Fish Finders**: these are probably good when angling in deep water (over 25 feet) but I find them of limited value in shallow water. As discussed in Chapter 4, trout will sometimes shy away from the sonar signals of these devices. I once had a friend with a fish finder troll by me several times. On about the fifth pass he commented that he wasn't seeing any fish on the finder. At the same time, I hooked a Rainbow about 20 feet from his boat and I had been consistently getting fish in the same area. The fish finder simply didn't show the Rainbows in the shallow water among the weeds. The best use for these devices is to locate shoals or drop-offs in unfamiliar lakes or lakes with murky water.

➢ **Extra Leader Material**: you may get a tangle or otherwise break off a large piece of tapered leader. In your fly vest or fishing bag, you should have leader material in a sufficient variety of sizes to replace anything you loose.

Fishing Tip
Use flies slightly larger than the bug being imitated. They will stand out and are more likely to attract the trout's attention in a crowd.

➢ **Pee Bucket**: keep a plastic container with a lid in your boat. If necessary, you can use this to take a leak and dump the bucket later. It will also serve as a bailing bucket. Boating regulations usually require that you keep a bailing bucket on board your boat but this way you have a dual purpose piece of equipment.

➢ **Soap**: I keep a small piece of soap wrapped in cloth in my fishing vest. If my leader won't sink, I rub it over the soap. Soap will break the surface tension of the water and allow the leader to sink. Rainbows don't seem to mind a smell of a small amount of soap.

➢ **Insect Repellant & Suntan Oil**: you may need to use these but don't keep these in your fly vest or fishing bag. They can damage the fly line and tend to repel the trout. Keep this stuff in a separate location and wash your hands if you use one of these products.

➢ **Aquarium Net**: some folks carry a small aquarium net to dip bugs for determination of size, type and color. I carry one but usually use it to catch bugs for taking pictures.

➢ **Thermometer**: some anglers use a thermometer to determine the underwater temperature at various depths. This can help find the depth of the ideal water temperatures for Rainbows or determine if a lake is in turnover. When searching for food, I find trout are often in water that is at temperatures other than ideal. I don't use the thermometer.

Some Tips on Fishing

You've planned when and where to go fishing. Your gear is ready and it's time to get on a lake. As intermediate to advanced anglers, there probably isn't a lot about this aspect of the sport that you don't already know. However, let's go through the process from start to finish and maybe you will find a tip or two that is useful.

Getting on the Water

You've turned off the highway and are making the final approach to the lake. The dirt road is dusty and in your mirror, you see a car is now behind you. The rule on these back roads is to always pull over and let a faster vehicle pass. If they have caught up to you then they are obviously going faster. At the first opportunity, pull over and let them pass rather than speeding up. After all, we are out to relax and enjoy. Slow down until the dust clears and then carry on. As a side note, if you see a loaded logging truck coming down the hill, it has the right-of-way.

> As the available room for camping increases, so does the likelihood that some yahoo will be camped in the middle of the only available boat launch.

When you reach the lake and approach the boat launch, try to park to one side or the other so that another vehicle can launch beside you. You don't have to rush but don't dally while unloading your boat and gear. Get everything unloaded and then park your vehicle somewhere besides the boat launch before setting up your gear. Never leave your vehicle parked at the launching site. Even if it seems out of the way, another angler may have a trailer or otherwise need that room to turn around.

If you use a boat motor, get that set up before assembling your fly rod. If you need bug spray or suntan lotion, get that applied at the start. You don't want to get gasoline, battery acid, suntan lotion or bug spray on your rod and line. After you have the "dirty" stuff taken care of, rinse your hands thoroughly at the boat launch. You don't want any repulsive smells on your flies or fly gear. This also gives you a chance to peek into the water to see what bugs may be moving about. If nobody is waiting to launch, I often walk a little way along the shoreline looking for bugs or discarded shells from bugs that are hatching.

> If you talk to an angler leaving the lake, you will always find that the fishing was better yesterday than it is today.

With clean hands, you can get your fly rod assembled. Once you have your reel attached to the rod, don't place it on the ground to get the fly line through the rod guides. Place the reel end of the rod inside your boat or another clean place where you won't get sand and grit into the reel. Strip about ten feet of fly line from the reel.

Run the fly line (not the leader) through the rod guides and pull any remaining leader through afterwards. If you need to fix or change anything with your tapered leader, now is the time to do it. Unless you were fishing yesterday, you will most likely need to straighten coils out of the leader. Stretching the leader across your pants or over a piece of leather should remove the coils.

Select a fly you suspect may be good. Attach it to the leader and then place the fly in the fly keeper or a guide on your rod. You may decide on a different fly before you start fishing but this fly will ensure your line and leader don't fall back through the rod guides. Carefully place the rod in your boat where it won't get stepped on. After making sure everything is where you want it, we are now ready to get on the water.

Examining Conditions

While planning the trip and choosing a lake, you probably looked over the seasonal graphs, the lunar graphs and the environmental conditions that each type of bug prefers. So you probably have a good idea of what invertebrates to expect. If you're lucky, the short walk along the boat launch will have confirmed your suspicions. But you also need to be observant and examine the other particular conditions of this day.

> If you are observant, it will improve your success as well as your enjoyment of the sport.

From the time you arrive at the boat launch, you should be looking over the conditions on the lake. That will have helped in the determination of which fly line and fly to start with.

➤ **Wind Strength**: if the wind is strong, you may need to start with a sinking line since it is easier to cast in windy conditions. Or, if the invertebrates you have seen or expect are best fished with a dry line, you may need to keep your tapered leader short. If it's only breezy, you may decide to start with a dry line and long leader. With suitable wind conditions, this is often a good first choice.

➤ **Wind Direction**: if winds are from the North or East, the fishing is likely to be slow and difficult. You may want to start with a sinking line and an attractor fly. While at the boat launch, you also need to note if the wind is blowing from the right, the left, at you or away from you. This helps in

> Always try to anchor where you are casting with the wind.

determining the best general location on the lake to start. For example, if the wind is from the right while you are at the boat launch, it will probably be better to anchor on the boat launch side of the lake or at the left end of the lake (assuming you are right handed). Either will allow you to cast into the shallows or along the drop-off without need to cast the fly on your up-wind side. If you go to the far side or the end of the lake or to your right, you will need to anchor in the shallows and cast toward the deep or strictly work the drop-off. These may be suitable options but should be considered while at the boat launch.

243

➤ **Sunshine**: if the lake has clear water and it's sunny, you may need to fish in relatively deep water. If there is cloud cover or the water is cloudy to murky, the shoals will probably be a good first choice. Sunshine conditions will probably affect your first choice of fly line and fly as well.

➤ **Fish Activity**: while getting ready, did you see fish moving around the lake? If so, how many and where? Even after leaving the boat launch, I always watch for rise lines and other signs of active fish. Knowing where the fish are active is the first clue for getting into the right location. You can usually tell if the fish are shallow, near the drop-off, out deep or evenly scattered around the lake. Sometimes they are even active over one area of the lake and not the rest. If you don't see any surface activity, it is a sign that the best fishing will probably be on or near the bottom in moderate to deep water.

Fishing Tip
If you have trout swirling at your strike indicator but not taking your fly, then you may be presenting the fly too deep in the water column. Try shortening your leader to get the fly nearer the surface.

➤ **Bug Activity**: in addition to my short walk near the boat launch, I always watch for signs of invertebrates as I'm moving around the lake. It's possible to find Chironomid, Caddis or Mayflies hatching on one shoal and not another. It also helps to observe the size of bugs the trout are likely to be feeding on and then match your fly to that size or use a slightly larger fly.

➤ **Angler Activity**: watch what other anglers are doing, especially if they are successful. Even from a distance, you can usually judge the water depth, whether they are using a floating or sinking line and the speed of their retrieve. That may help you get the right combination. If the successful angler is talking to others, you may be able to hear what is being said and get some useful hints. If all else fails, you can even ask. Many anglers are willing to share the information provided you haven't crowded into their fishing spot. If you see an angler scooting from location to location, odds are that he or she isn't hooking any fish.

Removing the barb doesn't necessarily decrease your effectiveness.

➤ **Other Environmental Factors**: exam the other environmental factors we discussed in Chapters 6 and 7 to assist in your assessment of what fly to use and how to present it. You now have the tools so use them to increase your success.

Anchoring to Fish

After leaving the boat launch and watching conditions on the lake, you will finally select a place to start angling. The spot you select shouldn't crowd other anglers. If you are using a motor, turn it off and row onto a shoal or over a drop-off. The wind should be at your back or left side when looking at the intended fishing area. You should be able to cast into your selected spot directly with the wind or cast across the wind provided it isn't coming from the same side as your casting arm. With the wind coming from the same side as your casting arm, you are likely to get a fly in the ear or your fly vest.

Especially on my first stop, I like to select a spot that allows me to cast to both the shallows and drop-off. This offers the best odds to find out where the fish are feeding. You can also watch for invertebrates in the various water depths. Naturally, if you see a rise line you won't need to guess where the fish are feeding. You can select a spot that allows the best casts into an obvious feeding zone. Then it's just a matter of finding the right fly and line with the proper retrieve.

When you find the perfect spot to anchor, don't just drop the anchor. Lower the anchor to the lake bottom. The low frequency vibrations of a heavy anchor crashing into the bottom muck can temporarily spook the fish and cause habitat damage. Sure, the trout will get over it but this avoidable mistake may have cost you 20 or 30 minutes of prime fishing time. If you have depth markings on your anchor rope, you should also note how deep the water is. This will help you in determining how close to the bottom your fly is getting. Knowing the depth may also be helpful if you are successful and then move to another location.

> The closer you anchor to shore, the greater the odds that someone will troll between you and the shoreline.

If necessary, fine tune the boats positioning in the water so that waves don't make a slapping noise against the side of the boat. This can be annoying and tends to make the trout overly cautious. Tie off the anchor and make sure everything is in its place. You don't want anything near your feet that may entangle the line. Fly lines are guaranteed to wrap around anything loose on the floor of the boat. Get comfortable and get ready to cast.

Casting for Fish

> If you go to a lake intending to fish a specific location, you will always find at least three boats already anchored in that spot.

When ready, strip enough line off the reel for a moderately long cast. Stripping the line will also let you know how tight the drag is set. Adjust if necessary. Make the first cast wherever it is easiest to deliver the line. After the fly line is out, check to see if the line is straight. You will probably find there are squiggles in the line from being stored on the reel. If so, straighten the fly line. This can be done by firmly stretching and holding an arms length of fly line for about two seconds. Then grab the next section of fly line and repeat until you have straighten the entire fly line. I usually lay the rod down in my canoe to stretch the line delivered on my first cast. If the line has been stored for a long time, you may need to repeat the process to get the line straight.

Now you are ready to start the actual process of fishing. The distance of the cast doesn't need to be long. The first time I took my wife out, she could only cast about 10 feet with 8.5 feet of that being fly rod. She patiently twitched the fly as instructed and the rod tip suddenly went completely under the canoe. She looked at me and said that she thought she might have a bite. She landed a four pound Rainbow, but the important point is about casting distance. If you are quiet, the trout will come close and may even shelter under your boat much the same as they would a wharf or floating dock. If you are quiet, the trout can be expected to come in close to your place of anchorage and you don't need long casts. My casts tend to be about 60 or 70 feet because I find that comfortable and easy. With more effort, I could get more line out but it usually isn't needed and I'm there to relax.

As already mentioned, the wind can be an important factor in casting. If the fly is being cast on your up-wind side, sooner or later you will hook yourself, your clothing or your boat. I call the area into which you can cast without fighting the wind the "effective casting zone". The radius of this zone is a function of wind strength, casting distance and leader length. The type of fly line will also play a minor role.

> Those who quietly row, flipper or paddle are the ones most likely to enter your back-cast zone. Watch for these folks.

> Those who spit, piss or cast into the wind are usually wet behind the ears.

If the wind is coming directly toward your back, then straight ahead is 12 o'clock, directly left is 9 o'clock and right is 3 o'clock. Assuming you are right handed and the wind is blowing, most of your casting will be in the zone from 9 o'clock to 12 o'clock. That's where you can place your fly line with the least worry of the wind directing the fly into the back of your head. Often, I turn to face the 9 o'clock position. That seems to offer the most trouble free casting. In very strong winds, you may be limited to the 10 o'clock to 11 o'clock positions.

You probably shouldn't consider casting into the 3 o'clock position even on breezy days unless you are using a short leader. As you shorten leader length, there is less chance of the wind redirecting your fly. With shorter leaders, you can expand your effective casting zone. If the wind is calm or if there is just a light breeze, you can usually cast in any direction around your boat, even with a long leader.

> Flies do not make very good earrings, especially if you've never had your ears pierced.

When you start casting, the first couple of casts should be into a spot you consider likely to produce a Rainbow. If that's unsuccessful, then start a searching pattern within your effective casting zone.

As a last note about casting, it isn't a good idea to cast a fly line between two folks in the same boat. Someone is liable to be wearing a fly earring. When I have two in my canoe, I adjust how I anchor so the canoe sits somewhat sideways to the wind. This can be achieved by tying the anchor to the side of the canoe and closer or further from the center. The person in front then casts to the left side (9 to 10 o'clock position) and the person in back casts more or less with the wind (11 to 12 o'clock position).

The Retrieve

While retrieving your fly, the rod tip should be held close to the water. That allows you to raise the rod tip to set the hook when you have a strike. If the rod tip is already high, you don't have a way to tighten the line and set the hook. I don't suggest pointing the rod directly at your fly during the retrieve. Instead, the rod should be pointed about 30 degrees away from the location of your fly. That's to prevent a Rainbow from breaking your leader within the first two seconds after taking the fly. You need the spring action in the rod to cushion the strike and prevent a leader break. Sometimes the trout will take the fly on the run and if your rod is pointed directly at the fish, it will almost certainly result in a broken leader. Also, remember that Rainbows can accelerate to full speed in less than a second. As fast as you can say 'one thousand one' the trout may already be traveling at 25 mph and the spring action in the rod is needed to keep your leader intact.

> Don't wade into chest deep waters if you are only wearing hip waders.

If you are fishing an imitator fly, the retrieve should range from slow to very slow to virtually still. Aquatic invertebrates simply don't move very fast. When fishing Chironomid pupa, many folks don't move the fly or move it as slow as possible. The old saying with Chironomid fishing is "if you think your retrieve is slow enough, then slow it down some more". An effective way to fish Chironomid patterns is to cast to the 9 o'clock position, don't retrieve and just let the wind drift your dry line.

Attractor flies can be fished with whatever retrieve suits the angler. Fast retrieves often entice the trout via the visual trigger. With a slow retrieve, the trout can visually key on components of the fly and mistake it for a bug of interest. Attractor flies are the most versatile for trying retrieves of different speeds or styles.

> Swarming and mating in flight isn't all that it's cracked up to be.

The method of fly retrieval is very important. It can mean the difference between catching and not catching fish. I once saw a person catching fish. Two unsuccessful anglers asked what he was using. He told them which fly and line. They were still unsuccessful so he called them over. He gave each of them one of his flies and even moved down the lake so they could fish in his spot. A while later he returned to find they still hadn't caught any fish. The unsuccessful pair moved so the helpful angler could have his spot back. Once again, this angler was into fish. The only difference in technique was in how these folks retrieved their flies. I would go so far as to say that the retrieve is more important than what fly you select.

As you retrieve the fly line, it should neatly coil on the bottom of the boat. Try not to step on your line as it sits on the floor of the boat. Accidentally stepping on your line wears it out much quicker than using it for fishing. Don't let the line wrap around anything on the boat bottom including your feet. When we started to cast, we straightened out the line. Part of the reason was to make casting easier but the other part was so the line would coil well while retrieving. The looping effect from being stored on the reel will cause the fly line to tangle. You don't want a tangle trying to flow through the rod guides while you have a big fish. It doesn't work and you will probably loose the fish.

When to Change

If you are unsuccessful in your approach then try something different. If you expect a fly to be successful, give it about 15 to 20 minutes before trying a different fly. That's usually enough time to cast through a full search pattern in the effective casting zone. If you haven't completed the search pattern, you may want to leave that fly on a little longer. Then it's time to try a new fly and cast that through another search pattern.

In 30 to 45 minutes, you will probably have tried two or three flies. If you still haven't had any success, then it may be time to try another location or a different fly line. If you see lots of fish activity where you are casting, then the problem isn't a lack of fish. That should be a clue to try a different fly line, or a different leader length and maybe a different retrieve.

> If you rock the boat or make waves, expect the skittish fish to scatter.

If you don't see any fish activity, it's possible you simply didn't find the active fish on your first stop. Another location may prove more productive. When you move, it may be wise to try water that is a little shallower or a little deeper. Keep watching for those rise lines when you move. After you have worked through a second stop without success, then it's time to try a different fly line and a totally different approach.

> Forty minutes no trout
> Then look about
> For another place to try
> Where fish may come by.

You probably arrived at the lake expecting a particular set of invertebrates to be on the trout's menu. Your first few flies were probably imitations of those bugs. To keep the retrieve slow enough, the odds are that you were using a floating line. Since the fish haven't yet cooperated, it may be time to put on a sinking line and an attractor fly. If most of the imitator flies were small, then try a large attractor fly combined with faster or variable retrieves. If we appeal to the trout's visual trigger, maybe we can get them interested.

What do you do after you have gone through a full complement of fly lines, leader lengths and fly types? I would suggest you do something other than fish. If you are on a day trip, then have lunch, take pictures, or go home. If you are staying at the lake, then wait until later in the day. I have often found that when Rainbows aren't feeding during the day, they usually feed in the evening.

Getting a Fish

After this lack of success, you go back out on the lake. This time you find the right location, you have the right presentation and the Rainbows are taking the fly. So what do you do to set the hook and get the trout to the boat?

When Rainbows strike the fly, the take can range from soft and almost imperceptible to a strike that just about rips the rod from your hand. Hard strikes are more common with large attractor flies. These hard strikes usually occur when the trout are aggressively attacking the fly rather than feeding on it. Very soft strikes occur when the trout essentially inhales the fly as a food item.

With hard strikes, trout essentially set the hook without your assistance. Hard strikes are felt because the trout has rapidly swam at the fly. As the trout engulfs the fly and its motion carries on, the line tightens and sets the hook. All you need to do is raise you rod tip and begin to play the fish.

With a very soft strike, the trout is just slurping in your fly as it cruises along. The trout isn't moving fast or far enough to cause the line to tighten and set the hook on its own. You need to tighten the line before the trout discovers the fly isn't a real bug and spits it out. A smooth but rapid lifting of the rod tip is usually all that is needed to

> **Did You Know**
> The greatest number of large fish caught per day is in the month of June. However, this is closely followed by October. The fewest large fish per day of fishing occurs in the month of August.

set the hook. Sometimes the trout will even bite down on the fly if it thinks a bug is getting away. Setting the hook shouldn't be a hard fast jerk of the rod. A snapping motion can break off the fly or yank the fly out of the trout's mouth. The smooth but rapid lifting of the rod is all it takes.

The angler needs to watch a floating fly line very closely to detect these soft strikes. With a dry line, you won't always feel the strike through the rod as you would with a

> About 80% of the big fish stories are created by folks with big imaginations.

sinking line. With the line floating, there is actually a lot of slack line between you and the fish. You need to watch the end of the fly line for slight hesitations or the tip of the line to be drawn below the surface. If this happens, set the hook. It's because of these very soft strikes that many anglers have begun to use strike indicators.

When discussing reels, I mentioned that the fly line is usually stripped through the index finger of the hand holding the rod. The finger can then be pressed against the rod to serve as a brake. The other hand is pulling on the fly line to retrieve the fly or bring in the fish. When setting the hook, the brake needs to be applied to tighten the fly line. However, be prepared to release that brake with only an instants advance warning. The trout may go into a powerful run at any time after the hook is set. If so, release the brake and let the trout run. Frequently, a beginner will panic and actually apply the brake harder rather than releasing it. Even the intermediate angler will sometimes forget to release the brake quick enough and break off a nice fish.

With the hook set and the rod tip high, we can begin to bring the fish to the boat. The trout is brought to the boat by alternating what your hands are doing. Strip line and then apply the brake while you reset to strip some more line. You need to "feel" the fish through the rod to judge how hard you can

> **Fishing Tip**
> When the trout are moving in very shallow water, try presenting a Chironomid on a dry line with about 12 to 18 inches of leader.

pull. If you pull too hard, the leader may break. If you let slack into the line, the trout may throw the fly. The objective is to land the fish without over exertion and lactic acid build up in the fish. If a trout is played too long, it may not survive being released.

Through the rod, you can feel what the trout is doing. If the trout runs directly at you, then you need to increase the speed of retrieving your line. Try to avoid slack line between you and the fish. If the trout is running away from you, then let it have line. Eventually the trout will tire and let you bring it near the boat without too much resistance. But be prepared as the trout nears your boat. When they see you and the boat, the trout often make another series of runs and possibly jumps.

> Don't use electronic bug zappers. They kill many of the night flying aquatic insects such as Caddis and Mayflies.

Now it's time to net the fish. I usually get the landing net out and ready before the final attempt to land the fish. You can apply brake with the rod hand while getting the net with the other hand. If the net is dry, you may want to wet it before trying to bring it under the fish. Cautiously lower your rod toward the trout. Apply the brake and gently raise the rod upward. This should drag the fish toward you. Slip the net under the fish. Lift the net while lowering your rod tip and you should have the trout. If it's a big fish, try to get the fish going into the net head first. I have seen a number of fish lost by folks trying to net large fish tail first.

If you are going to keep the fish, then kill it quickly with a sharp blow to the head. If you are going to release the fish, try to keep it in the net and in the water while removing the hook. If you want a picture before releasing the fish, then be careful not to harm the trout in the process. It's preferably to take the picture of the trout in the net while in the water. However, if you want to lift the trout out of

> For some reason, the peaks in bug availability tend to occur around the tenth day of the month.

the water, then grab the trout around tail section. With the other hand, support (don't squeeze) the trout's belly just behind the head and lift. The belly portion needs the support while out of the water so that it's internal organs aren't damaged. Take the picture quickly and gently return the trout to the water.

The Top 10 Considerations

Let's conclude this book with a look at what I consider the ten most important aspects of angling for Rainbows. With difficulty, I've attempted to prioritize these. They will give you some idea of what I consider important. Others may disagree with these but that's okay. I changed my mind several times in making this list and it's only presented as food for thought.

#1 – Location (Find the Fish)

I consider location to be the most important factor in fishing for Rainbows in pristine lakes. Even with perfect conditions, a good presentation and feeding fish, you aren't likely to get a trout unless you are angling where the fish are located. In pristine lakes, Rainbows often move around the lake in large groups or packs. They may be in one place today and somewhere else tomorrow. These groups may be one or more age classes and they may or may not feed according to pecking order. Naturally, some Rainbows won't stay in a group but the anglers best odds are with finding a concentration of fish.

> Depth, structure and shoals
> Are the fly fishers' goals.
> Remove any one
> And the fishing's not fun.

Certain places on the lake have a prime feeding shoal, near deep holding water. These locations usually contain an abundance of fish. Even in this limited area, the trout may be on the shoal, in the deep, or along the drop-off. The angler still needs to find just the right location.

Fishing Tip

If it's now harder to cast 60 feet of line than a 70 foot cast used to be, then you probably need to clean your fly line. While you're at it, try cleaning the guides on your rod.

Last Fall I made several trips to one lake over a period of several days. After several moves, I found the fish that first day. The next trip I didn't get Rainbows in that same location. After a little exploring, I found they had moved several hundred yards down the lake. On the third trip, I tried both places in vain. Again, I found they had moved another short distance down the lake. It was almost as if this large group of Rainbows gradually moved around the lake perimeter, eating all available food and then moving on. To me it highlighted the importance of finding the fish. I also consider the choice of lake to be a part of being at the right location. Lakes at different elevations with different water clarity and food chains can affect the angler's success.

#2 – Rainbow Motivators (Are They Hungry?)

In Chapter 5, we discussed what motivates Rainbows and their subsequent behavior. In my opinion, the second most important consideration to catching Rainbows is where the trout are fitting into the Rainbow Hierarchy as shown in Figure 25. Try to assess what is motivating the trout while you are fishing and adjust your presentation

251

to suit an expected behavior pattern. Remember that hunger is a primary motivator in this hierarchy.

> What many anglers call "enticing" trout is simply providing motivation. With the right motivation, you can catch most trout.

If you go to a lake containing too many fish and too little food, the trout are guaranteed to be hungry if not starving. In those circumstances, catching fish is just about a sure thing regardless of other factors or conditions. Conversely, if you go to a lake where the Bows are well fed and content then the fishing will surely be difficult. You would also expect a vast difference in the size of Rainbows from each of these lakes. Even within one lake, conditions will change and the trout will be motivated at different levels throughout the season.

Except for appealing to the trout's visual trigger, the angler can only assess what is motivating the trout and estimate the expected behavior patterns. The angler who is aware of these differences can then adjust approach and techniques to fit the circumstances.

#3 – Environmental Factors

Environmental factors are third on my list of important angling considerations. Lakes in turn-over, a wind from the east or hot, sunny conditions aren't things we can control. We can only adjust to the situation.

In Chapter 6, we saw how weather, water and other factors affected the Rainbows and fishing success. In Chapter 7, we saw how these same factors affected the bugs that Rainbows feed on. These environmental conditions have significant impacts on the trout and everything in their

> Always observe what is happening around you. It will increase your enjoyment of the sport as well as your success.

ecosystem. By using the tools provided in those chapters, an angler can adjust to environmental conditions and hopefully improve their angling success. For example, if fishing in October with a wind from the north and foul weather, the angler should probably select Shrimp or Bloodworm fly patterns rather than ones to imitate Waterboatmen. We saw that Waterboatmen are not fond of those conditions. As another example, we found that in warm water conditions the trout are usually found at or below the thermocline. These are the types of adjustments an angler can make to the environmental factors to help improve angling success. An angler needs to be familiar with how Rainbows and bugs respond to the environment.

#4 – Cyclic Timing

The seasonal and lunar cycles are more important than some other considerations in angling. Cycles occur throughout nature and most anglers don't understand these rhythms. Many anglers simply go to a lake hoping that the cyclic timing will produce good fishing on that day. The graphs presented in Chapter 7 not only help you to select a time that is likely to be productive but will also help you select which invertebrates have the best odds of catching Rainbows.

Many anglers probably wouldn't rank the cyclic rhythms so high in the top ten considerations. Those same anglers probably wouldn't fish with a Caddis fly pattern in April or a Waterboatman pattern in mid July and they probably know the Damselflies will be hatching in late June. Whether they are aware of it or not, they are

> Advice on what to use or where to go is usually based on last weeks fishing stories and thus, is out-of-date.

considering the cycling timing of the bugs. I have said several times that the best fishing is at the start of a new hatch rather than fishing the middle or end of a hatch. Even the feeding intervals of Rainbows Trout are a cyclic process. Use some of the cyclic rhythms provided in this book to help improve your success.

#5 – The Angler

What the angler does is an important factor in the equation for successfully hooking Rainbows. Anglers should be observant, informed and shouldn't advertise their presence to the trout. I've mentioned these aspects throughout the book and consider them a part of the top ten considerations.

> **Fishing Tip**
> Placing carpet in the bottom of your boat not only helps to muffle unwanted noise, it helps protect your fly line as it coils on the floor and you accidentally step on it.

The angler needs to avoid unnecessary noise, especially in an aluminum boat. Wash your hands and keep foreign smells off your flies and equipment. Avoid rapid movement in your boat that might startle the trout. Row the last little distance onto a shoal rather than motor into the spot you intend to angle. Try to keep the shadows of yourself and your rod out of the areas into which you are casting. Lower your anchor gently rather than dropping it. In other words, don't put a scare into the trout before trying to catch them.

The angler also needs to be observant and informed. You should watch for rise lines and other signs of Rainbow activity. Examine the bugs and be informed enough to know which will likely be on the trout's menu. Watch the lake and determine where the trout and bug activity are located. The angler needs to assess conditions and determine the best approach. Correctly assess what's happening to be among the 20% of anglers that catch 80% of the Rainbows.

> A trout, that is an inefficient forager, may get hungry and feed on non-typical foods.

#6 – The Presentation

After finding the right location, dealing with the various natural factors and not scaring the trout, it becomes important to present an offering that is appealing to the trout. The angler needs to select the right fly line, leader length and retrieve to get the trout interested. I'm not yet considering the specific fly pattern as part of the presentation. Two different flies could produce the same results with the right presentation.

The angler needs to decide if a fly is going to be presented on the surface or below and at what depth. Should you use a big fly or a small fly? Should the fly be retrieved up, down, horizontally or diagonally through the water column? Should the fly be moved fast, slow or not at all? An angler must select the right

> If refraction in the water allows you to see a trout, you can be sure that the trout can also see you.

equipment and technique to get the desired presentation. Sometimes the presentation doesn't matter but often it can be the difference between success and failure.

#7 – Rainbow Feeding Preferences

Even though a specific bug is abundant and readily available doesn't mean it will be on the trout's menu today. The trout may be after a minor component of the available bugs because of a preference for that bug. In fact, the bug might not even be available yet. The trout may be anticipating a hatch and searching for that invertebrate. The preference may be because of bug taste, size or amino acid content. Whatever the cause, Rainbows prefer certain bugs at certain times. That old saying of "match the hatch" may result in fewer fish than the angler might otherwise have caught.

> **Fishing Tip**
> Many anglers are using loops to tie fly to leader because these knots allow the fly to move freely. In fact, the fly often hangs vertical in the water. That's great for Chironomid fishing, but not when you want the fly to be horizontal or at some other angle.

I went fishing during the 1993 World Fly Fishing Championships even though I wasn't a contestant. I just wanted to watch. I found the trout were after Caddis pupa even though it was early June. I saw one adult Caddis in the morning and tried the pupa. I hit 42 fish in six hours. Sedges were the preferred food for the day. The contestants landed very few fish because most angled with Chironomids that were hatching at the time. Matching the hatch didn't work. This is a good example of a Rainbow food preference. Hopefully it will alert anglers that sometimes another fly might work better.

#8 – The Schreckstoff Factor

Many anglers don't seem aware that Rainbows give off chemical warnings to other trout when they are injured or alarmed. I have watched anglers catch a few fish and then the action stops. However, the angler patiently sits in the same location waiting for more strikes. I've

> Nobody needs to angle with more than one line or one fly (such as a dropper fly) especially if they are proficient at their sport.

seen this scenario often enough that I consider it one of the top ten considerations in fly fishing.

When you've been catching fish in one location and they stop, it may simply be because the hooked fish gave off the Schreckstoff warning. With the chemical warning of danger in the water, the trout will move away until the warning dissipates. In the meantime, you can simply move a couple of casting distances down the lake and probably be back into fish. After a while, you can move back to your original location and the odds are that the trout will have returned. Rather than facing a lull while the Schreckstoff dissipates, you can be into continuous good fishing.

#9 – The Visual Trigger

I consider the visual trigger as one of the top ten considerations in fly fishing on pristine lakes. Knowing that a trout can be enticed into striking a fly when they otherwise wouldn't is important. It can affect how you tie flies (contrast or hackle for vibrations) as well as how you fish certain flies. The angler who knows about the visual trigger can sometimes be into fish when others aren't.

I have even used the visual trigger while Chironomid fishing even though Chironomids are usually fished very slowly. Rainbows will often examine and then reject a fly for whatever reason. However, they will frequently take the fly when it tries to escape. Try occasionally lifting your rod tip while Chironomid fishing. A trout that has just examined and rejected your fly is likely to turn and take it because of the rapid

> In the early spring, as bugs come out of hibernation, they tend to be large but slim. In the fall, the new generation tends to be small, short and fat. You might consider this in fly selection.

movement imparted by lifting your rod tip. It's a part of the genetic instinct involved with the visual trigger. Many times the fish caught while trolling are reacting to the visual trigger.

#10 – Selection of a Fly Pattern

Many anglers will be surprised that I list the selection of a fly pattern as last in this list. It probably goes against the grain of those who spend half an hour tying just the right qualities into a fly pattern. But have you ever noticed that when lots of folks are catching fish they are often using different fly patterns. When conditions are good, the trout often take a variety of flies and bugs. Even when the trout are more selective, they will take a variety of flies with the correct visual keys even though the fly patterns presented are different.

> **Did You Know**
> While it isn't about fly fishing, Izaac Walton wrote the Complete Angler in 1653. Some of the earliest written confirmation of fly fishing dates back to the second century AD with the ancient Romans and Macedonians.

Also, consider the contents of Rainbows feeding samples. When you examine what is in the Rainbow's stomach you usually find more than one type of bug. Unless the trout are in the mode of seeking a preferred food item, they often take whatever comes along. Sometimes you need just the right fly, but most of the time that isn't the case.

End Notes

That brings us to the end. This book has provided you with lots of facts, data and food for thought. I hope you have found many tips to help improve your enjoyment of the sport. As you no doubt found, angling is a science as well as an art. The scientific aspects can help you be among the 20% of anglers that catch 80% of the fish. Most angling books present the artistic or fanciful side of fishing. With this text, you have been presented with many years of research and fishing data that can be put to good use while fishing. I encourage you to take this information and improve your success.

There is still a lot about Rainbows in pristine lakes that we don't know or simply don't understand. My data spans about 30 years of detailed record keeping. Now, with each year's additional data, the graphs and trends may change slightly but the data has essentially stabilized. Therefore, I'm reasonably certain that all the provided information is reliable. That doesn't mean, however, that I've quit examining the data for more or better information. For example, look at the information in Appendix 8 to see what I'm currently investigating.

With this kind of information, you should be able to determine why the trout behave as they do on certain days. Maybe you have even found something that will turn a poor day of fishing into a good one. I certainly hope so. That has been my intention. But now, it's up to you use this information or ignore it. Either way, I hope you enjoy your angling.

Ron Newman

Glossary of Terms

- **Adult**: sexually mature.
- **Aerobic:** requiring free oxygen for respiration.
- **AFTMA:** American Fishing Tackle Manufacturers Association. An association which standardizes fly line weights to match with fly rods.
- **Alga:** singular of algae.
- **Algae:** non-vascular (no vessels or channels) aquatic plants. Typically, these are single celled, free floating and contain chlorophyll.
- **Amino Acid:** a component of proteins produced by living cells in many organisms. These are necessary parts of a trout's diet.
- **Anaerobic:** living or existing in the absence of free oxygen.
- **Aquatic Invertebrate:** any of the creatures in a trout's diet that lack a vertebra including insects, crustacean, snails, arachnids, etc.
- **Artificial Fly:** various materials (fur, feathers, etc) tied onto a fish hook and designed to be cast with a fly rod and line without external weights.
- **Attractor Fly:** an artificial fly that isn't designed to imitate a specific invertebrate. It may not look like any invertebrate or it may visually represent two or more bugs (also see imitator fly).
- **Backing:** extra (back-up) line between the fly line and the fly reel. Often this is braided nylon line of 20 pound test.
- **Biological Clock:** A term used to describe the ability of many organisms to keep track of time and denote cyclic events through environmental cues.
- **Binocular Vision:** seeing with both eyes and thus depth perception is present.
- **Boat Charging:** a learned Rainbow behavior where the fish rapidly swims toward the angler in an attempt to throw the fly.
- **Bug:** strictly, an insect but loosely used in this text to refer to any of the aquatic invertebrates.
- **Butt Section:** the portion of a tapered leader that attaches to the fly line. This portion is usually the heaviest and thickest portion of the leader.
- **Carnivore:** an animal that eats other living animals.
- **Casting:** getting the line away from the angler and into the water.
- **Chlorophyll:** the green material of plants used to convert sunlight into energy and food. Chlorophyll needs the reds from the light spectrum.
- **Circadian:** referring to a 24 hour cycle typically of day and night.
- **Complete Metamorphosis:** the typical stages of insect development from egg, to larva, to pupa, to adult.
- **Cone Cells:** the cells in the eye that collect colored light.
- **Cruiser:** a Rainbow that leisurely patrols the shoals and drop-offs of its territory.
- **Cyclic:** an event that systematically repeats itself at given intervals or after specific external prompts.
- **Distant Touch:** the ability to "feel" or detect objects without contact via the lateral line system.

- **Decibels:** a measure of sound intensity much like the Richter scale for earthquakes.
- **Dorsally Compressed:** flattened from top to bottom like a hockey puck.
- **Drag:** to troll a fly behind the boat rather than cast the fly. Also, the tension setting on a reel to determine how much pressure is needed to cause the reel's spool to spin. The "drag" prevents free spooling and thus tangles.
- **Drop-Off:** the transition from a shoal (or shore) to deep water and defined by a steeper slope than typically found on a shoal or the lake bottom.
- **Dry Fly:** a fly that is designed to float on the water surface.
- **Dry Line:** a fly line that floats.
- **Dystrophic:** a faulty nutritional status but usually applies to ponds rather than lakes.
- **Effective Casting Zone:** the area you can cast into while casting with the wind rather than against it. For right handed folks, this is typically to your front or left side with the wind at your back.
- **Electroreception:** the ability to detect electric current.
- **Epilimnion:** the layer or zone of relatively warmer water near the surface of the lake in summertime.
- **Eutrophic Lake:** a lake rich in dissolved nutrients and is typically geologically old.
- **Feeding Interval:** the time it takes between meals. Rainbows will often eat their fill and then rest to digest that meal before eating again.
- **Feeding Sample:** a post-mortem examination of the content in a trout's stomach to determine the quantity and types of food it has been eating.
- **Fishing Season:** from ice-off until ice-over or as the fishing season is otherwise restricted in the fishing regulations.
- **Floating Fly or Line:** see dry fly and dry line.
- **Fly Pattern:** the model, design or blueprint of an imitator or attractor fly.
- **Fly Shy:** when a Rainbow becomes very cautious about taking a fly pattern that it previously took.
- **Food Availability:** the accessibility of invertebrates or other food that the trout can locate and feed on. Certain protective mechanisms and factors such as hibernation or size can restrict the trout's ability or desire to feed on certain invertebrates at specific times.
- **Habitat:** the place or environment where plants or animals normally live and grow.
- **Hatch:** when invertebrates change from one metamorphic stage to another. Sometimes used to indicate an egg "hatching" into a larva or nymph. At other times, it indicates a pupa or nymph "hatching" into an adult. The term is also loosely used to indicate a time of availability for any of the aquatic insects.
- **Hatch Forecasting:** the ability of Rainbows to predict and await specific hatches of insects.
- **Herbivore:** an animal that eats plant material.
- **Hypolimnion:** the layer or zone of relatively colder water near the bottom of the lake in summertime.
- **Ichthyology:** the study of fish.
- **Imitator Fly:** an artificial fly that is designed to represent the visual keys of one specific invertebrate.

- ➤ **Incomplete Metamorphosis:** lacking the typical metamorphic development of egg, larva, pupa and adult. These insects go from egg to nymph to adult.
- ➤ **Insectivorous:** feeding on insects or insect-like creatures. In this content, that includes the aquatic invertebrates within the food chain of a lake.
- ➤ **Invertebrate:** not having a backbone. Usually inferring bugs that trout feed on in this text.
- ➤ **Larva:** (plural = larvae) the first stage of development after the egg for insects with complete metamorphosis and typically looks like a grub or worm.
- ➤ **Lateral Line:** often refers to the main trunk of the Octavolateralis system but the entire system has 16 parts and detects low frequency vibrations in water.
- ➤ **Laterally Compressed:** flattened from side to side. The trout and freshwater shrimp are laterally compressed. Also, see dorsally compressed.
- ➤ **Leader Shy:** when fish refuse a fly because they see, and are spooked, by the leader. This normally only happens in very clear water with timid fish.
- ➤ **Limnetic Zone:** the lake zone above the profundal zone. This zone receives sufficient sunlight to carry out photosynthesis but does not contain any lake bottom on which to support the growth of rooted plants.
- ➤ **Limnology:** the study of lakes.
- ➤ **Littoral Zone:** the portions of a lake which are sufficiently shallow to allow the penetration of sunlight to carry on photosynthesis and thus support the growth of rooted plants.
- ➤ **Lunar:** referring to the moon.
- ➤ **Lunar Cycle:** the time it takes from New moon to New moon or Full moon to Full moon. This takes approximately 29.5 days.
- ➤ **L-serine:** a substance found in the skin of mammals. Rainbows are very sensitive to the smell of this substance and dislike it intensely.
- ➤ **Lux:** a measure of light illumination similar to a foot-candle.
- ➤ **Maiden Trout:** a Rainbow that appears fully grown but is not yet sexually mature (adult).
- ➤ **Marl:** a loose or crumbling lake bottom deposit containing lots of calcium carbonate classically in the form of snail and crustacean shells. Note that Chironomid tubes also contain calcium that helps to form marl or marl shoals.
- ➤ **Mesotrophic Lake:** a geologically mature lake with a moderate amount of dissolved nutrients.
- ➤ **Metamorphosis:** the changing of physical form and in this text meaning those changes from egg to adult in aquatic invertebrates.
- ➤ **Monocular Vision:** only seeing with one eye and thus no depth perception.
- ➤ **Moon Day:** the number of days after a New moon. The New moon is day zero and progresses to 28 or 29 days (29.5 day cycle) before the next New moon.
- ➤ **Moon Phase:** the four quarters of the moon which includes: New moon, First Quarter moon, Full moon and Third Quarter moon.
- ➤ **Neuromast:** a cell that detects sensory input such as sound or vibrations and then sends signals to the brain for interpretation.
- ➤ **Nymph:** an immature developmental stage of an insect species that has incomplete metamorphosis. Nymphs do not radically change appearance as do insects with complete metamorphosis (egg, larva, pupa, adult)

259

➢ **Oligotrophic Lake**: a lake deficient in dissolved nutrients and typically geologically young. Often contains abundant oxygen.
➢ **Omnivore**: an animal that eats both plants and animals.
➢ **Palming**: using the palm of a hand against the spool of the fly reel to act as a braking system when a fish is taking out line.
➢ **pH**: a measure of the alkalinity or acidity. Neutral water is 7.0 with acidic water being lower and alkaline water being higher.
➢ **Photosynthesis**: the process of chlorophyll in plants converting sunlight into energy and food. The plant absorbs the sugars and gives off oxygen.
➢ **Phytoplankton**: the plant component of plankton (also see zooplankton).
➢ **Plankton**: very small plant and animal life that is usually free-floating or swimming in water.
➢ **Pupa**: (plural = pupae) the metamorphic stage just prior to adult for insects with complete metamorphosis.
➢ **Predator**: an animal that hunts and eats other animals.
➢ **Preferred Food**: a menu item that trout will seek out in preference to other available foods.
➢ **Presentation**: how the fly is offered to the fish. This usually includes the type of fly and type of line along with the depth and speed of retrieve.
➢ **Primary Invertebrates**: the seven bugs of primary importance as Rainbow food in pristine lakes and of importance to the angler. These include the freshwater Shrimp, Chironomid, Caddis (Sedge), Dragonflies, Damselflies, Mayflies and Waterboatmen.
➢ **Pristine Lake**: a moderate to small size lake with good shoal development, productive water, and insectivorous Rainbows but lacking other competing fish species.
➢ **Profundal Zone**: the deeper water zone in a lake where the penetration of sunlight is insufficient to support photosynthesis.
➢ **Reflection**: the act of bending back or returning light or sound (as a mirror).
➢ **Refraction**: the bending of light as it passes from a medium of one density into a medium of different density.
➢ **Representational Fly**: an attractor fly that represents two or more bugs as opposed to not looking like any invertebrate.
➢ **Respiration**: the opposite of photosynthesis that occurs at night. The plant gives off carbon dioxide and water.
➢ **Retrieve**: after the cast, bringing the fly and line back toward the angler. The angler can retrieve the line fast, slow still, jerky, smooth and so forth.
➢ **Rise Line**: the observed action of trout rising to the surface in specific locations, often because of suitable environmental factors in that location. A rise line will frequently follow the "line" of a drop-off but may be circular or any other shape.
➢ **Rises**: when Rainbows disturb the water surface. The fish are not always feeding when they "rise" and this doesn't include trout jumping out of the water.
➢ **Rod Cells**: the cells in the eye primarily responsible for black and white vision.
➢ **Scavenger**: an animal that eats dead or decaying plants and/or animals.

- **Schreckstoff:** An alarm substance given off by fish when they are injured or alarmed and this gives a warning to other fish.
- **Sedge:** local vernacular for "Caddis" or members of the Trichoptera family.
- **Sediment:** any living or non-living material that settles to the lake bottom.
- **Setting the hook:** pulling the hook and line with the rod to get the hook firmly embedded in the trout's mouth.
- **Shoal:** relatively shallow water near the shore which can support rooted plants. These areas contain the bulk of a lakes biomass and serve as a Rainbow's main feeding grounds.
- **Shore:** the boundary between the land and water.
- **Sinking Fly or Sinking Line:** see wet fly or wet line.
- **Sinking Tip:** a type of fly line designed to float except for the last few feet of line which will sink
- **Skunked:** angler slang for "not catching any fish".
- **Sound Trigger:** the possible stimulation of trout to begin feeding due to sounds, such as the noise of other trout feeding.
- **Strike:** when the trout takes, hits or otherwise ingests the fly.
- **Strike Indicator:** a small "bobber" or float attached to the leader that the angler can watch to determine if they have a strike.
- **Sunken Island:** a shoal that is separated from the shore by deep water.
- **Synchronized Rises:** when many fish begin or stop rising at about the same time.
- **Terrestrials:** any of the bugs that normally develop on land rather than as aquatic invertebrates.
- **Thermocline:** the layer or zone of transition between the epilimnion and the hypolimnion characterized by rapidly changing water temperature.
- **Tippet:** the very last section of a tapered leader that attaches to the fly. This section is usually the thinnest in diameter.
- **Troll:** using the boat to pull the line rather than casting and retrieving.
- **Turnover:** the spring and fall process of water dropping and raising in the water column due to its maximum density occurring at 39.2 degrees F.
- **Visual Key:** the primary characteristics of an invertebrate that trout quickly examine before ingesting that bug or fly. This may include size, shape, movement and/or specific characteristics such as eyes or tails.
- **Visual Trigger:** the physical excitation of a Rainbow causing the "feed or flee" phenomenon brought on by movement or unusual contrast.
- **Visual Window:** the circular area that a trout or other critters can see above the waters surface. At more than 40 degrees, light is reflected off the bottom of the surface prohibiting above surface vision.
- **Wet Fly:** a fly that sinks below the water surface.
- **Wet Line:** a fly line that sinks in the water. There are different types of wet or sinking lines that drop at different rates in the water.
- **Wind Knot:** a knot in your leader. Knots significantly reduce leader strength. They are usually caused by casting errors rather than the wind.
- **Zooplankton:** the animal portion of plankton (also see zooplankton).

Appendix 1

A Fly Fishers Code of Ethics

In recent years, there has been a rise in the number of anti-hunting and anti-fishing groups who actually think they are helping the resource by limiting animal harvest or even prohibiting these sports. It becomes imperative that we police our own activities before someone else forces their opinions into our sport. Following are a set of Fly Fishing Ethics that should help us keep and improve our sport.

1. The ethical fly fisher will actively support the enforcement of sound fisheries regulations and habitat management through:
    - knowing, obeying and exceeding the requirements of any fishing regulations;
    - observing, recording and reporting any adverse environmental impacts or infractions of the fishing regulations;
    - co-operating with fisheries enforcement and management efforts;
    - disassociation with any person who knowingly damages the fisheries resource or violates fishing regulations.
2. The ethical fly fisher will conduct their fishing and associated activities in a manner which inspires respect for the individual and the sport of fly fishing through:
    - their courtesy, integrity and helpfulness on and around the fishing waters;
    - the avoidance of misleading or exaggerated statements;
    - limiting the number of fish kept to those needed for personal consumption;
    - releasing, unharmed, those fish that are spawners, illegal, undersized or otherwise not needed;
    - respecting the rights and needs of other resource users;
    - respecting the intrinsic values of nature, the fish and the fish habitat;
    - avoiding any unnecessary disturbances to wildlife including spawning fish, nesting birds and aquatic insects.
3. The ethical fly fisher will promote the art and science of fly fishing through:
    - the sharing of techniques, skills, knowledge and other information relevant to the sport;
    - actively encouraging the use of flies and fly fishing equipment where suited;
    - taking time from fishing to honestly and helpfully answer someone who asks "what fly are you using".
4. The ethical fly fisher will work to maintain and enhance the natural aquatic and terrestrial ecosystems integral to the fisheries habitat through:
    - the anticipation and prevention of adverse environmental impacts on the fisheries resource;
    - promoting management that will produce quality fisheries which are compatible with the inherent capability and natural diversity of the aquatic and terrestrial ecosystems;
    - encouraging fisheries projects directed at ensuring the future productivity, quality and diversity of the fisheries;
    - fostering opportunities to preserve the fish and their habitat requirements;
    - recognizing that human understanding of nature is incomplete and working to maintain options for the future.

Appendix 2

Catch and Release Guidelines

These days most anglers release Rainbows not intended for use on their dinner table within a short while. This practice puts fish back into the lake for another angler to catch and is commonly called "Catch & Release". It is recycling of the resource if you like. However, I wouldn't suggest you follow the release practices shown on many of the sportfishing shows on TV. Some of these shows follow correct release techniques but many of these so-called professional anglers do virtually everything wrong and it is unlikely those fish will survive for another angler to catch. Following are a few of the basic rules to follow in Catch & Release fishing.

> **Did You Know**
> About eighty to ninety percent of trout properly released will survive.

> - Bring in the fish for release as soon as possible. The exertion of trying to escape causes "lactic acid" to build up in the muscles of the fish. If the fish becomes over-exerted this lactic acid can be lethal.
> - Keep the fish in the water and avoid handling as much as possible. Not supporting the stomach area of the fish can cause internal injuries. Handling can remove scales which allow access points for bacteria or fungal infections. And naturally the trout can't breathe while out of the water.
> - Always use barbless hooks. These hooks lack the barb making it easy for removal from the trout's mouth. You will also find that using barbless hooks does not increase the number of fish you lose.
> - Never, ever, under any circumstances put your fingers through the gill slits of the Rainbow or even have your fingers contact the gills. These organs can be easily damaged and sentence the fish to a slow agonizing death. If you must lift the fish for a picture then hold it just in front of the tail, cradle the belly area in the other hand and gently lift. Don't squeeze or keep the fish out of the water longer than a moment.
> - Remove the hook by pulling it in the opposite direction from which it entered. This is usually toward the throat of the fish. Using a pair of needle nose pliers will move the hook in that direction much better than your fingers. If the hook is too deeply embedded then it is better to cut the leader and release the fish with the hook still attached. Within a couple of weeks the acid in the trout's mouth will dissolve the hook.
> - When releasing a fish into the water don't just toss it overboard. Trout often require a minute or two to recover. Hold the fish around the narrow part just forward of the tail and place it in the water until it struggles to escape. If necessary, slowly move the fish back and forth to get oxygen bearing water moving over the gills.

> **Did You Know**
> It takes a Rainbow several hours to die from Lactic Acid poisoning. It may seem fine when released but could die later.

Appendix 3

The Use of Stomach Pumps

A growing trend among fly fishers is to use a stomach pump to check out the latest food items that a trout has eaten and then release the fish. It sounds like a useful tool. Determine what the trout are feeding on, choose a fly to match, then release the fish and hopefully improve your fishing success. However, you may want to re-think the usefulness of this tool and the conservation ethics of this practice.

Contrary to its name, the stomach pump should not be rammed all the way down into the trout's stomach. If placed into the stomach it is likely to damage the valve that stops water in the esophagus from entering the stomach. If that happens the trout may be severely injured and die. The stomach pump should remain within the esophagus (throat) and not enter the stomach.

However, keeping the pump within the esophagus limits the usefulness of this tool. Only smaller food items (chironomids, smaller shrimp, etc) will remain within the esophagus for any length of time. Larger food items (dragonflies, larger Caddis, etc) will quickly pass into the stomach due to the muscular contractions of the esophagus on these larger items. Larger foods may also be too large to enter the end of the pump. Therefore, a stomach pump may likely give false readings on the primary foods the trout are seeking.

We normally expect ten to twenty percent of trout to die even with proper "catch & release" techniques. I don't have verified data but I expect the survival rate is only around 50% when the fish are subjected to a stomach pump analysis. Even in the hands of an expert the extra handling, extra pressure needed to hold fish, the extra time out of water, the trauma of an internal inspection, etc, is bound to increase fish mortality. And what is even worse is that some knowledgeable fly fishers promote the use of stomach

> **Did You Know**
> The common Darner Dragonfly nymph usually grows to a size of 30 – 50 mm in length and a bug that size is not likely to fit into your average stomach pump.

pumps to novice fly fishers who don't know how to use the tool or properly handle a fish. Undoubtedly that will increase the mortality of released fish to even higher levels.

I know it goes against the grain of many fly fishers who use this device, but in my humble opinion, the use of stomach pumps should be outlawed. Anyone who gives the idea a little logical thought will most likely agree with me. So please refrain from using this device and actively discourage others from doing so.

Appendix 4
Example of Primary & Secondary Pecking Order Distribution in a Lake

# Yrs in Lake	Primary Pecking Order	Typical Number of Fish by Secondary Pecking Order Within Class				Typical Size of Fish (Lbs) by Pecking Order Within Class		
		Aggressive Order	Cautious Order	Meek Order	Total	Aggressive Order	Cautious Order	Meek Order
0	6	2500	1500	1000	5000	0.2	.02	0.2
1	5	1340	1340	670	3350	1.2	1.0	0.8
2	4	502	838	335	1675	2.4	2.0	1.6
3	3	134	402	134	670	3.6	3.0	2.4
4	2	20	141	40	201	4.8	4.0	3.2
5	1	2	32	6	40	6.0	5.0	4.0
			Total Fish in Lake		10,936			

In the above table, we can see how aggressive fish tend to grow faster but their numbers also decline faster than fish that are cautious or meek. The meek fish tend to avoid predation and capture better but they don't grow as rapidly in size. The cautious fish shall inherit the lake.

Appendix 5

Estimated Levels of Sound Underwater

Sound In Air			Sound Intensity	Sound In Water		
Typical Sound Comparison	Relative Loudness	Air Decibels	Air -Watts/M2 Water - Micropascals	Water Decibels	Relative Loudness	Typical Sound Comparison
	na	na	1E-18	1	0	**Water Reference**
	na	na	1E-17	11		**Possible**
Known	na	na	1E-16	21		**Trout**
Human	na	na	1E-15	31		**Hearing**
Hearing	na	na	1E-14	41	1	Faintest Noises
	na	na	1E-13	51	2	Rustling Leaves
Air Reference	0	0	1E-12	61	4	Whisper
Faintest Noises	1	10	1E-11	71	8	Rain Falling
Rustling Leaves	2	20	0.000,000,000,1	81	16	Heavy Footsteps
Whisper	4	30	0.000,000,001	91	32	Two People Talking
Rain Falling	8	40	0.000,000,01	101	64	Busy Traffic
Heavy Footsteps	16	50	0.000,000,1	111	128	Vacuum Cleaner
Two People Talking	32	60	0.000,001	121	512	Niagara Falls
Busy Traffic	64	70	0.000,01	131	1,024	Orchestra
Vacuum Cleaner	128	80	0.000,1	141	2,048	Train
Niagara Falls	512	90	0.001	151	4,096	Rock Concert
Orchestra	1,024	100	0.01	161	8,192	Pain Threshold
Train	2,048	110	0.1	171	16,400	Jet Engine
Rock Concert	4,096	120	1	181	32,800	
Pain Threshold	8,192	130	10	191	65,400	Physical Damage
Jet Engine	16,400	140	100	201	130,800	
	32,800	150	1,000	211	261,600	
Eardrum Bursts	65,400	160	10,000	221		
	130,800	170	100,000	231		
	261,600	180	1,000,000	241		

It is estimated that Rainbows can hear noises that are about 61 decibels below the range of human hearing. In the above table, humans (left) are compared to trout (right).

Appendix 6

Sample of a Form for Recording Fishing

Lake:

WEATHER			Month	Day	Year

Sun / Temperature / Wind / Wind From... / Barom.

Sun	Temperature	Wind	Wind From...	Barom.
( ) Sunny	( ) Hot	( ) VWindy	N NW	( ) High >
( ) L. Cloud	( ) Warm	( ) Windy	S SE	( ) Mod
( ) Cloud	( ) Mild	( ) S Breeze	E NE	( ) Low <
( ) H Cloud	( ) Cool	( ) Breeze	W SW	( ) Change
( ) Overcst	( ) Cold	( ) L Breeze	Calm Var.	
( ) Rain	WATER	( ) Var	Rising	FISH	Feeding

Level	Temperature	Clarity	Rising	FISH	Feeding
( ) High	( ) Warm	( ) V.Clear	( ) Many	( ) Heavy
( ) > Avg.	( ) Mild	( ) Clear	( ) Mod	( ) Light
( ) Average	( ) Cool	( ) Cloudy	( ) Few	( ) V. Light
( ) < Avg.	( ) Cold	( ) Merky	( ) V Few	( ) None
( ) Low	( ) V.Cold	( ) V Merky	( ) None	( ) Var.
			( ) Var.	

FOOD Species Seen	Samples	Cows Standing	Birds Active
Many	Many	( ) Most	( ) Many
Mod	Mod	( ) Some	( ) Some
Few	Few	( ) V Few	( ) V Few
V.Few	V.Few	( ) Turn Over	
	None	Moon	

Time Fished	Hrs	Killed	Release	Lost	Missed	TOTAL	Rate
to							
to			CAUGHT & Missed				

TIME	Landed?	SIZE (lbs)	Fly	Location	Line	Retrieve

My Success	Others	Comments
( ) VG >4.5	( )	
( ) G < 4.5	( )	
( ) M < 3.5	( )	
( ) F < 2.5	( )	
( ) P < 1.5	( )	
( ) VP < 0.5	( )	

The above is a sample Fishing Record form that I use. It allows me to record lake and date with check-off boxes for weather and water conditions along with fish rising and feeding activity. I use codes, such as Shrimp = Sh and Sedge = Sg, to record bugs seen or in feeding samples. The time fished is recorded and lots of room is left to record catch info for each fish including time, fish size, fly and line used with retrieve information. I have a box for the day of the moon and some miscellaneous info I am tracking. Plenty of room is provided for comments. You can design your own form based on the good (or bad) points you see on this form. Whatever you decide on, you will find it worthwhile to keep fishing records.

Appendix 7 - The 80% Rules

Many aspects of fly fishing for Rainbow Trout in pristine lakes can be explained by an 80% or 20% split. Following are some examples of what I mean.

➢ 80% of the fish are caught by about 20% of the anglers.

➢ 80% of Rainbows are caught over shoals or at drop-offs. Of the 20% caught in deep water, many of those are caught during the summer downers.

➢ Expect 80% of your trout to be two pounds or smaller.

➢ About 80% of Rainbows will survive being released if properly handled.

➢ If you use a variety of imitator flies, about 80% of the fish caught on these will be on Shrimp, Chironomid or Caddis.

➢ 80% of fly fishing is location and presentation.

➢ 80% of large Rainbows become fly shy.

➢ 80% of broken leaders happen within 20 seconds of the strike.

➢ 80% of flies provide more appeal to the angler than the fish.

➢ 80% of the noise made in your boat is preventable.

➢ 80% of the time, imitator flies are retrieved too fast.

➢ 80% of the time, Rainbows can be taken on the dry line.

➢ 80% of the aquatic life lives within the littoral zone.

➢ 80% of Rainbows are cautious and efficient foragers. The other 20% are either timid or aggressive.

➢ 80% of your fish can be caught on black or very dark flies.

➢ 80% of the time, estimated trout weight is at least 20% more than actual weight.

➢ 80% of feeding Rainbows are within five feet of the lake bottom.

➢ 80% of Rainbows are not landed as quickly as possible (for release).

➢ Angling is good to excellent on 20% of the days fished but those days are when you get 80% of your fish.

Appendix 8

Fishing Success by Moon Altitude

Moon Altitude	Fishing Success
Degrees Above/Below Horizon	Number of Strikes Per Hour
60	1.52
50	1.52
40	1.54
30	1.70
20	2.16
10	2.29
0	1.89
-10	2.00
-20	1.97
-30	1.87
-40	1.82
-50	1.76
-60	1.60

The table to the left shows preliminary results for the latest information I'm working on. I'm examining fishing success by the altitude of the moon above (or below) the horizon.

This data isn't finalized. However, it looks as if the height of the moon in the sky may have an impact on fishing success.

By way of explanation, if the moon were straight overhead, it would be at 90 degrees. When the moon is at the horizon, not coming over a mountain, it would be at zero degrees. The negative numbers indicate that the moon is a certain distance below the horizon. Note that around Kamloops, the moon never gets more than about 60 degrees above or below the horizon.

As you can see from these preliminary results, it appears as if fishing is better when the moon is near the horizon and declines as the moon gets higher. However, I'm at a loss to explain why success drops just when the moon is "on" the horizon.

This is a work in progress so I won't yet stand by the numbers. However, I thought many anglers would be interested and may check their own success against moon altitude. If you are interested, the US Navy provides a good internet site on moon position which provides moon altitude at any time of a given day.

Appendix 9 – Bug Rank and Seasonal Rate

Any fly can catch a fish at any time of the year… but the following should improve your odds. **Time Period and Seasonal Comments**	Sunrise (am) Sunset (pm) Kamloops	Waterboatmen WB	Shrimp Sh	Chironomid Ch	Bloodworm BW	Dragonfly Dr	Damselfly Da	Caddis (Sedge) Sg	Mayfly Ma	Large Attractors (Doc Sprat, Leech) LA	Small Attractors (Halfback, fullback) SA
April 1 to 15	Rank >	2	1	3	6	4	9	10	8	7	5
Ice-off to 2,800 feet then turn over. Water cold & few bugs.	6:25 am 7:45 pm	G	G	F	F	G	VP	VP	VP	P	M
April 16 to 30	Rank >	4	3	1	6	2	9	10	8	5	7
Ice-off to 3,800 feet then turn over. Dragonflies migrate.	5:50 am 8:10 pm	G	F	M	M	VG	F	VP	F	G	F
May 1 to 15	Rank >	9	5	1	3	2	8	10	4	7	6
Ice-off to 4,800 feet. Bug sbecome active.	5:25 am 8:35 pm	F	P	VG	G	G	G	VP	VG	M	M
May 16 to 31	Rank >	10	2	1	8	4	9	6	5	3	7
Ice-off over 4,800 feet. Chironomids active.	5:05 am 8:55 pm	P	M	VG	F	M	M	P	G	G	F
June 1 to 15	Rank >	10	3	1	9	8	5	2	4	7	6
Lakes finished turn over. Many bugs.	4:50 am 9:10 pm	VP	M	VG	P	F	VG	G	VG	M	M
June 16 to 30	Rank >	10	3	2	9	4	7	1	5	6	8
Watch for Caddis and Damselfly hatches.	4:50 am 9:20 pm	VP	F	G	VP	M	G	VG	M	F	F
July 1 to 15	Rank >	10	3	2	9	4	7	1	6	5	8
Alga blooms start and Caddis peak	5:00 am 9:15 pm	VP	M	M	VP	G	M	VG	M	M	P
July 16 to 31	Rank >	10	2	4	9	3	8	1	6	5	7
Bugs at a seasonal low. Day time fishing is often slow.	5:15 am 9:00 pm	VP	M	F	VP	G	M	G	G	G	F
August 1 to 15	Rank >	9	2	4	10	3	8	5	7	6	1
Water temps high. Fish attractor flies deep.	5:40 am 8:35 pm	VP	F	F	VP	G	P	F	M	VG	VG
August 16 to 31	Rank >	8	1	6	10	2	9	3	7	4	5
Evenings start to cool. Dragonfly hatches peaking.	6:00 am 8:05 pm	P	G	P	VP	VG	VP	M	M	VG	G
September 1 to 15	Rank >	5	1	8	7	3	10	2	9	4	6
Cooling temps & Cinnamon Sedge hatches in eve	6:30 am 7:30 pm	M	G	VP	P	VG	VP	G	VP	VG	G
September 16 to 30	Rank >	2	1	8	4	6	10	5	9	7	3
Boatmen mate and fish move into shallows.	6:50 am 6:55 pm	VG	G	VP	F	F	P	F	VP	G	VG
October 1 to 15	Rank >	5	1	6	2	7	4	8	10	9	3
Cool water and bloodworms bring on good fishing.	7:15 am 6:25 pm	M	G	P	VG	F	VG	F	VP	F	VG
October 16 to 31	Rank >	2	1	5	3	7	6	8	9	10	4
Frosts and shrimp are plentiful	7:40 am 5:55 pm	VG	VG	P	VG	VP	VG	P	VP	P	G
November 1 to 15	Rank >	4	1	5	3	6	8	10	9	7	2
Pre Ice-Over. Still some good fishing	7:15 am 4:15 pm	F	VG	P	G	VP	VP	VP	VP	VP	VG

In the above generalized table, "Rank" indicates the relative importance of a bug during a specific period with 1 best and 10 least. The "Seasonal Rate" is provided below the Rank with VG = Very Good, G = Good, M = Moderate, F = Fair, P = Poor and VP = Very Poor.

Appendix 10

Morning and Evening Fishing Times

For Kamloops, British Columbia
DAYLIGHT SAVINGS TIME

Month	Day	SunRise	SunSet	Length Of Day	Morning Rise		Evening Rise	
Apr	3	6:35 AM	7:40 PM	13:05	5:55 AM	6:45 AM	7:30 PM	8:35 PM
Apr	8	6:25 AM	7:45 PM	13:20	5:45 AM	6:35 AM	7:35 PM	8:40 PM
Apr	13	6:10 AM	7:55 PM	13:45	5:30 AM	6:20 AM	7:45 PM	8:50 PM
Apr	18	6:00 AM	8:00 PM	14:00	5:15 AM	6:10 AM	7:50 PM	8:55 PM
Apr	23	5:50 AM	8:10 PM	14:20	5:05 AM	6:00 AM	8:00 PM	9:10 PM
Apr	28	5:40 AM	8:20 PM	14:40	4:55 AM	5:50 AM	8:10 PM	9:20 PM
May	3	5:30 AM	8:25 PM	14:55	4:45 AM	5:40 AM	8:15 PM	9:30 PM
May	8	5:25 AM	8:35 PM	15:10	4:40 AM	5:35 AM	8:25 PM	9:45 PM
May	13	5:20 AM	8:40 PM	15:20	4:35 AM	5:30 AM	8:30 PM	9:55 PM
May	18	5:10 AM	8:50 PM	15:40	4:25 AM	5:20 AM	8:40 PM	10:10 PM
May	23	5:05 AM	8:55 PM	15:50	4:15 AM	5:15 AM	8:45 PM	10:15 PM
May	28	5:00 AM	9:00 PM	16:00	4:10 AM	5:10 AM	8:50 PM	10:25 PM
Jun	3	4:55 AM	9:05 PM	16:10	4:05 AM	5:05 AM	8:55 PM	10:30 PM
Jun	8	4:50 AM	9:10 PM	16:20	4:00 AM	5:00 AM	9:00 PM	10:35 PM
Jun	13	4:50 AM	9:15 PM	16:25	3:55 AM	5:00 AM	9:05 PM	10:40 PM
Jun	18	4:50 AM	9:20 PM	16:30	3:50 AM	5:00 AM	9:10 PM	10:45 PM
Jun	23	4:50 AM	9:20 PM	16:30	3:50 AM	5:00 AM	9:10 PM	10:45 PM
Jun	28	4:50 AM	9:20 PM	16:30	3:55 AM	5:00 AM	9:10 PM	10:40 PM
Jul	3	4:55 AM	9:15 PM	16:20	4:00 AM	5:05 AM	9:05 PM	10:35 PM
Jul	8	5:00 AM	9:15 PM	16:15	4:05 AM	5:10 AM	9:05 PM	10:30 PM
Jul	13	5:05 AM	9:10 PM	16:05	4:10 AM	5:15 AM	9:00 PM	10:25 PM
Jul	18	5:10 AM	9:05 PM	15:55	4:20 AM	5:20 AM	8:55 PM	10:15 PM
Jul	23	5:15 AM	9:00 PM	15:45	4:25 AM	5:25 AM	8:50 PM	10:10 PM
Jul	28	5:25 AM	8:50 PM	15:25	4:35 AM	5:35 AM	8:40 PM	9:55 PM
Aug	3	5:30 AM	8:45 PM	15:15	4:45 AM	5:40 AM	8:35 PM	9:50 PM
Aug	8	5:40 AM	8:35 PM	14:55	4:55 AM	5:50 AM	8:25 PM	9:40 PM
Aug	13	5:50 AM	8:25 PM	14:35	5:05 AM	6:00 AM	8:15 PM	9:30 PM
Aug	18	5:55 AM	8:15 PM	14:20	5:10 AM	6:05 AM	8:05 PM	9:15 PM
Aug	23	6:00 AM	8:05 PM	14:05	5:20 AM	6:10 AM	7:55 PM	9:05 PM
Aug	28	6:10 AM	7:55 PM	13:45	5:30 AM	6:20 AM	7:45 PM	8:50 PM
Sep	3	6:20 AM	7:40 PM	13:20	5:40 AM	6:30 AM	7:30 PM	8:35 PM
Sep	8	6:30 AM	7:30 PM	13:00	5:50 AM	6:40 AM	7:20 PM	8:25 PM
Sep	13	6:35 AM	7:20 PM	12:45	5:55 AM	6:45 AM	7:10 PM	8:15 PM
Sep	18	6:40 AM	7:10 PM	12:30	6:00 AM	6:50 AM	7:00 PM	8:00 PM
Sep	23	6:50 AM	6:55 PM	12:05	6:10 AM	7:00 AM	6:45 PM	7:45 PM
Sep	28	7:00 AM	6:45 PM	11:45	6:20 AM	7:10 AM	6:35 PM	7:35 PM
Oct	3	7:05 AM	6:35 PM	11:30	6:25 AM	7:15 AM	6:25 PM	7:25 PM
Oct	8	7:15 AM	6:25 PM	11:10	6:35 AM	7:25 AM	6:15 PM	7:15 PM
Oct	13	7:20 AM	6:15 PM	10:55	6:40 AM	7:30 AM	6:05 PM	7:05 PM
Oct	18	7:30 AM	6:05 PM	10:35	6:55 AM	7:40 AM	5:55 PM	6:50 PM
Oct	23	7:40 AM	5:55 PM	10:15	7:05 AM	7:50 AM	5:45 PM	6:40 PM
Oct	28	7:45 AM	5:45 PM	10:00	7:10 AM	7:55 AM	5:35 PM	6:30 PM

If you like to fish the morning or evening rise, you can calculate your own rise times for these periods. Find out when sunrise, sunset and length of twilight times are for your location. The time of twilight up to sunrise or the length of twilight after sunset approximates the rise times.

Appendix 11 – Trout Feeding by Day of Moon

Moon Phase	Day of Moon	Bug >	Shrimp	Chiromonid	Caddis (Sedge)	Dragonfly	Damselfly	Mayflies	Waterboatmen	Large Attractors	Small Attractors
New	0		Avg	VG	VP	G	Avg	G	Avg	VG	VP
New	1		Avg	VG	VP	P	Avg	G	VG	VG	VP
	2		Avg	VG	VP	P	Avg	VG	VG	Avg	P
	3		Avg	VG	P	P	G	VG	VG	VP	P
	4		Avg	VG	Avg	P	G	G	G	VP	P
	5		Avg	VG	G	P	Avg	VP	Avg	P	P
	6		Avg	G	G	Avg	Avg	VP	Avg	Avg	VP
1/4	7		Avg	Avg	G	G	Avg	Avg	Avg	Avg	VP
1/4	8		G	Avg	Avg	G	Avg	VG	Avg	Avg	VP
	9		G	P	P	G	Avg	VG	VG	Avg	P
	10		VG	Avg	P	Avg	VG	VG	VG	Avg	P
	11		VG	G	P	G	VG	G	G	Avg	P
	12		VG	G	VP	VG	Avg	Avg	G	Avg	P
	13		G	Avg	VP	VG	VP	Avg	G	G	Avg
Full	14		G	P	P	G	VP	Avg	VG	G	G
Full	15		G	VP	Avg	Avg	VP	P	VG	G	G
Full	16		Avg	VP	G	Avg	VP	VP	Avg	G	G
	17		P	P	VG	Avg	VP	P	P	Avg	G
	18		VP	Avg	VG	Avg	VP	P	VP	Avg	G
	19		VP	Avg	VG	P	VP	P	VP	P	G
	20		P	P	VG	VP	P	VP	P	P	G
3/4	21		P	P	G	VP	P	VP	P	VP	Avg
3/4	22		P	VP	G	P	P	VP	P	VP	Avg
3/4	23		P	VP	VG	P	P	VP	P	VP	Avg
	24		Avg	VP	G	VP	Avg	Avg	VP	P	G
	25		Avg	P	Avg	VP	Avg	G	VP	Avg	VG
	26		G	Avg	Avg	Avg	G	VG	P	G	VG
	27		VG	Avg	Avg	G	VG	VG	P	G	VG
New	28		G	G	Avg	VG	VG	G	P	VG	Avg
New	29		G	VG	P	VG	VG	G	P	VG	VP

Avg = Average, G = Above Average, VG = Well Above Average, P = Below Average, VP = Well Below Average

The above table summarizes feeding activity on the seven primary invertebrates plus the two types of attractor flies. A Rainbow feeding on certain flies or bugs is not necessarily the same as you seeing those bugs. Hatches or other periods of availability can occur that trout simply ignore. It is much better to know when the trout are feeding on those bugs.

Use Appendix 9 or the Seasonal Graphs in Chapter 7 to determine the best time of year to fish specific flies. Then determine the day of the moon to fine tune your estimates with the above table. The shaded moon days are below average for each type of fly so target those days without shading. Naturally, "Very Good" (VG) days will provide the best chance of success. For example, flies imitating Waterboatmen are best fished before moon day 17 during the Spring and Fall.

About the Author

Ron Newman:

In 1949 my dad was in the Air Force and took me fishing. He put a dough-ball on a hook, tied about twenty feet of fishing line to the big toe of my left foot, sat me on a dock and threw everything but me into the Panama Canal. That was when I first began to fish and I've been at it ever since.

Like many people, I progressed through worms, grasshoppers, trolls and lures to finally arrive at fly fishing in 1973. Shortly after I first cast a fly I became involved with the Kamloops Fly Fishers Association and started asking questions. An old timer named Karl Haufler took me under his wing and systematically helped me to understand the sport. My mentor saw my interest in the scientific aspects of fly fishing and suggested I start to keep fishing records. For two years I kept records of which lake I went to, on what date, how many fish I caught and on what fly. As I began to try and use these records I soon realized that I wasn't collecting enough information.

So I went overboard. I began to keep track of virtually anything that may have affected the fishing on a certain day. This began in 1976 and I've been keeping detailed records ever since. I collect data on the weather, water, fish activity, hatches, moon position, fishing success, etc. This data is now computerized and forms a "very" comprehensive set of statistics that's easy to analyze. Any time I want to test a theory about fishing I make a few key strokes on my computer and then examine the results.

However, my data gave rise to another whole set of questions regarding Rainbow Trout. For example, why do trout feed at a certain time, how do they know a hatch is beginning or what the heck is a lateral line anyway? I began to delve into articles, textbooks, technical research papers, Internet sites and so on. Before I knew it, more than 25 years had elapsed. While there is still a lot to learn, I decided it was time to summarize all that information and observation into an easy to follow book for other anglers and especially other fly fishers.

I have fly fished the world famous trout lakes around Kamloops, British Columbia since 1973. I've written articles and shorts for magazines, newspapers, the internet and books. I have given presentations on Rainbow Trout, Aquatic Entomology and taught fly tying and fly casting.

Hopefully the above provides some assurance that I have more than a basic understanding about fly fishing. I present this section because I think it important that you know a little about my credentials and fishing background.

Ron Newman